D1707606

Travellers to the Middle East

Travellers to the Middle East from Burckhardt to Thesiger: An Anthology

Edited by

GEOFFREY NASH

ANTHEM PRESS
LONDON · NEW YORK · DELHI

Anthem Press
An imprint of Wimbledon Publishing Company
www.anthempress.com

This edition first published in UK and USA 2009
by ANTHEM PRESS
75-76 Blackfriars Road, London SE1 8HA, UK
or PO Box 9779, London SW19 7ZG, UK
and
244 Madison Ave. #116, New York, NY 10016, USA

British Library Cataloguing in Publication Data
A catalogue record for this book is available from the British Library.

Library of Congress Cataloging in Publication Data
A catalog record for this book has been requested.

ISBN-13: 978 1 84331 792 0 (Hbk)
ISBN-10: 1 84331 792 3 (Hbk)

1 3 5 7 9 10 8 6 4 2

For my Wife

TABLE OF CONTENTS

ACKNOWLEDGEMENTS

The author and publisher gratefully acknowledge the following for permission to quote copyrighted material:

Extract from *The Road to Oxiana* by Robert Byron (© Robert Byron 1937) is reproduced by permission of PFD (*www.pfd.co.uk*) on behalf of the Estate of Robert Byron.

Extract from *Letters from Palestine, 1932–1936* by Thomas Hodgkin is reproduced by permission of Quartet Books Ltd.

Extract from *The Cruel Way* by Ella K. Maillart (Virago Press 1986) is reproduced by permission of David Higham Associates.

Extract from *Ibn Sa'oud: His People and His Land* by Ameen Rihani is reproduced by permission of the Rihani family.

Extract from *The Gates of Southern Arabia* by Freya Stark (© Freya Stark 1936) is reproduced by permission of Mr John Murray.

Extract from *Arabian Sands* by Wilfred Thesiger (© Wilfred Thesiger 1959) is reproduced with permission of Curtis Brown Ltd, London on behalf of the Estate of Wilfred Thesiger.

INTRODUCTION

In his introduction to *Travel Writing in the Nineteenth Century*, subtitled 'Filling the Blanks Spaces', Tim Youngs states that the motivation for travel in places like Africa and South America was to fill the blank spaces on the map and 'once "discovered", many of those places would be exploited for their commercial potential' (Youngs 2006:2). To the imaginative draw of the blank spaces and the desire to exploit them economically should be added the urge to establish political control over them, directly or indirectly. The entire process is of course comprehended in the terms imperialism and colonization. Nineteenth century travel writing – especially in a region like the Middle East – is inextricably linked to the spread of European power, although that does not mean every traveller in this period set out on their journey with the express intention of building or adding to the British Empire. Nevertheless, the geographical and chronological divisions adopted in this volume largely conform to political realities. Britain's progressive entrenchment in India focalized the Middle East for her politicians. The Ottoman Empire, which comprised the lands known to European travellers as the Near East,[1] included Egypt and the Holy Land as well as many of the sites of classical antiquity, but became as a result of Britain's imperial interests in India the nexus of her foreign policy. Persia, which suddenly acquired strategic significance during the Napoleonic period precisely because Britain feared Napoleon wanted to penetrate it and then advance on India, was thereafter assigned only a peripheral importance until George N. Curzon raised the issue of the Great Game at the end of the century in a work of travel literature (*Persia and the Persian Question*) whose motivation was primarily political. As for the Arabian Peninsula, this was the Middle East's only blank space but as it remained for much of the nineteenth century largely unexplored, in political terms its importance was nugatory. Travel theory often emphasises how

---

[1] The terms 'Near East' and 'Middle East' are broadly interchangeable. The former is the older. Billie Melman (2002: 105) identifies the latter as a neologism coined by a US naval historian in 1902 'to designate the sea and land stretching between a farther East – India – and a nearer one, extending towards westernmost territories of Asia and the eastern Mediterranean.'

European imperial expansion entailed looking at old societies with new eyes and penetrating hitherto unknown ones. However, the Turkish Empire, which embraced the entire Islamic world of the Near East up to the borders with Persia, far from being a blank space was an area that contained in the Bible lands and its sites of classical antiquity Europe's foundation narratives. In the European psyche it was therefore less an area to be explored in the expectation of new knowledge emerging, and more an old place whose meanings had been fixed for all time and required merely to be correlated with the biblical text. Sceptic though she was, Harriet Martineau progressed through Palestine and Egypt as though the Bible were her handbook while George N. Curzon was depressed to find the holy places failed to live up to their biblical originals or inspire new faith (Ronaldshay 1928: I. 87–88). Because the lands occupied by the Ottomans had once belonged to the true faith but were now lost they comprised an area of darkness. Christian beliefs mixed with ideas of national freedom cohered around political causes such as freeing Greece from the Turkish yoke in the 1820s, punishing Turkey for its putative perpetration of the 'Bulgarian Horrors' in the 1870s and Armenian massacres in the 1890s, and in the Balkan Wars of the early twentieth century finally executing Gladstone's call to expel Turkey 'bag and baggage' from Europe. Robert Curzon's wish, as expressed in *Visits to Monasteries of the Levant*, that the Turkish flag be run down and a Christian one be raised over Jerusalem in its stead is unequivocally religious in tone. And though Alexander Kinglake's 'prophecy' in *Eothen* of the English takeover of Egypt nearly forty years before the fact is secular in character rather than Christian-inspired (Kinglake being a declared unbeliever), in *Modern Egypt* Cromer enlists it in a humanitarian cause (the rescue of the *fellahin* from oriental despotism) that clearly does possess Christian overtones. Likewise the rationalist Harriet Martineau, having only recently witnessed slavery in America, expressed her horror at the treatment of the women in a Muslim harem in Egypt by adopting an emancipation discourse that is indebted to evangelical sources.[2]

In addition to calling upon Christian rhetoric to support political and social crusades against an Islamic empire, travellers of a more intellectual hue than the simple tourist also used the racial stereotypes of the age to back up their arguments. The French invasion of Egypt precipitated John Malcolm's first embassy to Persia in 1800 and this contact led in turn to further diplomatic activity which eventuated in a flurry of travel publications on that country. These came too early to incorporate the century's big idea about

---

[2] 'The treatment of polygamy and domestic slavery in *Eastern-life* is neither historical nor scientific, drawing, as it does, on Martineau's experience of the North-American system of slavery and her commitment to Abolitionism' (Melman 1992: 138).

Persians: that they were, as Major Turton would later cynically remark of the Indians, our 'Aryan Brother'. Britons first acquired cognisance of the Persians' Aryan credentials through British governance of India, but it was in France that the Indo-European theories propounded by German philologists of the early nineteenth century were absorbed and recycled in the racial ideas of figures like Arthur Gobineau and Ernest Renan.[3] Renan, who travelled on a government expedition to Greater Syria in 1860 where he was able to imaginatively construct the natural environment that features so prominently in his *Life of Jesus*, was a fervent opponent of Islam, which he pronounced the creed of a motley agglomerate of undistinguished races, with the exception of the Aryan Persians.[4] He extended the philological meaning of the term *sémitisme* both to categorize and denigrate the Pharisaic religion of the Jews and the equally fanatical Islam of the Arabs, and by comparison to exalt the Sufi and Shi'ih counter-Islam of the Aryan Persians. Gobineau authored a travel work on Persia, *Three Years in Asia*, and in 1865 published *Religions and Philosophies of Central Asia*, which was even more influential than Renan's writings in pointing out Persian religious departure from orthodox Islam, especially in his narrative of the short-lived efflorescence of the Babis.[5] These ideas filtered through to erudite travellers like George N. Curzon, Edward Browne and Gertrude Bell (Nash 2005: Ch 4–5).

France, however, only penetrated to the Arabian heartland of 'Semitic' Islam by proxy. That is through Napoleon III's sponsorship of foreign spies such as the Italian Carlo Guarmani, and the half-Jewish Englishman William Gifford Palgrave, who both travelled through Central Arabia in disguise in the early 1860s. British travellers to Arabia were hardly influenced at all by Renan's contempt for 'Semitic' culture and religion, although their feelings towards Islam ranged from Richard Francis Burton's proposition of its superiority to Christianity to Charles Doughty's aggressive advocacy of the opposite. Burton, as Kathryn Tidrick points out, read into the racial theorizing

---

[3] On the evolution of Bopp's linguistic use of the term 'Indo-European' till it 'became absorbed in the crazy doctrine of "racial anthropology"', see Poliakov (1974: 193). On Aryanism in the British Empire see Ballantyne who argues (2002: 5) that it was Sir William Jones who first 'mapped a new vision of global history and established a common Indo-European cultural heritage (even though the term Indo-European would not be coined until 1813).'

[4] Renan partly derived his ideas on race and on Aryan Persia from Gobineau's *Essay on the Inqualities of the Human Race*, although he did not choose to acknowledge it. His anti-semitic bigotry operated from a space secularism took over from the Catholic Church. See Nash (2010).

[5] From his first tour of diplomatic duty in Persia Gobineau acquired the material for *Three Years in Asia*, part one of which is devoted to travel, part two to close social observation of Persia. See Gobineau (1983) and Nash (2009).

of his time, notably J.C. Prichard's *The Natural History of Man*, and among other things distinguished the Egyptians, who he considered related to the African Negro, from 'such exemplars of racial purity as the Anaza Bedouin and the inhabitants of Nejd' (Tidrick 1989: 79, 81). The Bedouin were at the heart of the English romance with Arabia, but whether or not they were considered aristocrats of the desert and, as the Blunts felt, custodians of an ancient model of governance, the shepherd kingdom, had more to do with the English class system and a displaced sense of *noblesse oblige* than ethnographic reality.

The aftermath of the first major Ottoman crisis of the century – the Greek War of Independence – drew to Greece, Albania and Istanbul travellers following in the footsteps of Byron. In the case of David Urquhart, who went to fight for the Greeks but stayed on to help establish the post-war boundaries, it helped turn a Philhellene into a Turkophile. Urquhart wrote a seminal work of travel on the Ottoman Empire – *Spirit of the East* – and was from the beginning engaged with the politics of its survival. He saw this as inextricably bound to European power and diplomacy, which he argued was under the baneful influence of Russia and worked against the Turks who he argued were tolerant and flexible rulers and if allowed space to reform themselves they would see off the Russians on their own. Urquhart's pro-Turk propagandizing shadowed the diplomacy of Stratford Canning, which strove to bolster Turkey against Russia and other European predators. In private though, Canning was extremely sceptical about Ottoman governance and its capacity for reform (Kedourie 1956: Ch 1). Still Urquhart was not without heirs who believed in the qualities of the Turks as a stolid imperial race not wholly unlike the British. This view continued into the twentieth century and we can see it in the writings of politicians and travellers of the ilk of Mark Sykes and Aubrey Herbert, and in the novelist and convert to Islam, Marmaduke Pickthall. Chosen affiliations with Middle Eastern nationalities and races, Arabs, Turks and Persians (Nash 2006; 2007), demonstrate one instance of how individual travellers took with them preconceptions from home that structured their reports of target cultures.

Said's theories on Orientalism still present the most coherent attempt to produce a cultural reading of 'Western conceptions of the Orient'.[6] Said allowed for both an academic and an imaginative Orientalism: the former 'made the Orient epistemologically visible to Europe, the aesthetic form made it culturally significant' (Behdad LTE: 888). However, the view that discourses of religion and race, as well as class and gender, continually inform travel writing has led some to criticize or attempt revisions of *Orientalism* (1978) as being monolithic and

---

[6] For a concise resumé of *Orientalism* and its significance for Middle East travel writing see Ali Behdad's article in *Literature of Travel and Exploration: An Encyclopaedia*.

unresponsive to many domestic preoccupations.[7] I have already mentioned
Christian and Christian-derived secular chauvinism above. According to Said
othering of the Orient incorporated long established stereotypes of violence,
sensuality, backwardness, irrationality, and effeminacy. However, he elided
Christian hatred of and anxiety about Islam, only representing this briefly in the
early pages of *Orientalism* as a medieval phenomenon that was presumably
replaced by a hegemonic Western Orientalist discourse fathered by the
Enlightenment and disseminated through imperial power.[8]

Orientalism has also been found lacking from a gender point of view. 'As
many feminist critics have pointed out...[Said's] theories construct the
position of enunciation in colonialist or Orientalist discourse as essentially
male' (Foster and Mills 2002: 7). Lisa Lowe (1991) Billie Melman (1992) and
Reina Lewis (2004) have amply filled in the gender dimension omitted by
Said. What differences then, if any, might we expect to encounter in women
travel writers as distinct from males? Arguing that feminist theories of
language can be extended 'to the production of travel writing in the context
of imperialism', Wendy Mercer (1999) proposes two discrete 'masculine' and
'feminine' discourses. The first constructs a masculine subject who displays
the urge to explore, conquer and subjugate the other, which we associate with
colonialism. However, where male travel narratives purport to be objective
and scientific, we would expect to find in travel writing by women a

different 'feminine' set of values appearing in the text: the boundaries
between subject and surroundings would be less clear, 'objective' analysis
would give way to involvement, mind to body. There would be a refusal
to prioritise and judge or to measure and order: this would constitute an
example of what Hélèn Cixous terms 'écriture féminine' (147–8).

---

[7] Lisa Lowe (1991: 8) writes: 'The Orient as Other is a literary trope that may reflect a
range of national issues: at one time the race for colonies, at others class conflicts and
workers' revolts, changes in sexual roles during a time of rapid urbanization and
industrialization, or postcolonial crises of national identity.'

[8] A selection from the writing of critics of *Orientalism* can be found in Macfie (2000). Another
departure is to be found in the work of anti-imperialist, pro-Islamic British writers and
travellers which demonstrate that Orientalism did not go unchallenged (Nash 2005).
A.L. Macfie (2007) also suggests that the career and myth of T.E. Lawrence are somewhat
different to the archetypal Orientalism Said correctly identified in the early chapters of *The
Seven Pillars of Wisdom*: that is, Lawrence's characterization of the Arabs as weak and effeminate,
alongside a racist dismissal of the Turks, and his projection of his own masterful energetic
control of the Arabs. However, Macfie goes on to argue, there are other facets to Lawrence's
text and indeed subsequent presentations of him by Lowell Thomas, which are ambiguous
about Lawrence's myth as a hero and also do not fit into an 'official' Orientalist mode.

In particular, we might expect to find greater sympathy with the colonized other in such 'feminine' writing. Having tested these assumptions against the work of two nineteenth-century French travel writers, one male, one female, Mercer however finds that such simple distinctions are not easy to uphold and concludes that other factors such as social forces come in to play. Adding the category race, Foster and Mills state: 'it helps us to recognize that in a colonialist context...there are various positions of enunciation which women may occupy, *in which gender is not the sole defining factor*' (3; my italics). Looking at writing by women travellers in the Middle East it should soon become apparent that factors such as class and race frequently intersect with and connect to the discourse of male travellers. At the same time discursive constraints – 'the range of "rules" and systems of representation and meaning within which writers negotiate in order to write' (Foster and Mills: 5) – can also prevent women travellers from adopting, for example, the authoritative voice found in male writers. Behdad (1994) argues for a gendering of tasks in the writing of the Blunts such that Wilfrid adopts the voice of Orientalist authority, and Anne that of his helper. Lucy Duff Gordon, who though without Gertrude Bell's university education still came from an intellectual family, supplies the more obvious example of *écriture féminine* in a British female writer on the Middle East, which the reader will need to search hard to find in Bell. Even the masculine tones of Harriet Martineau's writing are modulated by a Western (colonial?) feminist disdain for the harem. In the chapter 'Three Noble Ladies' in *Persian Pictures* (1928) Bell scarcely comes close to displaying sympathy for natives of her own sex, in this case the confined Persian women she has just visited who as royalty are from a higher class to her own. Her parting sentiments appear to exult in her own privileged freedom: 'Their prisoned existence seemed to us a poor mockery of life as we cantered homewards up the damp valley, the mountain air sending a cheerful warmth through our veins.' Even the far more sympathetic Freya Stark is dismayed to find herself in a women-only section of an Arab (Yemeni) wedding where she is angrily referred to as a 'Nasrani'. Afraid to be part of female ritual 'so ancient and fundamental, so far more tenacious in its dim, universal roots than the transitory effort of the incurably educational creature, Man,' she escapes, clinging to an honorary maleness. On the other hand, emphasizing how travel brought freedom to Victorian and Edwardian women travellers in general, Dea Birkett adds:

The women adventurers did not feel threatened by the opposite sex. 'Their apparent defencelessness is a passport, especially among born gentlefolk like the Arab and Druzes,' said one *Times Literary Supplement* commentator in 1907, a sentiment with which Middle East travellers Gertrude Bell and Freya Stark would have concurred. (Birkett 2004a: 37).

True as this is, we would certainly need to consider factors such as class and privilege in our scrutiny of the discourse of many women travellers to Middle East. Of the eccentric, Lady Hester Stanhope Sarah Searight comments:

> there is no denying...that she enjoyed remarkable respect and prestige for several years among the Druzes of Mount Lebanon... [and] the Arabs at Palmyra, but...both were largely the result of extravagant spending and the prestige disappeared with the pennies (Searight 1979: 216).

Prestige, class and race most likely account for the fact that, despite the common practice of male travellers of venturing into the deserts of Arabia in disguise, few of the women seem to have been tempted to indulge in cross-dressing, either of the cultural or gender kind, with the exception of Lady Hester, Isabelle Eberhardt in her travels in North Africa, and Rosita Forbes in Libya.[9] 'On what grounds, if their symbols of white masculine power were shared, could they maintain the unprecedented freedom and authority these trappings allowed?' (Birkett 2004b: 156).

So far I have discussed Middle East travel writing broadly in terms of cultural factors. I would like now to make some observations that specifically relate to literary genre. Tim Youngs has stressed the protean character of travel writing and the way in which it utilizes similar rhetorical literary techniques as those found in the genres of autobiography and fiction (Youngs 2006: 4). For example, he juxtaposes Stanley's *Through the Dark Continent* (1878) and Conrad's *Heart of Darkness* (1879) and raises the issue of how in the blank space they adopt the same trope by which to map areas of Africa. Writers, of course, have long employed similar material and literary techniques in both the genres of fiction and travel writing. Several generations before Robert Louis Stevenson, and therefore much earlier than Graham Greene or V.S. Naipaul, James Morier and James Baillie incorporated comparable characters and settings in their fiction and travel works. Morier has been praised for achieving a more vivid likeness of Persia and Persians in his fiction than in his more voluminous travel writings (Javardi 2005: 122–136). In fact he is responsible for originating one of the two recurring motifs about these in nineteenth-century travel writing. In his fictional anti-hero Hajji Baba Morier passed into circulation an unflattering image of 'the Persian character' that had a great influence on the way later generations of travellers saw Persia, greater probably than the Aryan myth. A strong intertextual

---

[9] Another exception might be Grace Ellison who includes her photograph as a veiled Turkish woman in *An Englishwoman in a Turkish Harem*. On the ambiguity of her attitude towards here Turkish sisters see Lewis (2004).

influence also operates across fiction to travel writing in the case of Walter Scott's novels. This impacted at the very least on Urquhart's narrative of his adventures among Greeks and Albanians in the Pindus Mountains, and Layard's in the Persian Zagros Mountains and plains of Khuzestan.

Another literary device shared between travel writing, autobiography and fiction is the letter home. Lucy Duff Gordon's letters to her family, Isabella Bird's to her sister, and Gertrude Bell's to her stepmother are obvious examples. In the shaped literary form in which they were published they bare obvious comparison with the most celebrated work in this format: Lady Wortley Montagu's *Turkish Embassy Letters* (1763). Such polishing of original material penned at the time of travel might be compared with 'unfinished' posthumously published writing such as Byron's letters from his Levant journey of 1809–10, Disraeli's *Home Letters* covering much the same terrain a generation later, and, included in this anthology, Thomas Hodgkin's *Letters from Palestine* (1986). A distinction between the 'worked-up' letters and the largely unedited ones is that in the latter the 'I' of the traveller is less smoothed out and, at least as far as his/her feelings and opinions are concerned, more immediate. Critics have also pointed out the prevalence in Middle East travel writing of the quest motif, or the journey of inner self-discovery – more grandly signified as 'pilgrimage' in titles by Burton, Anne Blunt, or implied though not stated in Robert Curzon's visit to Jerusalem and the monasteries of Mt. Athos. Melman, for example, believes the Blunts' journey in *A Pilgrimage to Nejd* (1881) is 'explicitly modelled on Bunyan's *Pilgrim's Progress*' (Melman 2002: 115).

*

The political, as implied above, is a key but by no means exhaustive signpost through the huge corpus of travel literature on the Middle East of this period.[10] This selection of travel writings of course reflects my interests and

---

[10] Readers with different interests can always consult the following: An anthology specifically covering the Middle East in the Romantic period is part I, vol. 4 in Pickering and Chatto's *Nineteenth Century Travels, Explorations and Empires, Writings from the Era of Imperial Consolidation, 1835–1910, The Middle East*, edited by Tijar Mazzeo, general editor P.J. Kitson. *Early Modern Tales of Orient: a Critical Anthology*, edited by Kenneth Parker (Routledge, 1999) is a compendium of early 16th and 17th Century English texts. On gender, Reina Lewis and Nancy Mickelwright, eds., *Gender, Modernity, Middle East and Western Women's Writings: a Critical Sourcebook*, (I.B. Tauris, 2006) deal with the late 19th early 20th centuries. A more general anthology is Elizabeth Bohls and Ian Duncan, *Travel Writing: An Anthology, 1700–1830* (Oxford World Classics, 2005) which covers the seven continents very broadly. See also: *Travel Narratives from the Age of Discovery: An Anthology*, edited by Peter Mancell (Oxford University Press, 2006) and *The Oxford Book of Exploration*, selected by Robin Hanbury-Tenison, (Oxford University Press, 2005). Lastly, an old favourite but out of print, is Gerald de Gaury and H.V.F. Winston, *The Spirit of the East* (Quartet, 1979).

omissions are unavoidable. For coherence's sake 1939 would probably have been a better stopping point, but that would have meant excluding Wilfred Thesiger, a writer who is spiritually connected to the great Victorian desert travellers. His political beliefs were formed in the colonial service where he learned to 'treat the men with whom he lived and traveled as companions instead of servants'.[11] Chronologically and from a thematic point of view, Thesiger completes the circle begun by John Lewis Burckhardt. The last great explorer of Arabia lived in his final years to see 'most of the places he traveled and dwelled in...lost' and felt responsible 'as a man who charted some of the territories technology has now laid waste to. He grieves for the old ways, for the freedoms only wild places and traditional societies allow.'[12] When the British Empire's power was fast receding, Thesiger filled in the last blank spaces on the map, before oil and American modernity blew away the whole episode of the Englishman's love affair with Arabia and the larger Middle East. In terms of the territories covered I am also aware of an imbalance. Turkey, Egypt, Central Arabia and Hijaz are well represented; Palestine features in several narratives, while two whole sections are devoted to Persia/Iran. This leaves a gap with respect to the Fertile Crescent – Iraq and Syria – and the Gulf States (excluding Oman and south Yemen). These omissions are perhaps to be accounted for by gaps in my own reading, but they also reflect to some extent a canon of Middle East travel writing that has been formed.[13]

---

[11] Alexander Maitland, 'Wilfred Thesiger,' *Dictionary of National Biography*, 2004.

[12] Mark Tredinnick, 'Wilfrid Thesiger,' *Literature of Travel and Exploration*, 1973.

[13] Melman (2002) adopts a similar division for the Arab world. A comprehensive overview of British travellers' perspectives of the entire region can be found in the early, yet perhaps still to be superseded, *The British in the Middle East* (1979) by Sarah Searight.

Part One

THE COMING OF EMPIRE
1800–1879

THE OTTOMAN EMPIRE AND EGYPT

Historical Background

The interventions of Christian powers in Islamic lands, starting with the Napoleonic invasion of Egypt in 1798 and the British counter-attack of 1799–1802, had a profound psychological effect on Muslim states as far a field as Persia. Ottoman decline had been in evidence since the eighteenth century: military reverses and economic stagnation had reduced her territory and made her vulnerable to the expansive European powers, most importantly Russia. Ottoman Turkey at the beginning of this period had become for Europeans the problematic core of the 'Eastern Question' and would remain so for the rest of the nineteenth century. Attempts at reform by successive Ottoman Sultans seemed to most European outsiders only a staving of inevitable collapse. In 1807 Selim III was deposed and later murdered after the Janissaries – who with the *ulama* formed a bastion of reaction – rose to resist his military reorganization. Mahmud II eventually managed to destroy the Janissaries in 1826 and to institute wholesale reform of the army, but not before Serbia had won autonomy (1813) and Greece her independence (1830). Another potentially critical secession was forestalled in Albania by a massacre of dissident pashas and their supporters in 1830. Ottoman weaknesses had contributed to the rise of a rival power in Egypt, which the Albanian Muhammad Ali took over in 1805. Though nominally under Turkish suzerainty, the armies of the Egyptian pasha expanded into the Hijaz and Central Arabia, and under the command of Muhammad Ali's son Ibrahim completed the occupation of Syria in 1833. Only intervention of the European Powers prevented the fall of Istanbul and ended Muhammad Ali's control of Syria in 1840. Later conflicts and diplomacy, notably the Crimean War (1854–56) and the Eastern Crisis that culminated in the Treaty of Berlin of 1878, saw Ottoman power and territorial possessions further denuded. By the 1870s both the Sublime Porte at Istanbul and Muhammad Ali's successors in Egypt had accrued massive debts to European capitalists further undermining the coherence and independence of the states over which they claimed jurisdiction.

Travellers and their Narratives

English connections with Turkey went back to the era of Suleyman the Magnificent. Trade with the Ottoman Empire began to flourish in the second half of the sixteenth century. The Turkey, later Levant, Company had been founded by royal consent in 1581, and its representative in Istanbul appointed as Queen Elizabeth's 'messenger, deputie and agent' to the Ottoman court (Searight 1979: 17). Lady Wortley Montagu's flattering and, from the point of view of gender, challenging portrayal of Istanbul society in her *Turkish Embassy Letters*, written during her husband's period as ambassador from 1717–18, but published in 1763, helped 'a positive, almost apologetic strain of thought about Turkey' to emerge (Paterson LTE: 893). But the debate over the civility of the Ottoman Turks remained polarised up to 1880 and beyond. William Eton, in *A Survey of the Turkish Empire* (1807), characterised them as 'unredeemable barbarians affecting a "haughty conceit of superiority arising from the most narrow and intolerable bigotry." He...spoke scathingly of the harem, the faithlessness of Turkish wives, and the sexual perversions of the men which... had led to the depopulation of the country' (Schiffer 1999: 371–2). When Stratford Canning became ambassador at the beginning of the nineteenth century trade with the Ottoman Empire became secondary to concern about its political viability. Dangers to European travellers had subsided by the time Lord Byron made his first visit to the Levant in 1809–10, but revived during the decade 1820–30, mostly owing to the Greek War of Independence. David Urquhart, the Scottish radical and later briefly Member of Parliament.– who would become notorious as the Turks' closest friend – arrived in the Ottoman capital as the new decade began, at almost the same time as the flamboyant future Tory Prime Minister and bolsterer of Turkey, Benjamin Disraeli.

With the onset of the Victorian age ever increasing numbers of visitors continued to arrive in Ottoman domains either en route to India via Egypt, or as pilgrims or sightseers to the holy land, while in the 1840s the start of Thomas Cook tours to the Upper Nile by steamer heightened Egypt's appeal as a tourist destination (Gregory: 1999; Kark: 2001). The genre of travel writing was irrevocably altered by one of these visitors. Alexander Kinglake set out for Ottoman domains in 1834 but the account of his travels, *Eothen*, was not published until 1844. In spite of – or more probably because of – his refusal to reproduce stale geographical and historical information as well as stereotypical 'political disquisitions' and 'moral reflexions', Kinglake's work quickly became a much imitated model in its own right, an early example being his friend Eliot Warburton's, *The Crescent and The Rose* (1844). As Edward

Said (1978:193–4) pointed out: *Eothen* also set the standard for an arrogant disdain of native orientals which was part of an emerging British imperial identity also to be observed in Thackeray's *Notes of a Journey from Cornhill to Grand Cairo* (1846). A less secular, more Protestant chauvinism, albeit of an ambivalent kind, is present in Robert Curzon's *Visits to Monasteries of the Levant* (1849). On the other hand, Lucy Duff Gordon's *Letters from Egypt* (1865) and *Last Letters from Egypt* (1875), which at the time of their publication approached Kinglake and Warburton in popularity, challenged the impact of commercialism and Eurocentrism on Egypt, this despite the fact that, owing to their criticism of the Khedive and the Turko–Circassian ruling class, Duff Gordon's letters were 'used as propaganda to legitimize British rule after 1882' (Lockwood LTE: 351).

DAVID URQUHART (1805–1877)

Son of a Scottish laird by his second wife, after being educated partly abroad, Urquhart spent a few months at Woolwich Arsenal where, according to the 1898 DNB entry, he 'acquired some knowledge of gunnery.' Whilst at Oxford he was advised by Jeremy Bentham to travel in the Levant (Maehl, 1981: 512). His association with Ottoman Turkey began in 1827 when he fought briefly for the Greeks in their war of independence. After the war had ended he gained a name for himself by his report on the borders of the new state. In 1831 he accompanied Ambassador Extraordinary Sir Stratford Canning to Istanbul where he became first secretary at the British embassy. So began a career that saw Urquhart exercise an important influence on the public mind in the early and mid-Victorian periods as a propagandist for Turkey and a virulent enemy of Russia and Lord Palmerston. The 1830s was a decade in which he swapped diplomacy for political pamphleteering and intrigue and also succeeded in publishing *The Spirit of the East: a Journal of Travels through Roumelia*, a work that mixes unobtrusive political commentary with romantic descriptions of the wild and sublime scenery of Greece and Albania, and celebration of Ottoman culture and civility. From thereon political writings far outnumber works of travel – *Lebanon: A History and a Diary* of 1860, is a rare combination of the two. Urquhart's promotion of the Turkish bath in England created a perhaps more lasting legacy than his brushes with Chartism and foreign policy, although, as W.S. Blunt observed, a 'School of Urquhart' that questioned Britain's dealings with other states continued into the 1880s, the very moment when Blunt himself began agitating against his country's interventions in the Middle East (Kedourie 1956: Ch 1).

From:

The Spirit of the East (1838)

Here the reader is presented with two juxtapositions that contrast the effects of ignorant cross-cultural encounter. First, the young Turkish nationals who ape European customs and manners are as a consequence 'denationalize[d]'.

Second, the Frankish visitor to the East through his boorishness only succeeds in blundering his way into a pasha's selamlik.

Social Intercourse with the Turks

Among a class of young men in the capital, chiefly belonging to the regular troops, there is an affectation to every thing European. Among them it is no extraordinary thing for a European to find himself treated, as he supposes, with every external mark of courtesy; but a position which is only to be gained by a change that remains to be effected, and cannot be so without difficulty and without danger, and the sphere of which is limited and insignificant, is scarcely worthy of observation. To establish the fact that a European may place himself within the pale of the national feeling, is I conceive, of the deepest importance, either as throwing light on the Turkish character, or as affording a new means of action on the Turkish nation.

I make these observations after two years intercourse with Mussulmans, on the footing of the most entire and perfect equality. It is true that many of my friends, for a long time, severally, believed that they alone were in the habit of treating me in such a manner; that such conduct was in violation of the precepts of their religion, and was only justified in my case from a supposed difference with other Europeans. It is perhaps superfluous to add, that in the faith of Islamism there is not the slightest ground for this supposition. Had it been so, Constantinople never could have been theirs. As a notable instance of the reverse, the Conqueror of Constantinople not only got up to receive the Greek Patriarch, his subject and a Christian, but accompanied him to the door of his palace, and sent all his ministers on foot to conduct him home.[*]

But, whatever have been the wrongs, feelings, or habits of the past, a reaction has now taken place in Turkey in favour of Europe. The change of dress, in imitation of those nations whose policy has been so injurious to them, exhibits great docility of mind, and proves that there has existed, unobserved by us, or, at all events, that there now exists among them, a spirit of imitativeness, which, in a nation (if well directed) contains the element of progress and amelioration. And, as if to render this proof the more conclusive, that which they have imitated has neither inherent merit nor

---

[*] What a contrast with the Western feelings regarding religious toleration is exhibited in the conquest of Constantinople by the Turks and by the Latins. When Dandolo planted the banner of St. Mark on the dome of St. Sophia, the Christian invaders placed in mockery, on the patriarchal throne, a prostitute, wearing on her brows the mitre, and holding in her hand the pastoral crook which Constantine had bestowed.

external attractions. Now a new duty devolves upon us,—that of directing their docility, and assisting their selection.

At present, among the Turks, there is no individual possessed of a thorough knowledge of Europe; and yet no man, not perfectly and equally conversant with the ideas, instruction, and institutions of the East and of the West, can reason to a satisfactory conclusion respecting what they ought, or ought not, to imitate. Amongst us there is no one sufficiently acquainted with *their* institutions and character to be able to become their guide. However beneficial, therefore, this change of disposition might be, were we in knowledge equal to the position offered us, it is to me a subject, under actual circumstances, of alarm rather than congratulation. Their imitation of Europe will be without knowledge or discrimination. That which we possess of value can only be obtained by years of labour, after adopting the fit direction, which a superior mind alone can give: that which is valueless is easily adopted and mimicked, if not copied. The former is scientific and practical knowledge; the latter is manners, vice, and taxes. Whatever, therefore, the Turks easily and rapidly adopt from Europe is not only bad in itself, but destructive of that which is good and estimable amongst themselves. That which it is advantageous for them to imitate is slow in acquisition, silent in its progress, and laborious in its course—it is useful and practical knowledge. Such knowledge is to be obtained in two ways,—lst, by sending young men to Europe; 2ndly, by carrying to the East men of letters and professors of science.

The first process is open to the most serious objections; it denationalizes these young Easterns, and will send them home depraved in morals, presumptuous in disposition, and intractable to the habits and customs of their compatriots. They will have lost also their simplicity of mind: they will carry back the mental maladies of Europeans.

Having been the first myself to bring young Turks to Europe for the purpose of education, I am induced to state these conclusions, not only as having been confirmed by observation and my own experience, but as having preceded the experiment. The young men I brought with me, I scarcely ever allowed out of my own sight. It was my constant endeavour to maintain their self-respect, and to make them sensible, at the same time, of all that was bad and injurious in our habits and customs, while cultivating their respect for our real merits. In this most anxious and laborious undertaking I was, however, actuated not by the desire of seeing young Turks sent to Europe (as has been the result), but of preparing the way for the second process of communication, which I have above alluded to, *viz.* selecting men of scientific acquirements to go to Turkey, with the view of their studying the genius of that people before entering on the duties of public instruction there. To this project the author lent his warm support, and even authorized its execution; but the apprehension of the insidious and powerful means directed to thwart every attempt to strengthen Turkey, or to cement its union with England, induced me to postpone the execution until possessed of surer guarantees of its success, and fortunate it was that I did so.

It is impossible that a people should adopt a double type of distinct customs, nor can they admit a new impression without disturbing and destroying the old; and as custom is the regulator and symbol of thoughts, feelings, and duties, nothing can be more dangerous to the constitution of a state, and the morality of a people, than a change of custom. In dealing with this question, I am equally impressed with the importance of this truth, and with the difficulty of rendering it intelligible to those I am addressing.

Custom, in English, conveys an idea which we despise; *Adet*, in Turkish, that of a venerated authority paramount to all others. Every thought, therefore, of the one people on this subject is unintelligible to the other, and every expression of the one conveys an imperfect or false idea to the other.

Presentation of a European in Eastern Society

The European arrives, probably on foot, attended by an interpreter; he has nothing about him of the state and style which commands respect; he meets with none, he expects none; his approach is perfectly unheeded. He ascends the staircase in his tight and meagre costume — the costume of the despised class of the country. Some of the attendants, in reply to his inquiries, point to the door of the Selamlik. A shuffling is then heard by those seated within; the Frank is getting off his boots[*] and putting on his slippers, or drawing slippers on above his boots; when he gets up with a reddened face, and escapes from the door-curtain, which has fallen on his head and shoulders, he comes tripping into the room in his inconvenient chassure, and is certain to stumble, if not before, on the step at the bottom of the room.

Ushered in thus to the party, he looks with a startled air all round, to find out which is the master of the house; he does not know what salutation to make, he does not know where to make it; he does not know whether he ought to be saluted by the host first; and his bewilderment is completed by the motionless composure of every thing around him. He then retreats abashed to the lower part of the room, or, in modest ignorance, not wishing to put himself forward, retires to the *corner* which has been left vacant by the mutual

---

[*] The command to Moses to take off his shoes before the burning bush, because *the ground whereon he stood was holy*, shows the antiquity of this custom. Shoes are put off, on coming into a carpeted apartment, because they have been in contact with the soiled earth: to put off the shoes therefore because the soil itself, the source of pollution, was sanctified, conveys a thought and produces an effect not to be understood or appreciated in Europe.

deference of two grandees. He then either perches himself, like an Egyptian statue, on the very edge of the sofa, or throws himself lolling backwards, with his legs spread out; an attitude scarcely less indecorous than elevating the legs on the table would be in England. These are incidents which may deprive a stranger of consideration, though they do not render him disagreeable or offensive; but, unfortunately, too often our countrymen make a display of awkwardness and presumption, by no means calculated either to smooth the way for themselves, or to leave the door of friendship open to future travellers. Nothing is more common than treading upon bowls of pipes; knocking over the coal or the ashes on an embroidered carpet, or upsetting a *narguillé*; scattering the fire about, while it rolls over pouring the water on the floor: and many a stranger, who considers himself degraded by putting on slippers, will walk in with an assuming and stately air with his boots on, which is revolting alike to every feeling of cleanliness, and every principle of decorum.[*]

No sooner is the Frank seated, than his health is inquired after by the master of the house, and by those present. Observing that the first is speaking to him, he turns an enquiring look upon his interpreter, to ascertain what the nature of the communication may be, while at the same moment the interpreter is endeavouring to call his attention to the salutations from the guests, all round the room: this completely puzzles him; he twists and turns backwards and forwards, looking one of the most ridiculous figures it is possible to conceive. My own gravity has repeatedly sunk under such a trial; but I never saw a Turk betray the slightest symptom of surprise or merriment, which could be construed into a breach of politeness, or become a source of embarrassment to the stranger. This is no sooner over than the Frank (for he cannot be silent) begins putting questions, which are rendered more or less faithfully, but generally less than more so; and, if he is very talkative or inquisitive, the interpreter takes leave to introduce matter or to omit, or gives a significant wink to the master of the house.

But when there are several Europeans together, then does the effect become truly lamentable. The slips of awkwardness, and the chances of mistake, though multiplied, are nothing compared, as their Eastern observers would conclude, to the rudeness of their mutual intercourse, the harshness of tones, loudness of voice, and shortness of manner, in addressing each other, and the

---

[*] We have recently in India enacted some regulation to make the natives wear their shoes in the courts of justice. The possession of an immense country by a handful of foreigners who, I will not say have not the habit of respecting, but who have not the facility of understanding CUSTOM, is a phenomenon only to be explained by the character for power which England owed to her former European station. Yet, what might England not be in Asia, and therefore in Europe, did she possess a slight insight into Eastern institutions and character.

differences of opinion that are constantly arising. The distracted Dragoman, overwhelmed by the multiplicity of questions directed by the European party to him, can only shrug his shoulders, and say to the Turks, "They are mad;" while he calms the restlessness of his employers, by saying "They won't answer you;" or, "they are fools;" or, "they don't understand." The effect produced on an Eastern, by such exhibitions, is humiliating in the extreme; but it can only be estimated by one who has sate looking on as a spectator, knowing the feelings of both parties. If this were a position of necessity, we might submit to it with patience; but what aggravates the case is, that any traveller who chooses, for a couple of days, to attend to customs, will find his position wholly altered.

The Dragoman of Mahmoud Hamdi, Pasha of Larissa, spoke both English and French. An English man-of-war touched at Volo, and two officers were sent with a message to the Pasha: a lieutenant, I believe, and a midshipman. The Pasha directed the interpreter not to know English: one of the officers fortunately knew a few words of French, and their observations were conveyed by this circuitous route to the Pasha. This difficulty of communication they made up for with quaint observations in their native tongue, on every thing they heard and saw. They evinced the greatest anxiety to see the Pasha's pipes arrive. The Pasha, on understanding this, ordered two of the richest and longest to be brought; their admiration knew no bounds; the dimensions were calculated, and the value estimated; and the envy of the gun-room and the cockpit anticipated, if the precious objects could be carried off. This, of course, was faithfully reported to the Pasha, with other discourse, in that schoolboy style which unfortunately is not confined to inmates of the cockpit, but is become the general characteristic of Englishmen in other lands.

The Pasha thus gave himself the gratification which an English spinster might have had in sending to a circulating library for a volume of Travels in Turkey; drew equally profound conclusions respecting the English character, and by the same process of reasoning which has established our opinions regarding his country, Mahmoud Pasha arrived at an equally just conclusion respecting the piratical disposition of the English navy. The story was told me by the Pasha himself, who, of course, only had the Dragoman's report; I, therefore, by no means undertake to vouch for its accuracy.

ALEXANDER WILLIAM KINGLAKE
(1809–1891)

For a writer often credited with radically changing the style of earlier nineteenth-century English travel writing, Alexander William Kinglake had a surprisingly conventional background and upbringing, and lived the largely uneventful life of a Victorian gentleman. Born into a well-off family in Taunton Somerset, like his father he went into the law, though without any great success. Eton and Cambridge would have strengthened a predilection for Classics first given him by his mother and which is inscribed in the Greek title ('from the East') of his celebrated work of travel. *Eothen, or, Traces of Travel Brought Home from the East* was published in 1844, a decade after its author set out on a tour of the Levant. It is the product of a young, unattached Englishman confident in the superiority of his class, race and nation. Rejected by the publisher John Murray on account of its irreverent style, 'it had undergone more than thirty printings by the end of the century' (Corwin, DLB/166: 191). In the preface Kinglake made it clear he had intentionally produced a travel book that 'was quite superficial in character' having 'discarded from it all valuable material derived from the work of others.' However, while displaying his 'egoism and colonial attitudes' these are 'continually undercut by his irony' (Baker LTE: 677) and self-mockery. At the Catholic church in Tiberias, for example, the English gentleman sneers at the genuflections of a local ministrant only to break into a lament over 'the fleas of all nations' consuming his flesh. Podsnapian in his attitudes to foreigners, straightforward if apologetic about his lack of religious faith, Kinglake's chauvinistic cleverness and embrace of the bustle of the steam-age covers a precarious sense of uncertainty. In Lebanon, looking westwards from a static East to the striving West, he writes: 'My place upon this dividing barrier was as a man's puzzling station in eternity, between the birthless Past, and the Future that has no end.' The remainder of Kinglake's life was spent writing an eight-volume history of the Crimean War, and contributing articles to the *New Monthly Review*; he published no further travel literature.

From:

Eothen **(1844)**

The type of treatment of Eastern peoples Urquhart would have loathed is here on view. Totally ignorant of Eastern languages and manners but possessing in abundance the chauvinist's self-assurance, the English traveller makes a virtue of his power and assertiveness. He seems totally unembarrassed by a feudal extraction of provisions from the native, usually Muslim, population through whose villages he passes. Kinglake goes so far as to recommend a 'peremptory method', which he acknowledges amounts to 'intimidation.' This is accomplished by the agency of his dragoman – here, as was frequently the case, a Greek, though he might have come from any of the other Levantine Christian communities.

Gaza to Nablous

Passing now once again through Palestine and Syria, I retained the tent which I had used in the Desert, and found that it added very much to my comfort in travelling. Instead of turning out a family from some wretched dwelling, and depriving them of rest without gaining rest for myself, I now, when evening came, pitched my tent upon some smiling spot within a few hundred yards of the village to which I looked for my supplies—that is, for milk, for bread (if I had it not with me), and sometimes also for eggs. The worst of it was that the needful viands were not to be obtained by coin, but only by intimidation. I at first tried the usual agent—money; Dthemetri, with one or two of my Arabs, went into the village near which I was encamped, and tried to buy the required provisions, offering liberal payment, but he came back empty-handed. I sent him again, but this time he held different language; he required to see the elders of the place, and, threatening dreadful vengeance, commanded them upon their responsibility to take care that my tent should be immediately and abundantly supplied. He was obeyed at once; and the provisions refused to me as a purchaser soon arrived, trebled or quadrupled, when demanded by way of a forced contribution. I quickly found (I think it required two experiments to convince me) that this peremptory method was the only one which could be adopted with success; it never failed. Of course, however, when the provisions have been actually obtained, you can, if you choose, give money exceeding the value of the provisions to *somebody;* an English—a thoroughbred English traveller will always do this (though it is contrary to the custom of the country), for the quiet (false quiet though it be) of his own conscience; but, so to order the matter that the poor fellows who have been forced to contribute, should be the persons to receive the value of their supplies, is not possible; for a traveller to attempt anything so grossly just as that, would be too outrageous. The truth is that the usage of the East in old times, required the people of the village at their own cost to supply the wants of travellers; and the ancient custom is now adhered to—not in favour of travellers generally—but in favour of those who are deemed sufficiently powerful to enforce its observance; if the villagers, therefore, find a man waiving this right to oppress them, and offering coin for that which he is entitled to take without payment, they suppose at once that he is actuated by fear (fear of *them*, poor fellows!), and it is so delightful to them to act upon this flattering assumption, that they will forgo the advantage of a good price for their provisions rather than the rare luxury of refusing for once in their lives to part with their own possessions.

The practice of intimidation, thus rendered necessary, is utterly hateful to an Englishman; he finds himself forced to conquer his daily bread by the pompous threats of the Dragoman, his very subsistence, as well as his dignity and personal safety, being made to depend upon his servant's assuming a tone of authority which does not at all belong to him. Besides, he can scarcely fail to see that, as he passes through the country, he becomes the innocent cause of much extra injustice—many supernumerary wrongs. This he feels to be especially the case when he travels with relays. To be the owner of a horse or a mule within reach of an Asiatic potentate, is to lead the life of the hare and the rabbit—hunted down and ferreted out. Too often it happens that the works of the field are stopped in the day-time, that the inmates of the cottage are roused from their midnight sleep, by the sudden coming of a Government officer; and the poor husbandman, driven by threats and rewarded by curses, if he would not loose sight for ever of his captured beasts, must quit all, and follow them: this is done that the Englishman may travel; he would make his way more harmlessly if he could, but horses or mules he *must* have, and these are his ways and means.

The town of Nablous is beautiful; it lies in a valley hemmed in with olive-groves, and its buildings are interspersed with frequent palm trees. It is said to occupy the site of the ancient Sychem. I know not whether it was there, indeed, that the father of the Jews was accustomed to feed his flocks, but the valley is green and smiling, and is held at this day by a race more brave and beautiful than Jacob's unhappy descendants.

Nablous is the very furnace of Mahometan bigotry; and I believe that only a few months before the time of my going there, it would have been madly rash for a man, unless strongly guarded, to show himself to the people of the town in a Frank costume; but since their last insurrection, the Mahometans of the place had been so far subdued by the severity of Ibrahim Pasha, that they dared not now offer the slightest insult to an European. It was quite plain, however, that the effort with which the men of the old school refrained from expressing their opinion of a hat and a coat was horribly painful to them. As I walked through the streets and bazaars, a dead silence prevailed; every man suspended his employment, and gazed on me with a fixed, glassy look, which seemed to say, 'God is good, but how marvellous and inscrutable are his ways that thus he permits this white- faced dog of a Christian to hunt through the paths of the faithful!'

The insurrection of these people had been more formidable than any other that Ibrahim Pasha had to contend with; he was only able to crush them at last by the assistance of a fellow renowned for his resources in the way of stratagem and cunning, as well as for his knowledge of the country. This personage was no other than Aboo Goosh ('the father of lies'[1]). The man had been suddenly taken out of prison, and sent into his native hill-country, with orders to procreate a few choice falsehoods and snares for entrapping the rebellious mountaineers, and he performed his function so well that he quickly enabled Ibrahim to hem in and extinguish the insurrection; he was rewarded with the Governorship of Jerusalem, and this he held when I was there. I recollect, by the by, that he tried one of his stratagems upon me. I had not gone to see him (as I ought in courtesy to have done) upon my arrival at Jerusalem, but I happened to be the owner of a rather handsome amber tchibouquepiece; this the Governor heard of, and having also by some means contrived to see it, he sent me a softly-worded message with an offer to buy the pipe at a price immensely exceeding the sum I had given for it. He did not add my tchibouque to the rest of his trophies.

There was a small number of Greek Christians resident in Nablous, and over these the Mussulmans held a high hand, not even allowing them to speak to each other in the open streets; but if the Moslems thus set themselves above the poor Christians of the place, I, or rather my servants, soon took the ascendant over *them*. I recollect that just as we were starting from the place, and at a time when a number of people had gathered together in the main street to see our preparations, Mysseri, being provoked at some piece of perverseness on the part of a true Believer, coolly thrashed him with his horsewhip before the assembled crowd of fanatics. I was much annoyed at the time, for I thought that the people would probably rise against us. They turned rather pale, but stood still.

The day of my arrival at Nablous was a *fête*—the new year's day of the Mussulmans.[2] Most of the people were amusing themselves in the beautiful

---

[1] This is an appellation not implying blame, but merit; the 'lies' which it purports to affiliate are feints and cunning stratagems rather than the baser kind of falsehoods. The expression, in short, has nearly the same meaning as the English word 'Yorkshireman'.

[2] The 29th of April.

lawns and shady groves without the city. The men were all remotely apart from the other sex. The women in groups were diverting themselves and their children with swings. They were so handsome that they could not keep up their yashmaks; I believed that they had never before looked upon a man in the European dress, and when they now saw in me that strange phenomenon, and saw, too, how they could please the creature by showing him a glimpse of beauty, they seemed to think it more pleasant to do this, than to go on playing with swings. It was always, however, with a sort of zoological expression of countenance that they looked on the horrible monster from Europe; and whenever one of them gave me to see for one sweet instant the blushing of her unveiled face, it was with the same kind of air as that with which a young timid girl will edge her way up to an elephant, and tremblingly give him a nut from the tips of her rosy fingers.

ELIOT WARBURTON (1810–1852)

Born in Aughrim Co. Galway the son of a former inspector of constabulary in Ireland, Bartholomew Elliot Warburton was privately educated in Yorkshire before proceeding to Eton, where he met Kinglake, and Trinity College Oxford from where he graduated in 1834. Though called to the Irish bar in 1837 he 'abandoned the law to superintend his Irish estates, travel and write' (DNB) adopting the soubriquet 'Eliot Warburton' for his works of fiction and travel. His tour of Syria, Palestine and Egypt was conducted some years after Kinglake, in 1843, but *The Crescent and The Cross, or, Romance and Realities of Eastern Travel* appeared only a year after *Eothen*, the former strongly imitating the latter as well as rivalling it in popularity during the Victorian period. Warburton died en route to South America when the steamer *Amazon* caught fire off Lands End.

From:

***The Crescent and the Cross* (1845)**

Chapter VII diverges from Kinglake in its generalizing observations on Egyptian religion and society. Even though Warburton states he intends to write only about the 'common-place' mid-nineteenth century – 'glimpses of men and things in our time are all I can hope to offer' – he proceeds to reproduce many of the Orientalist and racial categorizations that become typical of much later Victorian writing on the Egyptian scene and indeed on the Middle East overall. His knowledge of Egypt comes more from Edward Lane than from his own observation.

The Moslem

> Where'er the sun before them shone,
> And paved the world with gold,
> They passed. Round Earth's most favoured zone
> Their chief his turban rolled.

From Hagar's desert, Ishmael's plains,
To Ocean's western fold,
They reared their crescent-crowned fanes,
And cloistered fountains cold.

AUBREY DE VERE

How comes it that almost every event of vivid romance, and visible chivalry, and poetry of action,* belongs to the olden time of man: while woman, his inspiration— his goddess as a pagan, his idol as a Christian—remains, to this day, in being and in influence the same? from the garden of Eden to the throne, ay, and the village-green of Europe, she has ever exercised despotic influence over the destinies of her "lord and master." At this day, we might meet Rebeccas at many a well, and Hagars in every desert of the East; Ediths, moreover, it may be, and Erminias in the cities thereof; but where is the hunter Ishmael to be found? where the rash, generous Esau— outlaw of the Israelitish fold! where are the chivalrous Saracen and the bold Crusader now? Alas! the two former are represented by a swindling, camel-jobbing Sheikh, who will try to cheat you on Mount Sinai; the latter by the slavish Arab of the Nile, and the travelling dandy who employs him.

Far pleasanter would it be to enlist the reader as the follower of Mahomet through the following chapter, to take up the standard of the Prophet, and accompany it in its marvellous progress over the wide East, until it waved upon the towers of Jerusalem, and saw its green folds reflected in the waters of the Nile. Pleasanter would it be to go back to the old times of Egypt's mysterious history, when men were blended and confounded with the Gods, and the dreamlike glories of Karnak seemed almost to justify such presumption. However visionary the pursuit, and however faint the approximation to the truth, it is still pleasant to be humbugged by the priests with Herodotus; to go "body-snatching" in kingly tombs with brave Belzoni; or even to pick beetles, and read "handwriting on the walls" with Rosellini, Champollion, and Sir Gardner Wilkinson—pleasanter would any of these subjects be than the dry discussion of common-place life in these commonplace times. But the attempt to introduce such subjects into these slight pages would be as vain as to embroider tapestry with Cleopatra's Needle: glimpses of men and things in our own time are all that I can hope to offer; and if not vivid and comprehensive, they shall be at least faithful, as far as in me lies.

The graceful garb, the flowing beard, and the majestic appearance of Orientals, are very imposing to a stranger's eye. The rich colouring, the antique attitudes, the various complexions, that continually present themselves,

---

* "Sir Philip Sidney's life was poetry turned into action."—. CAMPBELL.

form an unceasing series of "tableaux vivans" in an Eastern city. And when over these is poured the brilliant sunshine of their climate, now making strong shadow of a palm-tree or a pile of Saracenic architecture, now gleaming upon jewel-hilted scimitars or gorgeous draperies, daily life wears an interest and picturesqueness unknown in this cloud-stricken land of hats and macintoshes.

The population of Cairo is composed of the descendants of Æthiopians, Romans, Greeks, Persians, Saracens, Arabs, and modern Europeans: the general maternity of the middle classes is Abyssinian. The variety of feature, form, colour, and character, resulting from such a mingling of races may be easily conceived. With respect to colour, the effect is pretty much the same as if all the tints in a paint-box were mixed up together, a variously modified brown being the result. In the women especially, the eye soon becomes accustomed to this complexion; and, as the Eastern people never become reconciled to ours, it would appear that we are not of the "right colour," after all; that our swarthy brethren have plausible grounds for asserting that Adam and Eve were copper-coloured, or something more; and that pallor of skin first appeared when Cain was questioned as to the cause of his brother's death. One fact relating to colour struck me as singular, that the Turks and Arabs were no darker in the face than on the arms or other parts usually protected from the sun. On our return from Nubia, we found ourselves, on our first glimpse in a looking-glass after two months' absence, daguerreotyped into a very magpie complexion—face, neck, and hands, were Arab-dark; while forehead and arms looked white as a woman's from the contrast.

The Turk seems to suffer little change from the climate, notwithstanding the light-brown colour of his hair and moustaches; and his olive-coloured complexion never assumes that yellowish tinge that seems peculiar to the people of Lower Egypt. As you ascend the river, the colour of the natives deepens so gradually, that you might almost calculate the latitude by their shade. Strange to say, however, after you have arrived at, and passed through, a nation as black as midnight, with coarse, crisp hair, you emerge, farther on, amongst a people of light olive colour, with smooth, shining tresses; these characteristics show the Abyssinian, who appears to be the purest and most distinct race in Africa. As the Egyptian generally has his family by Abyssinian wives or slaves, instead of, or in addition to, his Arab wives, he degenerates, in every generation, from the pure Arab race. The Bedouin requires a chapter to himself; the Osmanli, or Turk, will be introduced under the head of Constantinople; the Copt will appear in better company than he deserves, in speaking of the missionary schools; and our present concern is only with the Moslem-Egyptian-Arab of the cities and the villages along the Nile.

The childhood of this luckless specimen of man is passed in his mother's hareem in languor and effeminacy; he is not weaned for eighteen months, and his infancy is proportionately prolonged. At school, his education is limited chiefly to reading and writing, with sometimes a little arithmetic. Those who go to the University (in the mosque of el Azhar) acquire little more instruction of any practical utility. If an Egyptian can read, write, and repeat the greater part of tile Koran, he is considered learned; if to this he adds some knowledge of Arab poetry, he is a very accomplished and "promising young man."

The chief studies in the University are Mahomet's religion, and Heaven knows whose jurisprudence: medicine, chemistry, astronomy, and other sciences which are derived from the East, are very little cultivated. This, however, is to be understood only of the Egyptian when left to himself: Mehemet Ali has recently established numerous schools for boys: of these I shall speak when discussing the character of the Pasha.

An Egyptian infant is the most ill-favoured object in human creation; a name is applied to him with as little ceremony as a nickname is with us; and, indeed, there are not perhaps twenty different names distributed among the 200,000 Moslem inhabitants of Cairo; they are almost all taken from the Prophet or his immediate relations and followers. In our crew of ten men, we have five Mahmouds, or Mohammeds, two Ibraheems, three Abdallahs, and a Jad. As the Egyptian grows into childhood, he appears still more deformed, and extremely corpulent; but in manhood he becomes well-proportioned, stalwart, and sinewy; those at least who are employed upon the river. The city Egyptian never takes any active exercise, and passes nearly all his time squatted on his divan or counter. Many of the shopkeepers at Cairo are merely amateur tradesmen, being possessed of private property, and carrying on business, as good young ladies do in our bazaars, principally for amusement.

Along the river, and among the villages, the poor man is occupied with agriculture, boat-building, or the most laborious occupation of pumping up water to irrigate the fields. His children of both sexes run about naked, or nearly so; and if the little girls *have* a rag upon them, they coquettishly cover their *faces* with it. The peasant's utmost exertions scarcely suffice to earn two-pence a day; and even this pittance is often wrung from him for the Pasha, when some neighbour has failed in the taxes, for which the community is answerable. Yet happy does he consider himself, if allowed even thus to struggle on through life. The bright sun shines, and the cool river flows for him, however deep his poverty; and the faint shadow of freedom that he then enjoys gives energy to his labour. But the Pasha must have workmen for his factories, and labourers for his crops. Conscription, for these purposes, then seizes those whom that for war had spared; and the fellah is torn from his home, to work under the lash of a taskmaster, for the nominal wages of two-pence halfpenny a day. This is sometimes two years in arrear, and even then paid half in kind, at the Pasha's valuation of whatever he has least occasion for.

Such is the Egyptian peasant's lot, aggravated by privations that are incredible. If sick, be has no medicine or medical advice, and he dies; if starving, he must steal from his own crop, which the Pasha has set his seal upon, and he suffers the bastinado. If a conscript for war, he is kept in camp until no longer fit for service: then thrown upon the world to beg and die.

This is a dreary picture, but it is too true; and yet, under all these miseries, even here "the human heart vindicates its strong right to be glad:" amongst the most wretched hovels, under the most abject appearance of misery, I thought I could observe about the same proportion of merriment and amusement, sorrow and indifference, as in joyous Italy, or in our own favoured islands. No people, when exiled, suffer more from the *mal du pays* than the Egyptian, though his attachment to the soil be simply feline: all the factitious luxuries of Europe cannot compensate to him for his own voluptuous climate, his loved river with its indolent flow, the whispers of the palm-forest, bending with his favourite fruit. The Pasha and the Sheikh may rob him to the uttermost; his sense of Destiny and unconsciousness of wrong will make him submit to tyranny and oppression without repining;—leave him but his liberty, such as it is and his sunny home, and he asks no more on this side of Paradise.

In no other people, perhaps, is their history so clearly legible as in the Egyptian character: his loyalty is slavishness; his courage is ferocity; his religion, superstition; his love, sensual; his abstinence, pharisaical; his resignation, a dastard fatalism. Yet, let us rather—remembering his disadvantages—wonder that any virtues should survive their effects, than that vices should abound.

When young, the Egyptian is remarkably precocious in intellect, and learns with facility. As he grows up, his intelligence seems to be dulled or diminished; he has no genius for discovery, and, though apt in acquiring rudiments, he is incapable of generalising. He fills subordinate departments well, but appears incapable of taking or of keeping a lead.

The dress of the middle classes consists of a red cloth skull-cap, over which is wound a turban of green, or black, or white muslin, according to the station or the creed of the wearer. The first is only worn by descendants of the Prophet; the second by the Copts, or Egyptian Christians; the third is open to any who chooses to adopt it. A chemise of cotton is covered by a silk waistcoat, and very loose cotton drawers; over this is worn a loose robe of striped silk, with wide sleeves, confined round the body by a rich silken scarf, and over all is generally worn another loose robe of cloth, or darker coloured silk. A pair of yellow slippers is worn within another pair of a red colour, which they put off on entering a mosque or private dwelling.

The Mahommedan faith is strictly Unitarian: the Prophet is only prayed to as an intercessor. The religious Moslem performs his devotions five times a day, and sometimes twice in the night besides; he is strictly observant of numerous and trying fasts; he distributes alms in large proportion to his means; every act of his life is prefaced by a prayer, and yet he trusts to God's mercy alone for his hopes of heaven. He is ever conscious of the invisible and future world, and takes pride in acts of devotion that seem to him a vindication of his claims to a connection with that world. For this reason he despises the Protestant, whom he calls the "prayerless;" as he looks down on the Roman Catholic and the Greek as idolaters, on account of their processions, and their worship of saints and images.

Unfortunately, this familiarity with the name of the Deity leads to its introduction on the most irrelevant and irreverent subjects; and he often prefaces with "Please God," or "God prosper me," an observation that the "prayerless" Protestant would blush to listen to.

The resignation of the Islamite is the most respectable part of his religion; the most sudden and bitter misfortune is received as sent from God, and to be borne with humble patience. Death itself, cowardly as he seems in other respects, is encountered and undergone by the Moslem with dignity and fortitude: in setting out to travel, he is more anxious to provide himself with a shroud, than any other "change" of linen: if he is ill by the wayside, the caravan, which waits for none, moves on, and his death is inevitable; the sufferer then performs "the ablution" with sand, clothes himself with his shroud, and exercises his remaining strength in scraping a grave, with a heap of sand on the windy side. Then, trusting to the desert blast to cover him, he quietly lies down to die, with a parting prayer that his lonely grave may not be forgotten by the Resurrection Angel at the last day.[*]

The Moslem of the cities, also, when his last hour is come, turns himself in the direction of Mecca, and dies with as much resignation as if he did it on purpose; then his family raise cries of lamentation, such as "Oh, my camel!" "Oh, my lion!" "Oh, my only one!" These ejaculations become more striking as they proceed: "Oh, my buffalo!" does not sound pathetic, though it means simply that the dead was their support; and "Oh, my jackass!" sounds ambiguous, until the addition of "bearer of my burdens" turns it into eloquence.[†] The wailing-women and the grave-men now arrive, and, laid upon a bier, he is carried, all coffinless, to his last resting-place, and laid literally on the shelf, in the vault of his family.

In Paradise he finds the extreme of sensual enjoyment, as a reward for the mortification of the senses in this life; so that his self-denial on earth is only

---

[*] The angel Gabriel is the minister of divine vengeance. Azräel receives the parting soul. Israfel sounds the judgment trumpet, and opens the grave.
[†] I have taken the greater part of these observations from Mr. Lane's invaluable work— the highest authority.

an enlargement of the heroic abstinence of an alderman from luncheon on the day of a city feast. His heavenly hareem consists of 300 houris, all perfect in loveliness. What chance has his poor wife of being required under such circumstances!—it is *supposed* she has a heaven of her own, in some place or other, but as to *her* substitute for Houris the Koran is discreetly silent. In Paradise is to be found every luxury of every appetite, with every concomitant, except satiety and indigestion.

I have dwelt thus long on the incidents and character of Egyptian life, as it concerns us not a little politically as well as otherwise. The relations of his country are becoming daily more involved with those of England, and it concerns us not a little how he lives, how he acts and feels towards his present government. See him reduced from man's proud estate—divested of all interest in the land which is but farmed by a foreign adventurer—excluded from all share in politics—without a ray of freedom to light him onward through thought to action. Within the precincts of his hareem alone he feels himself a man, and there all his thoughts and ambition dwell imprisoned: not daring to mount a horse, lest it should draw upon him the attention of the taxgatherer or his spies, the descendant of the desert chieftains betakes himself to a donkey, and goes forth to his counter, his only business; or squats in a gloomy coffee-house, his only place of public resort. There he sits and smokes with downcast eyes, unless the voice of the story-teller strikes upon some chord of fancy not yet quite numbed; and, in the adventures of his forefathers, he is roused to feel an interest that nothing in his own dull life can waken. Can this man's fate be worse—can any change bring additional suffering or humiliation upon this fallen race?

The Turks, or Osmanlis, are of small number, but high consideration in Egypt. They are to the Arabs what the Normans were to the Irish five hundred years ago—a proud, privileged class, without a sympathy for their vassals, except such as their religion may impose. They are, for the most, ignorant of Arabic, considering it derogatory to learn the language of a conquered race. Endowed with an instinct and power of command, in which the Egyptian is utterly deficient, they occupy all posts of trust throughout the Pasha's provinces. They are also less avaricious than the Egyptians who are placed in authority; and, though equally lax in their ideas of justice, they seldom exercise the same grinding oppression that the Arab inflicts upon his fellow countrymen when in his power.

The Turk is vain, ignorant, presumptuous, and authoritative (I speak of the governors and officers, who are the only Osmanlis of Egypt of whom I have had any experience); yet in society he is courteous, affable, and gentlemanlike. He never, or very rarely, intermarries with Egyptians; and, as it is a well-known fact that children born of other women in this country rapidly degenerate or die, there are few instances of indigenous Turks in Egypt.[*] Through the long reign of the Mamelukes, there was not one instance, I believe, of a son succeeding to his father's power and possessions. The Mamelukes were young Georgian or Circassian slaves, adopted by their owners, and adopting others in their turn; this Dynasty of Foundlings ruled for many years in the land of the Pharaohs, and is now extinct; some few survived the massacre under Mehemet Ali, but they have gradually died away. When I arrived, the last of them was to be seen at Alexandria, with snow-white beard and bended form, but an eye that, in extreme old age, retained all its youthful fire. This last of a persecuting and persecuted race is now at rest, with a turban carved in stone above his tomb.

---

[*] Mehemet Ali's large family would appear to be a remarkable exception. Ibrahim, however, is of European birth, and the others form slight exceptions to the rule of degeneracy.

HARRIET MARTINEAU (1802–1876)

Martineau's life represents a triumph over early adversity. Overcoming poverty and ill health in childhood, and despite advancing deafness as an adult, she supported her siblings and established a career by writing for the *Daily News* and the *Edinburgh Review*. Born into a Unitarian family her radicalism – especially her antislavery principles and concern for the conditions of women – is incorporated into her travel writing, beginning with *Society in America* (1837), an account of a tour of both the southern and northern states of the USA. Martineau even went so far as to produce a manual for travellers, *How to Observe Morals and Manners* (1838). Her write up of her journeys in Egypt and Palestine of 1846–47, *Eastern Life, Present and Past*, appeared in 1848. As an observer of the East her Victorian social reformist principles and espousal of the 'higher criticism' of religion appeared to leave little room for her to connect with local people and their customs. She saw the world of the Middle East 'as frozen in biblical history' (Harper DLB/166: 255). Pointing out that only five of the twenty-four chapters of *Eastern Life* are concerned with 'modern' Egyptians, Billie Melman dubs Martineau as belonging to the 'mythopically ethnocentric' type of traveller: 'Time and again she discloses her total lack of interest in the Muslim Orient and in contemporary Egypt' (Melman 1992: 63, 242).

From:

Eastern Life, Present and Past **(1848)**

This chapter on the harem, based on several cursory visits made in Cairo, reveals Martineau at her most censorious and may have been influenced by her experience of slavery in North America rather than research into Eastern life; a paragraph after this extract she draws a direct comparison between Carolina and Cairo. Duff Gordon was right to consider Martineau's models atypical of native Egyptian marriages. The examples Martineau inscribes may represent the exceedingly circumscribed lives of women married into the Turco-Circassian elite that other Victorian women found aspects to admire in (See Melman 1992, Ch 5).

The Hareem

At ten o'clock one morning, Mrs. Y. and I were home from our early ride, and dressed for a visit to a hareem of a high order. The lady to whose kindness we mainly owed this opportunity accompanied us, with her daughter. We had a disagreeable drive in the carriage belonging to the hotel, knocking against asses, horses and people all the way. We alighted at the entrance of a paved passage leading to a court, which we crossed: and then, in a second court, we were before the entrance of the hareem.

A party of eunuchs stood before a faded curtain, which they held aside when the gentlemen of our party and the dragomen had gone forward. Retired some way behind the curtain stood, in a half circle, eight or ten slave girls, in an attitude of deep obeisance. Two of them then took charge of each of us, holding us by the arms above the elbows, to help us upstairs.—After crossing a lobby at the top of the stairs, we entered a handsome apartment, where lay the chief wife,—at that time an invalid.—The ceiling was gaily painted; and so were the walls, the latter with curiously bad attempts at domestic perspective. There were four handsome mirrors; and the curtains in the doorway were of a beautiful shawl fabric, fringed and tasselled. A Turkey carpet not only covered the whole floor, but was turned up at the corners. Deewáns extended round nearly the whole room,— a lower one for ordinary use, and a high one for the seat of honour. The windows, which had a sufficient fence of blinds, looked upon a pretty garden, where I saw orange trees and many others, and the fences were hung with rich creepers.

On cushions on the floor lay the chief lady, ill and miserable looking. She rose as we entered; but we made her lie down again and she was then covered with a silk counterpane. Her dress was, as we saw when she rose, loose trowsers of blue striped cotton under her black silk jacket: and the same blue cotton appeared at the wrists, under her black sleeves. Her head-dress was of black net, bunched out curiously behind. Her hair was braided down the sides of this head-dress behind, and the ends were pinned over her forehead. Some of the black net was brought round her face, and under the chin, showing the outline of a face which had no beauty in it, nor traces of former beauty, but which was interesting to-day from her manifest illness and unhappiness. There was a strong expression of waywardness and peevishness about the mouth, however. She wore two handsome diamond rings; and she and one other lady had watches and gold chains. She complained of her head; and her left hand was bound up: she made signs, by pressing her bosom, and imitating the dandling of a baby, which, with her occasional tears, persuaded my companions that she had met with some accident and had lost her infant. On leaving the hareem, we found that it was not a child of her own that she was mourning, but that of a white girl in the hareem: and that the wife's illness was wholly from grief for the loss of this baby ;—a curious illustration of the feelings and manners of the place! The children born in large hareems are extremely few: and they are usually idolised, and sometimes murdered. It is known that in the houses at home which morally most resemble these hareems (though little enough externally), when the rare event of the birth of a child happens, a passionate joy extends over the wretched household:—jars are quieted, drunkenness is moderated, and there is no self-denial which the poor creatures will not undergo during this gratification of their feminine instincts. They will nurse the child all night in illness, and pamper it all day with sweetmeats and toys; they will fight for the possession of it, and be almost heartbroken at its loss and lose it they must; for the child always dies,—killed with kindness, even if born healthy. This natural outbreak of feminine instinct takes place in the too populous hareem, when a child is given to any one of the many who are longing for the gift: and if it dies naturally, it is mourned as we saw, through a wonderful conquest of personal jealousy by this general instinct. But when the jealousy is uppermost,—what happens then?—why, the strangling the innocent in its sleep,—or the letting it slip from the window into the river below,—or the mixing poison with its food;—the mother and the murderess, always rivals and now fiends, being shut up together for life. If the child lives, what then? If a girl, she sees before her from the beginning the nothingness of external life, and the chaos of interior existence, in which she is to dwell for life. If a boy, he remains among the women till ten years old, seeing things when the eunuchs come in to romp, and hearing things among the chatter of the ignorant women, which brutalise him for life before the age of rationality comes. But I will not dwell on these hopeless miseries.

A sensible-looking old lady, who had lost an eye, sat at the head of the invalid: and a nun-like elderly woman, whose head and throat were wrapped in unstarched muslin, sat behind for a time, and then went away, after an affectionate salutation to the invalid.—Towards the end of the visit, the husband's mother came in,—looking like a little old man in her coat trimmed with fur. Her countenance was cheerful and pleasant. We saw, I think, about twenty more women,—some slaves,—most or all young—some good-looking, but none handsome. Some few were black; and the rest very light:—Nubians or Abyssinians and Circassians, no doubt. One of the best figures, as a picture, in the hareem, was a Nubian girl, in an amber-coloured watered silk, embroidered with black, looped up in festoons, and finished with a black bodice. The richness of the gay printed cotton skirts and sleeves surprised us: the finest shawls could hardly have looked better. One graceful girl had her pretty figure well shown by a tight-fitting black dress. Their heads were dressed much like the chief lady's. Two, who must have been sisters, if not twins, had patches between the eyes. One handmaid was barefoot, and several were without shoes. Though there were none of the whole large number who could be called particularly pretty individually, the scene was, on the whole, exceedingly striking, as the realisation of what one knew before, but as in a dream. The girls went and came in, but, for the most part, stood in a half circle. Two sat on their heels for a time: and some went to play in the neighbouring apartments.

Coffee was handed to us twice, with all the well-known apparatus of jewelled cups, embroidered tray cover, and gold-flowered napkins. There were chibouques, of course: and sherbets in cut glass cups. The time was passed in attempts to have conversation by signs; attempts which are fruitless among people of the different ideas which belong to different races. How much they made out about us, we do not know: but they inquired into the mutual relationships of the party, and put the extraordinary questions which are always put to ladies who visit the hareems.—A young lady of my acquaintance, of the age of eighteen, but looking younger, went with her mother to a hareem in Cairo (not the one I have been describing), and excited great amazement when obliged to confess that she had not either children or a husband. One of the wives threw her arms about her, entreated her to stay for ever, said she should have any husband she liked, but particularly recommended her own, saying that she was sure he would soon wish for another wife, and she had so much rather it should be my young friend, who would amuse her continually, than anybody else that she could not be so fond of. Everywhere they pitied us European women heartily, that we had to go about travelling, and appearing in the streets without being properly taken care of— that is, watched. They think us strangely neglected in being left so free, and boast of their spy system and imprisonment as tokens of the value in which they are held.

The mourning worn by the lady who went with us was the subject of much speculation: and many questions were asked about her home and family. To appease the curiosity about her home, she gave her card. As I anticipated, this did not answer. It was the great puzzle of the whole interview. At first the poor lady thought it was to do her head good: then, she fidgetted about it, in the evident fear of omitting some observance: but at last, she understood that she was to keep it. When we had taken our departure, however, a eunuch was sent after us to inquire of the dragoman what "the letter" was which our companion had given to the lady.

The difficulty is to get away, when one is visiting a hareem. The poor ladies cannot conceive of one's having anything to do; and the only reason they can understand for the interview coming to an end is the arrival of sunset, after which it would, they think, be improper for any woman to be abroad. And the amusement to them of such a visit is so great that they protract it to the utmost, even in such a case as ours to-day, when all intercourse was conducted by dumb show. It is certainly very tiresome; and the only wonder is that the hostesses can like it. To sit hour after hour on the deewán, without any exchange of ideas, having our clothes examined, and being plied with successive cups of coffee and sherbet, and pipes, and being gazed at by a half-circle of girls in brocade and shawls, and made to sit down again as soon as one attempts to rise, is as wearisome an experience as one meets with in foreign lands.—The weariness of heart is, however, the worst part of it. I noted all the faces well during our constrained stay; and I saw no trace of mind in any one, except in the homely one-eyed old lady. All the younger ones were dull, soulless, brutish, or peevish. How should it be otherwise, when the only idea of their whole lives is that which, with all our interests and engagements, we consider too prominent with us? There cannot be a woman of them all who is not dwarfed and withered in mind and soul by being kept wholly engrossed with that one interest,—detained at that stage in existence which, though most important in its place, is so as a means to ulterior ends. The ignorance is fearful enough: but the grossness is revolting.

At the third move, and when it was by some means understood that we were waited for, we were permitted to go,—after a visit of above two hours. The sick lady rose from her cushions, notwithstanding our opposition, and we were conducted forth with much observance. On each side of the curtain which overhung the outer entrance stood a girl with a bottle of rose-water, some of which was splashed in our faces as we passed out.

We had reached the carriage when we were called back;—his Excellency was waiting for us. So we visited him in a pretty apartment, paved with variegated marbles, and with a fountain in the centre. His Excellency was a sensible-looking man, with gay, easy, and graceful manners. He lamented the mistake about the interpreter, and said we must go again, when we might have conversation. He insisted upon attending us to the carriage, actually passing between the files of beggars which lined the outer passage. The dragoman was so excessively shocked by this degree of condescension, that we felt obliged to be so too, and remonstrated, but in vain. He stood till the door was shut and the whip was cracked. He is a liberal-minded man, and his hareem is nearly as favourable a specimen as could be selected for a visit; but what is this best specimen? I find these words written down on the same day in my journal: written, as I well remember, in heaviness of heart:—"I am glad of the opportunity of seeing a hareem: but it leaves an impression of discontent and uneasiness which I shall be glad to sleep off. And I am not conscious that there is prejudice in this. I feel that a visit to the worst room in the rookery in St. Giles's would have affected me less painfully. There are there at least the elements of a rational life, however perverted; while here humanity is wholly and hopelessly baulked. It will never do to look on this as a case for cosmopolitan philosophy to regard complacently, and require a good construction for. It is not a phase of natural early manners.

It is as pure a conventionalism as our representative monarchy, or German heraldry, or Hindoo caste; and the most atrocious in the world."

And of this atrocious system Egypt is the most atrocious example. It has unequalled facilities for the importation of black, and white slaves, and these facilities are used to the utmost; yet the population is incessantly on the decline. But for the importation of slaves, the upper classes, where polygamy runs riot, must soon die out, so few are the children born, and so fatal to health are the arrangements of society. The finest children are those born of Circassian or Georgian mothers; and but for these we should soon hear little more of upper class in Egypt.—Large numbers are brought from the south,—the girls to be made attendants or concubines in the hareem, and the boys to be made, in a vast proportion, those guards to the female part of the establishment whose mere presence is a perpetual insult and shame to humanity. The business of keeping up the supply of these miserable wretches—of whom the Pasha's eldest daughter has fifty for her exclusive service—is in the hands of the Christians of Asyoot. It is these Christians who provide a sufficient supply, and cause a sufficient mortality to keep the number of the sexes pretty equal, in consideration of which we cannot much wonder that Christianity does not appear very venerable in the eyes of Mohammedans.

ROBERT CURZON (1810–1873)

Son of Viscount Curzon and Baroness de la Zouche and educated at Charterhouse and Christ Church Oxford, Robert had an uneasy relationship with his parents whose long lives precluded him from entering into his inheritance – the family estate at Parham, Sussex – until three years before his own death in 1873. He first travelled in the Levant in 1833–34 after losing his seat as M. P. following the Reform Act of 1832. His troubled relations with his parents partly accounts for his time in the Middle East, which resumed in 1837 with a visit to Egypt, the Natron Lakes in the Libyan Desert, then on to Istanbul, Albania and Greece where he visited the monasteries of Mt. Athos. His time abroad continued with his appointment as Sir Stratford Canning's private secretary at the Istanbul embassy in 1841. The following year he started out for Armenia where he helped resolve border disputes. Together with A. W. Kinglake and Eliot Warburton – with whom he is often compared – Curzon published an account of travel in the Middle East that can be said to have chimed with the early Victorian public mood. As in the work of the other two writers, the voice of *Visits to Monasteries in the Levant* (1849) might be characterized as confident and proprietary in regard to the land and peoples it describes. What distinguishes Curzon's writing from theirs is a deeper knowledge of the region acquired through longer stays there. If his connection with Eastern monasteries as a collector of old manuscripts furnished the context for his first travel work, the period spent defining the boundaries between Ottoman Turkey and Persia resulted in his second work, *Armenia: A Year at Erzeroom, and on the Frontiers of Russia, Turkey, and Persia* (1854). Overall, there is variation in Curzon's discursive positions – at times chauvinistic, at others critical of the nostrums of Western Christendom. His style ranges from affable condescension in the Kinglake mode, and acquiescence in Oriental decay, to sudden engagement with Islamic culture – the muezzin's call to prayer being better than 'the clang and jingle of our European bells.' He was a strong admirer of Ibrahim Pasha, who in the 1830s had extended Muhammad Ali's power from Egypt into Syria. *Visits to Monasteries in the Levant* commends the disinterested exercise of power by

Ibrahim in Curzon's classic account of the riot in the church of the Holy Sepulchre and of 'the gruesome night that followed' (Hogarth 1983: xii) in which hundreds of worshippers died in a stampede during the miracle of the holy fire. With apparent reluctance Curzon also approved of the Turks: 'I do not respect them as a nation, still I cannot help admiring their calmness and self-possession in moments of difficulty and danger.'

From:

Visits to Monasteries in the Levant (1849)

A subject resonant with emotional significance at any time, a description of an English pilgrim's first sight of Jerusalem written in the third decade of the nineteenth century possessed added significance when European power was in the ascendant and Muslim power in decline. Curzon's religious chauvinism appears to be confirmed in his invocation of the Crusader spirit: 'I longed to tear down the red [Ottoman] flag and replace it with the banner of St. George.' A Protestant note is also detectable in his remarks on the Greek Christians' 'detestation of everything connected with the Latin Church [that] exceeds their aversion to the Muhammadan creed.'

Jerusalem

We left our camels and dromedaries, and wild Arabs of the desert, at Gaza; and being now provided with horses, we took our way across the hills towards Jerusalem.

The road passes over a succession of rounded rocky hills, almost every step being rendered interesting by its connection with the events of Holy Writ. On our left we saw the village of Kobab, and on our right the ruins of a castle said to have been built by the Maccabees, and not far from it the remains of an ancient Christian church.

As our train of horses surmounted each succeeding eminence, every one was eager to be the first who should catch a glimpse of the Holy City. Again and again we were disappointed; another rocky valley yawned beneath us, and another barren stony hill rose up beyond. There seemed to be no end to the intervening hills and dales; they appeared to multiply beneath our feet. At last, when we had almost given up the point, and had ceased to contend for the first view by galloping ahead, as we ascended another rocky brow we saw the towers of what seemed to be a Gothic castle; then, as we approached nearer, a long line of walls and battlements appeared crowning a ridge of rock which rose from a narrow valley to the right. This was the valley of the pools of Gihon, where Solomon was crowned, and the battlements which rose above it were the long-looked-for walls of Jerusalem. With one accord our whole party drew their bridles, and stood still to gaze for the first time upon this renowned and sacred city.

It is not easy to describe the sensations which fill the breast of a Christian when, after a long and toilsome journey, he first beholds this, the most interesting and venerated spot upon the whole surface of the globe—the chosen city of the Lord, the place in which it pleased Him to dwell. Every one was silent for a while, absorbed in the deepest contemplation. The object of our pilgrimage was accomplished, and I do not think that anything we saw afterwards during our stay in Jerusalem made a more profound impression on our minds than this first distant view.

It was curious to observe the different effect which our approach to Jerusalem had upon the various persons who composed our party. A Christian pilgrim, who had joined us on the road, fell down upon his knees and kissed the holy ground; two others embraced each other, and congratulated themselves that they had lived to see Jerusalem. As for us Franks, we sat bolt upright upon our horses, and stared and said nothing; whilst around us the more natural children of the East wept for joy, and, as in the army of the Crusaders, the word Jerusalem! Jerusalem! was repeated from mouth to mouth; but we, who consider ourselves civilised and superior beings, repressed our emotions; we were above showing that we participated in the feelings of our barbarous companions. As for myself, I would have got off my horse and walked barefooted towards the gate, as some did, if I had dared; but I was in fear of being laughed at for my absurdity, and therefore sat fast in my saddle. At last I blew my nose, and, pressing the sharp edges of my Arab stirrups on the lank sides of my poor weary jade, I rode on slowly towards the Bethlehem gate.

On the sloping sides of the valley of Gihon numerous groups of people were lying under the olive trees in the cool of the evening, and parties of grave Turks, seated on their carpets by the road-side, were smoking their long pipes in dignified silence. But what struck me most were some old white-bearded Jews, who were holding forth to groups of their friends or disciples under the walls of the city of their fathers, and dilating perhaps upon the glorious actions of their race in former days.

Jerusalem has been described as a deserted and melancholy ruin, filling the mind with images of desolation and decay, but it did not strike me as such. It is still a compact city, as it is described in Scripture; the Saracenic walls have a stately, magnificent appearance; they are built of large and massive stones. Windsor Castle multiplied by ten would have very much the appearance of Jerusalem as seen from this point of view. The square towers, which are seen at intervals, are handsome and in good repair; and there is an imposing dignity in the appearance of the grim old citadel, which rises in the centre of the line of walls and towers, with its batteries and terraces one above another, surmounted with the crimson flag of Turkey floating heavily over the conquered city of the Christians. I wonder whether in these times any portion of that spirit could be revived which animated our ancestors in the romantic days of the Crusades. I longed to tear down the red flag with its white crescent, and replace it with the banner of St. George. Nothing would please me more than to—

'Chase these pagans, in those holy fields,
Over whose acres walked those blessed feet,
Which *eighteen* hundred years ago were nail'd,
For our advantage, on the bitter cross.'[3]

We entered by the Bethlehem gate: it is commanded by the citadel, which was built by the people of Pisa, and is still called the castle of the Pisani. There we had some parleying with the Egyptian guards, and, crossing an open space, famous in monastic tradition as the garden where Bathsheba was bathing when she was seen by King David from the roof of his palace, we threaded a labyrinth of narrow streets, which the horses of our party completely blocked up; and as soon as we could, we sent a man with our letters of introduction to the superior of the Latin convent. I had letters from Cardinal Weld and Cardinal Pedicini, which we presumed would ensure us a warm and hospitable reception; and as travellers are usually lodged in the monastic establishments, we went on at once to the Latin convent of St. Salvador, where we expected to enjoy all the comforts and luxuries of European civilisation after our weary journey over the desert from Egypt. We, however, quickly discovered our mistake; for, on dismounting at the gate of the convent, we were received in a very cool way by the monks, who appeared to make the reception of travellers a mere matter of interest, and treated us as if we were dust under their feet. They put us into a wretched hole in the Casa Nuova, a house belonging to them near the convent, where there was scarcely room for our baggage; and we went to bed not a little mortified at our inhospitable reception by our Christian brethren, so different from what we had always experienced from the Mohammedans. The convent of St. Salvador belongs to a community of Franciscan friars; they were most of them Spaniards, and, being so far away from the superior officers of their order, they were not kept in very perfect discipline. It was probably owing to our being heretics that we were not better received. Fortunately we had our own beds, tents, cooking utensils, carpets, etc.;

---

[3] Henry IV., Part I.

so that we soon made ourselves comfortable in the bare vaulted rooms which were allotted to us, and for which, by the by, we had to pay pretty handsomely.

The next morning early we went to the church of the Holy Sepulchre, descending the hill from the convent, and then down a flight of narrow steps into a small paved court, one side of which is occupied by the Gothic front of the church. The court was full of people selling beads and crucifixes and other holy ware. We had to wait some time till the Turkish doorkeepers came to unlock the door, as they keep the keys of the church, which is only open on certain days, except to votaries of distinction. There is a hole in the door, through which the pilgrims gave quantities of things to the monks inside to be laid upon the sepulchre. At last the door was opened, and we went into the church.

On entering these sacred walls the attention is first directed to a large slab of marble on the floor opposite the door, with several lamps suspended over it, and three enormous waxen tapers about twenty feet in height standing at each end. The pilgrims approach it on their knees, touch and kiss it, and prostrating themselves before it, offer up their adoration. This, you are told, is the stone on which the body of our Lord was washed and anointed, and prepared for the tomb.

Turning to the left, we came to a round stone let into the pavement, with a canopy of ornamental ironwork over it. Here the Virgin Mary is said to have stood when the body of our Saviour was taken down from the cross.

Leaving this, we entered the circular space immediately under the great dome, which is about eighty feet in diameter, and is surrounded by eighteen large square piers, which support the front of a broad gallery. Formerly this circular gallery was supported by white marble pillars; but the church was burnt down in 1808, through the negligence of a drunken Greek monk, who set a light to some parts of the woodwork, and then endeavoured to put out the flames by throwing aqua vitae upon them, which he mistook for water.

The Chapel of the Sepulchre stands under the centre of the dome. It is a small oblong house of stone, rounded at one end, where there is an altar for the Coptic and Abyssinian Christians. At the other end it is square, and has a platform of marble in front, which is ascended by a flight of steps, and has a low parapet wall and a seat on each side. The chapel contains two rooms. Taking off our shoes and turbans, we entered a low narrow door, and went into a chamber, in the centre of which stands a block of polished marble. On this stone sat the angel who announced the blessed tidings of the resurrection.

From this room, which has a small round window on each side, we passed through another low door into the inner chamber, which contains the Holy Sepulchre itself, which, however, is not visible, being concealed by an altar of white marble. It is said to be a long narrow excavation like a grave or the interior of a sarcophagus hewed out of the rock just beneath the level of the ground. Six rows of lamps of silver gilt, twelve in each row, hang from the ceiling, and are kept perpetually burning. The tomb occupies nearly one-half of the sepulchral chamber, and extends from one end of it to the other on the right side of the door as you enter; a space of three feet wide and rather more than six feet long in front of it being all that remains for the accommodation of the pilgrims, so that not more than three or four can be admitted at a time.

Leaving this hallowed spot, we were conducted first to the place where our Lord appeared to Mary Magdalene and then to the Chapel of the Latins, where a part of the pillar of flagellation is preserved.

The Greeks have possession of the choir of the church, which is opposite the door of the Holy Sepulchre. This part of the building is of great size, and is magnificently decorated with gold and carving and stiff pictures of the saints. In the centre is a globe of black marble on a pedestal, under which they say the head of Adam was found; and you are told also that this is the exact centre of the globe; the Greeks having thus transferred to Jerusalem, from the temple of Apollo at Delphi, the absurd notions of the pagan priests of antiquity relative to the form of the earth.

Returning towards the door of the church, and leaving it on our right hand, we ascended a flight of about twenty steps, and found ourselves in the Chapel of the Cross on Mount Calvary. At the upper end of this chapel is an altar, on the spot where the crucifixion took place, and under it is the hole into which the end of the cross was fixed: this is surrounded with a glory of silver gilt, and on each side of it, at the distance of about six feet, are the holes in which the crosses of the two thieves stood. Near to these is a long rent in the rock, which was opened by an earthquake at the time of the crucifixion. Although the three crosses appear to have stood very near to each other, yet, from the manner in which they are placed, there would have been room enough for them, as the cross of our Saviour stands in front of the other two.

Leaving this chapel, we entered a kind of vault under the stairs, in which the rent of the rock is again seen; it extends from the ceiling to the floor, and has every appearance of having been caused by some convulsion of nature, and not formed by the hands of man. Here were formerly the tombs of Godfrey de Bouillon and Baldwin his brother, who were buried beneath the cross for which they fought so valiantly: but these tombs have lately been destroyed by the Greeks, whose detestation of everything connected with the Latin Church exceeds their aversion to the Mohammedan creed. In the sacristy of the Latin monks we were shown the sword and spurs of Godfrey de Bouillon: the sword is apparently of the age assigned to it: it is double-edged and straight, with a cross-guard.

LUCIE DUFF GORDON (1821–1869)

Daughter of radical parents who were close friends of Jeremy Bentham, James Mill and the Carlyles, Lucie Austin was perhaps destined to follow the career path of her mother Sarah as a translator of German literature, having as a child travelled in Germany and lived for a period in France. Her marriage with minor aristocrat Alexander Duff Gordon in 1840 brought love and entry into fashionable social and literary circles if little money. However, nearly twenty years into her marriage and after having given birth to three children, Lucie discovered she had tuberculosis. In summer 1861 she set sail for South Africa, unaware that her exile 'would be the bridge to a different kind of wholeness, the route to another identity' (Frank 1994: 206). In the summer of 1862 she returned briefly to England but soon left for warmer climes, eventually arriving in Egypt in the autumn. She would live there until her death in 1869. There she acquired a new Egyptian household, led by her personal assistant, guide and translator Omar, which substituted her English one. Except for her married, eldest daughter Janet, who for a while came out to Alexandria, she thereafter rarely saw any of her own family. Published a year after *Letters from the Cape* (1864), *Letters from Egypt* 'ran through three imprints in the first year' (Searight 1983: xii). They coincided with and helped feed a burgeoning British fascination with Egypt, and even led to their infirm author having to fend off trophy hunters from her home in Luxor in Upper Egypt (ibid, xvi). Lucie's emotional investment in the people around her and criticism of the modernization schemes of Khedive Ismail and their exploitative impact on the native Egyptians created an appealing mix. In their affective treatment of human relationships the *Letters* diverge from the masculine urge to produce the type of objective 'scientific' description seen in the work of an author like Edward Lane. They graduate from a derivative Orientalist vision of Egypt and Egyptians to an intimate one that nevertheless still 'romanticize[s] Arabs and highlights herself as their benefactor' (Lockwood LTE: 351).

From:

Letters from Egypt (1865)

Typical of *Letters from Egypt* in the way in which it domesticates and thus humanises the Egyptians, the extract foregrounds Duff Gordon's solicitude for them (seen here especially in her care of the dying sheykh), and intentionally deconstructs European notions of Muslim fanaticism, in particular Harriet Martineau's 'attack upon hareems.'

To Sir Alexander Duff Gordon.
Wednesday, January 20, 1864

.... Mr. Arrowsmith kindly gave me Miss Martineau's book, which I have begun. It is true as far as it goes, but there is the usual defect—the people are not real people, only part of the scenery to her, as to most Europeans. You may conceive how much we are naturalized when I tell you that I have received a serious offer of marriage for Sally.* Mustapha A'gha has requested me to 'give her to him' for his eldest son Seyyid, a nice lad of nineteen or twenty at most. As Mustapha is the richest and most considerable person here, it shows that the Arabs draw no unfavourable conclusions as to our morals from the freedom of our manners. He said of course she would keep her own religion and her own customs. Seyyid is still in Alexandria, so it will be time to refuse when he returns. I said she was too old, but they think that no objection at all. She will have to say that her father would not allow it, for of course a handsome offer deserves a civil refusal. Sally's proposals would be quite an ethnological study; Mustapha asked what I should require as dowry for her. Fancy Sally as Hareem of the Sheykh-el-Beled of Luxor!

I am so charmed with my house that I begin seriously to contemplate staying here all the time. Cairo is so dear now, and so many dead cattle are buried there, that I think I should do better in this place. There is a huge hall, so large and cold now as to be uninhabitable, which in summer would be glorious. My dear old captain of steamer XII would bring me up coffee and candles, and if I 'sap' and learn to talk to people, I shall have plenty of company.

The cattle disease has not extended above Minieh to any degree, and here there has not been a case. *Alhamdulillah!* Food is very good here, rather less than half Cairo prices even now; in summer it will be half that. Mustapha urges me to stay, and proposes a picnic of a few days over in the tombs with his Hareem as a diversion. I have got a photo, for a stereoscope, which I send you, of my two beloved, lovely palm-trees on the river-bank just above and looking over Philæ.

---

* Lucie's servant.

Hitherto my right side has been the bad one, but now one side is uneasy and the other impossible to lie on. It does not make one sleep pleasantly, and the loss of my good, sound sleep tries me, and so I don't seem well. We shall see what hot weather will do; if that fails I will give up the contest, and come home to see as much as I shall have time for of you and my chicks.

To Mrs. Austin.

Sunday, February 7, 1864

DEAREST MUTTER,

We have had our winter pretty sharp for three weeks, and everybody has had violent colds and coughs—the Arabs, I mean.

I have been a good deal ailing, but have escaped any violent cold altogether, and now the thermometer is up to 64°, and it feels very pleasant. In the sun it is always very hot, but that does not prevent the air from being keen, and chapping lips and noses, and even hands; it is curious how a temperature, which would be summer in England, makes one shiver at Thebes—*Alhamdulillah!* it is over now.

My poor Sheykh Yussuf is in great distress about his brother, also a young Sheykh (*i.e.*, one learned in theology and competent to preach in the mosque). Sheykh Mohammed is come home from studying in 'El-Azhar' at Cairo— I fear to die. I went with Sheykh Yussuf, at his desire, to see if I could help him, and found him gasping for breath and very, very ill. I gave him a little soothing medicine, and put mustard plasters on him, and as it relieved him, I went again and repeated them. All the family and a lot of neighbours crowded in to look on. There he lay in a dark little den with bare mud walls, worse off, to our ideas, than any pauper; but these people do not feel the want of comforts, and one learns to think it quite natural to sit with perfect gentlemen in places inferior to our cattle-sheds. I pulled some blankets up against the wall, and put my arm behind Sheykh Mohammed's back to make him rest while the poultices were on him, whereupon he laid his green turban on my shoulder, and presently held up his delicate brown face for a kiss like an affectionate child. As I kissed him, a very pious old moollah said *Bismillah* (In the name of God) with an approving nod, and Sheykh Mohammed's old father, a splendid old man in a green turban, thanked me with effusion, and prayed that my children might always find help and kindness. I suppose if I confessed to kissing a 'dirty Arab' in a 'hovel' the English travellers would execrate me; but it shows how much there is in 'Mussulman bigotry, unconquerable hatred, etc.,' for this family are Seyyids (descendents of the Prophet) and very pious. Sheykh Yussuf does not even smoke, and he preaches on Fridays. You would love these

Saeedees, they are such thorough gentlemen. I rode over to the village a few days ago to see a farmer named Omar. Of course I had to eat, and the people were enchanted at my going alone, as they are used to see the English armed and guarded. Sidi Omar, however, insisted on accompanying me home, which is the civil thing here. He piled a whole stack of green fodder on his little nimble donkey, and hoisted himself atop of it without saddle or bridle (the fodder was for Mustapha A'gha), and we trotted home across the beautiful green barley-fields, to the amazement of some European young men out shooting. We did look a curious pair, certainly, with my English saddle and bridle, habit, hat and feather, on horseback, and Sidi Omar's brown shirt, brown legs and white turban, guiding his donkey with his chibouque. We were laughing very merrily, too, over my blundering Arabic.

Young Heathcote and Strutt called here, but were hurrying on up the river. I shall see more of them when they come down. Young Strutt is so like his mother I knew him in the street. I would like to give him a fantasia, but it is not proper for a woman to send for the dancing-girls, and as I am the friend of the Maōhn (police magistrate), the Kadee, and the respectable people here, I cannot do what is indecent in their eyes. It is quite enough that they approve my unveiled face, and my associating with men; that is 'my custom,' and they think no harm of it.

To-morrow or next day Ramadan begins at the first sight of the new moon. It is a great nuisance, because everybody is cross. Omar did not keep it last year, but this year he will, and if he spoils my dinners, who can blame him? There was a wedding close by here last night, and about ten o'clock all the women passed under my windows with crys of joy 'ez-zaghareet' down to the river. I find, on inquiry, that in Upper Egypt, as soon as the bridegroom has 'taken the face' of his bride, the women take her down to 'see the Nile.' They have not yet forgotten that the old god is the giver of increase, it seems.

I have been reading Miss Martineau's book; the descriptions are excellent, but she evidently knew and cared nothing about the people, and had the feeling of most English people here, that the difference of manners is a sort of impassable gulf, the truth being that their feelings and passions are just like our own. It is curious that all the old books of travels that I have read mention the natives of strange countries in a far more natural tone, and with far more attempt to discriminate character, than modern ones, e.g., Neibuhr's Travels here and in Arabia, Cook's Voyages, and many others. *Have* we grown so *very* civilized since a hundred years that outlandish people seem like mere puppets, and not like real human beings? Miss M.'s bigotry against Copts and Greeks is droll enough, compared to her very proper reverence for 'Him who sleeps in Philæ,' and her attack upon hareems outrageous; she implies that they are brothels. I must admit that I have not seen a Turkish hareem, and she apparently saw no other, and yet she fancies the morals of Turkey to be superior to those of Egypt. It is not possible for a woman to explain all the limitations to which ordinary people do subject themselves. Great men I know nothing of; but women can and do, without blame, sue their husbands-in-law for the full 'payment of debt,' and demand a divorce if they please in default. Very often a man marries a second wife out of duty to provide for a brother's widow and children, or the like. Of course licentious men act loosely as elsewhere. *Kulloolum Beni Adam* (we are all sons of Adam), as Sheykh Yussuf says constantly, 'bad-bad and good-good'; and modern travellers show strange ignorance in talking of foreign natives *in the lump*, as they nearly all do.

Monday.—I have just heard that poor Sheykh Mohammed died yesterday, and was, as usual, buried at once. I had not been well for a few days, and Sheykh Yussuf took care that I should not know of his brother's death. He went to Mustapha A'gha, and told him not to tell anyone in my house till I was better, because he knew 'what was in my stomach towards his family,' and feared I should be made worse by the news. And how often I have been advised not to meddle with sick Arabs, because they are sure to suspect a Christian of poisoning those who die! I do grieve for the graceful, handsome young creature and his old father. Omar was vexed at not knowing of his death, because he would have liked to help to carry him to the grave.

I have at last learned the alphabet in Arabic, and can write it quite tidily, but now I am in a fix for want of a dictionary, and have written to Hekekian Bey to buy me one in Cairo. Sheykh Yussuf knows not a word of English, and Omar can't read or write, and has no notion of grammar or of *word for word* interpretation, and it is very slow work. When I walk through the court of the mosque I give the customary coppers to the little boys who are spelling away loudly under the arcade, *Abba sheddeh o nusbeyteen, Ibbi sheddeh o hefledeen*, etc., with a keen sympathy with their difficulties and well-smudged tin slates. An additional evil is that the Arabic books printed in England, and at English presses here, require a 40-horse power microscope to distinguish a letter. The ciphering is like ours, but with other figures, and I felt very stupid when I discovered how I had reckoned Arab fashion from right to left all my life and never observed the fact. However, they 'cast down' a column of figures from top to bottom.

I am just called away by some poor men who want me to speak to the English travellers about shooting their pigeons. It is very thoughtless, but it is in great measure the fault of the servants and dragomans who think they must not venture to tell their masters that pigeons are private property. I have a great mind to put a notice on the wall of my house about it. Here, where there are never less than eight or ten boats lying for full three months, the loss to the *fellaheen* is serious, and our Consul Mustapha A'gha is afraid to say anything. I have given my neighbours permission to call the pigeons mine, as they roost in flocks on my roof, and to go out and say that the Sitt objects to her poultry being shot, especially as I have had them shot off my balcony as they sat there.

I got a note from M. Mounier yesterday, inviting me to go and stay at El-Moutaneh, Halim Pasha's great estate, near Edfoo, and offering to send his dahabieh for me. I certainly will go as soon as the weather is decidedly hot. It is now very warm and pleasant. If I find Thebes too hot as summer advances I must drop down and return to Cairo, or try Suez, which I hear is excellent in summer—bracing desert air. But it is very tempting to stay here—a splendid cool house, food extremely cheap; about £1 a week for three of us for fish, bread, butter, meat, milk, eggs and vegetables; all grocery, of course, I brought with me; no trouble, rest and civil neighbours. I feel very disinclined to move unless I am baked out, and it takes a good deal to bake me. The only fear is the Khamaseen wind. I do not feel very well. I don't ail anything in particular; blood-spitting frequent, but very slight; much less cough; but I am so weak and good for nothing. I seldom feel able to go out or do more than sit in the balcony on one side or other of the house. I have no donkey here, the hired ones are so very bad and so dear; but I have written Mounier to try and get me one at El-Moutaneh and send it down in one of Halim Pasha's corn-boats. There is no comfort like a donkey always ready. If I have to send for Mustapha's horse, I feel lazy and fancy it is too much trouble unless I can go just when I want.

I have received a letter from Alexandria of January 8. What dreadful weather! We felt the ghost of it here in our three weeks of cold. Sometimes I feel as if I must go back to you all *coûte qui coûte*, but I know it would be no use to try it in the summer. I long for more news of you and my chicks.

ARABIA

Historical Background

Mainly a desert terrain, in 1800 the Arabian Peninsula had a population of perhaps no more than 1 million, a large part of which – excluding those living in the mountainous areas of Oman and Yemen where agriculture was practised – was pastoral, herding sheep, goats, or horses. Apart from the oases towns the major centres of population were on the coasts (Yapp 1987: 173). At the close of the eighteenth century most of the Arabs in the peninsula were independent of – and some actively hostile to – Ottoman rule. Wahhabis in Central Arabia, and in the South East Ibadis in Oman and Zaydis in Yemen, each functioned beyond Ottoman authority. In the Hijaz the Sherifs of Mecca ruled the holy cities but there was an Ottoman governor at Jeddah (Hourani 1991: 251, 253). In this period Arabia was therefore isolated but subject to expansive forces from within. The Wahhabis, whose power emanated from an alliance between the puritanical doctrine of the religious reformer Abdul Wahhab (1703–92) and the political leadership of the al-Saud clan, were the dominant political force in the subcontinent before Muhammad Ali's campaigns against them (1811–8). By 1840 the Egyptians had withdrawn leaving Central Arabia under Wahhabi control; an Ottoman return in Arabia was slow in coming and only took off after 1880 (Yapp: 174–5).

Besides Muhammad Ali and the Ottomans a third external force seeking to impact on Arabia was that of the European Powers. For the British, intent on bolstering their empire in the East: 'All the faster routes to India passed through the Middle East' and took in the peripheries of Arabia (Searight 1979: 151). Of particular interest was the Arabian Gulf, where piracy would be a concern up to the end of the century, and Southern Arabia, where Britain acquired a foothold with the annexation of Aden in 1839. The opening of the Suez Canal in 1869 amplified the importance of the 'Egyptian route' to India via the Red Sea. For the French, whose power and influence were expanding in North Africa and the Levant, the Arabian Peninsula was largely of theoretical interest only, but in the 1860s Napoleon III sent spies to report back on the political balance in Central Arabia, two of whom, the Italian Carlo Guarmani, and the Englishman William Gifford Palgrave, became well known Arabian travellers.

Travellers and their Narratives

Throughout most of this period Europeans were only acquainted with the peripheries of the Arabian Peninsula. Its large interiors remained unknown to them until the great desert journeys of the English explorers of the 1860s and 70s. 'To expand the information given in the Bible and to extrapolate between the biblical patriarchs and contemporary bedouin was one of the main goals of the first scientific expeditions sent to the Arabian Peninsula' (Öhrnberg LTE: 34). At the beginning of the century, though he had seen but a small part of the peninsula, the legacy of the German Carsten Neibuhr, who accompanied the ill-fated Danish-sponsored scientific expedition of the early 1760s about which he wrote in his *Travels in Arabia* (English edition 1792), still shone brightly. Neibuhr romanticized the Bedouin though he had had little contact with them (Tidrick 1989: 16). The *Travels of Ali Bey* (1816) were read for their account of a pilgrimage to Mecca made in 1807 by the Catalan Domingo Badia y Leblich (1766–1818) who adopted the persona of Ali Bey al-Abbasi. Ali Bey worked for the French, while Ulrich Jasper Seetzen, who accomplished the same feat in 1809, spied for the Czar (Öhrnberg LTE: 32). As Tijar Mazzeo (2001) puts it: 'It is surprising to discover the degree to which [early nineteenth-century] Middle Eastern travel narratives were connected with war and the military expansion of empire, whether as propaganda or intelligence' (xxviii). However Nigel Leask's remarks (2002: 3) about the period after 1815 which saw Britain's acquisition of a second empire – 'travel writers celebrated their emancipation from the necessity of cultural disguise alongside an increased sense of separation from indigenous peoples' – definitely do not apply to Arabia. The Egyptian ruler Muhammad Ali was convinced John Lewis Burckhardt was an English spy, while the Russian-educated Orientalist George Augustus Wallin, who after a spell in Egypt in 1845 went several times to Arabia disguised as a horse-dealer, was in the pay of the Egyptian Foreign Office (Trench 1986: 96). Spying for the French, the Italian Carlo Guarmani visited Central Arabia in 1864 under the same disguise.

But if Arabia 'emerged late as a destination of exploration…[it] quickly became an object of economic and political interests and an iconic place' ((Melman 2002: 108). Melman posits the Arabian travel narratives of this period as conforming to two primary formats: the first was a modernized version of the millennium-old paradigm of pilgrimage. Burton and the Blunts use the term in the titles of their two best-known travel works. The second was 'ethnography of modern everyday life' of Muslim Arabs (Melman 2002: 110). Victorian (especially male) travellers frequently incorporated into their narratives the discourse of the scientific report in the case of hitherto unexplored territories and their inhabitants. This was also linked to the expansion of empire and to metropolitan organizations like the Royal Geographical Society (Driver 2001: Ch. 2). James Wellsted combined political commentary with engaged, some have said sympathetic, observation of the customs and beliefs of Arabs in Oman. Ali Behdad (1994) sees Wilfrid Scawen and Anne Blunt's later journeys to Central Arabia as an exercise in colonial ethnography. Blunt did indeed address the Royal Geographical Society on this topic in 1880, but by the 1890s he was condemning the Society for its involvement in imperialist expansion (Finch 1938: 294). The political motive however does not alone account for the attraction the Arabian deserts exerted upon the English male – and in Lady Anne Blunt the one notable female – traveller during the latter part of this period. The Blunts, along with Palgrave and to varying degrees Burton and Doughty, expressed an aesthetic of the desert as a desolate purifying place inhabited by noble Arab nomads. Each sought an elsewhere to counteract the anomie of modernity (Behdad: 16). Each found in the desert a space in which they could test aspects of their own personalities, be it the sense of their physical and intellectual prowess, racial superiority, aristocracy, humanity, spirituality or whatever else they might have been searching for.

JOHN LEWIS BURCKHARDT (1784–1817)

Born Jean Louis Burckhardt into a wealthy Swiss manufacturing and trading family, Burckhardt was forced to leave Switzerland as a result of his father's falling out with the new order thrown up by the French Revolution. After studying at Leipzig and Göttingen universities he moved to England (1806) where he gained employment with the Association for Promoting the Discovery of the Interior Parts of Africa (1808). He studied Arabic at Cambridge University before travelling to Syria staying in Aleppo for two years (1809–11) where he acquired a scholarly knowledge of Arabic and the Qur'an. He also travelled in Lebanon and Palestine before reaching Cairo in September 1812. Burckhardt's identity therefore twice shifted: the new ruler of Egypt, Muhammad Ali, believed the Swiss to be an English spy, even though he had adopted the persona of Sheykh Ibrahim, a poor Muslim scholar of Aleppo. Journeys in Upper Egypt and Nubia followed, before Burckhardt determined to put his Arab identity to the ultimate test by going to Mecca and Medina where he eventually stayed for two years (1814–15). Travelling in reduced circumstances and plagued by ill health, a combination of his remarkable knowledge of written and spoken Arabic and the ambiguous protection of Muhammad Ali ensured that he succeeded in taking sufficient notes to be able later to write his seminal *Travels in Arabia* (1829) This and two other works, *Travels in Nubia* (1819) and *Notes on the Bedouins and Wahabys* (1822), were published posthumously under the auspices of the Africa Association, Burckhardt having died of dysentery in Cairo in 1817. Acquiring a place in the growing travel canon on the Middle East, Burckhardt's writings were influential in promoting the myth of the noble Bedouin Arab started by Neibuhr. *Travels in Arabia* was admired especially by Burton who paid tribute to its author by quoting his meticulous observations on the hajj in his own *Narrative of a Pilgrimage to El-Medinah and Mecca* (1855).

From:

Travels in Arabia **(1829)**

Summoned to Taif by Muhammad Ali who had known him in Egypt, 'Sheykh Ibrahim' has his disguise openly challenged by the Qadi of Mecca. Fearful of England's imminent invasion of Egypt and believing Burckhardt to be spying for the English, the Pasha has to set the opprobrium of his own people for allowing a Christian to penetrate the Islamic holy places against the realpolitik of protecting an Englishman in the East.

Residence at Tayf

I arrived at Tayf about mid-day, and alighted at the house of Bosari, the Pasha's physician, with whom I had been well acquainted at Cairo. As it was now the fast of Ramadhan, during which the Turkish grandees always sleep in the day-time, the Pasha could not be informed of my arrival till after sun-set. In the mean while, Bosari, after the usual Levantine assurances of his entire devotion to my interests, and of the sincerity of his friendship, asked me what were my views in coming to the Hedjaz. I answered, to visit Mekka and Medina, and then to return to Cairo. Of my intention respecting Egypt he seemed doubtful, begged me to be candid with him as with a friend, and to declare the truth, as he confessed that he suspected I was going to the East Indies. This I positively denied; and in the course of our conversation, he hinted that if I really meant to return to Egypt, I had better remain at head-quarters with them, till the Pasha himself should proceed to Cairo. Nothing was said about money, although Bosari was ignorant that my pecuniary wants had been relieved at Djidda.

In the evening Bosari went privately to the Pasha at his women's residence, where he only received visits from friends or very intimate acquaintances. In half an hour he returned, and told me that the Pasha wished to see me rather late that evening in his public room. He added, that he found seated with the Pasha the Kadhy of Mekka, who was then at Tayf for his health; and that the former, when he heard of my desire to visit the holy cities, observed jocosely, "it is not the beard* alone which proves a man to be a true Moslem;" but turning towards the Kadhy, he said, "you are a better judge in such matters than I am." The Kadhy then observed that, as none but a Moslem could be permitted to see the holy cities a circumstance of which he could not possibly suppose me ignorant, he did not believe that I would declare myself to be one, unless I really was. When I learnt these particulars, I told Bosari that he might return alone to the Pasha; that my feelings had already been much hurt by the orders given

---

* I wore a beard at this time, as I did at Cairo, when the Pasha saw me.

to my guide not to carry me through Mekka; and that I certainly should not go to the Pasha's public audience, if he would not receive me as a Turk.

Bosari was alarmed at this declaration, and in vain endeavoured to dissuade me from such a course, telling me that he had orders to conduct me to the Pasha, which he could not disobey. I however adhered firmly to what I had said, and he reluctantly went back to Mohammed Aly, whom he found alone, the Kadhy having left him. When Bosari delivered his message, the Pasha smiled, and answered that I was welcome, whether Turk or not. About eight o'clock in the evening I repaired to the castle, a miserable, half-ruined habitation of Sherif Ghaleb, dressed in the new suit which I had received at Djidda by the Pasha's command. I found his highness seated in a large saloon, with the Kadhy on one hand, and Hassan Pasha, the chief of the Arnaut soldiers, on the other; thirty or forty of his principal officers formed a half-circle about the sofa on which they sat; and a number of Bedouin sheikhs were squatted in the midst of the semicircle. I went up to the Pasha, gave him the "Salam Aleykum," and kissed his hand. He made a sign for me to sit down by the side of the Kadhy, then addressed me very politely, inquired after my health, and if there was any news from the Mamelouks in the Black country which I had visited; but said nothing whatever on the subject most interesting to me. Amyn Effendi, his Arabic dragoman, interpreted between us, as I do not speak Turkish, and the Pasha speaks Arabic very imperfectly. In about five minutes he renewed the business with the Bedouins, which I had interrupted. When this was terminated, and Hassan Pasha had left the room, every body was ordered to withdraw, except the Kadhy, Bosari, and myself. I expected now to be put to the proof, and I was fully prepared for it; but not a word was mentioned of my personal affairs, nor did Mohammed Aly, in any of our subsequent conversations, ever enter further into them than to hint that he was persuaded I was on my way to the East Indies. As soon as we were alone, the Pasha introduced the subject of politics. He had just received information of the entrance of the allies into Paris, and the departure of Bonaparte for Elba; and several Malta gazettes, giving the details of these occurrences, had been sent to him from Cairo. He seemed deeply interested in these important events, chiefly because he laboured under the impression that, after Bonaparte's downfall, England would probably seek for an augmentation of power in the Mediterranean, and consequently invade Egypt.

After remaining for two or three hours with the Pasha in private conversation, either speaking Arabic to him, through the medium of the Kadhy, who, though a native of Constantinople, knew that language perfectly, or Italian, through Bosari, who was an Armenian, but had acquired a smattering of that tongue at Cairo, I took my leave, and the Pasha said that he expected me again on the morrow at the same hour.

August 29th.—I paid a visit to the Kadhy before sun-set, and found him with his companion and secretary, a learned man of Constantinople. The Kadhy Sádik Effendi was a true eastern courtier, of very engaging manners and address, possessing all that suavity of expression for which the well-bred natives of Stamboul are so distinguished. After we had interchanged a few complimentary phrases, I mentioned my astonishment on finding that the Pasha had expressed any doubts of my being a true Moslem, after I had now been a proselyte to that faith for so many years. He replied that Mohammed Aly had allowed that he (the Kadhy) was the best judge in such matters; and added, that he hoped we should become better acquainted with each other. He then began to question me about my Nubian travels. In the course of conversation literary subjects were introduced: he asked me what Arabic books I had read, and what commentaries on the Koran and on the law; and he probably found me better acquainted, with the titles, at least, of such works than he had expected, for we did not enter deeply into the subject. While we were thus conversing, the call to evening prayers announced the termination of this day's fast. I supped with the Kadhy, and afterwards performed the evening prayers in his company, when I took great care to chaunt as long a chapter of the Koran as my memory furnished at the moment; after which we both went to the Pasha, who again sat up a part of the night in private conversation with me, chiefly on political affairs, without ever introducing the subject of my private business.

After another interview, I went every evening, first to the Kadhy, and then to the Pasha; but, notwithstanding a polite reception at the castle, I could perceive that my actions were closely watched. Bosari had asked me if I kept a journal; but I answered that the Hedjaz was not like Egypt, full of antiquities, and that in these barren mountains I saw nothing worthy of notice. I was never allowed to be alone for a moment, and I had reason to suspect that Bosari, with all his assurances of friendship, was nothing better than a spy. To remain at Tayf for an indeterminate period, in the situation I now found myself, was little desirable; yet I could not guess the Pasha's intentions with respect to me. I was evidently considered in no other light than as a spy sent to this country by the English government, to ascertain its present state, and report upon it in the East Indies. This, I presume, was the Pasha's own opinion: he knew me as an Englishman, a name which I assumed during my travels (I hope without any discredit to that country), whenever it seemed necessary to appear as an European; because at that time none but the subjects of England and France enjoyed in the East any real security: they were considered as too well protected, both by their governments at home and their ministers at Constantinople, to be trifled with by provincial governors. The Pasha, moreover, supposed me to be a man of some rank, for every Englishman travelling in the East is styled "My lord;" and he was the more convinced of this by a certain air of dignity which it was necessary for me to assume in a Turkish court, where modesty of behaviour and affability are quite out of place. Afraid as he then was of Great Britain, he probably thought it imprudent to treat me ill, though he did nothing whatever to forward my projects: As far as he knew, I could have only the five hundred piastres which he had ordered for me at Djidda, and which were not sufficient to pay my expenses for any length of time in the Hedjaz. Nothing was said to me either by him or Bosari of taking my bill upon Cairo, as I had requested him to do; but this favour I did not again solicit, having money enough for the present, and expecting a fresh supply from Egypt.

To remain for any length of time at Tayf, in a sort of polite imprisonment, was little to my taste; yet I could not press my departure without increasing his suspicions. This was manifest after my first interview with the Pasha and the Kadhy, and I knew that the reports of Bosari might considerably influence the mind of Mohammed. Under these circumstances, I thought the best course was to make Bosari tired of me, and thus induce him involuntarily to forward my views. I therefore began to act at his house with all the petulance of an Osmanly. It being the Ramadhan, I fasted during the day, and at night demanded a supper apart; early on the following morning I called for an abundant breakfast, before the fast re-commenced. I appropriated to myself the best room which his small house afforded; and his servants were kept in constant attendance upon me. Eastern hospitality forbids all resentment for such behaviour; I was, besides, a great man, and on a visit to the Pasha. In my conversations with Bosari, I assured him that I felt myself most comfortably situated at Tayf, and that its climate agreed perfectly with my health; and I betrayed no desire of quitting the place for the present. To maintain a person in my character for any length of time at Tayf, where provisions of all kinds were much dearer than in London, was a matter of no small moment; and a petulant guest is everywhere disagreeable. The design, I believe, succeeded perfectly; and Bosari endeavoured to persuade the Pasha that I was a harmless being, in order that I might be the sooner dismissed.

I had been six days at Tayf, but seldom went out, except to the castle in the evening, when Bosari asked whether my business with the Pasha was likely to prevent me much longer from pursuing my travels, and visiting Mekka. I replied that I had no business with the Pasha, though I had come to Tayf at his desire; but that my situation was very agreeable to me, possessing so warm and generous a friend as he, my host. The next day he renewed the subject, and remarked that it must be tiresome to live entirely among soldiers, without any comforts or amusements, unacquainted besides, as I was, with the Turkish language. I assented to this but added, that being ignorant of the Pasha's wishes, I could determine on nothing. This brought him to the point I wished. "This being the case," said he, "I will, if you like, speak to his Highness on the subject." He did so in the evening, before I went o the castle; and the Pasha told me, in the course of conversation, that as he understood I wished to pass the last days of Ramadhan at Mekka, (a suggestion originating with Bosari,) I had better join the party of the Kadhy, who was going there to the feast, and who would be very glad of my company. This was precisely such a circumstance as I wished for. The departure of the Kadhy was fixed for the 7th of September, and I hired two asses, the usual mode of conveyance in this country, in order to follow him.

As it was my intention to proceed afterwards to Medina, where Tousoun Pasha, the son of Mohammed Aly, was governor, I begged Bosari to ask the Pasha for a firman or passport, authorising me to travel through all the Hedjaz, together with a letter of recommendation to his son. In reply, Bosari told me that the Pasha did not like to interfere personally in my travels; that I might act as I pleased, on my own responsibility; and that my knowledge of the language rendered a passport unnecessary. This was equivalent to telling me, "Do what you please; I shall neither obstruct nor facilitate your projects," which, indeed, was as much, at present, as I could well expect or desire.

On the 6th of September I took my leave of the Pasha, who told me at parting, that if ever my travels should carry me to India, I might assure the English people there that he was much attached to the interests of the India trade. Early on the 7th the Kadhy sent me word that he should not set out till evening, would travel during the night, and hoped to meet me at Djebel Kora, midway to Mekka. I therefore left Tayf alone, as I had entered it, after a residence of ten days. At parting, Bosari assured me of his inviolable attachment to my interest; and I blessed my good stars, when I left the precincts of the town, and the residence of a Turkish court, in which I found it more difficult to avoid danger, than among the wild Bedouins of Nubia.

JAMES RAYMOND WELLSTED
(1805–1842)

After Carsten Neibuhr's visit to Muscat in 1764, James Wellsted, a naval officer who travelled there in 1834–5, was among the first to explore the important districts of inner Oman including the Jebel Akhdar mountain range. Dedicated to the young Queen Victoria, *Travels in Arabia* was published in 1838. Its political context was the British expedition against the Bani Bu Ali tribe, which had converted to Wahhabism and defeated a British force in 1821. Wellsted was part of General Lionel Smith's expedition of 1834 that all but wiped the tribe out. Wellsted characterizes Sultan of Oman Sayid Said bin Sultan as liberal, tolerant, personally abstemious, and a keen ally of the British – 'probably, if any native prince can with truth be called a friend to England it is the Imam of Maskat.' The Sultan received him warmly furnishing him with presents and promising every assistance. According to Robin Bidwell (1976), Wellsted 'had the greatest of all gifts in an explorer – an intuitive understanding of the people that he met and a sympathy with them' (207). An Austrian editor of *Travels in Arabia* (1838) writes: 'The description of Nizwa and above all the ascent of the Jabal Akhdar represents the highlight of Wellsted's book' (Scholz, 1978: XVI) Wellsted's writing visits some of the key themes of travellers to Arabia: Bedouin nobility, Arab treatment of women, and the freedom the desert gave.

From:

Travels in Arabia (1838)

This relates Wellsted's contact with the Bani Bu Ali in December 1835. The tribe seem to demonstrate no bitterness towards the English of whose *mores* particularly with respect to women they show some knowledge and curiosity. The narrative may be taken as establishing a model for British pacification of unruly Arab tribes but also evinces Wellsted's geniality and sensitivity as a traveller.

Travels in Omán

The Bení-Abú-'Alí tribe came originally from a small district in Nesjd, where a remnant of them is said still to exist. They accompanied those who separated from Alí's army during the struggle with Mowaiyah for the Caliphate, and continued to follow the Beazi tenets until the invasion of Abdul Uziz, in 1811, when they became converts to the Wahhábís faith. From that period they have been an object of the most deadly hatred to the other tribes in Omán ; and after Abdul Uziz was beaten back at Bedíah, their best efforts were necessary to prevent their total annihilation; but, continuing to temporise until they had erected a very strong fort, they, in return, became the aggressors, and, after carrying fire and sword into every part of the neighbouring district, became so formidable, that they were soon left in undisputed possession of their own and several of the neighbouring districts.

At a later period, several attempts were made by the Imám to dislodge or destroy them, but all his exertions proving ineffectual, in 1821 he made a requisition for assistance to Captain Thompson, who, after the fall of Rás-el-Khaïmah, in the preceding year, had been left with a small force of eight hundred men, principally sepoys, at the Island of Kishm[*]. Under an impression that some portion of the tribe had been engaged in extensive acts of piracy, that officer immediately dispatched a messenger with a letter of remonstrance to them, but he was massacred almost as soon as he landed. Captain Thompson, on the receipt of this intelligence, no longer hesitated to accompany a force which the Imám had already prepared to act against them, and, landing at Súr, he formed a junction, and they marched together against Bení Abú-'Alí, which is situated about fifty miles, in a direct line, from their place of disembarkment. The Bedowins retreated before them, and occupied the date grove which surrounds the fort. After our troops had passed Bení-Abú-Hasan, and were sweeping round a hill, the greater part being in a line parallel to the trees, the whole tribe, who had hitherto lain concealed beneath them, suddenly rushed forth with loud cries, and threw themselves headlong on the British force. Before the latter could be formed, or almost before the order could be given, the Bedowins were amidst them, the sepoys could not use their bayonets, but were hewn down by the long swords of their foes as they stood, and the whole soon became a mass of inextricable confusion. No quarter was given, and an officer, presenting his sword as a token of submission, was, at the same time, pierced through the back with a spear. They dragged the surgeon, who was sick, from his palanquin, and immediately butchered him; and the

---

[*] See Captain Thompson's Report, dated 18th November, 1820. —*Asiatic Journal*, vol. xi. p. 593.

British force, leaving two-thirds of their number dead upon the field, were compelled to retreat, and, after an undisturbed march of about eight days, Captain Thompson, two officers, and about one hundred and fifty men, the only survivors, succeeded in reaching Maskat[*].

Intelligence of this disaster was soon carried to Bombay, and a large force of three thousand men, under Sir Lionel Smith, again landed[†]. Nowise daunted by their superior numbers, the Bedowins, in concert with the Bení Geneba, planned a night attack, which, had it proved successful, would have placed the British force in a singular dilemma. The General and his staff were encamped at some distance from the army, and it was proposed by the Bedowins to cut off the whole of them. But, either through mistake or treachery, the latter were not at the rendezvous at the appointed time, and the former proceeded alone. Having reached the General's camp, they hamstrung several of the horses, and committed other damages, besides cutting down several men. They then effected their escape without the loss of one of their own number.

When our force on their march had nearly reached the fort, the Arabs met them on a large plain. Their number did not exceed eight hundred: many of their women had now joined their ranks, and they rushed on with the same impetuosity as before, but were met at every point by the bayonet: they, nevertheless, fought with amazing obstinacy and courage, and did not give up the contest until nearly the whole of them were slain or desperately wounded[‡]: amidst the latter was their Sheïkh, who, with the few survivors, was taken prisoner to Bombay. After being confined there for almost two years they were released; much attention was then shown them, and they were sent back to their own country with presents and with money to rebuild their town; but since the period of their defeat no European has entered their territory.

After my noon observation of the sun, a short journey of two hours brought me on to Bení-Abú-'Alí. A considerable crowd followed after me until I halted, when I was soon joined by the young Sheïkh and the principal men of the tribe. No sooner had I proclaimed myself an Englishman, and expressed my intention of passing a few days amidst them, than the whole camp was in a tumult of acclamation; the few old guns they had were fired from the different towers, matchlocks were kept going till sunset, and both old and young, male and female, strove to do their best to entertain me: they pitched my tent,

---

[*] The Imám, with the remnant of his army, accompanied our troops during their march, and it would be an injustice to the noble and gallant character of this prince, were I to omit mentioning the resolute bravery with which he maintained his ground, even when wounded, and his determination to retreat no farther than Beni Hasan, if he had not been deserted by a large portion of his army.

[†] In January, 1821.

[‡] In March, 1821.—*Asiatic Journal*, xii. 364.

slaughtered sheep, and brought milk by gallons. A reception so truly warm and hospitable not a little surprised me.

Before us lay the ruins of the fort we had dismantled,—my tent was pitched on the very spot where we had nearly annihilated their tribe, reducing them from being the most powerful in Omán to their present petty state. All, however, in the confidence I had shown in thus throwing myself amidst them, was forgotten.

Although so near the sea-coast, the Bedowins of this and the neighbouring districts have remained uncontaminated by any intercourse with strangers, for they neither intermarry nor mix with them; and there is, therefore, reason to believe that they preserve, in its strictest forms, all the simplicity and purity of the interior tribes.

It is to be regretted that we know so little of the character and habits of the true Bedowins. Those on the frontiers of Syria and Mesopotamia have been vitiated by their intercourse with the Turks and other nations. The same remark applies to the only parts of Hedjas and Yemen which our travellers have visited. Burckhardt, though well aware of, and as well calculated to supply this deficiency, was prevented by sickness from doing so, otherwise it was his intention to have passed a few months in the interior provinces. My object, therefore, while entering fully on what came under my observation during my stay amidst these tribes, now and on subsequent occasions, will be to furnish something towards this desideratum.

After their evening prayers, the young Sheïkh, accompanied by about forty men, came to the tent, and expressed his intention of remaining with me as a guard during the night. To ask the whole party in was impossible, and to invite a few only would have displeased others, so I took my carpet outside amidst them. It was one of those clear and beautiful nights which are only met with on or near the Desert: the atmosphere felt pleasantly cool, and we soon commenced an animated conversation. They were not wholly ignorant of our customs: some information on these points they had gathered from the men who had been prisoners of war in India; but their accounts were either so limited or exaggerated, that they served rather to increase than to allay the feelings of curiosity. The nature and observance of our religion formed, of course, their first subject of inquiry, and my opinion as to its comparative merits with the Mohammedan was demanded. It is generally a good maxim to allow yourself to be apparently beaten on questions of theology: I could not, however, at first, resist the temptation of leading to some of their least defensible doctrines, and stating the arguments which could be brought to bear against them; but they evinced so little prejudice or fanaticism on these points that I regretted having done so, and, to make amends, most willingly subscribed to the opinion of one of their old men, that either faith was best adapted for the country and people who practised it.

From this the conversation turned on our females. Was it true, they inquired, that those of high birth and condition danced in public, and went unveiled? Here they had me on the hip, as they fancied; and the rogues chuckled whilst awaiting my reply. I confessed it was, but we did not, like them, attach any indelicacy to it; that our females were never secluded, but were instructed in useful knowledge, and allowed equal liberty with the other sex, and that we found our advantage in doing so, for, instead of being objects of mere sensual desire, they then became companions. Here, however, I gained not a single convert. "Let them work," said they, "and attend to their household affairs. What business have they with reading and writing, which is only fit for Moolahs?"

"The women to the distaff, the men to their swords," said a venerable old man, with a white beard, repeating a proverb which was echoed by all present. I wished some of their dames had been within hearing, they would have pitched their note in a minor key.

The females of this tribe possess a considerable share of influence in all their councils, and in the absence of their Sheïkh, who had proceeded on the pilgrimage to Mecca, his wife and sister, at this moment, governed the tribe. Their remarks on some of our customs were highly amusing.

"We observed," said they, "that when you sat down to table each man had before him a small and a large glass; why apply to the small one so often when it would save so much trouble to fill the larger, and drink it off at once? Why did we send the ladies away before we had finished our wine, and yet rise up when they left?" &c., &c.

One of the slaves kept pounding coffee from the time they first arrived. The pestle on these occasions is made to strike the sides and bottom of the mortar in such time and manner as to cause it to resemble the chiming of bells, and the slave usually accompanies it with a song. As we chatted away, although Wahhábís, they drank their coffee as fast as it was brought, and we did not separate until a very late hour[*].

Saturday, December 5th. When I awoke this morning I found a man kneeling by me with a bowl of milk in his hand. I drank it off, and, accompanied by my escort, walked over the plain where the British had been encamped, and visited the scene of Captain Thompson's defeat; but, on either spot, every trace of the fierce encounter had disappeared. Near the former some rude graves were pointed out to me, but no "frail memorial" served to indicate whether their tenants were of the party of the victors or of the vanquished. It may serve to

---

[*] I had with me some cigars, but, knowing the aversion those of that sect have to the use of tobacco, I refrained from producing them;—but, by some means, they discovered they were in my possession and insisted on my smoking, which, to relieve myself from their importunities, I was compelled to do.

show the siccity, as well as purity of the atmosphere, to mention that the bodies of those slain on the first attack were found lying upon the sands untouched by worms, and showing not the slightest symptoms of decay.

The Bedowins evinced no disinclination to converse on the subject of the war, and their own defeat and losses they spoke of in the most perfect good humour. They were equally merry in their observations on the English during their stay in Jaïlán: their mode of attack, the arms and accoutrements of the soldiers, &c., being severally criticised with much shrewdness. To an Arab, who goes to war with no greater burden than his camel can well approach or retreat with, seldom, indeed, carrying anything beyond his arms, a small bag of moistened flour, and a skin of water, the quantity of baggage which accompanied our troops must have been not a little surprising; but what excited their utmost astonishment was, that we should carry casks of liquor for the men. This circumstance was afterwards frequently mentioned in Omán.

RICHARD FRANCIS BURTON
(1821–1890)

Burton's writings disclose his exceptional linguistic talents, deep knowledge of Islamic belief and practice, and a scientific accuracy worthy of the professional anthropologist and ethnographer. By temperament and upbringing – he spent much of his youth on the European continent – he was an outsider. Travel for him as for other Victorian explorers proffered the opportunity of escape from modern civilization and search for the primitive. He joined the East India Army in 1842, but upset his superiors by his reports, including one on the homosexual brothels of Sind. Sponsored by the Royal Geographical Society in April 1853 he embarked for Cairo on P.O. steamer *Bengal* disguised as a Persian, but changed his disguise in Egypt to that of an Afghan doctor, Mirza Abdullah. His account of his visit to the Muslim holy places, *Personal Narrative of a Pilgrimage to El-Medinah and Mecca*, was published in 1855. Burton was among the few modern Europeans to visit Mecca – before him the most notable were Ali Bey (Badia-y-Leblich) in 1807 and Burckhardt in 1814. He made much of the danger involved for a non-Muslim and the success of his disguise. Among his many later journeys the most celebrated was his exploration of the East African lakes with John Speke who without Burton discovered the source of the Nile. Like Palgrave, Burton's later career was spent in the diplomatic service. The only time he was able to employ his expertise in Arabic and Islamic studies, a period as consul in Damascus, 1869–71, nevertheless turned out a disaster. 'Burton was a man of many identities, but the basic core of his beliefs never really altered' (McLynn 1990: 98). His writings desiderate on the topic of race: he intervened on behalf of the Arab Bedouin who he saw as a 'noble savage' (Tidrick 1989) but wrote disparagingly of Africans. He was a passionate advocate of British imperialism, although a contemptuous critic of British colonial rulers, and displayed a wide conversance with Islamic literature, philosophy and culture. His reputation has been vitiated by his more extreme writings, especially those that now appear openly racist, sexist, and chauvinist in character.

From:

Personal Narrative of a Pilgrimage to El-Medinah and Mecca (1855)

Discourse on the Arabs of the desert as opposed to those of the towns and cities exercised travellers from Carsten Neibuhr onwards. To this Burton contributed his interest in race and 'the racial theorizing of his time', endeavouring to establish the racial characteristics of the 'true' Arab (Tidrick: 79). His extensive footnotes, which have been retained, demonstrate his pretension to scientific method and academic scholarship.

The Badawin of Al-Hijaz

The Badawi of the Hijaz, and indeed the race generally, has a small eye, round, restless, deep-set, and fiery, denoting keen inspection with an ardent temperament and an impassioned character. Its colour is dark brown or green-brown, and the pupil is often speckled. The habit of pursing up the skin below the orbits, and half closing the lids to exclude glare, plants the outer angles with premature crows'-feet. Another peculiarity is the sudden way in which the eye opens, especially under excitement. This, combined with its fixity of glance, forms an expression now of lively fierceness, then of exceeding sternness; whilst the narrow space between the orbits impresses the countenance in repose with an intelligence not destitute of cunning. As a general rule, however, the expression of the Badawi face is rather dignity than that cunning for which the Semitic race is celebrated, and there are lines about the mouth in variance with the stern or the fierce look of the brow. The ears are like those of Arab horses, small, well-cut, "castey," and elaborate, with many elevations aud depressions. The nose is pronounced, generally aquiline, but sometimes straight like those Greek statues which have been treated as prodigious exaggerations of the facial angle. For the most part, it is a well-made feature with delicate nostrils, below which the septum appears: in anger they swell and open like a blood mare's. I have, however, seen, in not a few instances, pert and offensive "pugs." Deep furrows descend from the wings of the nose, showing an uncertain temper, now too grave, then too gay. The mouth is irregular. The lips are either *bordés*, denoting rudeness and want of taste, or they form a mere line. In the latter case there is an appearance of undue development in the upper portion of the countenance, especially when the jaws are ascetically thin, and the chin weakly retreats. The latter feature, however, is generally well and strongly made. The teeth, as usual among Orientals, are white, even, short and broad—indications of strength. Some tribes trim their mustaches according to the "Sunnat"; the Shafe'i often shave them, and many allow them to hang Persian-like over the lips. The beard is represented by two tangled tufts upon the chin; where whisker should be, the place is either bare or is thinly covered with straggling pile.

The Badawin of Al-Hijaz are short men, about the height of the Indians near Bombay, but weighing on an average a stone more. As usual in this stage of society, stature varies little; you rarely see a giant, and scarcely ever a dwarf. Deformity is checked by the Spartan restraint upon population, and no weakly infant can live through a Badawi life. The figure, though spare, is square and well knit; fulness of limb seldom appears but about spring, when milk abounds: I have seen two or three muscular figures, but never a fat man. The neck is sinewy, the chest broad, the flank thin, and the stomach in-drawn; the legs, though fleshless, are well made, especially when the knee and ankle are not bowed by too early riding. The shins do not bend cucumber-like to the front as in the African race. The arms are thin, with muscles like whipcords, and the hands and feet are, in point of size and delicacy, a link between Europe and India. As in the Celt, the Arab thumb is remarkably long, extending almost to the first joint of the index[1] which, with its easy rotation, makes it a perfect prehensile instrument: the palm also is fleshless, small-boned, and elastic. With his small active figure, it is not strange that the wildest Badawi gait should be pleasing; he neither unfits himself for walking, nor distorts his ankles by turning out his toes according to the farcical rule of fashion, and his shoulders are not dressed like a drill-sergeant's, to throw all the weight of the body upon the heels. Yet there is no slouch in his walk; it is light and springy, and errs only in one point, sometimes becoming a strut.

Such is the Badawi, and such he has been for ages. The national type has been preserved by systematic intermarriage. The wild men do not refuse their daughters to a stranger, but the son-in-law would be forced to settle among them, and this life, which has its charms for a while, ends in becoming wearisome. Here no evil results are anticipated from the union of first cousins, and the experience of ages and of a mighty nation may be trusted. Every Badawi has a right to marry his father's brother's daughter before she is given to a stranger; hence "cousin" (*Bint Amm*) in polite phrase signifies a "wife.[2]" Our physiologists[3] adduce the Sangre Azul of Spain and the case of the lower

---

[1] Whereas the Saxon thumb is thick, flat, and short, extending scarcely half way to the middle joint of the index.

[2] A similar unwillingness to name the wife may be found in some parts of southern Europe, where probably jealousy or possibly Asiatic custom has given rise to it. Among the Maltese it appears in a truly ridiculous way, *e.g.*, "dice la mia moglie, *con rispetto parlando*, &c.," says the husband, adding to the word spouse a "saving your presence," as if he were speaking of something offensive.

[3] Dr. Howe (Report on Idiotcy in Massachussetts, 1848,) asserts that "the law against the marriage of relations is made out as clearly as though it were written on tables of stone."

animals to prove that degeneracy inevitably follows "breeding-in.[4]" Either they have theorised from insufficient facts, or civilisation and artificial living exercise some peculiar influence, or Arabia is a solitary exception to a general rule. The fact which I have mentioned is patent to every Eastern traveller.

After this long description, the reader will perceive with pleasure that we are approaching an interesting theme, the first question of mankind to the wanderer—"What are the women like?" Truth compels me to state that the women of the Hijazi Badawin are by no means comely. Although the Benu Amur boast of some pretty girls, yet they are far inferior to the high-bosomed beauties of Nijd. And I warn all men that if they run to Al-Hijaz in search of the charming face which appears in my sketch-book as "a Badawi girl," they will be bitterly disappointed: the dress was Arab, but it was worn by a fairy of the West. The Hijazi woman's eyes are fierce, her features harsh, and her face haggard; like all people of the South, she soon fades, and in old age her appearance is truly witch-like. Withered crones abound in the camps, where old men are seldom seen. The sword and the sun are fatal to

"A green old age, unconscious of decay."

The manners of the Badawin are free and simple: "vulgarity" and affectation, awkwardness and embarrassment, are weeds of civilised growth, unknown to the People of the Desert.[5] Yet their manners are sometimes dashed with a strange ceremoniousness. When two friends meet, they either embrace or both extend the right hands, clapping palm to palm; their foreheads are either pressed together, or their heads are moved from side to side, whilst for minutes together mutual inquiries are made and answered. It is a breach of decorum, even when eating, to turn the back upon a person, and if a Badawi does it, he intends an insult. When a man prepares coffee, he drinks the first cup: the *Sharbat Kajari* of the Persians, and the *Sulaymani* of Egypt[6], render this

---

He proceeds to show that in seventeen households where the parents were connected by blood, of ninety-five children one was a dwarf, one deaf, twelve scrofulous, and forty-four idiots—total fifty-eight diseased!

[4] Yet the celebrated "Flying Childers" and all his race were remarkably bred in. There is still, in my humble opinion, much mystery about the subject, to be cleared up only by the studies of physiologists.

[5] This sounds in English like an "Irish bull." I translate "Badu," as the dictionaries do, "a Desert."

[6] The Sharbat Kajari is the "Acquetta" of Persia, and derives its name from the present royal family. It is said to be a mixture of verdigris with milk; if so, it is a very clumsy engine of state policy. In Egypt and Mosul, Sulaymani (the common name for an Afghan) is used to signify "poison"; but I know not whether it be merely euphuistic or confined to some species.

precaution necessary. As a friend approaches the camp,—it is not done to strangers for fear of startling them,—those who catch sight of him shout out his name, and gallop up saluting with lances or firing matchlocks in the air. This is the well-known *La'ab al-Barut*, or gunpowder play. Badawin are generally polite in language, but in anger temper is soon shown, and, although life be in peril, the foulest epithets—dog, drunkard, liar, and infidel—are discharged like pistol-shots by both disputants.

The best character of the Badawi is a truly noble compound of determination, gentleness, and generosity. Usually they are a mixture of worldly cunning and great simplicity, sensitive to touchiness, good-tempered souls, solemn and dignified withal, fond of a jest, yet of a grave turn of mind, easily managed by a laugh and a soft word, and placable after passion, though madly revengeful after injury. It has been sarcastically said of the Benu-Harb that there is not a man

> "Que s'il ne voloit, voloit, tuoit, brûloit
> Ne fût assez bonne personne."

The reader will inquire, like the critics of a certain modern humourist, how the fabric of society can be supported by such material. In the first place, it is a kind of *société léonine*, in which the fiercest, the strongest, and the craftiest obtains complete mastery over his fellows, and this gives a keystone to the arch. Secondly, there is the terrible blood-feud, which even the most reckless fear for their posterity. And, thirdly, though the revealed law of the Koran, being insufficient for the Desert, is openly disregarded, the immemorial customs of the *Kazi al-Arab* (the Judge of the Arabs)[7] form a system stringent in the extreme.

The valour of the Badawi is fitful and uncertain. Man is by nature an animal of prey, educated by the complicated relations of society, but readily

---

The banks of the Nile are infamous for these arts, and Mohammed Au Pasha imported, it is said, professional poisoners from Europe.

[7] Throughout the world the strictness of the Lex Scripta is in inverse ratio to that of custom: whenever the former is lax, the latter is stringent, and *vice versâ*. Thus in England, where law leaves men comparatively free, they are slaves to a grinding despotism of conventionalities, unknown in the land of tyrannical rule. This explains why many men, accustomed to live under despotic governments, feel fettered and enslaved in the so-called free countries. Hence, also, the reason why notably in a republic there is less private and practical liberty than under a despotism, The "Kazi al-Arab" (Judge of the Arabs) is in distinction to the Kazi al-Shara, or the Kazi of the Koran. The former is, almost always, some sharp-witted greybeard, with a minute knowledge of genealogy and precedents, a retentive memory and an eloquent tongue.

relapsing into his old habits. Ravenous and sanguinary propensities grow apace in the Desert, but for the same reason the recklessness of civilisation is unknown there. Savages and semi-barbarians are always cautious, because they have nothing valuable but their lives and limbs. The civilised man, on the contrary, has a hundred wants or hopes or aims, without which existence has for him no charms. Arab ideas of bravery do not prepossess us. Their romances, full of foolhardy feats and impossible exploits, might charm for a time, but would not become the standard works of a really fighting people.[8] Nor would a truly valorous race admire the cautious freebooters who safely fire down upon Caravans from their eyries. Arab wars, too, are a succession of skirmishes, in which five hundred men will retreat after losing a dozen of their number. In this partisan-fighting the first charge secures a victory, and the vanquished fly till covered by the shades of night. Then come cries and taunts of women, deep oaths, wild poetry, excitement, and reprisals, which will probably end in the flight of the former victor. When peace is to be made, both parties count up their dead, and the usual blood-money is paid for excess on either side. Generally, however, the feud endures till, all becoming weary of it, some great man, as the Sharif of Meccah, is called upon to settle the terms of a treaty, which is nothing but an armistice. After a few months' peace, a glance or a word will draw blood, for these hates are old growths, and new dissensions easily shoot up from them.

But, contemptible though their battles be, the Badawin are not cowards. The habit of danger in raids and blood-feuds, the continual uncertainty of existence, the desert, the chase, the hard life and exposure to the air, blunting the nervous system; the presence and the practice of weapons, horsemanship, sharpshooting, and martial exercises, habituate them to look death in the face like men, and powerful motives will make them heroes. The English, it is said, fight willingly for liberty, our neighbours for glory; the Spaniard fights, or rather fought, for religion and the *Pundonor*; and the Irishman fights for the fun of fighting. Gain and revenge draw the Arab's sword; yet then he uses it fitfully enough, without the gay gallantry of the French or the persistent stay of the Anglo-Saxon. To become desperate he must have the all-powerful

---

[8] Thus the Arabs, being decidedly a parsimonious people, indulge in exaggerated praises and instances of liberality. Hatim Tai, whose generosity is unintelligible to Europeans, becomes the Arab model of the "open hand." Generally a high *beau idéal* is no proof of a people's practical pre-eminence, and when exaggeration enters into it and suits the public taste, a low standard of actuality may be fairly suspected. But to convince the oriental mind you must dazzle it. Hence, in part, the superhuman courage of Antar, the liberality of Hatim, the justice of Omar, and the purity of Laila and Majnun under circumstances more trying than aught chronicled in Mathilde, or in the newest American novel.

stimulants of honour and of fanaticism. Frenzied by the insults of his women, or by the fear of being branded as a coward, he is capable of any mad deed.[9] And the obstinacy produced by strong religious impressions gives a steadfastness to his spirit unknown to mere enthusiasm. The history of the Badawi tells this plainly. Some unobserving travellers, indeed, have mistaken his exceeding cautiousness for stark cowardice. The incongruity is easily read by one who understands the principles of Badawi warfare; with them, as amongst the Red Indians, one death dims a victory. And though reckless when their passions are thoroughly aroused, though heedless of danger when the voice of honour calls them, the Badawin will not sacrifice themselves for light motives. Besides, they have, as has been said, another and a potent incentive to cautiousness. Whenever peace is concluded, they must pay for victory.

---

[9] At the battle of Bissel, when Mohammed Ali of Egypt broke the 40,000 guerillas of Faisal son of Sa'ud the Wahhabi, whole lines of the Benu Asir tribe were found dead and tied by the legs with ropes. This system of colligation dates from old times in Arabia, as the "Affair of Chains" (Zat al-Salasil) proves. It is alluded to by the late Sir Henry Elliot in his "Appendix to the Arabs in Sind,"—a work of remarkable sagacity and research. According to the "Beglar-Nameh," it was a "custom of the people of Hind and Sind, whenever they devote themselves to death, to bind themselves to each other by their mantles and waistbands." It seems to have been an ancient practice in the West as in the East: the Cimbri, to quote no other instances, were tied together with cords when attacked by Marius. Tactic truly worthy of savages to prepare for victory by expecting defeat!

WILLIAM GIFFORD PALGRAVE
(1826–1888)

Adopting the diverse roles of spy, missionary, and Arabian explorer, like his contemporary Burton, Gifford Palgrave was an outsider who travelled both in order to test himself and in pursuit of an identity. Brought up in a conventional Anglican household though half Jewish through his father, Palgrave enjoyed a controversial reputation during his lifetime owing to perceived disloyalty to his country. After a brilliant academic career at Charterhouse and Oxford he surprised his family by giving up his studies to join the army in India in 1847. An even greater shock ensued when he converted to Catholicism and became a Jesuit in South India in March 1848, staying at Jesuit College, Negapatam, and then Collegio Romano, Rome until 1855. In the same year he travelled to Syria as Father Michel Sohail, where he witnessed in 1860 the massacre of Maronite Christians during their conflict with the Druze. By now well versed in Arabic language and culture, he went to Arabia as an agent of Napoleon III in the disguises of a Syrian doctor/merchant. He set out from Ma'an in June 1862 and traversed the heart of Central Arabia to Ha'il via Djowf and Jebel Shammar, then went on to Riyadh from where he crossed the Dahna desert to Hufuf, sailing around the northern coasts of Bahrain. Here Palgrave departed from his travelling companion, continuing to Qatar then through the straits of Hormuz, completing his journey in Muscat. In Riyadh Wahhabi ruler Abdullah Ibn Saud accused Palgrave and his companion of being 'Christians, spies and revolutionists.' This incident along with other adventures is to be found in *Narrative of A Year's Journey Through Central and Eastern Arabia* (1865). On returning from Arabia, Palgrave was refused permission to go on another Middle East mission, engendering a spiritual crisis that resulted in his renunciation of Catholicism in 1865. After accepting the position of Prussian proconsul at Mosul, which in the event he did not take up, Palgrave became British consul at Soukhoum Kale, 1866–67. There followed a series of diplomatic postings, none in Arabic speaking countries, until his death in 1888. Palgrave's restless transit through a series of conflicting religious and national causes left its trace in his writings. *Narrative of A Year's Journey* demonstrates a typically nineteenth-century preoccupation with race, revealing him as a virulent opponent of Islam, especially its Wahhabi form, but an enthusiastic supporter of the desert Arab kingdoms, particularly that of Ha'il ruled over by Talal ibn Rashid. However, in his later *Eastern Essays* (1870) Palgrave displays a sympathetic understanding of Islam in Ottoman Turkey (Nash 2005: Ch 2).

From:

Narrative of A Year's Journey Through Central and Eastern Arabia (1865)

Stronger in its narrative line perhaps than Burton's, and less encumbered by footnotes, Palgrave's style is equally assertive of his authority as an expert on Arab culture and social *mores*, though he and Burton disagreed as to who – the Nejdi town dweller or the Bedouin of the Syrian desert – was the 'true Arab.'

The Djowf

After taking our meal, we remained awhile where we were in question and answer. Having been previously informed that the governor Hamood resided in the town itself, we suggested to Ghāfil whether it might not be suitable for us to pay that important personage the compliment of a first visit at our very entrance. But the chief had several reasons, which my readers will afterwards learn, for not desiring our so doing. Accordingly he answered that we were his personal guests, and that he himself had in consequence the right to our first reception; that as for Hamood, we should visit him a little later, and in his own company; that it would be time enough for such ceremonies after a day or two, and that in the meanwhile he was himself a sufficient guarantee of the governor's good will.

But on this Dāfee put in his claim to be our host, saying that his house was the nearer at hand; that he also had come in person to meet us; and that in consequence he had as good a right as Ghāfil to have us for his guests. However, he was in his turn obliged to yield to the superior authority of his kinsman. We then all rode on slowly together, and when we were on the point of reaching the lower level of the valley, and had already begun to enter amid the deep shadows of the palmgroves, Dāfee tendered his apologies for letting us thus pass by his domicile without partaking its hospitality; and having added an invitation for the nearest day, he turned aside between the high garden walls to his abode, where we will leave him for the present. But on parting he gave a look of much meaning, first at Ghāfil, and then at us, the import of which we did not as yet fully understand.

Meanwhile we passed on in the company of our new host, who continued all the way his welcomes and protestations of readiness to render us every imaginable service, and leaving a little on our right the castle hill and tower, threaded between grove after grove, and garden after garden, till a high gateway gave us admittance to a cluster of houses around an open space, where seats of beaten earth and stone bordering the walls here and there formed a sort of Arab antechamber or waiting-room for visitors not yet received within the interior precincts, and thus bespoke the importance of the neighbouring house, and consequently of its owner.

Here Ghāfil halted before a portal high enough to admit a camel and rider, and, while we modestly dismounted to await further orders, entered alone the dwelling to see if all had been duly got ready for our reception, and then quickly returned, and invited us to follow him indoors.

We traversed a second entrance, and now found ourselves in a small courtyard, three sides of which were formed by different apartments; the fourth consisted of a stable for horses and camels. In front rose a high wall, with several small windows pierced in it (no glass, of course, in this warm climate) close under the roof, and one large door in the centre. This belonged to the K'hāwah, or G'hāwah, as they here call it, that is, the coffee-room, or reception-room, if you will; inasmuch as ladies never honour its precincts, I cannot suitably dignify it with the title of drawing-room. The description of one such apartment may suffice, with little variation, for all the K'hāwahs of Arabia; it is an indispensable feature in every decent house throughout the Peninsula from end to end, and offers everywhere very little variation, save that of larger or smaller, better or worse furnished, according to the circumstances of its owner. For this reason I shall now permit myself some minuteness of detail in Ghāfil's mansion; it may stand sample for thousands of others.

The K'hāwah was a large oblong hall, about twenty feet in height, fifty in length, and sixteen, or thereabouts, in breadth; the walls were coloured in a rudely decorative manner with brown and white wash, and sunk here and there into small triangular recesses, destined to the reception of books, though of these Ghāfil at least had no over-abundance, lamps, and other such like objects. The roof of timber, and flat; the floor was strewed with fine clean sand, and garnished all round alongside of the walls with long strips of carpet, upon which cushions, covered with faded silk, were disposed at suitable intervals. In poorer houses felt rugs usually take the place of carpets. In one corner, namely, that furthest removed from the door, stood a small fireplace, or, to speak more exactly, furnace, formed of a large square block of granite, or some other hard stone, about twenty inches each way; this is hollowed inwardly into a deep funnel, open above, and communicating below with a small horizontal tube or pipe-hole, through which the air passes, bellows-driven, to the lighted charcoal piled up on a grating about half-way inside the cone. In this manner the fuel is soon brought to a white heat, and the water in the coffee-pot placed above the funnel's mouth is readily brought to boil. This system of coffee furnaces is universal in Djowf and Djebel Shomer, but in Nejed itself, and indeed in whatever other yet more distant regions of Arabia I visited to the south and east, the furnace is replaced by an open fireplace hollowed in the ground floor, with a raised stone border, and dog-irons for the fuel, and so forth, just like what may be yet seen in Spain, and even in some old English manor-houses. This diversity of arrangement, so far as Arabia is concerned, is due to the greater abundance of fire-wood in the south, whereby the inhabitants are enabled to light up on a larger scale; whereas throughout the Djowf and Djebel Shomer wood is very scarce, and the only fuel at hand is bad charcoal, often brought from a considerable distance, and carefully husbanded.

This corner of the K'hāwah is also the place of distinction, whence honour and coffee radiate by progressive degrees round the apartment, and hereabouts accordingly sits the master of the house himself, or the guests whom he more especially delighteth to honour.

On the broad edge of the furnace or fireplace, as the case may be, stands an ostentatious range of copper coffee-pots, varying in size and form. Here in the Djowf their make resembles that in vogue at Damascus; but in Nejed and the eastern districts they are of a different and much more ornamental fashioning, very tall and slender, with several ornamental circles and mouldings in elegant relief, besides boasting long beak-shaped spouts and high steeples for covers. The number of these utensils is often ridiculously great. I have seen a dozen at a time in a row by one fireside, though coffee-making requires, in fact, only three at most. Here in the Djowf five or six are considered to be the thing; for the south this number must be doubled; all this to indicate the riches and munificence of their owner, by implying the frequency of his guests and the large amount of coffee that he is in consequence obliged to have made for them.

Behind this stove sits, at least in wealthy houses, a black slave, whose name is generally a diminutive, in token of familiarity or affection; in the present case it was Soweylim, the diminutive of Sālem. His occupation is to make and pour out the coffee; where there is no slave in the family, the master of the premises himself, or perhaps one of his sons, performs that hospitable duty; rather a tedious one, as we shall soon see.

Of slaves, and of their condition in central Arabia, I shall give a fuller account when we arrive at the central provinces, where these gentlemen are much more numerous than in the Djowf.

We enter. On passing the threshold it is proper to say, "Bismillah," *i.e.*, "in the name of God;" not to do so would be looked on as a bad augury alike for him who enters and for those within. The visitor next advances in silence, till on coming about half-way across the room, he gives to all present, but looking specially at the master of the house, the customary "Es-salamu 'aleykum," or "Peace be with you," literally, "on you." All this while every one else in the room has kept his place, motionless, and without saying a word. But on receiving the salaam of etiquette, the master of the house rises, and if a strict Wahhābee, or at any rate desirous of seeming such, replies with the full-length traditional formula, "W' 'āleykumu-s-salāmu, w'rahmat' Ullahi w'barakátuh," which is, as every one knows, "And with (or, on) you be peace, and the mercy of God, and his blessings." But should he happen to be of anti-Wahhābee tendencies, the odds are that he will say "Marhaba," or "Ahlan w' sahlan," *i.e.*, "welcome," or "worthy, and pleasurable," or the like; for of such phrases there is an infinite, but elegant variety. All present follow the example thus given, by rising and saluting. The guest then goes up to the master of the house, who has also made a step or two forwards, and places his open hand in the palm of his host's, but without grasping or shaking, which would hardly pass for decorous, and at the same time each repeats once more his greeting, followed by the set phrases of polite enquiry, "How are you?" "How goes the world with you?" and so forth, all in a tone of great interest, and to be gone over three or four times, till one or other has the discretion to say "El hamdu l'illāh," "Praise be to God," or, in equivalent value, "all right," and this is a signal for a seasonable diversion to the ceremonious interrogatory.

The guest then, after a little contest of courtesy, takes his seat in the honoured post by the fireplace, after an apologetical salutation to the black slave on the one side, and to his nearest neighbour on the other. The best cushions and newest-looking carpets have been of course prepared for his honoured weight. Shoes or sandals, for in truth the latter alone are used in Arabia, are slipped off on the sand just before reaching the carpet, and there they remain on the floor close by. But the riding stick or wand, the inseparable companion of every true Arab, whether Bedouin or townsman, rich or poor, gentle or simple, is to be retained in the hand, and will serve for playing with during the pauses of conversation, like the fan of our great-grandmothers in their days of conquest.

Without delay Soweylim begins his preparations for coffee. These open by about five minutes of blowing with the bellows and arranging the charcoal till a sufficient heat has been produced. Next he places the largest of the coffee-pots, a huge machine, and about two-thirds full of clear water, close by the edge of the glowing coal-pit, that its contents may become gradually warm while other operations are in progress. He then takes a dirty knotted rag out of a niche in the wall close by, and having untied it, empties out of it three or four handfuls of unroasted coffee, the which he places on a little trencher of platted grass, and picks carefully out any blackened grains, or other non-homologous substances, commonly to be found intermixed with the berries when purchased in gross; then, after much cleansing and shaking, he pours the grain so cleansed into a large open iron ladle, and places it over the mouth of the funnel, at the same time blowing the bellows and stirring the grains gently round and round till they crackle, redden, and smoke a little, but carefully withdrawing them from the heat long before they turn black or charred, after the erroneous fashion of Turkey and Europe; after which he puts them to cool a moment on the grass platter. He then sets the warm water in the large coffee-pot over the fire aperture, that it may be ready boiling at the right moment, and draws in close between his own trouserless legs a large stone mortar, with a narrow pit in the middle, just enough to admit the black stone pestle of a foot long and an inch and half thick, which he now takes in hand. Next, pouring the half-roasted berries into the mortar, he proceeds to pound them, striking right into the narrow hollow with wonderful dexterity, nor ever missing his blow till the beans are smashed, but not reduced into powder. He then scoops them out, now reduced to a sort of coarse reddish grit, very unlike the fine charcoal dust which passes in some countries for coffee, and out of which every particle of real aroma has long since been burnt or ground. After all these operations, each performed with as intense a seriousness and deliberate nicety as if the welfare of the entire Djowf depended on it, he takes a smaller coffee-pot in hand, fills it more than half with hot water from the larger vessel, and then shaking the pounded coffee into it, sets it on the fire to boil, occasionally stirring it with a small stick as the water rises to check the ebullition and prevent overflowing. Nor is the boiling stage to be long or vehement; on the contrary, it is and should be as slight as possible. In the interim he takes out of another rag-knot a few aromatic seeds called heyl, an Indian product, but of whose scientific name I regret to be wholly ignorant., or a little saffron, and after slightly pounding these ingredients, throws them into the simmering coffee to improve its flavour, for such an additional spicing is held indispensable in Arabia, though often omitted elsewhere in the East. Sugar, I may say, would be a totally unheard-of profanation. Last of all, he strains off the liquor through some fibres of the inner palm-bark placed for that purpose in the jug-spout, and gets ready the tray of delicate parti-coloured grass, and the small coffee cups ready for pouring out. All these preliminaries have taken up a good half-hour.

Meantime we have become engaged in active conversation with our host and his friends. But our Sherarat guide, Suleyman, like a true Bedouin, feels too awkward when among townsfolk to venture on the upper places, though repeatedly invited, and accordingly has squatted down on the sand near the entrance. Many of Ghāfil's relations are present; their silver-decorated swords proclaim the importance of the family. Others, too, have come to receive us, for our arrival, announced beforehand by those we had met at the entrance pass, is a sort of event in the town; the dress of some betokens poverty, others are better clad, but all have a very polite and decorous manner. Many a question is asked about our native land and town, that is to say, Syria and Damascus, conformably to the disguise already adopted, and which it was highly important to keep well up; then follow enquiries regarding our journey, our business, what we have brought with us, about our medicines, our goods and wares, &c. &c. From the very first it is easy for us to perceive that purchasers and patients are likely to abound. For my part, being still harassed by my intermittent fever, and very tired, I gave my comrade a hint to shirk the Esculapian topic, and to put the mercantile interest as much as possible in the foreground. Very few travelling merchants, if any, visit the Djowf at this time of year, for one must be mad, or next door to it, to rush into the vast desert around during the heats of June and July; I for one have certainly no intention of doing it again. Hence we had small danger of competitors, and found the market almost at our absolute disposal.

But before a quarter of an hour has passed, and while blacky is still roasting or pounding his coffee, a tall thin lad, Ghāfil's eldest son, appears, charged with a large circular dish, grass-platted like the rest, and throws it with a graceful jerk on the sandy floor close before us. He then produces a large wooden bowl full of dates, bearing in the midst of the heap a cup full of melted butter; all this he places on the circular mat, and says, "Semmoo," literally, "pronounce the Name," of God, understood; this means, "set to work at it." Hereon the master of the house quits his place by the fireside, and seats himself on the sand opposite to us; we draw nearer to the dish, and four or five others, after some respectful coyness, join the circle. Every one then picks out a date or two from the juicy half-amalgamated mass, dips them into the butter, and thus goes on eating till he has had enough, when he rises and washes his hands.

By this time the coffee is ready, and Soweylim begins his round, the coffee-pot in one hand, the tray and cups on the other. The first pouring out he must in etiquette drink himself, by way of a practical assurance that there is no "death in the pot;" the guests are next served, beginning with those next the honourable fireside; the master of the house receives his cup last of all. To refuse would be a positive and unpardonable insult; but one has not much to swallow at a time, for the coffee-cups, or finjans, are about the size of a large eggshell at most, and are never more than half filled. This is considered essential to good breeding, and a brimmer would here imply exactly the reverse of what it does in Europe; why it should be so I hardly know, unless perhaps the rareness of cup-stands or "zarfs" (see Lane's Modern Egyptians, Chapter V) in Arabia, though these implements are universal in Egypt and Syria, might render an over-full cup inconveniently hot for the fingers that must grasp it without medium. Be that as it may, "fill the cup for your enemy" is an adage common to all, Bedouins or townsmen, throughout the Peninsula. The beverage itself is singularly aromatic and refreshing, a real tonic, and utterly different from the black mud sucked by the Osmanli, or the watery roast-bean preparations of France. When the slave or freeman, according to circumstances, presents you with a cup, he never fails to accompany it with a "Semm'," "say the name of God," nor must you take it without answering "bismillah."

LADY ANNE NOEL (1837–1917) AND WILFRID SCAWEN BLUNT (1840–1922)

Granddaughter of Lord Byron, Anne Isabella Noel became Lady Anne Blunt on her marriage with Wilfrid Scawen Blunt in 1869. Together they formed a travelling couple, embarking on a series of journeys in the Muslim world beginning with Anatolia (1873) Algeria (1874) the Egyptian Western Desert (1876), Mesopotamia and Persia (1877–78) and the deserts of Central Arabia (1879). Lady Anne reports the last two in *Bedouin Tribes of the Euphrates* (1879) and *A Pilgrimage to Nejd* (1881). Her travel writings were developed from notes taken on the spot, and rewritten material initially based on impressions and dialogues (Hout DLB/174: 44). Wilfrid added introductions and also acted as 'editor', by no means an unusual practice given the unequal gender relations of the period, which required: 'a woman's representation of the exotic Other … to be authorized by a male orientalist', and demarcated roles 'between the woman as fieldworker and the man as analytical theorist' (Behdad 1994: 95, 97). These writings propose an ideal of an Arab aristocracy of the desert, initially stimulated by Palgrave and later by the Blunts' contact with sheykhs and emirs on their travels. They established a winter retreat, Sheykh Obeyd, in the desert outside Cairo from which Wilfrid was banned for several years after his involvement with the nationalist side in the Urabi revolution of 1881–2. They also assembled a stud of Arabian horses at Crabbet, their Sussex estate. Both husband and wife acquired a good command of Arabic, though Lady Anne's was superior, and in addition to their works of travel their mental partnership produced *The Seven Odes of Pagan Arabia* (1903). However Wilfrid's compulsive adulteries, laid out in detail in Elizabeth Longford's biography (1980), led to an estrangement that lasted for the decade or so before Anne's death in Cairo in December 1917.

From:

A Pilgrimage to Nejd (1881)

In his preface to *A Pilgrimage to Nejd* Blunt adduced his ideas on the 'Shepherd rule' which he claimed was to be found in Central Arabia. Lady Anne's account of their visit to Ha'il, then ruled by Muhammad ibn Rashid who had achieved power through the murder of his nephews, fleshes out this ideal form of government.

Haïl

Abdallah, and all the Ibn Rashid family, have been endowed with a large share of caution. No important enterprise has been embarked on in a hurry; and certainly at the present day affairs of state are discussed in family council, before any action is taken. It seems to have been always a. rule with the Ibn Rashids to think twice, thrice, or a dozen times before acting, for even Mohammed's violent deeds towards his nephews were premeditated, and thought over for many months beforehand. In their conduct with the Ibn Saouds and the Turkish Sultans, they have always waited their opportunity, and avoided an open rupture. It is very remarkable that so many members of this family should be superior men, for it is difficult to say who has been the ablest man of them, Abdallah, Obeyd, Tellál, Mohammed, or his cousin Hamúd. Nor is the rising generation less promising.

Having united into a sort of confederation all the Bedouin tribes of Northern Nejd, Abdallah became naturally supreme over the towns; but he was not satisfied merely with power, he aimed at making his rule popular. It is much to his credit, and to that of his successors, that none of them seem to have abused their position. Liberality and conciliation, combined with an occasional display of power, have been no less their policy with the townsmen than with the Bedouins, and they have thus placed their rule on its only secure basis, popularity. In early days the Ibn Rashids had to fight for their position at Haïl, and later in Jôf and at Meskakeh. But their rule is now acknowledged freely everywhere, enthusiastically in Jebel Shammar. It strikes a traveller fresh from Turkey as surpassingly strange to hear the comments passed by the townspeople of Haïl on their government, for it is impossible to converse ten minutes with any one of them without being assured, that the government of the Emir is the best government in the world. "El hamdu lillah, ours is a fortunate country. It is not with us as with the Turks and Persians, whose government is no government. Here we are happy and prosperous. El hamdu lillah." I have often been amused at this chauvinism.

In the town of Haïl the Emir lives in state, having a body-guard of 800 or 1000 men dressed in a kind of uniform, that is to say, in brown cloaks and red or blue kefiyehs, and armed with silver-hilted swords. These are recruited from among the young men of the towns and villages by voluntary enlistment, those who wish to serve inscribing their names at the castle, and being called out as occasion requires. Their duties are light, and they live most of them with their families, receiving neither pay nor rations, except when employed away from home on garrison duty in outlying forts and at Jôf. Their expense, therefore, to the Emir is little more than that of their clothes and arms. To them is entrusted any police work that may be necessary in the towns, but it is very seldom that the authority of the Emir requires other support than that of public opinion. The Arabs of Nejd are a singularly temperate race, and hardly ever indulge in brawling or breaches of the peace. If disputes arise between citizens they are almost always settled on the spot by the interference of neighbours; and the rowdyism and violence of European towns are unknown at Haïl. Where, however, quarrels are not to be settled by the intervention of friends, the disputants bring their cases to the Emir, who settles them in open court, the *mejlis*, and whose word is final. The law of the Koran, though often referred to, is not, I fancy, the main rule of the Emir's decision, but rather Arabian custom, an authority far older than the Mussulman code. I doubt if it is often necessary for the soldiers to support such decisions by force. Thieving, I have been repeatedly assured, is almost unknown at Haïl; but robbers or thieves taken redhanded, lose for the first offence a hand, for the second their head.

In the desert, and everywhere outside the precincts of the town, order is kept by the Bedouins, with whom the Emir lives a portion of each year. He is then neither more nor less himself than a Bedouin, throws off his shoes and town finery, arms himself with a lance, and leads a wandering life in the Nefûd. He commonly does this at the commencement of spring, and spring is the season of his wars. Then with the extreme heat of summer he returns to Haïl. The tribute paid by each town and village to the Emir is assessed according to its wealth in date palms, and the sheep kept by its citizens with the Bedouins. Four khrush for each tree is, I believe, the amount, trees under seven years old being exempt. At Haïl this is levied by the Emir's officers, but elsewhere by the local sheykhs, who are responsible for its due collection. At Jôf and Meskakeh, which are still in the position of territory newly annexed, Ibn Rashid is represented by a vakil, or lieutenant, who levies the tax in coin, Turkish money being the recognised medium of exchange everywhere. Without pretending to anything at all like accuracy we made a calculation that the Emir's revenue from all sources of tribute and tax may amount to £60,000 yearly, and that the annual passage of the pilgrimage through his dominions may bring £20,000 to £30,000 more to his exchequer.

With regard to his expenditure, it is perhaps easier to calculate. He pays a small sum yearly in tribute to the Sherif of Medina, partly as a religious offering, partly to insure immunity for his outlying possessions, Kheybar, Kâf and the rest, from Turkish aggression. I should guess this tribute to be £3,000 to £5,000, but could not ascertain the amount. The Emir's expenditure on his army can hardly be more, and with his civil list and every expense of Government, should be included within £10,000. On his household he may spend £5,000, and on his stable £1,000. By far the largest item in his budget must be described as entertainment. Mohammed ibn Rashid, in imitation of his predecessors, feeds daily two to three hundred guests at the palace; the poor are there clothed, and presents of camels and clothes made to richer strangers from a distance. The meal consists of rice and camel meat, sometimes mutton, and there is besides a. constant "coulage" in dates and coffee, which I cannot estimate at less than £50 a day, say £20,000 yearly, or with presents, £25,000. Thus we have our budget made up to about £45,000 expenditure, as against £80,000 to £90,000 revenue—which leaves a handsome margin for wars and other accidents, and for that amassing of treasure which is traditional with the Ibn Rashids. I must say, however, once more, that I am merely guessing my figures, and nobody, perhaps, in Jebel Shammar, except the Emir himself and Hamúd, could do more.

It will be seen from all this that Jebel Shammar is, financially, in a very flourishing state. The curse of money-lending has not yet invaded it, and neither prince nor people are able to spend sixpence more than they have got. No public works, requiring public expenditure and public loans, have yet been undertaken, and it is difficult to imagine in what they would consist. The digging of new wells is indeed the only duty a "company" could find to execute, for roads are unnecessary in a country all like a macadamised highway; there are no rivers to make canals with, or suburban populations to supply with tramways. One might predict with confidence, that the secret of steam locomotion will have been forgotten before ever a railway reaches Jebel Shammar.

With regard to the form of government, it is good mainly because it is effective. It is no doubt discordant to European ideas of political propriety, that the supreme power in a country should be vested in Bedouin hands. But in Arabia they are the only hands that can wield it. The town cannot coerce the desert; therefore, if they are to live at peace, the desert must coerce the town. The Turks, with all their machinery of administration, and their power of wealth and military force, have never been able to secure life and property to travellers in the desert, and in Arabia have been powerless to hold more than the towns. Even the pilgrim road from Damascus, though nominally in their keeping, can only be traversed by them with an army, and at considerable risk. Ibn Rashid, on the other hand, by the mere effect of his will, keeps all the desert in an absolute peace. In the whole district of Jebel Shammar, embracing, as it does, some of the wildest deserts, inhabited by some of the wildest people in the world, a traveller may go unarmed and unescorted, without more let or hindrance than if he were following a highway in England. On every road of

Jebel Shammar, townsmen may be found jogging on donkey-back, alone, or on foot, carrying neither gun nor lance, and with all their wealth about them. If you ask about the dangers of the road, they will return the question, "Are we not here in Ibn Rashid's country?" No system, however perfect, of patrols and forts and escorts, could produce a result like this.

In the town, on the other hand, the Bedouin prince, despotic though he may be, is still under close restraint from public opinion. The citizens of Jebel Shammar have not what we should call constitutional rights; there is no machinery among them for the assertion of their power; but there is probably no community in the old world, where popular feeling exercises a more powerful influence on government than it does at Haïl. The Emir, irresponsible as he is in individual acts, knows well that he cannot transgress the traditional unwritten law of Arabia with impunity. An unpopular sheykh would cease, *ipso facto*, to be sheykh, for, though dethroned by no public ceremony, and subjected to no personal ill-treatment, he would find himself abandoned in favour of a more acceptable member of his family. The citizen soldiers would not support a recognised tyrant in the town, nor would the Bedouins outside. Princes in Arabia have, therefore, to consider public opinion before all else.

The flaw in the system, for in every system there will be found one, lies in the uncertainty of succession to the Sheykhat or Bedouin throne. On the death of an Emir, if he have no son of full age and acknowledged capacity to take up the reins of government, rival claimants, brothers, uncles, or cousins of the dead man, dispute his succession in arms, and many and bitter have been the wars in consequence. Such, quite lately, was the quarrel which convulsed Aared on the death of Feysul ibn Saoud, and led to the disintegration of the Wahhabi monarchy, and such, one cannot help fearing, may be the fate of Jebel Shammar, on Mohammed's. He has no children, and the sons of Tellál, the next heirs to the throne, have a formidable rival in Hamúd. The Emir, however, is a young man, forty-five, and may live long; and if he should do so, seems to have the succession of the Wahhabi monarchy in his hands. He has effected, he and his predecessors, the union of all the Bedouin sheykhs, from Meshhed Ali to Medina, under his leadership, and is in close connection with those of Kasim and Aared. His authority is established as far north as Kâf, and he has his eye already on the towns still further north, if ever they should shake off the Turkish bondage. I look forward to the day when the Roala too, and the Welled Ali, shall have entered into his alliance, possibly even the Sebaa and Ibn Haddal; and though it is neither likely nor desirable that the old Wahhabi Empire should be re-established on its centralised basis, a confederation of the tribes of the north may continue its best traditions. Hauran and the Leja, and the Euphrates towns, were once tributary to the Ibn Saouds, and may be again one day to the Ibn Rashids. This is looking far afield, but not farther than Mohammed himself looks.

CHARLES MONTAGU DOUGHTY
(1843–1926)

With clergymen for father and maternal grandfather, and a navy tradition to boot, Doughty's family background seemed to predetermine him to a life of patriotic service and religious earnestness. But while these influences would leave their imprint on his life, other contingencies arose to conflict with them. He was an orphan by the age of six, developed a stammer, and his faith was confronted by doubts raised by his study of geology. The speech impediment barred him from a naval career and despite graduating from Cambridge with a natural science degree in 1865 this was not good enough for him to take his scientific work further. After literary study in England and travel in Europe, during which he laid the foundations for his later preoccupation with a literary style purged of modern adulteration, Doughty spent the period 1874–78 in the East. Having prepared himself by studying Arabic, he set off from Damascus in November 1876 with the intention of being the first European scholar to describe the carved monuments of Madain Salih. He accompanied the hajj as far as its vicinity, viewed and made notes on the site, but then instead of returning determined to continue his wanderings in Central Arabia. Attaching himself initially to the Fukara Bedouin, he went on to Ha'il, where he met Muhammad ibn Rashid, and thence to Khaybar, before turning back towards the Hijaz. Not far from Mecca he came perilously close to being murdered by a fanatic, but eventually arrived in Jeddah in August 1878. The major source of Doughty's problems, besides travelling without the approval of the British consul in Jeddah or a *laissez-passer* from the Ottoman authorities, was his refusal to don a disguise, his proud assertion of his Englishness, and open proclamation of his Christianity. *Travels in Arabia Deserta*, upon which Doughty worked for nearly six years, was published in 1888. It is a challenging work of some 600,000 words written in a style influenced by Chaucer and Spenser with a large complement of Arabic words and phrases. In spite of its author's avowed contempt for Islam, and its portrayal of his frequent humiliation at their hands, the work evidences a genuine humanitarian concern for the Bedouin, about whose way of life Doughty gained 'a greater insight...than any [European] before him' (Trench 1986: 135). Indeed some have seen in this the clue to Doughty's journey: he 'was attempting to work back to the origin of mankind' (Assad 1964: 125) as well as, perhaps, to expiate the guilt of 'betraying the simple faith of his childhood' (Tidrick 1989: 147). A social misfit and loner, Doughty's lifelong devotion to writing patriotic verse is almost entirely forgotten, while his one work on Arabia is now a canonical text of travel.

From:

Travels in Arabia Deserta (1888)

In observing the life and talk of the Fukara Doughty displays a humanitarian interest in primitive people and fascination for their language, as summed up in the phrases that open this extract.

Life in the Wandering Village

A pleasure it is to listen to the cheerful musing Beduin talk, a lesson in the travellers' school of mere humanity,—and there is no land so perilous which by humanity he may not pass, for man is of one mind everywhere, ay, and in their kind, even the brute animals of the same foster earth—a timely vacancy of the busy-idle cares which cloud upon us that would live peaceably in the moral desolation of the world. And pleasant those sounds of the spretting milk under the udders in the Arabs' vessels! food for man and health at a draught in a languishing country. The bowl brought in foaming, the children gather to it, and the guest is often bidden to sup with them, with his fingers, the sweet froth, *orghra* or *roghrwa, irtugh:* or this milk poured into the sour milk-skin and shaken there a moment, the housewife serves it forth again to their suppers, with that now gathered sourness which they think the more refreshing.

The nomad's eyes are fixed upon the crude congruity of Nature; even the indolence in them is austere. They speak of the things within their horizon. Those loose "Arabian tales" of the great border-cities, were but profane ninnery to their stern natural judgments. Yet so much they have of the Semitic Oriental vein, without the doting citizen fantasy, that many dream all their lives of hidden treasures; wealth that may fall to them upon a day out of the lap of heaven. Instead of the cities' taling, the Aarab have their braying rhapsodies, which may be heard in every wild nomad hamlet, as those of the Beny Helál. The Arabs are very credulous of all that is told beyond their knowledge, as of foreign countries. All their speech is homely; they tell of bygone forays and of adventures in their desert lives. You may often hear them in their tale quote the rhythms between wisdom and mirth of the *kasasîd* (riming desert poets without letters); the best are often widely current among the tribes. In every tribe are makers: better than any in this country were the kassâds of Bishr. The *kassâd* recites, and it is a pleasant adulation of the friendly audience to take up his last words in every couplet. In this poetical eloquence I might not very well, or hardly at all, distinguish what they had to say; it is as strange language. The word *shâer,* he that '*feeleth,*' a poet, is unused by them; the Beduins knew not the word, Zeyd answered "it is *nadêm.*" The Beduin singer draws forth stern and horrid sounds from the rabeyby or viol of one bass string, and delivers his mind, braying forcedly in the nose. It is doubtless a very archaic minstrelsy, in these lands, but a hideous desolation to our ears. It is the hinds, all day in the wilderness with the cattle, who sing most lustily in their evening home-coming to the humanity of the byût. I often asked for a *kasîda* of Abeyd Ibn Rashîd, and have found no singer in this country who was not ready with some of them. The young herdsmen of Zeyd's menzil would chant for the stranger the most evening-times the robust *hadû,* or herding-song. [This word *rabeyby* is perhaps the Spaniard's *rabel,* and that was in Ancient England *revel, rebibel.*] The Beduw make the instrument of any box-frame they may have from the towns: a stick is thrust through, and in this they pierce an eye above for the peg; a kid-skin is stretched, upon the hollow box; the hoarse string is plucked from the mare's tail; and setting under a bent twig, for the bridge, their music is ready.

The nomad's fantasy is high, and that is ever clothed in religion. They see but the indigence of the open soil about, full of dangers, and hardly sustaining them, and the firmament above them, habitation of the Divine salvation. These Ishmaelites have a natural musing conscience of the good and evil, more than other men; but none observe them less in all their dealings with mankind. The civil understanding of the desert citizens is found in their discourse (tempered between mild and a severe manly grace) and liberal behaviour. A few turns and ornaments of their speech, come suddenly to my remembrance: gently in contradiction, *la! Ullah yesellímk,* "Nay, the Lord give thee peace;" in correction, *la! Ullah hadîk,* "The Lord lead thee;" and in both, *Ullah yerham weyladeyk,* "The Lord show mercy to thy deceased parentage;" or *yuhâdy weyladeyk il' ej-jínna,* "Lead in thy parents to the paradise." Wonder, as all their Semitic life, has the voice of religion, *Ullah!* "The Lord!" *Ana ushhud,* "I do bear witness!" *Yukdur Ullah!* "The Lord is able." *Rahmat Ullah!* "The Lord His mercy!" and very often the popular sort will say, (a Beduinism that is received with laughter in the towns,) *ana efla youwella!*—which I leave to Arabists. When weary they sigh *ya Rubby!* "Ah my Lord!" Lovers of quietness at home, their words are peace, and still courteous in argument; *wa low,* "And if it were so;" *sellímt,* "I grant it you." Confession of faulty error through ignorance, *udkhul al' Ullah,* "If I said amiss, the Lord is my refuge." A word of good augury to the wayfaring and stranger; *Ullah yuwasselak b'il-kheyer,*

"God give thee to arrive well." *Insh' Ullah ma teshûf es-shurr,* "It may please the
Lord that you see not the evil!" *Ullah yethkirak b'il-kheyer?* "The Lord remember
thee for good!" Beduish giving of thanks are: *âfy aleyk, el-âfy,* "I wish thee
heartily health!" or, *jizak Ullah kheyer,* "God give thee good chance!" The
nomads, at leisure and lively minds, have little other than this study to be
eloquent. Their utterance is short and with emphasis. There is a perspicuous
propriety in their speech, with quick significance. The Arabian town-dwellers
contemn this boisterous utterance of the sons of the wilderness; they
themselves are fanatic sectators of the old koran reading. Asiatics, the Aarab
are smiling speakers. All Beduin talk is one manner of Arabic, but every tribe
has a use, *loghra,* and neighbours are ever chiders of their neighbours' tongue.
"The speech of them, they will say, is somewhat 'awry,' *awaj.*" In the mouth of
the Fukara sheykhs, was a lisping of the terminal consonants. The Moahîb talk
was open and manly. In that dry serenity of the air, and largely exercised
utterance of the many difficult articulations of their language, the human
voice, *hess,* is here mostly clear and well-sounding; unless it be in some husk
choking throat of heart-sore misery.

There is as well that which is displeasing in their homely talk. The mind is
distempered by idleness and malice; they will hardly be at pains to remember
suddenly, in speech, their next tribesman's name; and with this is their
barbarous meddling curiosity, stickling mistrust one of another and beggarly
haggling for any trifle, with glosing caresses, (would they obtain a thing, and
which are always in guile,) impudent promises and petulant importunity.
And their hypocrite iniquitous words, begetting the like, often end in
hideous clamour, which troubling "the peace of Ullah" in the nomad booth, are
rebuked by the silent impatience of the rest, of whom the better will then
proffer themselves as peace-makers. The herdsmen's tongue is full of infantile
raillery and, in sight and hearing of the other sex, of jesting ribaldry: they think
it innocent mirth, since it is God that has founded thus our nature. Semites, it is
impossible that they should ever blaspheme, in manner of those of our blood,
against the Heavenly Providence. Semitic religion is the natural growth of the
soil in their Semitic souls; in which is any remiss, farewell life's luck, farewell his
worldly estimation: their criminal hearts are capable of all mischief, only not of
this enormous desperation to lede the sovereign majesty of Ullah. Out of that
religious persuasion of theirs that a man's life should be smitten to death, who
is rebel unto God and despiser of the faith, comes the sharp danger of our
travelling among them; where of every ten, there is commonly some one,
making religion of his peevish bestiality, who would slay us, (which all men may
do religiously and help divine justice). But otherwise they all day take God's
name in vain (as it was perhaps in ancient Israel), confirming every light and
laughing word with cheerful billahs. The herdsmen's grossness is never out of

the Semitic nature, the soul of them is greedy first of their proper subsistence and then of their proper increase. Though Israel is scattered among the most polite nations, who has not noted this humour in them? Little Joseph is a tale-bearer to their father of his brethren's lewd conversation in the field; such are always the Semitic nomads. Palestine, the countries beyond Jordan and Edom, given to the children and nephews of Abraham, spued out the nations which dwelled before in them, and had defiled the land: the Beny Israel are admonished, lest the soil cast out them also. In Moses is remembered the nomad offence of lying with cattle; the people are commanded to put away guiltiness from the land by stoning them: in Arabia that is but a villanous mock, and which the elder sort acknowledge with groans and cursing. The pastoral race being such, Israel must naturally slide back from Moses' religion to the easy and carnal idolatry of the old Canaanites.

To speak of the Arabs at the worst, in one word, the mouth of the Arabs is full of cursing and lies and prayers; their heart is a deceitful labyrinth. We have seen their urbanity; gall and venom is in their least ill-humour; disdainful, cruel, outrageous is their malediction. "Curse Ullah, thy father (that is better than thou), the father of the likes of thee! burn thy father! this is a man fuel for hell-burning! bless thee not God make thee no partaker of His good! thy house fall upon thee!" I have heard one, in other things a very worthy man, in such form chide his unruly young son: "Ullah rip up that belly in thee! Curse the father (thy body) of that head and belly! Punish that hateful face!" And I have heard one burden another thus; "Curse thee all the angels, curse thee all the Moslemîn, let all the heathen curse thee!" The raging of the tongue is natural to the half-feminine Semitic race. The prophet prayeth against some which disquieted him: "Pour out their blood by the sword, let their children consume with famine, their women be childless and their wives widows: they shall cry out from the houses as the ghrazzu is suddenly upon them. Forgive not, Lord, their trespass, give to them trouble of spirit, destroy them from under the heaven, and let Thy very curse abide upon them." Another holy man curses to death petulant children. The Aarab confirm all their words by oaths, which are very brittle, and though they say *Wa hyât Ullah*, "As the Lord liveth," or a man swear by himself, *aly lahyaty*, or *Wa hyât dúkny*, "Upon (the honour of) my beard." He will perform such oaths if they cost him nothing, this is if he be not crossed in the mean while, or have become unwilling. If a man swear by his religion, it is often lightly and with mental reservation. For the better assurance of a promise they ask and give the hand; it is a visible pledge. So in Ezekiel, the sheukh of the captivity promise and plight their hands. A Beduin will swear to some true matter Wellâhi, or doubly, which is less to trust, Wellâhi-Billâhi. It is a word he will observe if he may, for nothing can bind them against their own profit; and they may lawfully break through all at an extremity. Another form is

Wullah-Bullah, often said in mocking uncertainty and hypocrisy. That is a faithful form of swearing which they call *halif yemîn:* one takes a grass stalk in his fist, and his words are: *"Wa hyât hâtha el-aûd,* By the life of this stem, *wa'r-rubb el-mabûd,* and the adorable Lord." When I have required new wayfaring companions to swear me this at the setting out, and add *inny mâ adeshurak,* "I will not (for any hap) forsake thee," they have answered, "Our lot is one whilst we are in the way, whether to live or die together; and what more can I say, I will conduct thee thither, but I die, and by very God I will not forsake thee." I laid hold on their hands and compelled them, but they swore (to a kafir) unwillingly; and some have afterward betrayed me: when then I reproached them to the heart, they answered me, "Oaths taken to a kafir be not binding!" Magnanimous fortitude in a man, to the despising of death, where his honour is engaged, were in their seeing the hardihood of a madman: where mortal brittleness is fatally overmatched we have a merciful God, and human flesh, they think, may draw back from the unequal contention.

To clear himself of an unjust suspicion one will say to the other, "There is nothing between us but Ullah." Like words we hear from gentle Jonathan's mouth, in his covenant with the climbing friend David. Certain oaths there are, which being received by the custom of the tribes as binding, are not violated by any honourable person. And, to tell the little which I have ascertained in this kind,—a Beduin, put in trust of another man's cattle, often some villager, will give up his yearly tale of the increase without fraud, under a solemn obtestation which he durst not elude, the owner having also traced a ring about him with his sword. If aught be missing in the nomad menzil, the owner of that which is lost or strayed may require of whom he will an oath of denial, as Ahab took an oath of his neighbours, who are called "every nation and kingdom," that his subject and enemy, Elias, was not found amongst them. I have seen some under an imputation go with the accuser to the hearth to give his answer; this they call to swear upon their swords. It is over certain lines, which they trace with their weapon in the ashes; a cross mark in a circle ⊕; therewith taking a handful from the ash-pit. It is an oath such, that the complainant must thereafter yield himself satisfied. Zeyd accused of devouring his neighbours' substance, which was not seldom, would cheerfully, with a faultless countenance, spread and smooth out upon the soil the lap of his mantle, and clapping down his flat palm upon it, he cried, "Ha!" and proffered himself all ready to swear that this was not so, there was nothing of the other's ownership, Wellah! in his hold. Oaths of the desert there are some held binding between enemies. I knew a B. Atîeh man guesting with the Moahîb, who in time when they lay friendly encamped together with the Fejîr, was admitted to converse freely amongst these his natural foemen, when he had sworn his oath at the hearth, before Motlog, that he would not practise against them. This matter of oaths is that in the nomad commonwealth which I have least searched out; even the solemn forms, conjuring quarter and a magnanimous protection. Although Beduins often questioned me, what our words were in these cases, yet ever, as God would have it, to the last, I neglected to enquire the like of themselves again. At every moment, when they gave me their minds, I had rather ascertain all that I might of the topography of their country; having less care of the rest, as never thinking to entreat for my life of any man.

Besides, there are certain gestures used among them, which are tokens of great significance. I smooth my beard toward one to admonish him, in his wrongful dealing with me, and have put him in mind of his honour. If I touch his beard, I put him in remembrance of our common humanity and of the witness of God which is above us. Beard is taken in Arabia for human honour, and to pluck it is the highest indignity; of an honest man they say, *lahyat-hu tâiba,* "His is a good beard;" of a vile covetous heart *mâ lihu lahya,* "He has no beard." The suppliant who may bind, as I have heard, a certain knot in the other's kerchief, has saved himself: and were the other the avenger for blood, yet he must forbear for God! Kiss an angry man's forehead, and his rancour will fall; but the adversary must be taken by surprise, or he will put forth stern hostile hands to oppose thee. Surely a very ancient example of the Semitic sacramental gestures is that recorded of Abraham, who bids his steward put the hand under his thigh, to make his oath sure. A simple form of requiring an honourable tolerance and protection is to say; *Ana nuzîlak,* "I have alighted at thy tent," or say where thou fearest treachery, *ana nusîk,* and again, *Ana bi wejhak ya sheykh,* "Sir, I am under thy countenance;" more solemnly, and touching him, *Terâny billah ya sheykh; wa bak ana dakhîlak,* which may signify, "By the Lord thou seest me, and I do enter, Sir, under thy protection." In my long dangerous wanderings in the Arabian Peninsula I have thrice said this one word *dakhîlak:* twice when, forsaken in the deserts, I came to strange tents of Heteym (they are less honourable than Beduins, and had repulsed me); once to the captain of the guard at Hâyil, when I was maltreated by the emir's slaves in the market-place. He immediately drove them from me; and in the former adventure it made that I was received with tolerance.

As above said, the nomads will confirm every word with an oath, as commonly *wa hyât,* 'By the life of;' but this is not in the Waháby country, where every oath which is by the life of any creature they hold to be "idolatry." They swear *wa hyât,* even of things inanimate; ' By the life of this fire, or of this coffee,' *hyâtak,* "By thy life," Wa *hyât rukbaty,* " By the life of my neck," are common affirmations in their talk. *Wa hyât ibny* men rarely say, and not lightly, "By my son's life." *Wa hyât weyladich,* "Life of thy child," is a womanish oath of Bíllî mothers one to another at every third word; and a gossip says tenderly, *wa hyât weylady,* "By my child's life:" I have heard a Beduin woman testify to her child thus, "By the life of thy father, who begat thee upon me!" In the biblical authors, Joseph makes protestation to his brethren "By the life of Pharaoh," and later that is common in them "as the Lord liveth;" Jehovah promises under the same form, "As I live, saith the Lord." In every tribe there is a manner, even in this part of their speech. The Moahîb, who, like their Bíllî neighbours, are amiable speakers, use to swear, not lightly, by the divine daylight and the hour of prayer, as *wa hyât el-missîeh hâtha*, "By this (little) sun-setting hour." The Beduw will put off importunity with much ill humour, saying, *furrka* or *furr'k ayn abûy*. Unruly children are checked with *subbak!* they will answer *yussbak ent*. Full of ribaldry, the Aarab will often say in a villanous scorn *kuss marrathu*, "his wife's nakedness for him," or *ummhu*, "his mother's nakedness." My Medina host at Kheybar, who otherwise was a good worthy man, would snib his only son tyrannically and foully with this reproach of his deceased mother, whom he had loved. The biblical Saul, justly incensed, also reviles his son by the nakedness of his mother, a perverse and rebellious woman, and Jonathan her son rose from his father's dish and departed in fierce anger.

The Aarab's leave-taking is wonderfully ungracious to the European sense, and austere. The Arab, until now so gentle a companion, will turn his back with stony strange countenance to leave thee for ever. Also the Arabs speak the last words as they have turned the back; and they pass upon their way not regarding again. This is their national usage, and not of a barbarous inhumanity; nay, it were for thee to speak when any departs company, saying: "Go in peace." You have not eaten together, there was nothing then between you why this must take his leave; all men being in their estimation but simple grains, under the Throne of God, of the common seed of humanity. But the guest will say as he goes forth, and having turned his face, with a frank simplicity, *nesellem aleyk*, "We bid thee peace." The Arabs are little grateful for the gift which is not food, receive they with never so large a hand; "So little they will say, put to, put to;" but the gentler spirits will cry out soon, *bess! Wâjed! keffy!* "enough, there is found, it sufficeth me heartily."

PERSIA

Historical Background

A long period of instability and fragmentation followed the end of the Safavid dynasty (1736) and the brief reign of Nadir Shah (1736–1747). Although Zand rule created order and prosperity in the southern part of the country for most of the second half of the eighteenth century, a unifying force only arose at the century's end in the form of the Qajars. Before his assassination in 1797 Aqa Muhammad Qajar, who ended the Zand dynasty, re-instated to the Persian Empire its former territories in the Caucasus. Acting to defend her interests in India by pre-empting Afghanistan's expansion into Persia and thence India, as well as possible French invasion, in 1799 Britain sent an embassy led by John Malcolm. This reached Tehran the following year and resulted in the signing of two Anglo-Persian treaties: one promised economic cooperation, the other British support in defending Persia against both Afghanistan and France. However when Russia attacked his kingdom's Caucasian provinces, Fath Ali Shah (ruled 1797–1834) turned in 1807 to France for help, signing a treaty and receiving a French military mission. But when Napoleon settled with Russia at Tilsit he left Persia prey once more to her northern neighbour. Diplomatic manoeuvres were then resumed by Britain. London sent Harford Jones who negotiated a new treaty with the Shah only for John Malcolm to arrive from India in February 1810. With the Napoleonic menace ended Britain lost interest in Persia, which then suffered humiliation and territorial emasculation at Russia's hands. Two disastrous wars fought in 1813 and 1826 resulted in the loss of Georgia, Armenia and northern Azerbaijan.

For the rest of the century and well into the next, Persia would be 'torn between the conflicting interests of Russia and Great Britain' (Wilbur 1963: 76). Russia continued to expand her presence in Central Asia thus threatening Persia's northern borders, while Britain consolidated her power in the Persian Gulf. Persian campaigns in Afghanistan aimed at the re-conquest of Herat, mounted in the reign of Muhammad Shah (1834–1848) and early in that of Nasir al-Din (1848–1896), were strongly opposed by Britain, who in 1856 went so far as to declare war against Persia over the issue. By the last quarter of the nineteenth-century European industrial products had begun to make an appearance in Persia's bazaars but economic development was greatly inferior to that in Turkey or Egypt. According to the economic historian Charles Issawi reasons behind this included weak central government, 'archaic administrative and fiscal systems', distance from Western Europe, and lack of indigenous groups who could mediate Western ways (Keddie 1980: 120). However Issawi also argued that Anglo-Russian rivalry played an important role in cancelling out schemes for economic development in Persia, an example being Baron de Reuter's 1872 concession to develop almost every aspect of her economy, which Russian opposition nullified.

Travellers and their Narratives

Travel books on early nineteenth-century Persia were more frequently than not authored by diplomats who used their knowledge and expertise to supplement their incomes. Mazzeo (2001: xxiii) states: 'Although Romantic exploration of Persia was largely conducted as part of diplomatic or military service, travel accounts of the region were typically more entertaining than useful.' The comedy of the rival British missions of 1810 left at least one legacy: Malcolm's lavish dispensing of gifts created expectations that subsequent travellers found it difficult to satisfy. In addition, as Marzieh Gail pointed out, Sir Gore Ouseley's reception in 1811 as Britain's first ambassador on Persian soil since the time of Charles I resulted in 'endless battles over ceremonial, and struggles to convince the Shah that the British sovereign, even though a limited, was not an inferior, monarch' (Gail 1951: 60). The literature on Persia written by the likes of William Ouseley, James Morier, and John Malcolm reproduces this clash of cultures, at the same time emphasizing a lavishness of ceremony that in the case of Morier in particular exemplifies 'the intimate relationship between Romantic rhetoric and empire building' (Mazzeo 2001: 154).

Into the Victorian period British officers on secondment from the Indian Army came to Persia with military considerations in mind while other visitors travelled as individuals 'out of curiosity or for pleasure' (Wright 1977: 149). In the latter category were the artist Ker Porter, author of *Travels in Georgia, Persia, Armenia and Ancient Babylonia*, which Curzon criticized for its 'ludicrous' and 'pompous' style (Curzon 1892: 1.25), and James Baillie Fraser, writer of four travel books as well as novels with Persian backdrops. Notable future Victorian diplomats and politicians who travelled in Persia as young men were Edward Eastwick, Henry Rawlinson, and Austen Henry Layard. For the last two, the draw of the ancient civilizations of Persia and Mesopotamia claimed genuine precedence over strategic reconnoitring. However, Layard's 1840 journey, narrated in *Early Adventures in Persia, Susiana and Babylon* (not published until 1887), nonetheless describes his intrigues on behalf of the Bakhtiaris, at the time in conflict with the Persian government and later to become protégés of the British.

Writing in 1895, George Nathaniel Curzon, who himself travelled to Persia as a young aspiring politician in the late 1880s, could still refer to the work of Malcolm and Morier as true to 'the salient and unchanging characteristics of a singularly unchanging Oriental people' (Curzon 1895: 128). Morier's fiction helped generate increasingly familiar and therefore oft-repeated stereotypes of Orientalism such as the devious and cowardly 'Persian character.' Such tropes were incorporated into the travel literature on Persia but were not exhaustive. Accounts of political and social movements and events in the country were inscribed into the corpus according to other preconceptions of the age. The Babi movement, for example, a manifestation of social unrest couched in religious messianism, which threatened the foundations of the Qajar state between 1848 and 1852, was encoded by an observer like Lady Sheil in *Glimpses of Life and Manners in Persia* (1856) according to home anxieties and preconceptions about communism and revolution in Europe. The Jewish–Hungarian Orientalist Arminius Vambery, who arrived in Persia en route to Central Asia in 1862, claimed he went to the East in order to establish which linguistic branch Hungarian belonged to. An ardent Turkophile, his *Travels and Adventures in Central Asia* (1864) won him international fame. Martin Kramer comments that though he was not free from prejudice, 'and often wrote sardonically about the customs and beliefs he encountered in the East', Vambery 'had a fundamental sympathy for the Muslim peoples' perhaps because of his own oppressed, Jewish origins (Kramer 1999: 9). Another sympathetic pen belonged to French diplomat Comte de Gobineau who was instrumental in bringing Babism to the attention of Europe and celebrated Persians and their history partly because of his racial theories, which grew out of his own alienation from modern Europe, as well as his contempt for British and Russian imperialism in the East.

JAMES JUSTINIAN MORIER (1780–1849)

Morier was the second son of a Swiss father who had become a naturalized British subject and moved to Smyrna (Izmir) where he worked for the Levant Company, later rising to become British consul-general in Istanbul. James was born in Smyrna but educated at Harrow entering the diplomatic service as secretary to Harford Jones' mission to Persia in 1808. After a preliminary treaty had been agreed Morier accompanied the Persian ambassador Mirza Abul Hasan to London where he acted as his guide through London society. Morier returned to Persia in 1811 in the role of secretary to the new British ambassador Sir Gore Ouseley, who Morier replaced briefly in 1814 before the embassy was closed. After a short mission to Mexico in 1815 Morier gave up diplomacy and concentrated on writing. He wrote up the Harford Jones' mission in *A Journey through Persia, Armenia and Asia Minor* (1812), published a sequel book of travel in Persia in 1818, and brought out his hugely successful picaresque novel, *The Adventures of Hajji Baba of Ispahan* in 1824. This too required a sequel: *The Adventures of Hajji Baba of Ispahan in England* (1824), a satire in the tradition of Montesquieu's *Persian Letters*. Further novels with oriental settings followed. Morier put his Persian experiences into both his travel works and his fiction, but Hasan Javardi is probably right that 'without noticing, [the] reader [of *Hajji Baba*] learns more about the Persians than he would from a travel book', although he also contends that Morier's 'obsession with the vices of the Orient produces a decidedly unbalanced portrayal of the Persian character' (Javardi 2005: 124, 129).

From:

A Journey through Persia, Armenia and Asia Minor (1812)

The extract describes the hospitality and entertainments staged in Shiraz for Harford Jones' mission. Extravagance is played up – 'such a fête costs a very considerable sum' – in order perhaps to inflate the self-esteem of both parties. But the speed with which the English throw off the *kalat* or ceremonial Persian dress at the end could be read as metonymic of their future imperial arrogance and callousness toward their hosts.

Shiraz

4th. At about one hour before sunset, we repaired to the house of the Minister, to partake of an entertainment which was given to the Envoy. We had scarcely dismounted from our horses at the Minister's gate, when the crowd, anxious to obtain admission, rushed forward, and long impeded the passage of the suite; until our *Mehmandar* himself commanded respect by administering a volley of blows with a stick on the heads of the surrounding multitude. As soon as the Envoy entered the court, (which appeared from the numbers already pressed into it, to be the scene of the amusement), the Persian music struck up, and a rope dancer, whose rope stood conspicuous in the centre, begun to vault into the air.

ABDULLAH KHAN, the Minister's Son, conducted us into the presence of his father, where we soon ranged ourselves among a numerous company of the Nobles of the place, who were invited to meet us. ABDULLAH KHAN, who is a man of about thirty, and a person of much consequence at *Shiraz*, never once seated himself in the apartment where his father sat, but, according to the Eastern customs of filial reverence, stood at the door like a menial servant, or went about superintending the entertainments of the day. As soon as we were settled, the amusements commenced; and at the same moment the rope-dancer vaulted, the dancing boys danced, the water-spouter spouted, the fire-eater devoured fire, the singers sung, the musicians played on their *kamounchas*, and the drummers beat lustily on their drums. This singular combination of noises, objects and attitudes, added to the cries and murmurs of the crowd around, amused, yet almost distracted us.

The rope-dancer performed some feats, which really did credit to his profession. He first walked over his rope with his balancing pole, then vaulted on high; he ascended the rope to a tree in an angle of forty- five degrees? but, as he was reaching the very extremity of the upper range of the angle, he could proceed no further, and remained in an uncertain position for the space of two minutes. He afterwards tied his hands to a rope-ladder of three large steps; and, first balancing his body by the middle on the main line let fall the ladder and himself, and was only brought up by the strength of his wrists thus fastened to their support. He next put on a pair of high-heeled shoes, and paraded about again; then put his feet into two saucepans, and walked backwards and forwards. After this he suspended himself by his feet from the rope; and, taking a gun, deliberately loaded and primed it, and, in that pendant position, took an aim at an egg (placed on the ground beneath him) and put his ball through it. After this he carried on his back a child, whom he contrived to suspend, with his own body besides, from the rope, and thence placed in safety on the ground. His feats were numerous (and as he was mounted on a rope much more elevated than those on which such exploits are displayed in England), they were also proportionably dangerous. A trip would have been his inevitable destruction. He was dressed in a fantastical jacket, and wore a pair of breeches of crimson satin, something like those of Europeans. The boys danced, or rather paced the ground, snapping their fingers to keep time with the music, jingling their small brass castanets, and uttering extraordinary cries. To us all this was tiresome, but to the Persians it appeared very clever. One of the boys having exerted himself in various difficult leaps, at last took two *kunjurs* or daggers, one in each hand; and with these, springing forwards, and placing their points in the ground, turned himself head over heels between them; and again, in a second display, turned himself over with a drawn sword in his mouth.

A negro appeared on the side of a basin of water (in which three fountains were already playing), and, by a singular faculty which he possessed of secreting liquids, managed to make himself a sort of fourth fountain, by spouting water from his mouth. We closely observed him: he drank two basins and a quarter of water, each holding about four quarts, and he was five minutes spouting them out. Next came an eater of fire: this man brought a large dish full of charcoal, which he placed deliberately before him, and then, taking up the pieces, conveyed them bit by bit successively into his mouth, and threw them out again when the fire was extinguished. He then took a piece, from which he continued to blow the most brilliant sparks for more than half an hour. The trick consists in putting in the mouth some cotton dipped in the oil of Naptha, on which the pieces of charcoal are laid and from which they derive the strength of their fire: now the flame of this combustible is known to be little calid. Another man put into his mouth two balls alternately, which burnt with a brilliant flame, and which also were soaked in the same fluid.

The music was of the roughest kind. The performers were seated in a row round the basin of water; the band consisted of two men who played the *kamouncha*, a species of violin; four, who beat the tamborin; one, who thrummed the guitar; one, who played on the spoons; and two who sung. The loudest in the concert were the songsters, who, when they applied the whole force of their lungs, drowned every other instrument. The man with the spoons seemed to me the most ingenious and least discordant of the whole band. He placed two wooden spoons in a neat and peculiar manner betwixt the fingers of his left hand, whilst he beat them with another spoon in his right.

All this continued till the twilight had fairly expired; when there commenced a display of fire-works on a larger scale than any that I recollect to have seen in Europe. In the first place, the director of the works caused to be thrown into the fountain before us a variety of fires, which were fixed on square flat boards, and which bursting into the most splendid streams and stars of flame, seemed to put the water in one entire blaze. He then threw up some beautiful blue lights, and finished the whole by discharging immense vollies of rockets which had been fixed in stands, each of twenty rockets, in different parts of the garden and particularly on the summits of the walls. Each stand exploded at once; and at one time the greater part of all the rockets were in the air at the same moment, and produced an effect grand beyond the powers of description.

At the end of this exhibition, a band of choice musicians and songsters was introduced into the particular apartment where we were seated. A player on the *komouncha* really drew forth notes, which might have done credit to the better instruments of the West: and the elastic manner with which he passed his bow across the strings, convinced me that he himself would have been an accomplished performer even among those of Europe, if his ear had been tutored to the harmonies and delicacies of our science. The notes of their guitar corresponded exactly to those of our instrument. Another sung some of the odes of HAFIZ, accompanied by the *kamouncha*, and in a chorus by the tamborins.

After this concert, some parts of which were extremely noisy and some not unpleasant even to our ears, appeared from behind a curtain a dirty-looking negro, dressed as a *fakeer* or beggar, with an artificial hump, and with his face painted white. This character related facetious stories, threw himself into droll attitudes, and sung humorous songs. Amongst other things he was a mimic; and, when he undertook to ridicule the inhabitants of *Ispahan* he put our *Shiraz* audience into ecstacies of delight and laughter. He imitated the drawling manner of speaking, and the sort of nonchalance so characteristic of the *Ispahaunees*. The people of *Shiraz*, (who regard themselves as the prime of Persians, and their language as the most pure, and their pronunciation as the most correct), are never so well amused as when the people and the dialect of *Ispahan* are ridiculed. Those of *Ispahan*, on the other hand, boast, and with much reason, of their superior cleverness and learning, though with these advantages indeed they are said to mix roguery and low cunning. The exhibition finished by the singing of a boy, the most renowned of the vocal performers at *Shiraz*, and one of the Prince's own band. His powers were great, descending from the very highest to the very lowest notes; and the tremulations of his voice, in which the great acme of his art appeared to consist, were continued so long and so violently, that his face was convulsed with pain and exertion. In order to aid the modulations, he kept a piece of paper in his hand, with which he did not cease to fan his mouth. When the concert was over, we collected our legs under us (which till this time we had kept extended at ease) to make room for the *sofras* or table-cloths, which were now spread before us. On these were first placed trays of sweet viands, light sugared cakes, and sherbet of various descriptions. After these, dishes of plain rice were put, each before two guests; then *pillaus*, and after them a succession and variety, which would have sufficed ten companies of our number. On a very moderate calculation there were two hundred dishes, exclusive of the sherbets. All these were served up in bowls and dishes of fine china; and in the bowls of sherbet were placed the long spoons made of pear-tree, (which I mentioned on a former occasion), and each of which contained about the measure of six common table-spoons, and with these every guest helped himself. The Persians bent themselves down to the dishes, and ate in general most heartily and indiscriminately of every thing sweet and sour, meat and fish, fruit and vegetable. They are very fond of ice, which they eat constantly, and in great quantities, a taste which becomes almost necessary to qualify the sweetmeats which they devour so profusely. The Minister NASR OALLAH KHAN had a bowl of common ice constantly before him, which he kept eating when the other dishes were carried away. They are equally fond of spices, and of every other stimulant; and highly recommended one of their sherbets, a composisition of sugar, cinnamon, and other strong ingredients. As the Envoy sat next to the Minister, and I next to the Envoy, we very frequently shared the marks of his peculiar attention and politeness, which consisted in large handfuls of certain favourite dishes. These he tore off by main strength, and put before us; sometimes a full grasp of lamb mixed with a sauce of prunes, pistachio-nuts, and raisins; at another time, a whole partridge disguised by a rich brown sauce; and then, with the same hand, he scooped out a bit of melon, which he gave into our palms, or a great piece of omelette thickly swimming in fat ingredients. The dishes lie promiscuously before the guests, who all eat without any particular notice of one another. The silence, indeed, with which the whole is transacted is one of the most agreeable circumstances of a Persian feast. There is no rattle of plates and knives and forks, no confusion of lacquies, no drinking of healths, no disturbance of carving, scarcely a word is spoken, and all are intent on the business before them. Their feasts are soon over; and, although it appears difficult to collect such an immense number of dishes, and to take them away again without much confusion and much time, yet all is so well regulated that every thing disappears as if by magic. The lacquies bring the dishes in long trays called *conchas*, which are discharged in order, and which are again taken up and carried away with equal facility. When the whole is cleared, and the cloths rolled up, ewers and basins are brought in, and every one washes his hand and mouth. Until the water is presented it is ridiculous enough to see the right hand of every person (which is covered with the complicated fragments of all the dishes) placed in a certain position over his left arm: there is a fashion even in this. The whole entertainment was now over, and we took our leaves and returned home. Such a fête costs a very considerable sum. Besides ourselves, all the Envoy's numerous servants, and all the privates of his body guard were invited to it, and eat and drank in different apartments. The same dinner which had been put before us was afterwards carried to them, and I understand that, even in the common domestic life of a Persian, the profusion which is exhibited on his table surprises the European stranger; and is explained only by the necessity of feeding his numerous household, to whom all his dishes are passed, after he has satisfied his own appetite.

5th. As we were at dinner on the following day, one of the Prince's own *feroshes* brought a dish composed of eggs, &c. made up into a species of omelette, with two small bowls of sherbet, and a plate of powdered spices, which he announced as a present from the Prince himself. These sort of attentions are frequent between friends in Persia, and, at the moment of dinner, it seems that the Prince, who is particularly fond of the dish, was anxious that the Envoy also should partake of it; though at the time of receiving it, the Envoy suspected, that it might have been the trick of some one who calculated on a more valuable largess in return.

6th. A *zeeafet* or entertainment was given this evening to the Envoy by MIRZA ZAIN LABADEEN, Chief Secretary and Private Minister to the Prince. This was so nearly a repetition of the former display, that any description may well be spared. One thing indeed may be remarked; as soon as the Prime Minister came into the room, he took the direction of the feast upon himself; and the master of the house, the real donor, sunk into the character of a guest. This is the case wherever the Minister goes, as he is supposed to be the master of every thing, and to preside in every place, next after the Prince his own immediate superior.

On the 7th, JAFFER ALI KHAN, (the English Agent at *Shiraz)* Mr. BRUCE and I, went by the Envoy's order to the Minister, to propose certain measures. We were introduced into the *Bagh-a-Vakeel,* a garden belonging to the Prince, and situated contiguous to his palace in the town. In the centre is a pleasure house called *Koola-frangee,* (and built on the model of the one of the same name in the *Bagh-a-Jehan Nemah,* on the outside of the city gates.) Here we conferred with the Minister, and as, in quitting him, we were going out of the garden, we chanced to meet the Prince himself, who asked us the common questions of civility, and passed on. In the evening, the Prince invited the Envoy to meet him on horseback at the *Maidan,* and expressed a wish to see the troop of cavalry go through some of its exercises and evolutions. We accordingly proceeded, and, when we perceived the Prince, we all dismounted from our horses for a moment, and when be waved his hand, we all mounted again, and rode close up to him. His manners and appearance were most elegant and prepossessing. He was dressed most richly: his outer coat was of blue velvet, which fitted tight to his shape; on the shoulders, front pocket, and skirts, was an embroidery of pearl, occasionally (in the different terminations of a point or angle,) enlivened with a ruby, an emerald, or a topaz. Under this was a waistcoat of pearl; and here and there, hanging in a sort of studied negligence, were strings of fine pearl. A dagger, at the head of which blazed a large diamond, was in his girdle. The bridle of his horse was inlaid in every part of the head with precious stones; and a large silver tassel hung under the jaws. The Prince was altogether a very interesting figure.

Cornet WILLOCK paraded his troop much to the Prince's satisfaction, and in the interval his own men ran their horses up and down the course, firing their muskets in various dextrous ways. Unfortunately one of his cavaliers met with a very dangerous fall.

ISMAEL BEG, the young Georgian favourite, also shewed off his horse. He carried the Prince's bow and arrows, which were placed on each side of him, in quivers covered with black velvet and thickly studded with pearls and precious stones. After this, the Prince ordered his Russian prisoners, thirty in number, to draw up and go through their exercise. These poor fellows, commanded by their officer (who goes by the name of *Rooss Khan*, or Russian Khan), went through every thing that they could do, and even formed a hollow square. To all this the Persians give the name of *bazee* or play. NASR OALLAH KHAN, the Minister, kept at a respectful distance, whilst the rest of the nobles and chief men were stationed in a crowd much further off. The Prince remained an isolated and unsocial being, never speaking but to command, never spoken to but to feel the servitude of others.

It is always the custom for the King and Princes to order their visitors away, which they do, either by a nod of the head or a wave of the hand. We received this kind of licence to depart, and returned to town in the order in which we came out.

8th. The last and most splendid entertainment was given this evening to the Envoy by our *Mehmandar,* MAHOMED ZEKY KHAN. His own house was not large enough to contain us and our numerous attendants; he received therefore the Prince's permission to give it in that of AGA BESHEER, the Queen's head Eunuch. The apartment, into which we were introduced, was still more elegant than any which we had yet seen, and if it could have been transported to England, would probably have excited universal admiration, and a new taste in the interior decoration of rooms. Like almost all the public rooms or *dewan khonéh* of a Persian house, it was in shape a parallelogram, with a recess formed by a Saracenic arch, in the centre of the superior line of the figure. The ground of the wall was of a beautiful varnished white, and richly painted in gold in ornaments of the most neat and ingenious composition. The entablature, if it may be so called, was inlaid glass placed in angular and prismatic positions, which reflected a variety of beautiful lights and colours. The ceiling was all of the same composition. In the arched recess was a chimney piece formed in front by alternate layers of glass and painting. The whole side fronting the arch was composed of windows, the frames of which opened from the ground; and, though of clumsy workmanship compared with frames in England, yet aided by the richness of the painted glass intermixed with the gilding of the wood-work, they filled up the space splendidly and symmetrically.

This fête corresponded in all it parts with the others that I have described; except that there was a greater variety of entertainments. Besides the rope-dancer, water-spouter, dancing boys, and fire-eater, we had an exhibition of wrestlers, a combat of rams, and a sanguinary scene of a lion killing an ox. The wrestling was opened by two dwarfs, about three feet and a half in height: one with a beard descending to his girdle, with deformed arms and hands, but with strong and muscular legs. The other, with bad legs, but with regular and well shaped arms. Both had the appearance of those animals represented in mythological pictures as satyrs, or perhaps of the *Asmodeus* of LE SAGE. The figure with the beard was the victor, and fairly tossed his antagonist into an adjoining basin of water. The professional wrestlers succeeded; the hero of whom threw and discomfited eight others, in most rapid succession. In this the combat of rams resembled that of the wrestlers: one bold and superb ram, belonging to the Prince, remained the undisputed master of the field, for although a great number of his kind were brought to meet him, none dared to face him after the first butt.

The scene of blood next begun. A poor solitary half-grown ox was then produced, and had not long awaited his fate, when a young lion was conducted before us by a man, who led him with a rope by the neck. For some time he seated himself by the wall regardless of the feast before him. At length, urged by the cries of his keepers, and by the sight of the ox, which was taken close to him, he made a spring and seized his victim on the back. The poor brute made some efforts to get loose, but the lion kept fast hold, until he was dragged away by his keepers. Both were again brought before us, when the ox fell under a second attack of the lion. An order was at length given to cut the throat of the ox, when the lion finished his repast by drinking heartily of his blood. A very small cub of a lion, not larger than a water-spaniel was carried out, and the vigour with which he attacked the ox, was quite amusing. He fed upon him, after he was dead, with a relish which showed how truly carniverous were his young propensities. This bloody scene was pleasing to the Persian spectators in general, although I thought that I perceived some who sympathized with us for the helplessness of the ox.

In the course of the morning the Prince's present to the Mission was brought by ISMAEL BEG. It consisted of a sword and two horses to the Envoy, and to each of the gentlemen *kalaats*, or dresses of gold brocade, a sash, and a shawl. Our appearance, when we wore our new dresses, which had not been made on purpose for us, was probably very ridiculous. We put the rich brocade Persian vest over our English clothes, having only taken off our coats: then wound the brocade sash round our waists, and lastly, put our shawls either over our shoulders, or fastened them into our cocked hats. This, with our red cloth stockings and green high-heeled shoes, completed the adjustment, in which we appeared before the Prince. The morning of the 9th had been fixed for our parting visit; dressed in these gifts with which he had honoured us, we were introduced to the Prince in a room called the private audience, in the *Bagh-a-Vakeel*. On walking through the garden we met one of his brothers, a little fellow about six years old, and who could just totter under the weight of the brocades, furs, and shawls with which he was hugely encumbered. Several Khans and men of consequence were standing before him, in the same attitudes of respect and humility, as they did before his elder brother, and attending to all his little orders and whims, with as much obsequiousness, as they would have shewn to a full-grown sovereign. It was singular that no notice was taken of an inadvertence which we committed: the dresses which we had received were honours to which a Persian looks forward through his whole life; but as they happened to be extremely inconvenient to us, we threw them off as soon as we left the Prince's presence. An Englishman just invested with an Order, would hardly so throw off the ribband at the gate of St. James's. In strictness, the *kalaat* of Persia should be worn three days, as we afterwards learnt, when again we had received a similar distinction at *Teheran*, and treated it with similar disrespect.

Before we left *Shiraz*, the merchants were all displeased with the Envoy, for they had been accustomed in former missions to sell immense quantities of their goods at exorbitant prices; while now all their offers were refused, as most of the presents which were given by Sir HARFORD in our progress, were made in coin. The amount of those presents indeed was not always satisfactory to the receivers.

JOHN MALCOLM (1769–1833)

Son of a small Eskdale farmer, Malcolm went to India as a boy soldier for the East India Company and his career took off there under the patronage of Lord Wellesley. A second career as a diplomat began when aged 30 he was sent as the Company's envoy to Persia in 1799. A speaker of Persian and admirer of Persian poetry with experience of the etiquette of the Persianized courts of the Indian Nawabs, Malcolm seemed well qualified to lead a diplomatic mission to Persia, and should his superiors have chosen to employ force he could equally have put to use his military skills. Although he negotiated a treaty with Persia in 1801 this was never ratified, and after the French gained a foothold in Persia in 1807, Malcolm sailed to Bushire with a military force to threaten dire consequences if the Shah did not expel them. The option was still open to seize Kharg Island in the Gulf; however Harford Jones pursued the diplomatic route, arriving in Tehran in 1809 to successfully negotiate a new treaty. Malcolm's mission to replace Jones and restore the preeminence of the Indian Government in Persian affairs was unfruitful. Knighted in 1815, he spent the last three years of his career as Governor of Bombay, retiring in 1830. Given his limited early education and soldier's background, Malcolm's achievement as a writer is all the more remarkable. The *History of Persia* (1815) filled a gaping hole in British knowledge about that country. In contrast, *Sketches of Persia*, published anonymously in 1827 and intended as a riposte to *Hajji Baba*, displays literary invention, wit and anecdotal detail to compare with Morier.

From:

Sketches of Persia (1828)

Written up from his journals, the extract re-captures Malcolm's first audience with Fath Ali Shah in 1800. The meeting set a standard for the struggles with the Persian court and its representatives over protocol encountered by subsequent envoys. (Traveling on his own even in 1821, James Baillie Fraser felt the need to take a stand on protocol). Adopting a separate narrative persona to the envoy or 'Elchee', Malcolm reports his own witty repartee with the Persian monarch. By holding back on 'the whole truth' of the English traveller Jonas Hanaway's earlier humiliation at the Persian court of Isfahan, Malcolm shows the altered power relations represented by his mission.

The Court of Fath Ali Shah

A canal flowed in the centre of a garden which supplied a number of fountains; to the right and left of which were broad paved walks and beyond these were rows of trees. Between the trees and the high wall encircling the palace files of matchlock-men were drawn up; and within the avenues, from the gate to the hall of audience, all the princes, nobles, courtiers, and officers of state, were marshalled in separate lines, according to their rank, from the lowest officer of the king's guard, who occupied the place nearest the entrance, to the heir apparent, Abbas Meerzâ, who stood on the right of his brothers, and within a few paces of the throne.

There was not one person in all this array who had not a gold-hilted sword, a Cashmire shawl round his cap, and another round his waist. Many of the princes and nobles were magnificently dressed, but all was forgotten as soon as the eye rested upon the king.

He appeared to be above the middle size, his age, little more than thirty, his complexion rather fair; his features were regular and fine, with an expression denoting quickness and intelligence. His beard attracted much of our attention; it was full, black, and glossy, and flowed to his middle. His dress baffled all description. The ground of his robes was white; but he was so covered with jewels of an extraordinary size, and their splendour, from his being seated where the rays of the sun played upon them, was so dazzling, that it was impossible to distinguish the minute parts which combined to give such amazing brilliancy to his whole figure.

The two chief officers of ceremonies, who carried golden sticks, stopped twice, as they advanced towards the throne, to make a low obeisance, and the Elchee at the same time took off his hat. When near the entrance of the hall the procession stopped, and the lord of requests said, "Captain John Malcolm is come, as envoy from the governor-general of India to your majesty." The king, looking to the Elchee, said, in a pleasing and manly voice, "You are welcome[*]."

---

[*] Khoosh Amedee.

We then ascended the steps of the hall, and were seated, as had been previously arranged. The letter from the governor-general, which had been carried in the procession on a golden tray, was opened and read. His majesty inquired after the health of the king of England and of the ruler of India. He desired particularly to know how the Elchee had been treated in his dominions, and whether he liked what he had seen of Persia?

To all these questions appropriate answers were returned; and we left his majesty, after being seated about twenty minutes, very much gratified by our reception, and with an assurance from our Mehmandar*, which was afterwards confirmed by the prime minister, that the king of kings was highly pleased with the mission, the state and splendour of which he could not but feel added to his reputation, and gave him fame and popularity with his own subjects.

Several days passed before our second visit to court, when the Elchee carried the presents from the governor-general, some of which were very valuable, particularly the pier-glasses, which have been already mentioned. A change was made in this second visit; we were not stopped as before at the room, where we were met by Sûlimân Khan Kajir, that chief having failed in showing the Elchee proper respect, by not rising when he went in or out of the apartment; and to prevent further disputes, the ceremony of stopping, in our progress towards the throne, was altogether dispensed with. The court was still more fully attended than before, and the king, if possible, more magnificently dressed.

After we had been seated a short time, the presents were announced. I was a little anxious when one of the ministers began to read the list. There had been a great desire to give them a name which denoted inferiority of rank on the part of the person from whom they were sent; but the Elchee would not allow of any such term being used, and he told the prime minister, that if any attempt of the kind were made, he would, notwithstanding the strict etiquette of the Persian court, instantly address the king, and tell him, that the presents he brought were neither tribute nor offerings, as his secretary had from inadvertence called them, but rarities and curiosities sent from the British ruler of India, in token of his regard and friendship for the king of Persia. This communication had the desired effect; our presents were termed rarities, and the high rank of the governor general, as a person intrusted with sovereign functions, was on this occasion upheld.

This visit was at its commencement very formal, but the king, evidently desirous to give it another character, said to the Elchee, "I have heard a report which I cannot believe, that your king has only one wife." "No Christian

---

* Fatteh Ali Khan Noovee.

prince can have more," said the Elchee. "O, I know that! but he may have a little lady*." "Our gracious king, George the Third," replied the Envoy, "is an example to his subjects of attention to morality and religion in this respect, as in every other." "This may all be very proper," concluded his majesty of Persia, laughing, "but I certainly should not like to be king of such a country."

A curious incident occurred as we left the palace. The king's giant, a man above eight feet high, and stout in proportion, was placed against one of the walls of the gate through which we were to retire, and he had in his hand a club of enormous dimensions. It was expected that the Elchee, on seeing him, would start with astonishment if not alarm; but he passed without taking any notice of this redoubtable personage, except by a slight glance. The fact was, as he afterwards confessed, it never entered into his imagination that it was a human being. Paintings of Roostem and his club (which the giant was dressed to imitate) are very common in Persia, and in the hurry of passing he took this to be one. He was first made sensible of his mistake by the praises of his Mehmandar. "Admirable!" said the latter to him: "nothing could be better: the fools wished to try to startle you with giants and clubs stuck up against a wall. They are rightly served; your eye hardly rested on him for a moment, evidently not thinking him worthy of your notice. I shall tell them" (he added, with a feeling that showed he considered his honour was associated with that of the person of whom he had charge) "that such men are quite common in your country, and that this giant would hardly be tall enough for one of the guards of the king of England."

Before we left Teheran the Envoy had several interviews with the king, at all of which his majesty was gracious; and at some which were private he spoke a great deal, and was very inquisitive into the habits and usages of England, and the character of its government.

Speaking of the empire of India, he asked, if it were true that ten ships were sent every year from that country to England loaded with gold and silver? The Elchee said it was very rare any bullion was sent from our territories in the East to England; that whatever went was, in merchandize. "What a lie," said his majesty "the Envoy† who preceded you told me; but," (seeing the Elchee annoyed), "do not vex yourself, it is not your shame but ours; your predecessor was a Persian, and we all exaggerate—you speak truth. But why did you send a Persian to my court? I suppose," continuing to answer himself, "it was to find out what kind of a being I was, and whether my country was settled, before you deputed one of your own nation."

---

* "Amma Keneezekee," the expression used by his majesty, means literally—But a little lady.
† Mehdee Ali Khan, a Persian, gentleman, who had been deputed the year before to Persia by Mr. Duncan, Governor of Bombay.

"Are the French," he asked, "a powerful people?" "Certainly," replied the Envoy; "they would not otherwise deserve to be mentioned as the enemies of the English." "There again," said the king, turning to his ministers, "you know we were told that the French were a weak and contemptible nation, which was incredible: the Elchee, by telling the truth, has done them justice, and raised his own country at the same time."

After a number of questions on the mines of South America, and the arts and manufactures of Europe, the king said, "All this is astonishing! Persia has nothing but steel." "Steel well managed," said the Elchee, "has, from the beginning of the world to the present day, commanded all other riches." "Very true," said the king, quite pleased with this compliment; "that is a very just observation, therefore we must not complain, but continue to be contented, as our ancestors have been, with our swords and our lances."

The king had learned that the Elchee, in his conversation with the minister, had displayed considerable acquaintance with the past history of his family at Asterabad, and his curiosity being excited, he sent to desire his attendance. We were received in a private apartment in which there were only a few courtiers, but there were several Kajir chiefs, and four or five elders* of that tribe.

The interrogation began; and as the Elchee derived his knowledge from that minute and truth-telling traveller, Jonas Hanway, his answers quite surprised all present; and when he informed them, not only of the events: which happened fifty-six[†] years before, but gave them accounts of the personal appearance, the dispositions, the connexions, and the characters of the different chiefs, the astonishment of the elders was expressed by the frequent repetition of "Yâ Ali," an ejaculation that, in the mouth of a Persian, attends all sudden emotions of wonder. The king was more than pleased, he was delighted; he evidently believed, from the Elchee's knowledge of the history of his family, that their fame had reached Europe, and that it was as well known to the nations of that quarter of the globe as to the Tûrkûmâns of Goorgân, or the natives of Mazenderan.

The Elchee on this occasion told the truth, but not the whole truth. The character of the court in which he was giving evidence did not perhaps require the latter, and it might have lessened the pleasure imparted, to have spoken of the plundered bales of cloth, and the dread of being made over to the Tûrkûmâns, which had so fixed the recollection of his majesty's family in the mind of poor Jonas Hanway. As it was, the king was delighted, and

---

* "Reesh-e-Seffeed," literally gray-beard, is the Persian term for an elder.
[†] Jonas Hanway was at Astrabad in 1744, during the rebellion of the ancestor of the present king.

conversed familiarly on various subjects. Amongst others, he inquired very particularly into the frame of the English government.

The Elchee explained it to him as well as he could. When he spoke of the liberty of the subject, his majesty was puzzled to understand what it meant; but on being told it implied, that no man was so high in England as to be able to do any thing contrary to the law of the land; and no man so low, but that he might do every thing not contrary to that law, he appeared to comprehend this, as well as the other points which had been explained to him.

"I understand all you have said," he observed; and after some reflection, he added – "Your king is, I see, only the first magistrate* of the country." "Your majesty," said the Elchee, "has exactly defined his situation" "Such a condition of power," said he, smiling, "has permanence, but it has no enjoyment: mine is enjoyment. There you see Sûlimân Khan Kajir, and several other of the first chiefs of the kingdom—I can cut all their heads off: can I not?" said he, addressing them. "Assuredly, 'Point of adoration of the world†,' if it is your pleasure."

"That is real power," said the king; "but then it has no permanence. When I am gone my Sons will fight for the crown, and all will be confusion: there is, however, one consolation, Persia will be governed by a soldier."

The king, at this visit, appeared in great good humour with the Elchee, and gratified the latter by showing him his richest jewels, amongst which was the "sea of light‡," which is deemed one of the purest and most valuable diamonds in the world. Many of the others were surprisingly splendid.

On the evening after this visit, my excellent friend, whom I have before mentioned as preferring a shot at a duck to a view of the ruins of Persepolis, said he would like to be king of Persia. Knowing that inordinate ambition had no place in his mind, I asked him what he would do if he attained that station: "Run away with my crown," was the prompt answer. We had a hearty laugh at the genuine simplicity of this expression.

---

* "Ket-khûdâ-e-avvel."

† "Kibla-e-Alem" is the universal term his subjects apply when speaking to the king of Persia. Kibla is the point to which Mahomedans turn when they pray: Alem signifies the world.

‡ The Deriâ-e-Noor, or sea of light, weighs 186 carats, and is considered to be the diamond of the finest lustre in the world. The Tâj-e-Mâh, or "crown of the moon," is also a splendid diamond; it weighs 146 carats. These two are the principal in a pair of bracelets, valued at near a million sterling. Those in the crown are also of extraordinary size and value.

JAMES BALLIE FRASER (1783–1856)

Born into a wealthy Edinburgh family, Fraser travelled in the East for both business and pleasure. Connected with India through his brother who was an employee of the East India Company, in 1821 he visited Persia on the way home to England. Arriving in Isfahan he proceeded to Meshed with the intention of continuing to Bukhara, but was prevented from doing so by the political situation in Central Asia. Instead he journeyed along the Caspian shores, thence from Tabriz to Baghdad via Kurdistan. These journeys provided material for two books of travel: *Narrative of a Journey into Khorasan in the Years 1821 and 1822* (1825) and *Travels and Adventures in the Persian Provinces on the Southern Banks of the Caspian Sea* (1826). Fraser returned to Persia a decade later to gather political intelligence, publishing *A Winter's Journey from Constantinople to Tehran* in 1838, and *Travels in Kurdistan, Mesopotamia etc* in 1840. George. N. Curzon praised Fraser for his 'admirable books of travel' that displayed 'broad acquaintance with and faithful portraiture of every aspect of modern Persian life' (1892: 1. 22, 24). However, in pointing out the critical view he took of the Qajars, especially the Princes he met on his journeys through the Caspian region, Denis Wright counts Fraser an early exponent of the 'jaundiced view of the Persians [which] helped to sow seeds of resentment and misunderstanding between the two countries' (1977: 154).

From:

Travels in the Persian Provinces of the Caspian (1826)

This chapter goes some way to placing Wright's remarks in context. It summarizes the outcome of the chief adventure recounted in Fraser's book: his detention in Gilan following a 'garbled account of my adventures' had reached the Shah in Tehran. Correctly reporting Fraser's 'rather scurvy' reception by the government of Resht, the story had fatefully identified him as a Russian envoy, causing embarrassment to those involved. Orders were therefore sent for him to be detained in Resht until the Prince-Governor and son of the Shah returned to look into the matter. Desperate to continue his journey to Tabriz, Fraser tried to escape only to be captured and roughly dealt with. Not surprisingly, the incident left its imprint on his view of Persians. As he states: 'There is something uncandid and mysterious about these people, which makes it painful to have any dealings with them; their actions are inconsistent with their profession; their explanations dubious and unsatisfactory.' Though recompensed for the indignities perpetrated against him, Fraser's low opinion of his hosts is confirmed when his 'friend', the English educated Mirza Reza, cadges part of his compensation money from him.

Resht

June 25th. I went about six this morning to wait on Meerza Tuckee, and though he was at prayers when I arrived, I was immediately shown up stairs into his private room, where he bid me take a seat until he should be finished. His prayers took up some little time, during which, he at intervals addressed a kind observation to me; his manner was greatly changed, it was now all graciousness. He prefaced the audience, by observing to me that M. Willock was a particular friend of his, and that as I was that gentleman's friend also, I must fully confide in him, and tell him every thing that had taken place. Thus encouraged, I related to him what had happened to me, from first to last, during which, he asked me many questions, made me repeat several circumstances over again, and was, or appeared to be, much shocked and surprized. I then showed him all my papers, which he carefully perused.

When he had fully satisfied himself, he told me he would lose no time in letting the prince know what had happened, and pledged himself that all should be made right: he desired me to make out a written list of the things taken from me by Mahomed Khan Massaul; said that he would himself see my horses, and if any of them had been wounded, or rendered unfit to pursue the journey, he would see to finding a remedy. I told freely of the shabby treatment and neglect I had suffered from mine host, the hadjee; adding the fact, that I had been forced to purchase all the food required for myself and my servants, during the time of my detention, as well as before it; and that consequently my finances had run so short, I feared I should not have a sufficient sum to carry me to Tabreez. To all this, and several other observations of mine, he remarked, that the country had been in a troubled state; that there had been great discontents and abuses; the master had been absent, and the servants had gone astray; that I must forget and I forgive a great deal of what I had suffered, under the explanation now given; that it had not been inflicted by the prince's wish, but contrary to his desire; and that he now would be disposed to make every thing up to me, and no doubt, would dismiss me with marks of his bounty. I could reply but little to this, further than by thanking the minister for the interest he had taken in my case, and expressing a hope that the prince would consider the long and ruinous detention I had already suffered, and not protract the period of my departure beyond what might be necessary.

One thing I felt it proper to premise to the minister; which was, that if the prince admitted me to an audience, I should be allowed a seat. This, the minister said, was impossible, because his royal highness had made a positive rule against such an indulgence. I replied, that in that case, I should entreat to be excused from waiting upon him; as he must be aware it was a privilege granted to all Englishmen who visit princes of the blood; that I had enjoyed it at Shiraz, at Tehrān, at Khorasān, and Mazunderān; and conceived that I should be betraying, as it were, the honour of my country, as far as an individual could so do, if I admitted in my own person of any unusual slight whatever. The minister, upon this positive adherence to my point, smiled, and said; "Well, well, we shall see what is to be done;" so again thanking him for his friendly conduct, I took my leave.

It may be proper here to enlarge a little more upon the reasons which induced me to insist so strongly upon what many may deem a trifle of no consequence, but which in Persia is really a matter of serious importance. Etiquette among Persians is one of the chief affairs of life, and their great study, particularly when dealing with strangers, is to gain, if they can, a point of this game in their own favour. That this was the case with all the embassies from England, may be seen in any account given of these missions, and it seems absolutely expedient to maintain the national dignity, not only by the means that are esteemed in Europe, but by those which carry weight in Asia. The influence of Britain in India has often been called that of opinion, though there we are armed with real power; how much more important must it be to keep up that species of influence in Persia, if indeed it is expedient to continue our relations with that country at all, where we can have little or no real power. Had I been able to pass under the disguise of a Persian, or had I succeeded in penetrating to remoter countries, where the fear of the British name is less felt, my conduct would have been very different; but in Persia, as a British subject, it appeared imperative on me to claim all the privileges of one, and to repel every thing like affront as a slight on the nation. Like a poor gentleman, in short, I was obliged to be much more punctilious than a richer man could afford to be: such a trifle as this was to be a sort of index, if I may say so, to my whole character, and if relinquished without a struggle, would have left me in worse plight than I really needed to be.

Meerza Reza called upon me this forenoon, and expressed much surprise at my having gone to see the minister before he had fully explained to him my character and situation: it was, he assured me, to the minister's ignorance on this important point, that I owed the cool reception I had met with the evening before; and in a like manner, it was to the information which he (the meerza) had given to the minister on these points, afterwards, that the more cordial and respectful reception of the morning was due. There is something uncandid and mysterious about these people, which makes it painful to have any dealings with them; their actions are inconsistent with their profession; their explanations dubious and unsatisfactory. This remark applies equally to the conduct of the princes and their ministers, as to that of Meerza Reza, in all their transactions with me: the motives for which, as well as the true causes of my detention in Gheelan, still remain to me a perfect mystery.

In reply to a written note of the articles which I sent to the minister according to his desire, he sent me a message to say, that a person had been dispatched to bring Mahomed Khan himself, or the things I had lost, and to desire my attendance at his levee next morning, when I should hear further.

June 26th. I waited on the minister, according to order, but was not again honoured with a private audience. I had to wait with others below for the appearance of the great man. He had no news to communicate; but told me he had sent for my things from Mahomed Khan, and had informed the prince of' my story: he assured me that his royal highness was much displeased at what had occurred, and that when my things arrived from Talish, I should be dismissed with marks of high favour. I ventured to express a hope that the persons who had so wantonly insulted and injured me, should meet with such reprehension as might be deemed proper, and that as every thing which occurred to me should be represented to his Persian majesty, through the English ambassador, I might have to express my satisfaction at the reparation offered to the injured subject of a friendly state. "Leave all that to me," said he, "the business is in my hands, and every thing that is proper shall be done." With this emphatic reply, he moved on the door, and we all made our bows, and separated.

June 28th. I learned this day, that the minister had made arrangements for my reception by the prince, who had given orders that I should receive a khelut, and as he was informed I had spent the greater part of my money in maintaining myself during my detention, he directed a sum of thirty tomauns to be given to me, to serve for my travelling expences to Tabreez. The minister further desired that Meerza Reza and myself should attend his levee the next morning, after which he should carry me to be presented to the prince, and procure my leave.

June 29th. Early in the morning, I went with Meerza Reza to the minister's house; but he was much occupied, and did not make his appearance till a late hour; when he did, he was wonderfully gracious, gave me a seat by his side, told me the prince was desirous to see me this very day, and that he had made such arrangements about my seat as I should be fully satisfied with. He said that as it was difficult to procure carriage from Resht to Tabreez direct, he would recommend my going by the Enzellee road, and had directed Baba Allee Khan (my old Enzellee friend), to send a person who should see me safe to Khal-Khal: he apologised for having deferred my business so long from the press of other matters on his hands; and concluded by hoping I would now forget all the vexation and trouble I had experienced in Gheelan, in consideration of the distracted state of the place, and its master's absence; and not give that master a bad name for what he was innocent of. I replied, by professing my sense of the great obligations I owed to him for the friendly regard and ready assistance he had afforded me, which I assured him I should faithfully report to his friend the English elchee; and I had now no doubt of every thing going on well, as it was in the hands of so good and so just a nobleman.

About noon the meerza and myself were roused by the arrival of an attendant, who came to tell us the prince desired our immediate attendance; we were accordingly introduced by a private door to the interior of the palace; and after more than the ordinary number of bows, were ushered into an apartment, at the upper end of which the prince himself was seated.

It was not without considerable curiosity that I examined the external appearance of a person who had exercised so great influence over my actions for some time past. His figure was comely, though slightly inclined to be fat, and his aspect grave, but far from unpleasing, with a good deal of the fine features of the royal family; he possessed a sweetness of expression, which, had it not been poisoned by an affectation of dignity, which all these princes deem it indispensable to assume, would have been rather prepossessing. He was seated upon a shawl cushion, and leaned his back upon a large silk pillow; his dress was plain, consisting only of an oemah or riding-coat of shawl, with a plain dagger stuck in his sash. He held in his hand a dervish's stick of ivory, perhaps indicative of his disposition towards the principles of that sect, which is said to be particularly strong.

There was here a greater affectation of state than I had observed at the court of any of his brothers; it did not consist in an assemblage of ragged toffunchees, or crowds of servants, but in the ceremony observed in approaching him; the only person present was the vizier, who was dressed in his robes of ceremony, which consisted of a splendid pelisse of green and gold silk, worked with rich embroidery and gold spangles, with rich fur upon the shoulders, and a high turban of shawls wound round his cap. He stood up at the lower end of the room opposite to the prince, waiting his commands. When we were introduced, he suffered us to stand for a time at the bottom of the apartment, but at last ordered me to be seated.

The conversation was much in the usual style; the questions of where I had been, whither going, where I lived, and what I had seen, led to the ten times told tale of my detention and suffering. He observed, it was strange I should have desired to leave the country without seeing him. I answered, that my having thought of doing so, and abandoning the hopes of seeing such a prince, sufficiently proved the urgent necessity under which I was, of hastening to Tabreez; and I took the opportunity to mention how severe a loss I might be subjected to, by the detention I had suffered. To this he replied, that the country had been in a distracted state in consequence of his own absence, and that I must forget what had happened, as it resulted entirely from this unsettled state of things. He made a good many enquiries respecting the state of Khorasān, of Reza Koolee Khan, and Nujjuff Allee Khan; my answers to which, as they coincided with his own opinions, appeared to please him. At length, after assuring me that he had given directions for expediting me on my way, and satisfying me in all respects, he gave us leave, and I left the presence.

I took an opportunity, on leaving the prince, to go and pay the compliments of leave-taking to the prince's uncle, who had always treated me with politeness; and who now congratulated me heartily on my honourable release, and wished me a safe and speedy journey.

June 30th. This morning I determined to send off my people and baggage, at least, and got every thing packed; and after waiting a long time for one of Baba Allee Khan's people, at last had the pleasure to see them once more file out of the court-yard of Hadjee Meer Ismael, under better auspices than the last. I retained Seyed Allee, with two horses, to follow when I should have procured my final dismissal, along with the necessary papers. These I had reason to expect in the course of this day, but the greater part of it passed without their appearance. As I lounged in the shop of my friend Hadjee Moolla Baba towards evening, I was hailed by Mahomed Reza Khan of Kiskar, who had been charged to recover my goods from the khan of Massaul, and with whom I had become acquainted at the minister's levee, who told me that my things had arrived from Mahomed Khan. Accordingly I was very soon saluted by one of my Talish guards, a little spare active fellow, a sort of page, or "Callum beg" to the wild Highland chief of Massāul, who, from a dirty old handkerchief produced my silver case of instruments, and other trinkets, all sorely broken; the remains of my medicines, in a sad state from rain; Seyed Allee's and my daggers; and eight tomauns in money of all descriptions. These I was requested to acknowledge the receipt of to the vizier, which I promised to do in the evening. I was not a little amused with the sly looks of the little henchman, who eyed me with a smothered smile, as if remembering the awkward situation in which he had formerly seen me, though now clear of his clutches.

The minister this evening received me with high favour, seating me by himself in presence of all the grandees of Resht, and handing me a plate of delicious ripe apricots, served in snow, which had just been brought in for himself, as if to compensate me for the slights which many of them had offered

me. My host Hadjee Meer Ismael was present, as well as Hadjee Reza, who
had refused me entrance into his house when I first came to Resht. He assured
me that my other things, my pistol (which had been traced to the possession of
Furz-Allee Beg, the gholaum who retook me), the two remaining tomauns,
with the prince's present and my passports, should all be sent early next
morning; and in my own presence, he gave orders to a meerza for writing a
letter to Mr. Willock, besides the usual order for soorsaut and protection, which
forms the passport. He then dismissed me, desiring me to come to him when
ready to depart.

July 1st. After waiting several hours in a state of readiness for departure,
a messenger came with the stray pistol, but neither passport or present made
their appearance; so that I was forced, after a further delay, to repair to the
durkhaneh myself, where I fortunately found the minister transacting business,
until the prince should come into public. Soliciting his orders for expediting my
departure, he called for the letters, signed them, gave them to me, and ordered
the prince's gift to be brought: then, saying he was obliged to attend the prince,
took leave in a very kind tone, and left me among the attendants, who appeared
little disposed to second his good intentions. Much time was unnecessarily
wasted, many pipes smoked, and many useless forms gone through, before a
receipt was handed me for thirty tomauns, which I was desired to seal.

I now discovered that the khelut, or dress of honour, was to be transformed
into the thirty tomauns, instead of accompanying them; but disgusted as I had
been with so much delay, I had no desire whatever to agitate a question, which
would not have been graciously received, and would have subjected me to still
further detention. It was not certainly for the value of the khelut, but I disliked
the apparent commutation for money; because, although the latter was but too
necessary to enable me to reach Tabreez, I did not by any means intend that
it should appear to be received as an indemnification for what had passed, but
only as a mark of the prince's bounty, given for the purpose of paying my
travelling charges to Tabreez, as had at first been intended. At last the thirty
tomauns in gold were handed to me; I received this acknowledgment of my
triumph in the very same room where I had been insulted and arrested. Not
one moment did I delay my "Khodah Hafiz," and I almost leaped with
impatience and joy, as I traversed the court, and re-crossed the ominous
threshold of the palace gates, I devoutly hoped never to enter them more.

After directing the horses to be saddled, I went to the house of Hadjee
Moolla Baba, to take leave of that kind and steady friend, and of Meerza
Reza. I found the latter, who had enjoyed an intermission of some hours,
labouring under a second violent attack of fever, and so uneasy, that in spite
of my impatience, and the favourable breeze that blew directly for Enzellee,
I was persuaded, at his instance, to remain with and nurse him through the

fit of this night; for there was no doubt that the fever was the common intermittent so prevalent in all marshy countries.

I advised him, as soon as the first strong and disabling succession of fits should be over, to lose no time in leaving Gheelan, and returning for change of air to Tabreez, as the only means of escaping a tedious and perhaps fatal disorder. This he promised to do, but my disinterested urgency on this occasion proved the means of furnishing me with a trait of the meerza's character, which was rather disappointing. He entered bitterly into invective against the prince's unhandsome and niggardly conduct to himself, in withholding from him the smallest supply of money, although, as he assured me, upwards of 800 tomauns of cash were already due to him as wages; and that, independent of the forced presents and peculations to which he had been subjected by the prince and his retainers, he had been obliged, not only to sell his clothes, shawls, and ornaments, but to get deeply in debt to his friends, and among the rest to the hadjee, for the means of subsistence. He said he was now almost pennyless; that he was unwilling to trespass further on the hadjee's generosity, and that as he was aware that I had just received thirty tomauns from the prince, which was more than sufficient (as he presumed) to carry me to Tabreez, he hoped I would do him the favour to lend him *ten* of these, and thus enable him also to move from this vile country; that he would give me an order on his brother at Tabreez for the same amount, which should be paid immediately on presentation.

I was somewhat staggered with this request, not on account of the money, though with my company and number of animals to provide for, allowing contingencies on the road, I could very ill spare it, but because it had a bad appearance. I had before occasionally remarked some traits indicating a certain degree of his country's meanness and selfishness in the meerza, but had dismissed these suspicions from me as unworthy, and was unwilling to believe there was any alloy of interestedness in the really great friendship he had shown me. This, however, was a measure of most suspicious appearance; he knew my circumstances well; he knew the heavy losses my detention had subjected me to, and the real necessity which had induced me to accept of the prince's present; so that I was the last person to whom he ought to have made such an application. But the poor man was very ill; perhaps the tale of his poverty was true, and that he should not be able to remove from a noxious climate without such assistance, might be equally so: there was no doubt that he had been of considerable service to me, the sacrifice therefore now required might be considered as the discharge of a debt; but, I confess, I should have been better pleased, had it been claimed in a more handsome manner. I gave him the money, and received from him what he told me was an order on his brother at Tabreez, and which turned out not worth a farthing; it never was paid; it did not even prove to be an order, but a mere acknowledgement of receipt, for the payment of which, the brother said, he could not consider himself liable in any degree.

The truth is, that the meerza in character was a Persian; like too many of his countrymen, he was thoughtless, extravagant, and very lax in both moral and religious principles, and from these defects was often led to be guilty of acts, which otherwise he might have scorned; for I believe, that he was naturally kind, and had many good dispositions. His English education, and intercourse with Englishmen, had no doubt a beneficial effect upon his character, but could not eradicate the evil implanted by early and continued habit.

LADY MARY LEONORA SHEIL (d. 1869)

Daughter of Stephen Woulfe, chief baron of the Irish Exchequer, Mary became the second wife of Lieutenant–Colonel (later Sir) Justin Sheil in 1849. She went with him to Persia where he had been serving in the British legation since 1836 (he was minister from 1844 to 1853) and where she bore him three children. Lady Sheil published *Glimpses of Life and Manners in Persia* in 1856, and it has been designated the first travel book on the country by a woman. Her narrative of the deposition and murder of Nasir al-Din's first Prime Minister, Amir Kabir Mirza Taqi Khan, is used as a primary source for this incident by Abbas Amanat in his biography of the Shah, *Pivot of the Universe* (Amanat 1997). An observant writer on her own account, she made full (sometimes verbatim) use of her husband's dispatches, especially with regard to the section in her book on the Babi movement which provides one of the earliest published accounts on the sect by a European.

From:

***Glimpses of Life and Manners in Persia* (1856)**

Lady Sheil's account of Babism explains this manifestation of acute social and religious unrest in Qajar Persia as the work of socialists, communists and anarchists, 'the opinion shared by almost all of the European colony in Tihran in 1850–52' (Momen 1981: 5).

Babeeism

September 6th.—This year has been remarkable for civil and religious wars waged in various parts of Persia. At Meshed, on the eastern extremity of the kingdom, a son of a maternal uncle of the Shah had for many months raised the standard of rebellion, and sustained a vigorous siege against his sovereign's forces. It terminated in his capture by treachery, which was succeeded by his execution, and that of one of his sons and two of his brothers. A few years ago a wholesale massacre would have followed this bold rebellion, but European influence and unceasing expostulation have softened Persian manners. It is curious, though I believe true, that the English press has had some share in producing this change. The strictures on Persian misgovernment, which sometimes appear in the English journals, are viewed with anger and alarm, particularly when the evil-doers are held up by name to public reprobation.

But a far more serious attempt at revolution has been in progress in various parts of the kingdom. Under the disguise of a new revelation, socialism and communism have made advances in Mazenderan, Yezd, Fars, and Zenjan, which would leave nothing to wish for in the aspirations of the reddest republican. Blood has flowed in torrents in crushing the malcontents, for terror and religious hate walked hand in hand. For the renegade there is no quarter in the Mahommedan code; far less when to apostasy are added the startling doctrines of universal spoliation, and, above all, of the relentless slaughter of all Mussulmans, in particular of moollas, kazees, &c. This amiable sect is styled Bābee, from Bāb, a gate, in Arabic, the name assumed by its founder, meaning, I suppose, the gate to heaven.

This celebrated person, whose real name was Syed Ali Mahommed, was born forty years ago in Sheeraz, where his father was a merchant. When fifteen years of age he was sent to prosecute his theological studies at Nejeff. Here he became acquainted with two derveeshes, with whom he was for a considerable period on terms of great intimacy. He was afterwards sent to Bushire to follow commercial pursuits, but he withdrew from society, and in a life of seclusion devoted himself to the religious exercises commonly observed by derveeshes. These mystic practices are supposed to have affected his intellect. After some changes he settled at Kazemein, near Bagdad, where he first divulged his pretensions to the character of a prophet. Incensed at this blasphemy, the Turkish authorities issued orders for his execution, but he was claimed by the Persian consul as a subject of the Shah, and sent to his native place. Here in a short time he collected so many disciples around him, that imprisonment followed an investigation into his doctrines. It was debated whether he was to be treated as a lunatic, or a blasphemer and unworthy descendant of the Prophet, but his life was saved by the voice of the Sheikh ool Islam on his making a public recantation of his errors from the pulpit of one of the principal mosques. He contrived to escape from prison, and made his way to Ispahan, where many people of distinction secretly embraced his opinions. Again arrested, he was sent to the fort of Cherek, in Azerbijan, and under the infliction of the bastinado he again recanted his errors. Six months afterwards, it having been ascertained that his doctrines were obtaining rapid diffusion among all classes, he was conveyed to Tabreez, and on the day of his arrival was brought out for execution in the great maïdan, or square. This was on the point of becoming a most remarkable event, which would probably have overturned the throne and Islamism in Persia. A company of soldiers was ordered to despatch Bab by a volley. When the smoke cleared away, Bāb had disappeared from sight. It had so happened that none of the balls had touched him; and, prompted by an impulse to preserve his life, he rushed from the spot. Had Bāb possessed sufficient presence of mind to have fled to the bazar, which was within a few yards of the place where be was stationed, he would in all probability have succeeded in effecting his escape. A miracle palpable to all Tabreez would have been performed, and a new creed would have been established. But he turned in the opposite direction, and hid himself in the guard-room, where he was immediately discovered, brought out, and shot. His body was thrown into the ditch of the town, where it was devoured by the half-wild dogs which abound outside a Persian city. Bāb possessed a mild and benignant countenance, his manners were composed and dignified, his eloquence was impressive, and he wrote rapidly and well.

It would appear that in the beginning of his career he did not wholly reject the established forms and doctrines of the Mahommedan faith, but he reduced these to proportions so small as to be equivalent to their annulment, and thus rendered his speculations acceptable to the multitude. As his disciples increased so did his views enlarge. — — was acquainted with one of his proselytes, who, however, adopted the principle of never avowing his faith even to him. This man was in a respectable condition of life, and his statements were subsequently confirmed, though with some exaggeration, by a moolla of eminence, who had been converted to Bābeeism but had recanted his errors. His conversion, according to his own affirmation, had only been feigned in order to be able to dive into all the secrets of the system. It was a strange circumstance that among those who adopted Bāb's doctrine there should have been a large number of moollas, and even moojteheds, who hold a high rank as expounders of the law in the Mahommedan church. Many of these men sealed their faith with their blood. Bāb's notions did not contain much originality. Atheism, under the disguise of pantheism, was the basis of his principles. Every single atom in the universe, he said, was actually God, and the whole universe collectively was God; not a representative of, or emanation from God, but God himself. Everything in short was God. Bāb was God, and every living creature down to each lowest insect. Death was not real—it was only another form of divinity, if such language has any signification at all. Virtue had no existence, neither had vice; they were necessarily wholly indifferent, as being portions or emanations of the Godhead. Rights of property had no existence, excepting in the equal division of all things among the godly. But this was a fiction, the real doctrine being the reign of the Saints,—that is, of the Bābees,—and their possession of the goods of the ungodly,—in other words, the non-Bābees. It was the simplest of religions. Its tenets may be summed up in materialism, communism, and the entire indifference of good and evil and of all human actions. There was no antipathy, it was affirmed, on the part of the Bābees to Christians, or to the followers of any other creed excepting Mahommedans, who, as they slew Bābees, ought to be exterminated. When the Bābee meerza was reminded of this being somewhat contrary to the doctrine of indifference of all human actions, he had no reply to make.

One of the proofs alleged against Bāb's claim to a divine mission was the ungrammatical Arabic of his revelations, which could not consequently have descended from heaven. The Koran is regarded as a miracle of style and composition.

In the maxims of Bāb there does not seem to be a material difference from the doctrines alluded to in a former page, as inculcated by Hassan Sābah at Alamoot. In the reign of Kei Kobad, five hundred years after Christ, Mazdak spread widely through Persia his atheistical doctrines, not dissimilar from those of Bāb. Among them was included the same principle of a division of property; and, strange to say, his creed was adopted by the monarch Kei Kobad. Nousheerwan, the son of that sovereign, put to death Mazdak, with thousands of his followers.

The present Shah shows no disposition to follow the example of his predecessor. Mazenderān, owing to its secluded position, is perhaps the province in Persia most infected with a fanatical attachment to the Mahommedan faith. It was here that, headed by the priesthood, the attack on the Bābees commenced; many hundred were slain in that province, fighting to the last, and sustaining with invincible fortitude all the barbarous inflictions which cruelty, fanaticism, and terror could invent. Scenes nearly similar, but with a diminution of cruelty and bigotry, were repeated in Fars and Yezd.

This year, seven Bābees were executed at Tehran for an alleged conspiracy against the life of the Prime Minister. Their fate excited general sympathy, for every one knew that no criminal act had been committed, and suspected the accusation to be a pretence. Besides this Bābeeism had spread in Tehran too. They died with the utmost firmness. Previously to decapitation they received an offer of pardon, on the condition of reciting the Kelema, or creed, that Mahommed is the Prophet of God. It was rejected, and these visionaries died stedfast in their faith. The Persian minister was ignorant of the maxim that persecution was proselytism.

In Zenjan the insurrection, or the religious movement, as the Bābees termed it, broke out with violence. This city is only two hundred miles from Tehran, midway to Tabreez. At its head was a moolla of repute and renown, who, with his associates, retired into an angle of the city, which they strengthened as best they could. For several months they defended themselves with unconquerable resolution against a large force in infantry and guns, sent against them from Tehran. It was their readiness to meet death that made the Bābees so formidable to their assailants. From street to street—from house to house—from cellar to cellar—they fought without flinching. All were killed at their posts, excepting a few who were afterwards bayoneted by the troops in cold blood.

Few believe that by these sanguinary measures the doctrines of Bāb will cease from propagation. There is a spirit of change abroad among the Persians, which will preserve his system from extinction; besides which, his doctrines are of an attractive nature to Persians. Though now subdued, and obliged to lurk concealed in towns, it is conjectured that the creed of Bāb, far from diminishing, is daily spreading; at the fitting time Bāb will come to life again. There will be either a resurrection, or else his successor will maintain that his death was a falsehood invented by the Mussulmans. Whenever that day of desolation arrives, wading in blood will not be a figure of speech in Persia.

ARMINIUS VAMBERY (1832–1913)

Born in a small town in Austro–Hungary into a poor Jewish family, Vambery distanced himself from his Jewish origins but not before acquiring a command of the Hebrew bible and the Talmud (Kramer 1999: 9). Excelling at languages, he left for Istanbul in 1857 where he earned his livelihood as a language teacher. After 'several years' residence in Turkish houses, and frequent visits to Islamic schools and libraries', he was 'transformed into a Turk – nay into an Efendi', as he claimed later in his introduction to *Travels in Central Asia* (1864). His journey to the East was stimulated, so he tells us, from a desire to prove his hunch that Hungarian was connected to the Turko–Tartaric language branch. In the guise of a Turkish gentleman he arrived in Tehran in July 1862 where he presented himself at the Turkish, French and British consulates. Finding his onward journey forestalled owing to the situation in Afghanistan, he spent the next six months in Persia. Eventually meeting a party of simple Tartar–Chinese pilgrims returning to their homeland, he decided to accompany them in the guise of a dervish. Sometimes placed in great peril, throughout his travels – which took him to Khiva, Bukhara, and Samarkand – he was stalked by fear of his disguise being penetrated. At the court of Herat the young ruler took him for an Englishman and the rumour rapidly spread to the bazaar. However Vambery managed to safely re-cross the Persian border and proceed to Meshed, his journey into Central Asia having taken ten months. On its publication, *Travels in Central Asia* (1864) earned its author international fame and acclamation paving the way for his eventual appointment as Professor of Oriental Languages at the University of Budapest. He became especially popular in Britain, calling the Englishman 'the real embodiment of the European spirit – the rightful civilizer of Asia' (Vambery 1973: 366)

From:

Travels in Central Asia (1864)

On his journey through the Caspian province of Mazandaran, Vambery saw the ill treatment meted out to the poor Turkic Sunni pilgrims with whom he was travelling by the bigoted and hostile Persian Shi'ihs. However, on crossing the border into Turcoman territory he discovers the extent of the Turcoman depredations in Persia. His sympathies now engaged by the young Persian men he witnesses enslaved there, he senses that the barbarism of the Turcoman hordes would best be dealt with by the Russians, who at this point were spreading their Central Asian empire into Turcoman territory. However he also noted the Persians' disinclination to embrace the Russian bear.

Persian Slaves

I was astonished to find many of my fellow-travellers, the poorest of the poor, in spite of the noble hospitality of which they had been partakers, were already weary of the Turkomans; for it would be, they said, impossible for men having the least sentiment of humanity to be eyewitnesses any longer of the cruel treatment to which the wretched Persian slaves had to submit. 'True, the Persians are heretics, and they tormented us terribly in our journey through their country; but what the poor wretches here suffer is really too much.' The compassion evinced by my fellow-travellers, in whose own country the slave-trade is not carried on, and the imprecations they used against the Karaktchi (robbers) for their inhumanity, convey the best impression of the sufferings to which the poor captives are exposed. Let us only picture to ourselves the feelings of a Persian, even admitting that he is the poorest of his race, who is surprised by a night attack, hurried away from his family, and brought hither a prisoner, and often wounded. He has to exchange his dress for old Turkoman rags that only scantily cover parts of his body, and is heavily laden with chains that gall his ancles, and occasion him great and unceasing pain every step he takes; he is forced upon the poorest diet to linger the first days, often weeks of his captivity. That he may make no attempt at flight, he has also during the night a Karabogra (iron ring) attached to his neck and fastened to a peg, so that the rattle betrays even his slightest movements. No other termination to his sufferings than the payment of a ransom by his friends; and, failing this, he is liable to be sold, and perhaps hurried off to Khiva and Bokhara!

To the rattle of those chains I could never habituate my ears; it is heard in the tent of every Turkoman who has any pretensions to respectability or position. Even our friend Khandjan had two slaves, lads, only in their eighteenth and twentieth year; and to behold these unfortunates, in the bloom of their youth, in fetters made me feel indescribable emotion, repeated every day. In addition, I was forced to listen in silence to the abuse and curses with which these poor wretches were loaded. The smallest demonstration of compassion would have awakened suspicions, as, on account of my knowledge of Persian, I was most frequently addressed by them. The youngest of our domestic slaves, a handsome black-haired Irani, begged of me to be so good as to write a letter for him to his relatives, praying them for God's sake to sell sheep and house in order to ransom him, which letter I accordingly wrote. Upon one occasion I thought, without being perceived, I might give him a cup of tea, but unluckily at the moment when he extended his hand to receive it some one entered the tent. I pretended to be only beckoning to him, and, instead of presenting him the tea, I felt constrained to give him a few slight blows. During my stay in Gömüshtepe no night passed without a shot echoing from the sea-shore to announce the arrival of some piratical vessel laden with booty. The next morning I went to demand from the heroes the tithes due to the Dervishes, or rather, let me say, to behold the poor Persians in the first moments of their misfortune. My heart bled at the horrid sight; and so I had to harden myself to these most striking contrasts of virtue and vice, of humanity and tyranny, of scrupulous honesty and the very scum of knavery.

I had stayed only a fortnight when, like my companions, I began to weary of the place, my eyes feeding with inexpressible longing upon the frontiers of Persia. Only a few leagues' separate the two countries, and yet the manners, customs, and modes of thinking amongst the Turkomans are just as different as if the two nations were a thousand miles asunder. How wonderful the influence of religion and of historical tradition upon mankind! I cannot refrain from laughing when I think that these Turkomans, in some particulars so cruel and so inhuman, were at this very time constantly giving entertainments, 'Lillah' (for pious ends), at which it was necessary that our entire company of pilgrims should be present. These invitations were repeated several times during the day. It was only the first and second that I was disposed to accept; from the third I showed by my manner that I wished to be excused; but my would-be host forced me by many pushes in the ribs to leave my tent. According to the rule of Turkoman etiquette, 'the harder the push, the more hearty the invitation.' On such festal occasions the Amphytrion threw down before the tent some pieces of felt—or, if it were his humour to be sumptuous, a carpet—whereupon the guests seated themselves in groups of five or six in a circle, and each group received, a large wooden dish proportioned in size and contents to the number and ages of those who were to share it. Into the dish every guest plunged his half-open fist, until emptied to the very bottom. The quality and dressing of the meats which were served to us are not calculated to interest much our 'gastronomes.' I merely remark, therefore, in passing, that horse-flesh, and camel-flesh were the order of the day: what other dishes represented our venison, I must, decline mentioning.

During my sojourn with Khandjan, he affianced his son (twelve years old, as before mentioned) to a maiden in her tenth year. This event was accompanied by a festival, from which, as his guests, we could not absent ourselves. On entering the tent of the 'fiancée,' we found her completely occupied with working a shawl. Her manner was that of one unconscious of the presence of others; and during our stay, which lasted two hours, I only once remarked from her furtive glance that she took any interest in our company. During the banquet, which, in my honour, consisted of rice boiled in milk, Khandjan observed that this festival had been fixed for the next autumn; but he had wished to turn to account the occasion of our presence, that the event might take place under our auspices and benedictions.

Let me not here forget to mention that we were entertained also on this occasion by a Karaktchi, who had, alone on foot, not only made three Persians prisoners, but had also by himself driven them before him into captivity for a distance of eight miles. He gave us the tithes of the spoil due to the Church, consisting of a small sum of two krans; and how happy he was when we with one voice intoned a Fatiha to bless him!

After having lingered, very much against my will, three weeks in Gömüshtepe, the hospitable Khandjan at last showed a disposition to aid our preparations for departure. We considered that the purchase of camels would entail too much expense; we consequently determined to hire one for every two of us to carry our water and our flour. This might have been very difficult, had we not been so fortunate as to possess in our cattle-dealer, Ilias Beg, a proper adviser for the purpose. He was not, perhaps, a religious person, nor had he much reverence for our Hadji character; but he only showed the more exactitude to fulfil the law of hospitality, and the more disposition to make the greatest sacrifices to give us satisfaction. Ilias is properly a Turkoman from Khiva, and of the tribe of the Yomuts; he makes a journey of business every year through the desert to Gömüshtepe, and during his stay is under the protection of Khandjan, without which his position is as insecure as that of any other stranger. He comes generally in autumn, and returns in spring, with twenty or thirty camels loaded with his own merchandise, or that of strangers. Having been induced this year to take back with him some extra camels, the small additional sum for hire of these camels was, as it were, a God-send. Khandjan had recommended us in the warmest manner, and the words, 'Ilias, you will answer with your life,' had clearly shown him in what degree of estimation we stood with our host. Ilias cast his eyes down to the ground, as the nomads are in the habit of doing when they appear most in earnest; and his answer, in a low tone, which seemed to issue from him without any movement of the lips, was, 'You surely do not know me.' The singular *sang-froid* of the two Turkomans, as they dealt together, began to irritate my still half- European character, ad forgetting that Hadji Bilal and my other companions were also present, and yet remained motionless, I made some remarks; but I soon had occasion to regret it, for even after having addressed them several times, my words remained without notice. Without, therefore, venturing to mix in the negotiation, it was determined that we should hire, a camel for two ducats to go as far as Khiva; and as for our flour and. water, Ilias declared that he would take it with him without compensation.

The small sum of money belonging to me, which I had sewn and hidden in different parts of my mendicant attire, together with the tolerably rich harvest of my Hadji dealings amongst the Turkomans, had abundantly provided for me, so that I was in a position to hire a camel for myself alone; but I was dissuaded by Hadji Bilal and Sultan Mahmoud, who remarked that an appearance of wretchedness calculated to excite compassion was the best guarantee for safety amongst these nomads; while their covetousness was sure to be excited by the slightest sign of affluence. A suspicion of wealth might convert the best friend into a foe. They named several of the Hadjis who were well provided with means, and who, nevertheless, for the sake of prudence, were obliged to wander on in rags and on foot. I admitted the necessity, and secured a joint share in a camel, only stipulating for permission to make use of a kedjeve (air of wooden baskets, hanging down from the two sides of the camel), as I should find it very fatiguing, with my lame foot and without cessation, to ride day and night forty stations, squeezed with another into the same wooden saddle. At first, Ilias objected, because, according to him (and he was indeed right), the kedjeve in the desert would have been a double burden for the poor beast. Khandjan, however, at last persuaded him, and he consented. On the journey to Khiva, which we were to perform in twenty days, and of which everyone spoke in a manner to make us feel fearful misgivings, I should at least have the consolation of being able now and then to sleep a little; but what pleased me most in the whole arrangement was, that I should have for my *vis-à-vis* and 'equipoise,' as the two kedjeve were termed, my bosom friend Hadji Bilal, whose society began by degrees to become indispensable for me. After the dialogue was over, we paid, as is the custom, the hire beforehand. Hadji Bilal said a Fatiha; and after Ilias had passed his fingers through his beard, consisting, it is true, of only a few straggling hairs, we had no occasion to take any other steps, and we but begged that the departure might be hastened as much as possible. This, however, he could not promise, as it depended upon the Kervanbashi of the Khan, who, with his buffaloes, was to place himself at the head of our karavan. In a few days we were ready to start for Etrek, our rendezvous. After the preparations had been completed I burnt with twofold ardour to quit Gömüshtepe: for, first, we had lost time here, and I perceived that the hot season was more and more advancing, and we feared that the rain-water, still to be found in the desert, would become scarcer; and secondly, I began to grow uneasy at the ridiculous reports which were in circulation respecting me. Whilst many saw in me merely a pious Dervish, others could not rid themselves of the idea that I was a man of influence, an envoy of the Sultan, in correspondence with the Turkish Ambassador in Teheran, who was bringing a thousand muskets with him, and was engaged in a plot against Russia and Persia. Had this come to the ears of the Russians in Ashourada, they would have certainly laughed at it, but still it might have led to enquiries respecting the singular stranger; and the discovery of my disguise might have involved a cruel, perhaps a life-long captivity. I therefore begged Hadji Bilal repeatedly at least to leave Gömüshtepe, but his previous impatience had given way to absolute indifference as soon as Ilias had engaged with us; on my urging him, he even answered how ridiculously childish it was for me to seek to anticipate the decrees of destiny. 'Thy haste,' said he to me, 'is all thrown away; thou must perforce remain on the Görghen's banks until the Nasib (fate) has decreed that thou shouldst drink water in another place; and no one knows whether this will occur at an early or a late period.' Only imagine what effect an answer so oriental was calculated to produce upon a mind that had just cause to feel impatience! I saw, however, but too well, the impossibility of escape, and so submitted to my fate.

About this time, it happened that some Karaktchi had, by treachery, in one of their depredatory expeditions, seized upon five Persians. One of these was a man of property. The robbers had sailed in a vessel up beyond Karatepe, under the pretence of purchasing a cargo from the village of the Persians. The bargain was soon made; and scarcely had the unsuspicious Persians appeared with their goods upon the sea-shore, than they were seized, bound hand and foot, buried up to their necks in their own wheat, and forcibly carried off to Gömüshtepe. I was present when these unfortunates were unpacked, so to say. One of them was also dangerously wounded; and I heard the Turkomans themselves characterise the act as a deed of shame. Even the Russians in Ashourada interested themselves in the affair, and threatened a landing if the prisoners were not immediately set at liberty. As the robbers resolutely refused to let their prize go, I thought that now the rest of the Turkomans, who run common risk from the Russians, would compel their countrymen to give way. Not at all; they ran up and down, distributing arms, in order, should the Russians land, to give them a warm reception. It may be interesting to know that I was also appointed to shoulder a musket, and great was my embarrassment when I reflected upon whom I should be expected to fire. Happily, no attempt was made to carry out the threat.[*] Next morning a

---

[*] Let not the reader be surprised by the equivocal attitude of the Russian authorities. Persia regards every landing of the Russian forces on the coasts as a hostile invasion of its own soil, and prefers to endure the depredations of the Turkomans rather than avail itself of the Russian arms, which might, it is true, in particular cases, be of service to them, but would not fail, on the whole, to be most detrimental.

Russian steamer came quite close to the shore, but the matter was disposed of by a political manœuvre; that is to say, the Turkomans gave hostages for the future, but the Persians remained in chains. The wealthy prisoner paid a ransom of 100 ducats; another, who was crippled in both hands and feet, and was not worth the sum of four ducats, was set free in honour of the Russians; but the three others—strong men—were loaded with still heavier chains, and led away to the usual place of torture for the slaves, at Etrek. The name of Etrek, which is given both to a river and the inhabited district in its vicinity, is a word of terror and a curse for the unfortunate inhabitants of Mazendran and Taberistan. The Persian must be very incensed when he allows the words 'Etrek biufti!' (May you be driven to Etrek!) to escape his lips. As it was fixed for the rendezvous of our karavan, I was soon to have the opportunity of seeing closely into this nest of horror. Khandjan had also had the goodness to recommend me as guest to Kulkhan the Pir (grey-beard) of the Karaktchi. He came to us very opportunely. The old sinner had a sombre repulsive physiognomy. He did not by any means meet me in a friendly manner when I was transferred to his hospitality. He examined my features a long time, occasionally whispering something in the ear of Khandjan, and seemed determined to discover in me more than other people had seen. The cause of this distrust I soon detected. Kulkhan had in his youth travelled through the southern parts of Russia, in company with Khidr Khan, who was in the service of the Czar. He had also long lived at Tiflis, and was pretty familiar with our European modes of existence. He remarked that he had seen many nations, but never the Osmanlis. He had heard it said of them that they had sprung from a tribe of Turkomans, whom besides they resembled in every respect; and that his astonishment was great to distinguish in me quite opposite characteristics. Hadji Bilal remarked that his own information upon the subject was not good, and that he had actually lived several years in Roum, without having occasion to make any similar observation; whereupon Kulkhan told us he would return two days afterwards, early in the morning, to his Ova in Etrek, recommended us to make ourselves ready for our journey, inasmuch as without his conduct we should be unable to travel hence to Etrek, although only a distance of twelve miles; and, in short, that he was only waiting the return of his son Kolman from the Alaman (predatory expedition) to the Persian frontiers, in quest of some fine mares. The return of his son from this piratical adventure was awaited by Kulkhan with almost the same feelings as those with which a father amongst us would expect his son coming home from an heroic expedition, or other honourable enterprise. He also informed us that we might walk forwards a little way down the banks of the Görghen, for his son was to return about this time, and we should then see something worth seeing. As I had nothing at that moment else to do, I was not displeased to comply with the invitation. I mixed with the crowd which was looking, with the greatest impatience, for the rest sight of the party. At last eight mounted Turkomans appeared on the opposite bank, bringing ten led horses with them. I thought that now the expectant multitude would give vent to their enthusiasm in hurrahs, but they uttered no sound; all measured with greedy eyes and speechless admiration those who were approaching. The latter dashed into the Görghen, across which in an instant, they swam to the bank on our side, where, dismounting, they extended their hands with indescribable earnestness to their relatives. Whilst the seniors were passing the spoil in review with the greatest attention, the young heroes were occupied in arranging their dress. Lifting their heavy fur caps, they wiped the sweat from head and forehead.

The whole spectacle was splendid. Whatever my contempt for the robbers and their abominable doings, my eye fell still with particular pleasure upon these young men, who, in their short riding dresses, with their bold looks, and hair falling to their breasts in curly locks as they laid aside their weapons, were the admiration of all. Even the gloomy Kulkhan seemed cheerful: he introduced his son to us, and after Hadji Bilal had bestowed his benediction upon him, we separated. The next morning we were to proceed from Gömüshtepe, accompanied by Kulkhan, his son, and stolen horses, to Etrek.

AUSTEN HENRY LAYARD (1817–1894)

Layard's main claim to fame was as an archaeologist, but he also had a career in public life, first as a Member of Parliament, and then as a diplomat, culminating in a period as ambassador to Turkey between 1877 and 1880. He is, however, most celebrated for his expeditions to Nineveh and the excavations he made there, described in *Nineveh and its Remains* (1849) and *Discoveries in the Ruins of Nineveh and Babylon* (1851). His *Early Adventures in Persia, Susiana and Babylonia* was published in 1887, more than four decades after the journeys it describes. While a young man Layard left a career in the law to travel in the East with his friend Edward Mitford. Determining on Ceylon as their destination, they set off across Turkey and Syria to Jerusalem, where they split, Layard exploring on his own the ancient sites of Petra and Jerash. Reunited, they proceeded to Baghdad then accompanied a caravan to Kermanshah where Layard resumed his investigations of ancient inscriptions. At a time of tension between Britain and Persia over the former's campaign in Afghanistan the companions were suspected of being spies. So in Hamadan they split for the second and last time, Layard proceeding south to Isfahan and the wild areas of Luristan where the Bakhtiari tribes lived and operated beyond the control of the Persian government. There Layard 'travelled far and wide, studying archaeological sites, copying rock-cut inscriptions, taking notes on tribal organization, exploring the possibilities of trade with India' (Wright 1977: 160). One modern writer sees *Early Adventures in Persia* as 'too narrowly anecdotal' claiming it 'frequently fails to achieve the wide historical sweep of the Nineveh books' (Birns DLB/166: 207). It is true that at points Layard's narrative reads 'more like fiction than fact' (Wright 1977: 157), with the hero's adventures resembling those of Walter Scott's English protagonist in *Waverley*, the Bakhtiari filling the role of rebellious Highlanders. As with Scott's Scottish novels, the piece at one level can be read as political allegory with an imperial dimension. Generations of Iranians have like the Bakhtiari chief Muhammad Taqi Khan found it difficult to believe the Englishman's motivation to travel in Persia was only 'love of adventure, and … a curiosity to visit new countries and to explore ancient remains.'

From:

Early Adventures in Persia, Susiana and Babylonia (1887)

The extract situates the young traveller in Isfahan, where he meets for the first time the eunuch-governor and villain of the piece Manuchir Khan, portrayed here as if an oriental monster from the *Arabian Nights*. The descriptions evoking the fallen splendour of Persia further intensify the exoticism, while the hero's first meeting with the Bakhtiaris suggests coming intrigue.

The Matamet

The many horsemen, and men and women carrying loads, whom I passed on the road showed me that I was approaching Isfahan; but nothing could be seen of the city, which was completely buried in trees. By constantly asking my way I managed to reach, through the labyrinth of walls which enclose the gardens and melon beds, the Armenian quarter of Julfa. I had letters for M. Eugène Boré, a French gentleman, and, not knowing where to find a lodging, I presented myself to him to ask for advice. He received me with great kindness, and insisted that I should he his guest.

Mr. Edward Burgess, an English merchant from Tabreez, who was at Isfahan on business, hearing that I had arrived, came to see me and offered to be of use to me. He proposed that we should present ourselves to the governor, Manuchar Khan, the Mu'temedi-Dowla, or, as he was usually called, 'the Matamet,'[*] to whom he was personally known.

I was anxious to deliver the letter which had been given to me by the Haji at Hamadan for this high personage, and at the same time to lodge a complaint against Imaum Verdi Beg, my mehmandar, for his exactions and his ill-treatment of the villagers on the road. He had left me as we approached the city, taking with him the horses and donkeys laden with rice, sugar, and other spoils which he had acquired by the use of my firman. I was determined to have him punished, and compelled to restore to their owners the animals that he had carried off, and to repay to the village chiefs the money he had levied from them.

Although very ill and weak, I rode with Mr. Burgess on the second day after my arrival to the governor's palace. The Armenian suburb of Julfa is at some distance from the main portion of the city, in which only Musulmans were then permitted to live. After passing through extensive gardens we reached the Mohammedan quarters, and threading our way between mud-built

---

[*] I spell this name as it was pronounced; Mu'temedi-Dowla means the 'one upon whom the State relies.'

houses, for the most part falling to ruins, through narrow, paved streets, deep in dust and mud and choked with filth and rubbish, we at length reached the Matamet's residence.

After entering, through a narrow dark passage, a spacious yard with the usual fountains, running water, and flowers, we passed into the inner court, where the governor gave audience. The palace, which at one time must have been of great magnificence, was in a neglected and ruined condition, but had been once profusely decorated with paintings, glass, and inlaid work, such as I had seen in the palace of Douletabad. The building was thronged with miserably clad soldiers, 'ferrashes,'* men and women having complaints to make or petitions to present, and the usual retinue and hangers-on of a Persian nobleman in authority.

The Matamet himself sat on a chair, at a large open window, in a beautifully ornamented room at the upper end of the court. Those who had business with him, or whom he summoned, advanced with repeated bows, and then stood humbly before him as if awestruck by his presence, the sleeves of their robes, usually loose and open, closely buttoned up, and their hands joined in front—an immemorial attitude of respect in the East. In the 'hauz,' or pond of fresh water, in the centre of the court, were bundles of long switches from the pomegranate tree, soaking to be ready for use for the bastinado, which the Matamet was in the habit of administering freely and indifferently to high and low. In a corner was the pole with two loops of cord to raise the feet of the victim, who writhes on the ground and screams for mercy. This barbarous punishment was then employed in Persia for all manner of offences and crimes, the number of strokes administered varying according to the guilt or obstinacy of the culprit. It was also constantly resorted to as a form of torture to extract confessions. The pomegranate switches, when soaked for some time, become lithe and flexible. The pain and injury which they inflicted were very great, and were sometimes even followed by death. Under ordinary circumstances the sufferer was unable to use his feet for some time, and frequently lost the nails of his toes. The bastinado was inflicted upon men of the highest rank—governors of provinces, and even prime ministers—who had, justly or unjustly, incurred the displeasure of the Shah. Husayn Khan, on his return from a special mission as ambassador to England and France, had been subjected to it on a charge of peculation.

Manuchar Khan, the Matamet, was a eunuch. He was a Georgian, born of Christian parents, and had been purchased in his childhood as a slave, had been brought up as a Musulman, and reduced to his unhappy condition. Like many of his kind, he was employed when young in the public service, and had by his

---

* The 'ferrash,' literally the 'sweeper,' is an attendant employed in various ways, from sweeping the rooms to administering the bastinado.

remarkable abilities risen to the highest posts. He had for many years enjoyed the confidence and the favour of the Shah. Considered the best administrator in the kingdom, he had been sent to govern the great province of Isfahan, which included within its limits the wild and lawless tribes of the Lurs and the Bakhtiyari, generally in rebellion, and the semi-independent Arab population of the plains between the Luristan Mountains and the Euphrates. He was hated and feared for his cruelty; but it was generally admitted that he ruled justly, that he protected the weak from oppression by the strong, and that where he was able to enforce his authority life and property were secure. He was known for the ingenuity with which he had invented new forms of punishment and torture to strike terror into evil-doers, and to make examples of those who dared to resist his authority or that of his master the Shah, thus justifying the reproach addressed to beings of his class, of insensibility to human suffering. One of his modes of dealing with criminals was what he termed 'planting vines.' A hole having been dug in the ground, men were thrust headlong into it and then covered with earth, their legs being allowed to protrude to represent what he facetiously called 'the vines.' I was told that he had ordered a horse-stealer to have all his teeth drawn, which were driven into the soles of his feet as if he were being shod. His head was then put into a nose-bag filled with hay, and he was thus left to die. A tower still existed near Shiraz which he had built of three hundred living men belonging to the Mamesenni, a tribe inhabiting the mountains to the north of Shiraz, which had rebelled against the Shah. They were laid in layers of ten, mortar being spread between each layer, and the heads of the unhappy victims being left free. Some of them were said to have been kept alive for several days by being fed by their friends, a life of torture being thus prolonged. At that time few nations, however barbarous, equalled— none probably exceeded—the Persian in the shocking cruelty, ingenuity, and indifference with which death or torture was inflicted.

The Matamet had the usual characteristics of the eunuch. He was beardless, had a smooth, colourless face, with hanging cheeks and a weak, shrill, feminine voice. He was short, stout, and flabby, and his limbs were ungainly and slow of movement. His features, which were of the Georgian type, had a wearied and listless appearance, and were without expression or animation. He was dressed in the usual Persian costume—his tunic being of the finest Cashmere cloth— and he carried a jewel-handled curved dagger in the shawl folded round his waist. He received us courteously, said a few civil things about the English nation, which he distinguished from the English Government, and invited us to come up into the room in which he was seated and to take our places on a carpet spread near him.

I handed him my firman and the letter from the Haji, and being unable to suppress my indignation against Imaum Verdi Beg, my mehmandar, for his ill-treatment of the villagers on the road, I denounced him at once in vehement terms, describing his misconduct and the insolent manner in which he had behaved to me when I had remonstrated against it. The Matamet applied a variety of opprobrious and foul epithets to the Ghulâm himself and to his mother and all his female relatives, after the Persian fashion, and promised that he should receive condign punishment. And he was as good as his word, for two days after Imaum Verdi came hobbling to me with a very rueful countenance, and his feet swollen from the effects of the bastinado which he had received. I was inclined to pity the poor wretch, although he had richly deserved his punishment; but I almost regretted that I had denounced him to the Matamet when he said to me in an appealing tone, 'What good, sir, has the stick that I have eaten done you? Who has profited by it? You and I might have divided the money and the supplies that, as the Shah's servant, I was entitled by his firman to obtain for you on our way. The villagers would have been none the worse, as they would have deducted the amount from their taxes. Do you think that they will get back their horses, or their donkeys, or their tomans? No, the Matamet has taken them all for himself. He is a rich man and does not want them; I am a poor man and do. He is the greater robber of the two. He goes unpunished and I have scarcely a nail left on my toes.'

After the Matamet had made the usual inquiries as to the object of my journey, and as to the route I desired to take and the places I wished to visit, he said that, had I been accompanied by a competent Ghulâm, I should have met with no difficulty in carrying out my original intention of crossing the Bakhtiyari Mountains to Shuster. He promised to send with me one of his own officers, who would conduct me to that city. A Bakhtiyari chief, named Shefi'a Khan, who happened to be present, confirmed what the governor had said, and informed me that one of the brothers of Mehemet Taki Khan, the great Bakhtiyari chief, was then in Isfahan. When I took my leave of the governor he told me that my new mehmandar would be ready to leave immediately, and that I should receive the letters he had promised me without delay.

The day after my interview with the Matamet I succeeded, after some trouble, in finding Shefi'a Khan, who had promised to introduce me to Ali Naghi Khan, the brother of the principal chief of the Bakhtiyari tribes. They both lodged in the upper storey of a half-ruined building forming part of one of the ancient royal palaces. The entrance was crowded with their retainers— tall, handsome, but fierce-looking men, in very ragged clothes. They wore the common white felt skull-cap, sometimes embroidered at the edge with coloured wools when worn by a chief, their heads being closely shaven after the Persian fashion, with the exception of two locks, called 'zulf,' one on each side of the face. The Bakhtiyari usually twist round their skull-caps, in the form of a turban, a long piece of coarse linen of a brown colour, with stripes of black and white, called a 'lung,' one end of which is allowed to fall down the back, whilst the other forms a top knot. In other respects they wear the usual Persian dress, but made of very coarse materials, and, as a protection against rain and cold, an outer, loose-fitting coat of felt reaching to the elbows and a little below the knees. Their shoes of cotton twist, called 'giveh,' and their stockings of coloured wools, are made by their women. A long match-lock—neither flint-locks nor percussion-caps were then known to the Persian tribes—is rarely out of their hands. Hanging to a leather belt round their waist, they carry a variety of objects for loading and cleaning their guns—a kind of bottle with a long neck, made of buffalo-hide, to contain coarse gunpowder; a small curved iron flask, opening with a spring, to hold the finer gunpowder for priming; a variety of metal picks and instruments; a mould for casting bullets; pouches of embroidered leather for balls and wadding; and an iron ramrod to load the long pistol always thrust into their girdles. I have thus minutely described the Bakhtiyari dress as I adopted it when I left Isfahan, and wore it during my residence with the tribe.

I had some difficulty in making my way to Shefi'a Khan through this crowd of idlers, who were not a little surprised at learning that I was a Christian, and especially a 'Feringhi,' as they had never seen one before, and were evidently not quite certain as to how they should treat me. I found the Khan in a small room at the top of a rickety wooden staircase. He received me very civilly, and conducted me at once to Ali Naghi Khan. The Bakhtiyari chief was seated on a felt rug, leaning against a bolster formed of his quilt and bed-clothes rolled up in a piece of chequered silk. In front of him was a large circular metal tray, on which were little saucers containing various kinds of sweetmeats and condiments. In one hand he held a small porcelain cup, from which he occasionally sipped 'arak,' and in the other a 'kaleôn,' from which he drew clouds of smoke. An effeminate youth was singing verses from Hafiz and other Persian poets, accompanied by a man playing a kind of guitar. Ali Naghi Khan had unwound the shawl from his waist, and had unbuttoned his shirt and his robe, and on his closely shaven head was a small triangular cap made of Cashmere shawl, jauntily stuck on one side. It was evident that the chief was indulging in a debauch with four or five friends who were seated near him. But he had still his senses about him. I was amused at seeing in one of the corners of the room a mullah squatted upon his hams, and rocking himself to and fro whilst reading from the Koran, and interspersing with the text loud ejaculations of 'Ya Allah!' and 'Ya Ali!' apparently unmindful of the violation of the laws of his religion by his drunken associates.

Ali Naghi Khan was the second brother of Mehemet Taki Khan who at that time exercised authority over the greater part of the Bakhtiyari Mountains. He was on his way to Tehran, to be kept as a hostage for the good conduct of the chief, whose loyalty was suspected, and who had recently been in open rebellion against the Shah. Shefi'a Khan had accompanied him with an escort of retainers as far as Isfahan, whence he was about to proceed to the capital with a few attendants. He was a short, thick-set man, of about forty years of age, not ill-looking, and with an intelligent, though somewhat false, countenance.

Shefi'a Khan, kneeling down by his side, whispered to him the object of my visit. As soon as he learnt that I was an Englishman, he begged me to sit on the felt rug by his side, bade me welcome in very cordial terms, and offered me a cup of iced Shiraz wine and sweetmeats, which I could not refuse. We soon became boon companions over the bottle. It was my object to establish friendly relations with him, as I hoped through his influence and the recommendations he might give me to his brother to enter the Bakhtiyari Mountains.

We had scarcely commenced a friendly conversation when attendants entered, bearing upon their heads trays containing various kinds of pillaus, savoury stews, and other dishes. The arak, the wine, and the sweetmeats were speedily removed, and the trays having been placed on the floor, the guests gathered round them, crouching on their hams. I was invited to partake of the breakfast, which was excellent. Persian cookery is superior to that of any other Eastern nation. As I was a Frank and an infidel, I had a tray to myself, an arrangement to which I by no means objected, although I could never altogether get over the sense of humiliation at being treated as unclean and unfit to dip my fingers into the same dish with true believers.

After the breakfast had been removed and the usual kaleôns smoked, the Khan spoke to me about my contemplated journey to the Bakhtiyari Mountains. He had already been at Tehran, where he had acquired the manners and the vices of the Persians who frequented the court. As he had seen Englishmen in the capital and had learnt something about their habits and customs, I was able to make him understand the object of my journey, and to remove the impression that might have existed in his mind that I was a spy, or that I was travelling in search of buried treasures, or for the discovery of a talisman which would enable the Franks to conquer his country—for such are the usual reasons assigned by wild tribes like the Bakhtiyari to the presence of Europeans amongst them. These suspicions have more than once led to fatal results. He very readily answered some questions I put to him as to various ruins of which I had heard, and when he was unable to give me the information I required he sent for such of his attendants as might be able to supply it. He expressed regret that he was not returning to the mountains, otherwise, he said, I should have accompanied him, but he promised to give me a letter to his brother, and suggested that I should join Shefi'a Khan, who would shortly leave Isfahan for Kala Tul, the residence of Mehemet Taki Khan. I gladly agreed to avail myself of his offer.

The Matamet had met my request to be allowed to proceed either through Yezd or Kerman to the Seistan with so absolute a refusal, that I thought it better to renounce for the time any attempt to reach that district from Isfahan. The news of the occupation of Afghanistan by the British troops had caused great excitement in Central Asia, and had added greatly to the insecurity of the country on the eastern borders of Persia. The death of Dr. Forbes, who had been murdered in an attempt to reach the Lake of Furrah, was known to the Matamet, and he was persuaded that I should meet with the same fate, and that he would be held responsible for anything that might happen to me if he permitted me to undertake so dangerous an expedition. As he had the means of preventing me from carrying out my intention of going to Yezd, I decided upon waiting until the state of affairs might enable me to persevere in it. In the meanwhile I could employ my time usefully in exploring the Bakhtiyari Mountains, and in endeavouring to solve some interesting geographical and archælogical problems. Such were the reasons which induced me to renounce for the time my original plan of reaching Kandahar through the Seistan, but I was still resolved to adhere to it unless I found insurmountable difficulties in my way. Alone, and without official protection—England being in a state of war with Persia—and suspected of being a spy or an English agent, I was under the necessity of acting with extreme prudence and caution, although I was prepared to run any risk that the object I had in view should appear to me to justify.

Although Shafi'a Khan had assured me that he was about to leave Isfahan at once, the days passed by without any signs of his departure. I was continually going to and fro to the caravanserai, a ruined building in the middle of the city, to which he had removed after the departure of Ali Naghi Khan. There he sat, imperturbably smoking his kaleôn, on a raised platform of brickwork in the centre of a dirty yard in which his horses and mules and those of other travellers were tethered, and in which the smells were consequently almost intolerable. He had always some excuse ready to explain the delay. At one time it was a hostile tribe that had closed the road; at another he was endeavouring to raise, by the sale of his effects, money to pay his bill at the khan and to provide for the necessary expenses of his journey. Then the mullah who was to accompany him had failed, after opening the Koran and other books and consulting the first words on the page,[*] to name the day on which it would be propitious to begin the journey. His detention was, however, mainly caused by discussions with the Matamet, who wished to

---

[*] This mode of ascertaining the propitious moment for commencing an undertaking or a journey prevails among Mohammedans, and is called 'Istikâra.'

send one of his officers to collect the tribute from the Bakhtiyari tribes, and who was disposed to retain the Khan as hostage for its payment.

The five weeks that, in consequence of this delay, I passed in Isfahan were not unprofitably or unpleasantly spent. I continued to study the Persian language, which I began to speak with some fluency. I frequently visited the mosques (into which, however, I could not, as a Christian, enter), and the principal buildings and monuments of this former capital of the Persian kingdom now deserted by the court for Tehran. I was delighted with the beauty of some of these mosques, with their domes and walls covered with tiles, enamelled with the most elegant designs in the most brilliant colours, and their ample courts with refreshing fountains and splendid trees. I was equally astonished at the magnificence of the palaces of Shah Abbas and other Persian kings, with their spacious gardens, their stately avenues, and their fountains and artificial streams of running water, then deserted and fast falling to ruins. It was not difficult to picture to oneself what they must once have been. Wall-pictures representing the deeds of Rustem and other heroes of the 'Shah-Nameh,' events from Persian history, incidents of the chase and scenes of carouse and revelry, with musicians and dancing boys and girls, were still to he seen in the deserted rooms and corridors, the ceilings of which were profusely decorated with elegant arabesques. In the halls, the pavements, the panelling of the walls, and the fountains were of rare marbles inlaid with mosaic. The rills which irrigated the gardens and avenues were led through conduits of the same materials. Even the great carpets, the finest and most precious which had issued from Persian looms in the sixteenth and seventeenth centuries—unequalled for the beauty and variety of their designs and the fineness of their texture—were still spread upon the floors. The neglected pleasure-grounds were choked with rose-bushes in full bloom. These gorgeous ruins—desolate and deserted—afforded the most striking proof of the luxury and splendour of the Persian court in former times.

Mr. Burgess had several acquaintances amongst the notables of the city, who invited us to their houses and hospitably entertained us with breakfasts and dinners, at which I became acquainted with a great variety of excellent Persian dishes. They were, unfortunately, almost always accompanied by a free use of wine or arak, which generally preceded such feasts—Easterns rarely drink them during and after a repast—unless the host was a rigorous Musulman who looked upon all that intoxicates, or even exhilarates, as forbidden. Music and dancing were rarely wanting. The odes of Hafiz and Saadi, which have almost the same effect upon a Persian as the wine of Shiraz, were sung by professional reciters, and occasionally by some one of the company—for most educated Persians have a rich store of them in their memory.

But the most characteristic and curious scenes of Persian life were those I witnessed in the house of a Lur chief who had left his native mountains and had established himself in Isfahan, professing to be a 'sufi,' or free-thinker. He was an intimate friend and a distant connection of Shefi'a Khan, by whom I was introduced to him. He invited me more than once to dinner, and I was present at some of those orgies in which Persians of his class were too apt to indulge. On these occasions he would take his guests into the 'enderun,' or women's apartments, in which he was safe from intrusion and less liable to cause public scandal. They were served liberally with arak and sweetmeats, whilst dancing girls performed before them. Many of these girls were strikingly handsome—some were celebrated for their beauty. Their costume consisted of loose silk jackets of some gay colour, entirely open in front so as to show the naked figure to the waist; ample silk 'shalwars,' or trousers, so full that they could scarcely be distinguished from petticoats, and embroidered skullcaps. Long braided tresses descended to their heels, and they had the usual 'zulfs,' or ringlets, on both sides of the face. The soles of their feet, the palms of their hands, and their finger- and toe-nails were stained dark red, or rather brown, with henna. Their eyebrows were coloured black, and made to meet; their eyes, which were generally large and dark, were rendered more brilliant and expressive by the use of 'kohl.' Their movements were not wanting in grace; their postures, however, were frequently extravagant, and more like gymnastic exercises than dancing. Bending themselves backwards, they would almost bring their heads and their heels together. Such dances are commonly represented in Persian paintings, which have now become well known out of Persia. The musicians were women who played on guitars and dulcimers. These orgies usually ended by the guests getting very drunk, and falling asleep on the carpets, where they remained until sufficiently sober to return to their homes in the morning.

I called once or twice on the 'mujtehed,' or head mullah of the great mosque and of the Musulman religion in Isfahan. Although a very strict Mohammedan, and unwilling to be seen seated on the same carpet with a Christian—any manner of contact with an infidel rendering a follower of Islam unclean—he received me very courteously, and appeared to take pleasure in conversing with me about European manners and discoveries, and upon general politics. I always carefully avoided the discussion of subjects connected with religion—and especially controversial matters— in conversing with him and any other Persian Musulman, as an unguarded expression might have brought me into very serious trouble. In those days the fanatical Persians were apt to deal very summarily with anyone who might have used words which could be construed into an insult to their religion, or as blaspheming their Prophet. A Christian thus offending would have caused a public tumult, and might even have been torn to pieces.

Part Two

COLONIALISM AND RESISTANCE 1880–1950

OTTOMAN AND FORMER
OTTOMAN TERRITORIES

Historical Background

European involvement in the Muslim world, which accumulated as the century progressed, came to a head with the French invasion of Tunisia in 1881 and the British occupation of Egypt in 1882. Colonel Urabi, leader of the revolt of 1881–1882 against foreign interference in Egypt that took his name, 'came to be seen in some quarters as representing the authentic voice of the Egyptian people' (Cleveland 2000: 99). Muslims were not forward in staging coherent resistance to imperialism, though the earliest articulations of opposition frequently combined Islamic and nationalist loyalties, as was the case in Egypt in the first decade of the twentieth century. A European invention, nationalism had been invoked earlier in the century against the last Muslim empire, the Ottoman, by its Christian subject peoples: Greeks, Serbs, Bulgarians, Romanians and Armenians. As these achieved autonomy or, backed by the force and diplomacy of the Christian powers, split away, the largest non-Turkish population left in the Ottoman Empire was the Arabs. Preponderantly Muslims, with the exception of a small politically conscious group from among the Christian minority, hardly any contemplated let alone actively pursued the break up of the Ottoman Empire. But the Syrian reformer Abdul Rahman Kawakibi 'suggested that the Ottomans were responsible for the corruption of Islam, [and thus] introduced a nationalist argument that had profound implications for the Ottoman-Islamic order in the Arab provinces' (Cleveland: 125). Arabs and Turks briefly joined together to celebrate the 1908 Young Turk Revolution that forced the despotic Sultan Abdul Hamid to revive the 1876 Constitution he had revoked in 1878. Once in power, however, the radical Committee of Union and Progress alienated the other nationalities in the empire. Their repression of an Arab leadership in Beirut and Damascus during the Great War, together with the British sponsored Arab Revolt in the Hijaz that broke out in 1916, resulted in the defection of many Arabs from the Turkish side. Turkey's defeat along with the

Axis Powers in 1918 finished off the Ottoman Empire for good, while the sultanate and Islamic caliphate were ended by the parliament of the new Turkish Republic under Ataturk in 1924.

Egypt, after more than thirty years of undeclared British rule, most of it under Lord Cromer, was made a Protectorate on the outbreak of war in 1914. Under Cromer's rule foreign tentacles continued to spread over her commercial life, taking un-Islamic practices such as the selling of alcohol beyond the city and deep into countryside. The arrival of cinema and in the both World Wars large numbers of British and Australian soldiers further exposed Egyptians to Western influences. Politically, the country emerged in the early 1920s with a viable nationalist party, the Wafd led by Saad Zaghlul, poised to form an independent government. The constitution granted by the British in 1923 in reality represented only a form of 'semi-independence' (Mansfield 1971). Nor did the Anglo-Egyptian Treaty of 1936 secure the removal of British forces, which remained in occupation of the Canal Zone until 1956. But nowhere was the unraveling of Britain's brief imperialist 'moment' in the Middle East more marked than in Palestine. Having in the Balfour Declaration of 1917 pledged to create a 'national home' for the Jews, at the same time as they had raised the hopes of self-determination for the Arabs by backing the Arab Revolt, the British steered their League of Nations mandate for the country from crisis to crisis until peremptorily laying it down in 1948, so assisting a disaster for the Palestinian Arabs.

Travellers and their Narratives

The 1882 occupation of Egypt, with all that this meant for future British relations with the Ottoman Empire and the wider Muslim world, is encapsulated in Blunt's *Secret History of the English Occupation of Egypt* (1907), which while containing reminiscences of travel is more a political memoir than a piece of travel literature. By the time of its publication, travellers had been engaging with political and social changes in the Ottoman Empire for some while. The Turks' advance toward modernity is plotted in diverse ways in travel narratives of the period. In *A Wandering Scholar in the Levant* (1896), David Hogarth implied that any reform of the Ottoman Empire could only be superficial and was doomed to fail. Influential head of the Cairo Arab Bureau during the Great War and mentor to T.E. Lawrence, Hogarth's sceptical levity (which recalls that of Kinglake and Robert Curzon but is better informed) is not very dissimilar to the conservative desire to preserve an imagined Ottoman authenticity to be found in Mark Sykes' *Dar al-Islam* and *The Caliphs' Last Heritage*. Though they did not get on, Sykes and Gertrude Bell both used their travels to prepare themselves for a role in determining the Middle East's destiny. If Bell's expeditions in Syria and Asia Minor in the decade before the Great War made her less of a Turkophile than Sykes and more an admirer of the desert hierarchy of the Arab Bedouin, she avoided the latter's *volte-face* of planning the break up of the Ottoman Empire in the East during the war.

The Young Turk Revolution of 1908, an event which was generally seen at the time as representing a radical break with the East's despotic past, naturally enough drew to Istanbul both admirers and more sceptical critics of Turkey. Among these were political figures like Charles Roden Buxton, author of *Turkey in Revolution*, and the sympathetic journalists and Turkophiles, Grace Ellison and Marmaduke Pickthall. The patronizing note that runs through much Victorian and Edwardian travel writing on the Middle East is not entirely absent from Buxton's observations on the honeymoon period that followed the Young Turk takeover. However, Ellison wrote more sympathetically of Turkey's embrace of modernity, at least as far as the position of women was concerned. Nearly two hundred years after Lady Wortley Montagu, and at the precise moment that women were campaigning for the vote in Britain, Ellison challenged (and at the same time indulged) Western stereotypes of the seclusion of women in the East. Like Marmaduke Pickthall, who in 1917 declared himself a Muslim, Ellison's sketches of life in Istanbul were printed in the press before being published as *An Englishwoman in a Turkish Harem* (1915). She also disparaged, though in a milder form than Pickthall, Britain's 'betrayal' of her former ally.

As far as Egypt and the Egyptians are concerned it may be correct to say that the standard colonial attitude towards them was 'at best patronizing affection and at worst contemptuous dislike' (Mansfield 1971: xii). European travel writing on Egypt, that appears so definitive in the succession of canonical tomes penned in the eighteenth and nineteenth centuries, falls away quite drastically after 1918. C.S. Jarvis' publications on Egypt between the two world wars now seem a parody of the attitude Peter Mansfield describes, employing a comical colonialist discourse on 'the Arab' as a supercilious counterpoint to the strange, fast evaporating 'English romance' with the Bedouin. In Palestine, Thomas Hodgkin, a young British graduate from an impeccable elite background, treading uncertainly in T.E. Lawrence's footsteps as a would-be archaeological research student, stumbled into the contradictions of the British mandate. The engaging product of his stay, *Letters from Palestine*, alludes to Kinglake and Gertrude Bell as well as Lawrence whilst responding to modern complexities with a self-consciousness and self-irony that recall his contemporary Robert Byron.

DAVID GEORGE HOGARTH (1862–1927)

Orientalist scholars with specialist knowledge about an essentialist Orient were pressed into service as Western 'territorial acquisition in the Orient increased' (Said 1978: 223). This was especially the case as Britain and France parcelled out Asiatic Turkey between themselves; Said listed David Hogarth among the key 'experts' who aided this process. Hogarth was an academic whose Classical interests drew him to the Eastern domains of the Ottoman Empire, as confirmed by the title of his travel narrative: *A Wandering Scholar in the Levant* (1896). He began his travels there in 1887 and as a specialist with interests in the ancient Hittites returned in 1890. Academic recognition came with the publication of *Phillip and Alexander of Macedon* in 1887, and in the same year Hogarth was appointed Director of the British School of Athens. Confirmation of his fame as an archaeologist came when he was made a fellow of the British Academy in 1905. His interest in the Arab lands developed in the early 1900s and he published his account of Western exploration of that region, *The Penetration of Arabia*, in 1904. But it wasn't until the summer of 1916, when he went to Jeddah as part of a British delegation to negotiate with Husayn Sherif of Mecca, that Hogarth actually set foot on the Arabian Peninsula. By this time he was director of the Cairo Arab Bureau 'of intelligence and diplomatic officers...[set up] to organize Britain's role in the Arab Revolt' (Mansfield 1992: 168). He was instrumental in promoting the career of T.E. Lawrence, who he first met when leading the archaeological dig at Carchemish in 1911, bringing him to Cairo to join the Arab Bureau. A convinced imperialist who opposed the Sykes–Picot agreement, Hogarth's attitudes most likely rubbed off on Lawrence and helped give him 'an abiding hatred of Turks and French, Britain's biggest rivals in the Middle East' (ibid).

From:

A Wandering Scholar in the Levant **(1896)**

Among the imperial elite attitudes towards Turkey, masterfully exposed by Elie Kedourie in *England and the Middle East: the Destruction of the Ottoman Empire*

(1956), underwent a shift in the 1890s. The emerging ideas ranged from the conservative Turkophile position of Mark Sykes, who argued that the importation of Western ways was killing the authentic genius of the Turks, to the condescending view expressed here by Hogarth that reforms implemented under Sultan Abdul Hamid were only skin deep, and doomed to fail: the Oriental was 'probably happiest under a mildly "corrupt" and "oppressive" Government.' Among the defeatist nostrums that Hogarth projected on to the Turks, one – 'He will never fight again as he fought then, for faith is weaker' – would return to haunt the British at Gallipoli and Kut.

The Anatolian

Who else can arrest the Anatolian death? Not the Ottoman rejuvenated by any political alchemy. His organs are wasted too far to be saved by any "reforms." Reforms! How many have we pressed upon the Sick Man, and what is to show now? What, indeed, could there be to show for the introduction of corporate responsibility where no western sense of individual responsibility exists? The forms of a civilisation based on the equality of all men before the law have been imposed on those who, by religion and custom immemorial, respect persons. A system, pre-supposing development and progressive adaptation, is entrusted to a people who regard human initiative in change as an insult to the Creator. Centuries of slowly widened identification of the individual with the common claim of humanity lie behind the effective working of the European machine of government: in the Ottoman East the individual is considered alone; there are no common claims of humanity.

Picture a mean, whitewashed barrack, with a long alignment of dingy panes, cracked and patched with paper. It is ten years old, but its unlevelled precinct remains a slough in winter, a dustpit in summer. The crazy doors open on a corridor, along whose walls runs an irregular dado of grease where frowsy heads have reposed, and the floor twinkles with fleas. Push aside the mat hanging before one of the little dens which open right and left, and look at the dozen men sitting on the cheap Manchester cottons of the *diván:* eleven have no business there, the twelfth, whose "office" this is, is doing no more than the eleven. An occasional coffee, a more frequent cigarette, the listless fingering of beads, make up the morning and the evening. It is the reduction to the absurdest of a western bureau, this parade of desks and ledgers and files. Coffee-cups and ash-trays monopolise the first; and pages of the second are stopping the wind from a broken pane. A memorandum is penned slantwise on the folded knee and records are turned out on the floor from a wide-mouthed bag. In such dens as this all European travellers have had-their weary experiences of Ottoman officialism, but they may reckon safely that for every hour and every piastre that they spend in getting merely a visa for a passport the poor native must spend days and pounds.

They are an evil unmixed, these semi-pauper officials, who all must live and form a predatory class in direct contact with their prey, the peasantry. Things were better under the powerful Bureaucracy, which fell in the present reign; then there was more local knowledge at headquarters and less harem intrigue; a greater responsibility and a truer dignity in the official. Centralization is slow death in such an Empire as the Ottoman, whose nervous system of wires and roads is not half-developed, whose brain cannot adequately direct the members. In this heterogeneous loose-knit state such a feudal system as the rule of the *aghas* a century ago is perhaps best. The local lords at least were sensitive to the condition of the peasantry and were punished directly by their disorders. Justice at the city gate was done rudely, often venally, but at least done, and something was given back indirectly in the shape of alms and entertainment for what was taken. The great families, that could put a thousand horse in the field and sleep under their own roofs at every stage from Stambul to Baghdad, were doubtless too often brigands and foes to trade, but the Anatolian sighs now with the Old Pindari—

I'd sooner be robbed by a tall man who showed me a yard of steel,
Than be fleeced by a sneaking Baboo with a belted knave at his heel.

Now the descendants of the *aghas* who entertained Pococke, and Chandler, and Leake have perished utterly or lost their nobility and its obligations in official rank. Here and there an old man survives in ever increasing poverty, still eager to welcome the stranger, to offer all his house, and serve him with his own hands; but for the feudal chieftain, who will roast whole sheep and bid godspeed with fifty horsemen at his back, one must go to the Kurds and Circassians.

The only form of government understood in the Ottoman East is immediate personal government. The introduction of an official system results merely in the multiplication of personal governors. Where the governed supported one before, now they support ten. They never complained that they should have to support the governor; they complain now that governors should be so many. What we of the West term corruption and venality means often not more to the East than a recognized system of *aliquid pro aliquo*. Fixed stipends and centralized taxation are things not less alien to Eastern tradition than the equality of all men before Law that altereth not. The peasant feels it no hardship to pay directly for the services of the governor in proportion to his own needs or the governor's personal tariff; he likes to have visible value for his money, one year to pay nothing, the next to escape a visible prison by paying treble, and he prefers, on the whole, that his contributions should vanish into visible pockets. The one thing in the beginning of our administration of Cyprus disliked by the Cypriotes more than the regularity of our taxation was the incorruptibility of our local officials. The Oriental is a born bargainer. Where railways are new to him, as in Upper Egypt, he will offer half as much for his ticket as the booking-clerk demands, and delay the train while he chaffers for ten minutes at the window. Once I scornfully asked a Greek trader, who had been haggling over a certain bargain for a whole week and gained thereby one piastre and a half on the price first offered, at what he valued his time. "My time!" he exclaimed, "what else should. I do with it?"

The Oriental, therefore, is probably happiest under a mildly "corrupt" and "oppressive" Government. His indolence prefers action that is inconstant; his gambling instinct is gratified by inconsistency; and his fatalism secures him against any very acute mental misery. A piggish contentment with their lot has been remarked by all travellers as characterizing the Anatolian peasantry, notwithstanding that there may be "corruption" abroad unbelievable except by a Russian. In 1891 at a certain centre of government I heard that the post of Provincial Receiver, tenable for two years only, at a stipend of 70 pounds Turkish, had been assigned lately to a candidate who offered 200 as entrance fee: the ex-Receiver was pressing a claim for a stray sum of 800 not yet paid over to him on an official bargain! It is commonly notorious that not one-third of the provincial credits for public works is spent on such works, and European would-be concessionaires of mining or railway undertakings make no secret of setting aside thousands out of subscribed capital for "commission" on the desired *firman*. There is withal "oppression" of the most arbitrary kind; forced labour on Government works with the accompaniment of the whip; quartering of police at free rations on the poorest peasantry; tax-gatherers seizing the plough-ox or the last sack of seed-corn; sudden imprisonments and long detentions until money is paid, not for release, but for the preliminary privilege of trial.

But, all this notwithstanding, there is no misery apparent in most Anatolian villages. The peasant's standard of living is not high, his wants are few, and such as earth supplies to little labour. Ordinary taxation, which he hates, is very low, extraordinary requisitions are not resented. Religion guarantees his exclusive possession of his women-folk, and a bare subsistence in any event. Not being highly developed, he does not feel acutely physical pain, but accepts a beating at the hands of a police trooper as a schoolboy takes a flogging. The gulf between prosperity and adversity is neither deep nor wide: the richest man of a village commonly lives in a similar house on like food and drink the same life of manual labour as the poorest: a roof, four walls, bread, water and sexual joys are all that either craves. The luxuries of Anatolian life are its necessities, slightly more abundant.

These nations of the East are in their childhood, but it is their second childhood. They began to live before us, and in a climate where there is no strenuous battle to fight with Nature have developed racially, as they develop individually, more rapidly than we. The Egyptian was adult while we were in the Caves, and the Anatolian was living in great cities when we were setting up shapeless monoliths on Salisbury Plain. Now they are all very old and cannot put on again their youthful energy, or fall into the ways of a later generation. How seldom do we realise this truth in thought or speech! It is a commonplace to regard the Eastern nations as children, to whom we are schoolmasters. India is to be taught Western methods, Egypt set in the path of our own development, Turkey regenerated in our image. Vanity of all vanities! here is the sheerest alchemy! It is *we* that are the children of these fathers; we have learned of them, but we shall surpass and outlive them, and our development is not just what theirs has been, even as development of a second generation is never quite like that of the first. When we speak of educating India or Egypt we are the modern son who proposes to bring his father up to date. We are dominant in those lands for the sake not of their but our own development, and in order to use them as our own "stepping-stones to higher things." It is possibly not amiss for our own moral nature that we should hug an altruistic illusion at home, and we find little difficulty in doing so; but it is less easy abroad. No one who has been long in Egypt appears ever to tall about the "political education" of the Egyptians.

The Old Man in Anatolia neither craves nor can thrive on our strong meats. He has lost all keenness of desire, and is not equal to a new line of life. The young West takes him in hand, shakes him out of his lethargy, pushes him hither and thither, and makes fuller the evening of his life; but likewise it makes it shorter. What more hopeful moral are we to draw from all the history of the concourse of civilised and uncivilised races? The Turk, indeed, is a little less obviously effete than some other Orientals, because his upper class has been reinvigorated continually from younger stocks, the debt of the ruling families of Stambul to their Caucasian wives passing all estimation. But, none the less, those who knew the Turk before the War and know him now speak of manifest decline. He will never fight again as he fought then, for faith is weaker. His extremities no longer answer the call of the brain, Yemen in revolt, the Hejaz indifferent, Egypt separated, Kurdistan defiant, the Balkan provinces under a suzerainty not a sovereignty. And all these people—Arabs, Kurds, Bulgars—are "younger" than that aboriginal stock which formed the backbone of his armies twenty years ago. Most significant of all signs, he has lost heart himself. Already he foretells the stations in the retreat of the Crescent—Stambul to

Brusa, Brusa to Aleppo, Aleppo to Baghdad; and Moslem mothers tell their children that this or that will come to pass as surely as a cross will be seen again on Santa Sophía. And, be sure, the Turk will make no effort himself to arrest his own decay; for as faith grows weaker, the original sin of fatalism waxes more strong—that fatalism which has been mistaken so often for a symptom of Islam, but preceded it and will survive.

MARK SYKES (1879–1919)

Believing his son's lungs should not be exposed to English winters, Mark Sykes' father took him with him on journeys through the continents of Europe, Asia, Africa and America in the 1880s and 1890s. These early travels may have contributed to Sykes' distaste for modernity and helped form the essentializing statements about the East we frequently find in his travel writings. In the late 1890s he traversed Palestine, Syria and Iraq and *Through Five Turkish Provinces*, a write-up of these journeys, appeared in 1899. Returning to Syria and eastern Turkey in 1903, he published *Dar-ul-Islam* the following year. Sykes had by now acquired a mannered jokey style à la Kinglake, with burlesque passages of dialogue that look forward to Robert Byron. To this he added an opinionated array of pseudo-authoritative observations on the racial characteristics of the diverse peoples of the eastern Ottoman lands. Strongly pro-Turk, he disparaged their subject races, especially the Armenians and Jews. *The Caliphs' Last Heritage* (1915) mixes an extensive history of the Ottomans with narrative of journeys through Ottoman territory made from 1906 almost yearly until 1913. As the title implies, Sykes saw the current Near East in terms of a noble but dying civilization; but not content with decrepitude 'instead of respecting their own traditions, Easterners had caught the Western contagion of progress' (Adelson 1975: 101). Ironically, by the time the book appeared Sykes had dropped his frenetic pre-war pro-Turk propagandizing in which he warned his country of the dangers of the fall of the Ottoman Empire. Now a member of a War Office Committee that recommended its partition among the allies, he was preparing the way for the notorious Sykes–Picot agreement that accomplished precisely this when the war was over.

From:

Dar-ul-Islam (1904)

Having passed through Syria into the mountains of eastern Turkey Sykes' party experiences harsh winter conditions. Always looking out for markers of racial distinctiveness Sykes congratulates himself on recognizing the Alawis who unlike the hardy Turkish soldier cannot be true Turks because they speak with animation. His stilted optimism on the situation of the Armenians in the Ottoman Empire would shortly prove disastrously incorrect; but in the early 1900s Sykes' pro-Turk views were paramount.

To Derendeh

We rode on to Yeni-yapalak, a village some four miles from Albistan, where the Shaykh, who was exceedingly hospitable, is the possessor of a very beautiful guest-room. We asked him if he would sell it us to take to England— 'Willingly,' he replied, 'if it were not that I should then have no place in which to receive another English Bey Effendi if he came.' It was again pleasing to see several Armenians in the Shaykh's house, whom he served with coffee with his own hands.

While stopping there I noticed the intelligence and vivacity of the company, which I could in no way associate with Osmanli stolidity, but which rather reminded one of the Arab. I enquired of what race were the inhabitants, and they stoutly answered that they were Turks; notwithstanding this, however, one of the Armenians winked very knowingly. On subsequent inquiry from the Zaptieh it appeared that they were Alawieh Shiahs. This curiously isolated people were until lately nomadic, but have been induced by the Government to live in villages. Their religion is supposedly Shiah, including that extraordinary reverence for Ali which appears to run into every kind of extravagance wherever it obtains.

The men, who never cut their beards, are strikingly handsome and exceedingly intelligent: their sense of humour approaches the Arab; their bright eyes, quick movements, and smartness in repartee make it easy to distinguish them from the slow, ponderous, and phlegmatic Turkish peasant, although their dress is precisely the same. Their women are remarkably good-looking, and their children beautiful.

They are excellent farmers, being as good as Circassians, using similar wheeled trucks. Their houses are well built; and I noticed in their villages that the snow was systematically cleared from the streets, a thing unheard of among the Turks or Kurds. Jacob remarked to me that they were, very like Druses; I was at once struck by the similarity and am curious to know if there is any relation between the two. Without any scientific data, and speaking only from observation, it seems to me that there might be some connection—the good looks, the progressive methods of cultivation, the superior intelligence and secret religion, serve as a hint which would be well worth following up. Lord Warkworth's description of the Avshars of Yalak in no way tallies with

the Alawieh, with whom I think some travellers have confounded them. It is
to be hoped that any one who is in the Taurus will make as much investigation
as possible concerning this interesting people.* The Shaykh accompanied us
a short way out of the village mounted on a pretty little stallion.

From New Yapalak to Old Yapalak is a ride of about three-quarters of an
hour; the latter village is inhabited by true Osmanlis—a remarkable contrast
to the cheerful Shiah.

Our ride from Old Yapalak to Yeni Keui, on the following day, bid fair to
be our last. We started with a fine frosty sun, the ground thawing pleasantly
beneath its rays. About three hours later on, however, the sky grew cloudy,
and signs of an approaching blizzard were not wanting, little cold puffs of
wind bringing small powdered flakes of snow and leaving soft woolly packs
following behind. Seeing this the Zaptiehs wisely advised us to abandon our
visit to the lions and make for Yeni Keui. To reach that village we were obliged
to leave the main track and make across the snow. This seemed no great feat,
but the going was so heavy that the horses plunged over their hocks in the
deep drifts. Just as our whole party were ploughing through a particularly
steep and difficult valley the blizzard broke with fearful violence, and for a few
moments one could hardly breathe or see. The wretched animals seemed
paralysed, and two lay down quite helpless. We struggled on, but when the
squall had passed, to our surprise and dismay, no village was in sight; only a
long-stretching vista of drifted snow hemmed in by rolling clouds close to the
ground, our old track completely hidden. The fact that we were hardly able
to move more than three-quarters of a mile an hour, with no sign of the
direction of our destination before us and the certain knowledge that if we
were out after nightfall a most unpleasant death awaited us—a death which a
great number of muleteers had suffered that very month—served to make a
sufficiently unpleasant situation. Luckily, however, we saw two men on foot
eight hundred yards to our left: to these we made signs of distress, and they
came to our assistance as quickly as they could and led us in the right
direction. Although we had only two miles and a half to go, we were three
hours in reaching the village; indeed, so exhausted were we on our arrival that
another half-mile would have been too much. We soon found an evil-smelling
hovel, where we were glad enough to lie down and rest.

Here we found three Zaptiehs awaiting us, having been despatched hither
from Derendeh.

The next day we walked out to the 'probably Hittite lions.' Only one is
standing; the other was overthrown, according to local report, by a European

---

* Antiquaries had better note that at New Yapalak there is a marble Ionic column which
looks as if there might be something worth digging for.

wit travelling in the neighbourhood. They are both fine examples of early impressionist work; indeed at first one is at some difficulty to distinguish the head from the tail, which is just what is wanted in a really artistic presentment; the spectator then gets in harmonic touch with the sculptor. These lions have every advantage of the Rodin School: they are repulsively ugly, hopelessly misshapen, their mouths are growing in the middle of their chests, and, further, they bear no more resemblance to lions than the bandy-legged, sinewy, simian green gentleman at South Kensington does to St. John the Baptist.

From the Rodinian lions we struggled on towards Derendeh, having left Halil behind with a horse that had fallen ill. The road was so heavy that we only reached Ashodeh about three o'clock, and were obliged to stop there.

Ashodeh is credited in the guide-book with two thousand houses. If this is correct, which I cannot doubt, the five hundred inhabitants, who form the total population, must be well off for lodgings. The Armenian church and convent were not destroyed during the massacres but were in ruins some years previously. According to the local Armenians things are now progressing very well, and there is no present cause for complaint.

Indeed, although one does not wish to be too sanguine, there certainly appears to be a decided improvement in the situation in the whole district, and if the Armenians are by no means in good circumstances, there is a prevailing tone of better feeling between them and the Moslems which has the outward appearance of a more hopeful time to come.

The following morning, about an hour after leaving Ashodeh, we reached Derendeh, the Mudir of the former town, a Circassian, insisting on accompanying us. On our arrival we were well entertained by the Kaimakam, who had received telegraphic instructions from the Vali of Sivas in anticipation of our arrival: two rooms were provided for us above the local café, and every care was taken that we should be comfortable. No sooner were we under cover than the snow came tumbling down in heavy flakes; half an hour later Halil entered, weeping, with the news that the sick horse was dead.* Poor beast! The snow and cold had been too much. This was our first casualty.

There are moments when one has doubts as to one's own intelligence, and when I found myself staring at the snow and smelt the café oozing through the floor, and blew my nose, in which there was a cold, and cleared my throat, in which there was a soreness, and shook my head, in which there was an ache, I pondered on the five snow-strewn days that lay between me and Malatia, and thought that if ever there was an obstinate, self-proved idiot he

---

* My dear wiseacre, although you have travelled in Turkey you are quite wrong—he brought the tail with him as a proof.

was an Englishman who rode through the Taurus in winter. I had been warned, and in my pride and folly had disregarded the warning, and now I was justly punished.

Similar thoughts were evidently passing through Jacob's mind as he glared at me, crying, 'Ah! sir, what evil have we done that our Lord God should have hardened our hearts to come into this accursed land of Kurds and Armenians and Turks—fools so simple that they do not flee from it, but remain here to starve!'

The town of Derendeh is not exactly described in 'Murray's Handbook,' which states, on p. 261, that 'the *old town*, now partly in ruins, lies on the narrowest part of the river gorge, and is dominated by a strong castle on the right bank.'

As a matter of fact, the strong citadel is a miserable heap of ruined mud buildings; the masonry, such as remains, is hardly more than dry stone walling, and the whole castle is not worth climbing the mountain to see. The ruined town still possesses a few houses and three mosques; the rest, a space of about 150 acres, is merely a mass of broken walls and fallen houses. The konak is situated in the ruined town, as also a small bazaar and large khan, which is still in use.

The new town straggles for about one hour and a half's walk down the gorge: it contains three hundred and sixty Armenian houses besides two thousand Turkish and Kurdish. It possesses some fine gardens, and in the future will be a large market for vegetables and fruit. The town is blessed with a boil, much the same as that of Aleppo but not quite so formidable; the scar it leaves. behind is not larger than a threepenny piece.

The inhabitants of the district have adopted the Circassian or Cossack flannel hood for winter wear—a curious innovation—and this sudden alteration of fashion in dress is very striking in the so-called unchanging East. As a matter of fact orientals often do alter their customs in a very curious and unexpected manner: tobacco and coffee, for instance, were adopted quite suddenly, although now it would be hard to imagine the East without either.

It was our evil fortune to encounter a fall of snow at Derendeh so heavy that every route was blocked, and we were caged like rats in a trap. Of all the dismal places to be snowed up in, a Turkish café is the worst: the temperature varies from stifling heat when the stove is lit to freezing point when it goes out: a feat it performs twice in each hour. A tinker kept a shop next door, who was tapping every tune one knew on his wares. The wretched dogs crept up to catch the warmth of the rooms, and huddled round the doors, snapping, snarling, and growling day and night. The smell of stale narghillies, bad cigarettes, and dirty hot water pervaded everywhere, and the tinker's tunes were only interrupted by the rattling of the backgammon board.

From my window the only sight I could see was the ever-falling snow and a tumble-down minaret, up which a worthy old gentleman climbed in all weathers. I could see his jaws moving, but either the wind was so high or he was so husky that he was inaudible.

Four days later it ceased snowing, and a thaw set in. A thaw in England is generally an unpleasant period—in the Taurus it is a damnable one. Although there are no water pipes to burst, yet every house is flooded; for the roofs, being flat and only plastered with mud, are turned into slushy poultices. The various dogs, cats, and mules that have perished in the streets during the frost, and which the snow has covered, begin to attract attention; the offal heaps, silent during the cold months, now proclaim with loud voices that 'there is no sanitary officer but the dog and the vulture,' and forthwith begin their appointed task of reducing the surplus population with enteric, typhus, and diphtheria. The brick-arched bazaars sag and fall in where the melting snow has weakened the keystones, crushing anybody whose Taqdir* provides them with a martyr's[†] death.

In the offices of the Valis and Kaimakans the water drips from the ceiling into files of official reports, and makes short work of those priceless manuscripts. In the houses of the rich the windows of the selamliks and harems are being patched with brown paper, while poorer inhabitants temporarily prop up their dwellings with poles, and begin seriously to contemplate building fresh ones. The mule tracks and chaussées are ripped and torn with floods; embankments slip down; culverts vanish; and bridges, tired of their stationary lot, slide gently off their piers, and hurry down stream; marshes and swamps appear in the most unexpected places—in the governor's reception-rooms, in the foundations of the barracks, in the floors of the cafés, and in the baker's ovens. Yet of all this discomfort the inhabitants make no complaint: the Vali is just as dignified on his divan if his secretary has to throw him reports and papers across a little stream in the centre of the room; the gossip and chatter in the cafés is none the less because the customers have to perch themselves on tables; the soldiers are not more miserable because a barrack-room collapsed, killing ten men the night before; the merchants are not distressed if caravans are delayed two or three weeks. No one shows any surprise; no one does anything to improve matters; everything goes on as usual. And it is for this reason that it is so hard for a European to understand an oriental. English people under the same circumstances would fret and fume, curse the Government, sweat and toil, until the authorities took some action; but in the East, not only do people do nothing themselves, but they would by no means be pleased if the Government did.

---

* Destiny, from Arab to decree, predestine.
[†] Anyone on whom a house shall fall is a martyr. Mohammedan belief.

The Government in India have had experience of this inexplicable trait during the plagues and epidemics, when the people have almost threatened rebellion unless they were suffered to rot in peace. Orientals hate to be worried and hate to have their welfare attended to—oppression they can bear with equanimity, but interference in their private affairs, even for their own good, they never brook with grace.

CHARLES RODEN BUXTON (1875–1942)

Charles Buxton came from a family that had acquired wealth in the brewing industry and after an illustrious career at Cambridge where he took a first in Classics was called to the bar. Liberal in politics, with a strong social conscience, in 1902 Charles became Principal of Morley College, an institute for workingmen and women in South London. The DNB comments: 'Christian principles informed Buxton's politics and all aspects of his life.' Together with his older brother, Noel, he helped form the Balkan Committee, a pressure group which promoted the cause of the Balkan Christian nationalities. Although he claimed the Committee had the 'sole objective of improving the condition of the European subjects of Turkey, Moslem and Christian alike' it was generally critical of Ottoman governments. Following the Young Turk revolution, Buxton went to Istanbul as an invited observer to be present at the opening of the new parliament. *Turkey in Revolution* captures the optimism of the early period of Young Turk rule, before the British political establishment became severely critical of the Committee of Union and Progress. The Balkan Committee actively sided with the Balkan nations in the wars that followed, the Buxton brothers journeying to Bulgaria in 1914 presumably to report further Turkish 'atrocities'.

From:

***Turkey in Revolution* (1909)**

Buxton's account of the opening of the first parliament in Istanbul since Abdul Hamid annulled the constitution thirty years previously focuses on the Sultan, 'for all his pomp [parliament's] prisoner and…puppet'. He also has the sagacity to point out 'it is the men in frock-coats who are going to make or mar, within these walls, the destiny of Turkey'.

The Opening of Parliament

A day of brilliant sun and cold, crisp air, contrasting delightfully with the weeks of gloomy weather which have preceded it; the whole population in the streets; joy in the most inexpressive faces; bright scarlet banners, with the crescent and star in white, waving from every window, with here and there a green one, to vary the almost universal red. Our road, which the procession will follow later, dips down from Pera, crosses the Old Bridge over the Golden Horn, where every ship is gay with flags, rises to the grand mosque of Suleiman, and then descends slowly towards the Palace of Justice, on the point of the peninsula, where stood the ancient city of Byzantium. There are soldiers, in couples, every twenty yards. On the site of the Forum of Theodosius, now the approach to the War Office, the road is lined by heavy cavalry on white Hungarian horses, their uniforms a dark grey, with red pennons at the points of their long upright lances. The mind goes back to the processions of old, the pomp of the Emperors of the East, with the long hierarchy of gorgeous officials, and the gold and silver plate, the priceless silken hangings displayed at the windows and balconies; far exceeding the procession of to-day in grandeur, but never equalling it in significance. We cross the Forum of Constantine, marking the spot where he planted his banner before the final victory over Licinius. Just to our right lies the Hippodrome, where Justinian stooped to take a part in the fierce factions of the circus. And as we push our way with difficulty into the great oblong space in front of the Parliament House—the Palace of Justice, where the Parliament met in 1877—we are treading the Augusteum, over-looked to-day, as it was fourteen centuries ago, by the vast but clumsy exterior of St. Sophia.

A moment's parleying among the high dignitaries at the gate, and we slip through, cross the court, ascend a broad stair to the first floor, and are installed in a low gallery at the side of the Chamber, like a big box at a theatre. By good fortune, it has a window, which looks down upon the open space through which we have just passed. We have time to take in the view.

The side to our right is formed by the lower domes of St. Sophia, to whose edges clusters of women in black or violet seem to be clinging somewhat precariously; there is just a glimpse of the huge central dome, culminating in its gilded crescent. The buildings on the left are hidden from us by the angle of a wall. Right in front, at the farther end where the procession will enter, is a huddle of houses rising up the hillside, and crowned by the solid Serasker tower, white against a cloudless sky.

The crowd is enormous. From above it seems all red—a sea of fezzes—save for the white turbans of the priests and the white flags borne by the students of the Law School. It sways to and fro excitedly, and the soldiers are pretty free with the butts of their rifles now and then, but it never resists, it is gentle and good-humoured, and not one serious accident is reported. The infantry in dark blue, four ranks deep, keep a wide path open down the middle for the procession—wide but winding, with a want of precision which adds greatly to the artistic effect. A place of honour by the gate is occupied by the khaki-clad "chasseurs" from the Macedonian garrison, who played a notable part in the Revolution. The bands play the new "Constitution hymn"; they play it again and again, as if the people could never have enough of it. At one point on the right the midday sun catches a group of brass instruments and makes a blinding glare of them.

From the window we watch the deputies arriving one by one. The military members are in uniform, which they will discard after the first sitting. Most are in fez and frock-coat; but here comes a Kurd, striding along in a long cape of black and white fur, and a black cap surrounded by a turban; and yonder the Arab deputy from the Yemen, his graceful *keffiyeh*, shot with green and faint purple, falling down on either side of a dark, black-bearded face, and his long black robe sweeping the ground. The Ministers come separately, in black Civil Service uniform, encrusted with gold, and set off by a broad green sash The *ulema*, the heads of the Moslem Church, in long, full robes of brilliant green, gold collar, and large white turban; the Sheikh-ul-Islam, all in white save for his turban of deep yellow; the Greek patriarch, in black, with a green collar, looking immensely dignified; the Armenian patriarch; the Bulgarian exarch; the representative of the Holy See, in flowing purple robe and cap; and, finally, the Diplomatic Corps, in plumed cocked hats and stiff, uncomfortable coats, advancing in order of seniority; these are among the chief of the guests. A special round of applause greets the English ambassador.

Within, the House fills rapidly. It is a square room of no great size, painted white, with curtains and upholstery of white and red—the national colours. The platform or tribune of the President, with the tables of the secretaries below, occupies most of one side. The deputies sit facing it, each with a desk before him; rows of red fezzes, relieved by from thirty to forty white turbans. There are galleries on each of the other three sides. Immediately below the President's tribune sit the senators and the dignitaries of the Church. Separate places were reserved for the Moslem and the Christian ecclesiastics; but the former invite the latter to sit with them, and the little symbol of fraternisation is appreciated. Ahmed Riza, the leader of the Young Turks, is kissed on the forehead by an ancient *mollah*. Several members of the Committee of Union and Progress, including Enver Bey, are accommodated on the floor of the House. The last of the deputies walk in and take their places. A pause ensues. The *mise-en-scène* is complete.

* * * * *

The climax came swiftly. A sudden clamour of bugles; the troops, with fixed bayonets, presented arms; the bands struck up (for the first time) the Hamidieh March; we turned towards the open space outside, and round the corner at the far end a squadron of cavalry, holding their white horses at a steady canter, their red pennons fluttering above, swung into the arena. They were through it in a moment, and had barely time to line up on either side of the entrance gate before the Sultan's carriage was passing through them at a fast trot—a light victoria with the hood up, drawn by four bays. Facing him sat his son, Burhan-ed-din, and the Grand Vizier. The speed of the procession, which had covered the four miles from Yildiz Kiosk in half an hour, made a regular order almost impossible, and one got but a fleeting impression of two or three other carriages, encompassed rather than followed by a cloud of horsemen—princes and aides-dc-camps, dazzling uniforms, a rapid advance, a sudden halt.

There was a pause while the Sultan and his suite came up the stair, and then, before we expected it, he was standing there before us, in a little square box to the President's left, lit at the back by electric light. The old man's silhouette was sharply defined; the simple fez, the head bent forward in melancholy lassitude, the short form clad in a thick military overcoat of dark grey, edged with red, with heavy epaulettes. He stood there saluting, and all the assembly stood in silence. Then he handed a roll of paper, the Speech from the Throne, to the Master of the Ceremonies, who carried it down to be read by the First Secretary of the Palace, while the Ministers, including the commanding figure of the Sheikh-ul-Islam, filed in to their places. "In spite of evil counsellors, we resolved to order the election of a new Parliament." There was a hoarse, almost a fierce, murmur of applause. These deputies knew well that the man at whose name, for thirty years, a whole empire trembled, stood there, for all his pomp, their prisoner and their puppet. He stood nervously, now raising a white-gloved hand to adjust his fez, but for the most part leaning forward, with hands clasped on his sword-hilt, shifting at intervals from one foot to the other. The speech ended; and the blare of trumpets and the dull boom of a hundred cannon announced to the city that the Parliament was opened.

Then the oldest of the *ulema* rose, and, turning towards the Sultan, prayed that God might bless the Sovereign and prosper the new Constitution; while all the assembly, and the Sultan himself, stood with arms outstretched and palms turned upwards. The voice was high and nasal, but full of feeling. The prayer was punctuated by low murmurs of approbation, suggesting oddly a revivalist meeting. And at the end the strange little figure in the box seemed to pull itself together, and quite unexpectedly (for it formed no part of the programme) spoke in a low voice a few quite simple but emphatic words; the left hand holding the sword, the right extended towards the deputies. It gave him "extraordinary" pleasure to see them assembled there; he prayed God for the continuance and success of the Parliament. Again he saluted slowly, and withdrew. It was over.

* * * * *

What were his thoughts? His eyes, wandering restlessly over the assembly, might have discerned men whom he had sent to exile a quarter of a century ago; men whose nearest and dearest had "disappeared" at his order. In a far corner he may have noted the little group of young officers at whose daring blow the whole structure of his despotism had tumbled like a house of cards. Did there penetrate into that unlettered brain, behind the high, abnormally narrow forehead, any sense of the strange vicissitudes of his fortune, and the depth of a nation's forgiveness? The drive from Yildiz, which he had so much dreaded, had been a triumph; the people, who would hardly have been blamed if they had torn him from limb to limb, had shouted themselves hoarse, delighted to see him once more in their midst; and here were their chosen representatives, in Parliament assembled; and here was he, the lord of a great empire still; and he was an old man; and the new *régime* seemed at any rate safer and pleasanter than the old. Did those impromptu words of his come with a sudden impulse from the heart?

*****

In the lobbies they are occupied with other questions than these. Why did the Sultan not renew his oath to observe the Constitution? There is some dissatisfaction over this, and the deputies refuse to take the oath of loyalty individually; it is merely read out by the President, and a general assent given by the whole House. The business begins; credentials are presented. The plumes and the sashes, the tinsel and the steel, are trivialities; it is the men in frock-coats who are going to make or mar, within these walls, the destiny of Turkey.

But all interest centres for the moment on the departure of the Sultan and the distinguished guests. The brilliant show melts gradually away, the crowd singling out its favourites for vociferous applause. The magnificent inauguration has had its uses, if it has impressed on the popular mind the greatness of the change, the glory of the new era of liberty. Before the sun goes down the city is already illuminated. As twilight deepens into dark, the swirling surface of the Bosphorus reflects the fairy-lights of a score of palaces; rockets shoot up from every quarter; the ships in the Golden Horn, lit up from stem to stern, flash their searchlights over roofs and domes and towers; little rings of light surround the muezzins' galleries at the summit of the tall minarets; while reckless holidaymakers discharge their revolvers into the air.

But the queerest thing about all this revelry is its short duration. Only those whose deeds are evil go out at night in Constantinople; and the habit of early sleep is not easily broken. By seven o'clock the lights have begun to wane. By nine the whole population is in bed, and we stumble home in the dark, while the watchman, according to immemorial custom, is tapping with his long staff the deserted pavements.

GRACE ELLISON (d.1935)

Journalist and feminist, Grace Ellison was a strong Turkophile who publicized the cause of Turkish women in newspaper articles written from within 'a Turkish harem'. She met Zeyneb Hanim, daughter of a government minister, in Istanbul in 1905. Zeyneb and her sister Melek had organised dinners in their home to discuss women's rights until forbidden by the government. The restless sisters then wrote to the French author Pierre Loti, who met them clandestinely and incorporated their stories into his sentimental novel, *Les Désenchantées*. Subsequently, Ellison visited the sisters in Paris where they had fled in fear of their lives. Together with Zeyneb she co-authored *A Turkish Woman's European Impressions* (1913). In the introduction Ellison wrote: 'I, who through the veil have studied the aimless, unhealthy existences of these pampered women, am nevertheless convinced that the civilization of Western Europe for Turkish women is a case of exchanging the frying-pan for the fire.' In *An Englishwoman in a Turkish Harem* (1915), published in *The Daily Telegraph* in the form of 'letters home', she described the sequestered day-to-day existence she led in the house of another Turkish friend, Makboulé Hanim, who she called Fatima. Ellison took pains to deconstruct the misconceptions of her fellow countrymen about the lives of Eastern women – she wrote she had been told not to use the word 'harem' in a public lecture because it might raise audience expectation of 'improper revelations'. Nevertheless, *An Englishwoman in a Turkish Harem* retains the word in its title and includes a photograph of the author as a veiled Turkish woman. According to Reina Lewis, Ellison remained 'captivated by the exoticism of Turkey and did not want to diminish the differences between East and West into a bland homogeneity' (Lewis 2004: 100). She was under no illusion concerning the 'ugly, unprotected existence of some of the women of my country'.

After the end of the First World War, Ellison returned to Turkey, writing two further books: *An Englishwoman in Angora* (1923), and *Turkey To-day* (1928), re-iterating her support for a reformed Turkey and expressing her admiration for Mustapha Kemal Atatürk.

From:

An Englishwoman in a Turkish Harem (1915)

When Ellison writes of the imperial harem – 'still…the harem about which Western readers expect to hear, the part of the Oriental house exclusively reserved for the use of women' – she is describing what for the West was a quintessential sign of the Orient but which had already become an anachronism. Still, in her closing remarks about the new Sultan – brother of the now deposed Abdul Hamid – 'He who was obedient to his brother is now obedient to the Constitution; perhaps for Turkey it is better he should be so' – we catch, in spite of Ellison's oft-pronounced support for the Young Turks and their feminist policy, a note of nostalgic ambivalence.

The Imperial Harem—A Reception by the Sultan

It has been the privilege of many foreigners visiting Constantinople to witness the ceremony of *baise-main*, which takes place at the Dolma Bagtché Palace, but it does not fall to the lot of every woman to see that imposing ceremony from the Imperial harem. This unique and interesting experience I owe to my hostess, Fâtima.

The ceremony of baise-main is too well known for me to describe it here, and those persons who were seated in the gallery reserved for the Corps Diplomatique would no doubt see to better advantage than I the throne-room, the Sultan, and the curious and many-coloured uniforms and costumes of the Ottoman subjects who paid their homage to the Kaliph of Islam. Through the lattice-work windows of the Imperial harem it was difficult to form more than a vague idea of the ceremony, for we were so many women huddled together on the cushions, so many who were trying to see, that after a few moments I gave my seat to another lady in order to wander at leisure through the Imperial harem, where Fâtima tells me I am the first Englishwoman to be admitted as a visitor.

It was the first day of Baïram. We were awakened at dawn by the plaintive cries of the sacrificed sheep. Réchad, the coachman, was chosen as vékil (sacrificer), because he is recognized by the whole household as the most pious of us all, and his forty-five years of service also demand that this privilege should be his. His, too, was the privilege of distributing the meat, the skin, and the horns of the four sheep which this Moslem household offered to the poor, who came in through the open gates like a pack of hungry wolves, and looked, with their poor ravenous eyes, as if they could tear the meat from the hands of the coachman. To me, standing on the balcony, it was like watching a scene from the Old Testament—a scene all out of focus with so many of the attempts at progress which I see around this beautiful and interesting capital.

How strange it seemed also to be dressing for Court at 6.30 in the morning! To be putting on thin silk evening dresses and slippers at that early hour, and driving away in the chilly morning to pay our homage to an Eastern monarch.

Fâtima's dress was of pink crêpe-de-chine embroidered in dull silver—a Paris creation—the last, however, she will ever have embroidered outside Turkey, for, like so many other ladies here, she has now awakened to the fact that the most costly embroideries of Europe are but poor imitations of the work of her own land. Round her hair she wore a pink and silver scarf, attached to the side by a silver rose, a charming variation of the curious turbans of flowers, feathers, and jewels which are worn by so many of the ladies attending the Ottoman Court. I asked Fâtima if the Court officials gave instructions to the ladies regarding their dress. "Provided their hair be decently covered," she replied, "etiquette is satisfied," and the Caliph has the "supreme" privilege of seeing all his subjects unveiled.

Like most of the ladies of the Court, we were attended by a slave, my negress, Miss Chocolate, an interesting personage in her Court attire. For this occasion she was dressed in pale blue satin, with a pale blue turban trimmed with pink roses, her fingers, arms, and neck being covered not only with all the jewellery she possessed, but the jewellery of the other slaves. It was her duty to follow us all the while, and during luncheon she stood inside the door with folded arms, in case her services should be required. It was she who took charge of our little bags, and in one of the "grandmother" pockets of her wide satin skirt were hair pins, safety pins, and handkerchiefs, in case of emergency. To drive to the Court, Miss Chocolate wore a white tulle veil which entirely covered her face, and a vivid blue satin feridji, covered with sequins and big white velvet pansies. How I wish I could have photographed her! Fâtima wore a yashmak, now, alas! only worn by Princesses and ladies attending the Court, for to me it is one of the most becoming of head-dresses, showing the eyes to very great advantage. She wore, also, a peacock-blue satin feridji, a hideous contrast to Miss Chocolate's electric blue.

The Imperial harem, in spite of certain changes and certain privileges accorded to the Imperial Ottoman Princes and Princesses, still remains the harem in the real sense of the word, the harem about which Western readers expect to hear, the part of the Oriental house exclusively reserved for the use of the women. Across its threshold no man may enter, and even as we drove into the big door, which is inside another wooden door, and which is opened to admit each carriage and shut again immediately, our footman had to descend and wait for us outside the door. The whole Imperial harem is surrounded by a wall so high that no passer-by can possibly see within. The coachman, too, having left us at the entrance door, had to drive out and wait outside the first door.

This is the first time since I have been back again in Turkey that I have felt myself really within a harem. Even when I wear a veil, even when I forget I am not in England and try to push back the fixed lattice windows, even when I take part in these Baïram dinners, where not even the master of the house may be present, I do not realize the atmosphere of the harem. But within the palace, amidst its curious assembly of slaves and eunuchs, and in spite of its wide corridors and immense salons, there is a most uncomfortable feeling of bondage which would turn me into a raving lunatic at the end of a week. It is true, Fâtima explains to me, that all these women are solemnly asked four times at the end of each year whether they would like to marry and leave the harem. I say to myself, then, if they stay it is because they wish to stay, and are therefore happy. Their existence, however, seems a most heartrending waste of human life, and as I sat watching them loitering along the exquisitely carpeted corridors, gossiping, smoking, carrying alternately coffee and water to the guests, I longed to break down for them the lattice-work which always is there between them and the sun, to fling the windows wide open, so that they could breathe in the fresh air, and open the doors so that they, too, might go out. And yet not one of these women seemed in the least to feel her slavery, and, no doubt, they would turn their backs in horror on the ugly, unprotected existence of some of the women of my country.

"But these slaves are perfectly happy," again and again Fâtima assured me, and, to judge from their smiling faces, I suppose they are. But waste is always sad—waste of youth, waste of beauty, waste of womanhood, especially when women are so sorely needed for the regeneration of this country.

Arrived at the central entrance door of the harem, Fâtima and I were helped out of our carriage by the attendant eunuchs. I was told that eunuchs were now a thing of the past, but certainly that remark could not have been made with reference to the Imperial harem. It is difficult for me, however, to remember that these poor mutilated anachronisms are great personages at the Ottoman Court, who, although they perform the menial service of opening the carriage doors and helping us up the stairs (one on either side and one behind, as though we were old ladies), are yet the masters of the establishment. Fâtima explained to me that they spoke to her with the exaggerated politeness of the Eastern courtier, because of their affection for her father, and all of them came to ask for news of him.

At the first turning of the central staircase we walked into the yashmak room, where a host of female slaves came forward to help us. I felt for a moment as though I had strayed behind the scenes at Drury Lane, so curious they looked, in their brightly coloured figured silks and clashing coloured turbans, but their dyed hair and blackened eyes should be my excuse for the poor compliment I am paying them. Some of the costumes, it is true, were made of those priceless Persian embroideries for which Fâtima and I have searched the market-place, but always the *tout ensemble* was spoilt by some vividly coloured and clashing turban, a vivid yellow dress with a bright pink head-dress, an electric-blue dress and an exaggeratedly blue turban, which made one's eyes ache. Behind the footlights, perhaps, such combinations could pass muster, but in the daylight, even in the dim daylight which comes through the latticed windows, they were a motley, uncomfortable spectacle. These dresses, however, defied both time and fashion, and were all cut on the same model; a long dress, with the train caught up to the waist, and a sack jacket.

Once the yashmak and our cloaks were removed the slaves took away the veils to iron them, and other slaves arrived to conduct us upstairs and announce our arrival to the lady Court officials, who wore costumes of different colours according to their rank. There was, first of all, the Hasnadar Ousta, or High Controller of the establishment, in white satin, trimmed with real gold embroidery at the foot of her dress and at the bottom of her coat. Her little white and gold turban suited her perfectly, and her jewels, if not beautiful, at least were original. On her breast was a bouquet of diamond flowers, which stretched almost from shoulder to shoulder. Another diamond ornament stretched across the front of her turban, and in her ears she wore birds the size of butterflies, each holding in its mouth a pearl the size of a cherry. She was an old lady, judging by her wrinkled face and bent back, rather than her golden hair, and after she had walked once or twice round the assembled ladies, kissing some and saluting others, leaning on her stick of office, she hobbled into the presence of one of the Princesses, leaving the real duties of the day to the younger officials.

I would have liked to ask one of the Court officials, had I dared, how our dresses appeared to them. The wife of the War Minister was wearing a dress of cerise *crêpe-de-chine*, so tight that she had to sit down carefully. All the ladies wore silk stockings and high-heeled shoes—most of them might have come straight out of the paper *Chiffons* which is carefully studied in up-to-date harems to-day. How strange we all must have looked to these uncorseted women, who made no attempt at a fashionable coiffure, who still remained faithful to the "babouches" (heelless slippers) and coloured stockings worked with gold, and whose dresses could have been made into three or four of our present-day creations.

Most of the Court officials wore the Grand Cordon of the Order of the Chefakat, the Order of Mercy given to ladies of high rank and distinguished lady visitors. Fâtima alone amongst the lady visitors wore that order. Every time the Court officials passed, the guests stood, as the Eastern etiquette demands they should in the presence of superiors and aged ladies. This, however, was rather uncomfortable for us, for the Assistant Treasurer had known Fâtima's family all her life, and frequently came and spoke to us. Seeing us about to rise, with Eastern politeness she ordered us to remain seated, but Eastern politeness also demanded that we should disregard her request and rise to speak to her.

The Assistant Hasnadar was particularly interested in me when, after much beating about the bush, Fâtima at last owned that I had never had a husband. "We are companions in distress," said the Hasnadar, which in her case was not true, as I have already explained. A husband would be found for her to-morrow if she wished. But the wherefore of my celibacy puzzled her. "It is nothing of which to be ashamed," I protested. "It is nothing of which to be proud," she answered, and, like an Eastern woman when unable to reply, I shrugged my shoulders and laughed. The joys of "single blessedness" are not understood in this country, and personally, outside these high Court officials, I have never met an old Turkish spinster.

But supposing any of these women should take advantage of the solemn asking once a year, whether or no they will marry, what becomes of them? We have at present living in our harem a slave who has just left one of the Princess's palaces. Fâtima has undertaken to keep her here until she and her friends can find a suitable husband for her. She is a contented, beautiful, useless creature, who eats with us when the young Bey is not here, and sings Oriental songs of exquisite pathos, accompanying herself on the oude.* And sometimes, when she sings, I ask Fâtima to interpret the words of them. "It is an old, old Turkish love-song," she said, "a beautiful old song, and I love to hear her sing it." "And what kind of love-song does a Turkish man sing to his unknown bride?" I asked. "That all the sorrows in the world may be his lot, if only all the joys may be hers." "And what is the most awful of all the sorrows?" I asked. "Solitude," answers Fâtima without hesitation.

We were a curious luncheon party that day—the wife of the Sultan's Master of Ceremonies, several of Fâtima's friends, and an Egyptian Princess, whose arrival at the Palace in a magnificent steam launch I had seen through the harem lattices. Most of these ladies, who spoke quite fluent French, were too timid to speak to me, a most distressing modesty, especially when it necessitates the constant employment of Fâtima as interpreter. If only they could hear how unmercifully most of us Englishwomen handle foreign languages, whilst they are really excellent linguists (the best in Europe, except, perhaps, the Russians), they surely would take courage.

The meal the Sultan offered us could scarcely be called a luncheon. There were cold meats of various kinds, sweatmeats, creams, and other delicacies,

---

* Oude: Turkish guitar played with a feather.

served in Sèvres dishes, but water was the only beverage. And after the meal was over, the slaves came round offering us glasses of water in beautifully cut crystal goblets, with gold lids, and served on little golden dishes. It was extraordinary to me to be bidden to an Emperor's feast and given only water to drink, and yet here water is so limpid and cold that it is often more acceptable than the best champagne, and often on the steamboat, when we travel, I call the water-seller, who frequently passes in and out of the harem part of the boat in which we travel, and purchase a penny glass of water.

The ceremony of baise-main in the Selamlic was finished about eleven. To the cry of "Oh, Sultan, be humble, and remember God is greater than you," from the assembled Court, the Sultan retired for a short rest before coming to the harem to receive the ladies of the Court. And, perhaps, he slept longer that day than he intended, for it seemed to us an eternity to wait. Eight hours at a Court, however, would be considered tiring in most countries, but most particularly in a harem where male conversation cannot be procured for untold gold. I begin to miss the society of the opposite sex: it is true we have men, far more men, in our Turkish home than in any other Turkish home I know, but I miss the men at the parties and picnics and meetings. And it does seem rather a waste of time to put on my prettiest gowns and make a particularly handsome coiffure to eat only with women. Zeyneb used to say that "men spoiled the look of our Western functions; that they crawled about our drawing-rooms and ball-rooms like great black-beetles." Surely she had forgotten the appearance of an Ottoman Court and the awful black-beetles that crawl about there, when she spoke so disparagingly of our Western assemblies.

Fâtima explained to me that the Court of the present Sultan in no way equals the Court of the ex-Sultan in magnificence. The embroidery which the slaves hold in front of the coffee tray whilst coffee is being served was only a plain gold embroidery, whilst in Abdul Hamid's time the cloth was studded with real stones. The coffee cups, too, and the jam service were only solid gold, whilst in Abdul Hamid's time jewelled coffee cups were always used. The Court, however, has become more democratic. Princesses walk about amongst the people as they were not allowed to do during the reign of Abdul Hamid, and but for their red enamel necklaces and large diamond orders, exclusively worn by members of the Imperial family, we should have scarcely known we were amongst the members of' the Imperial family. The Sultan's grand-daughter interested me particularly—not so much because of her rank, but because of her appearance. She is a short girl for her age, which, I believe, is about twelve, but her dress was long and wide, her hair dressed in a knot on the top of her head inside a diamond crown, and the front of her small body was covered with diamond orders and a diamond dog-collar encircled her little throat. But most curious of all was the long, thin hand, quite out of proportion to the size of her body, with which she acknowledged our *temenahs* (Eastern salutations), and on those curious hands she wore gold mittens studded with rubies and diamonds. It looked as though she had utilized a gold purse for that purpose. She had a charming and interesting face, this little Princess, though one of unending sadness. She looked to me not unlike a schoolgirl acting the part of Queen Elizabeth, and a striking contrast to the merry little Princesses of her age in our Western countries.

But what is most delightful to me in Turkish life, in the Court and out of the Court, in fact in every station of life, is the beautiful feeling of democracy. A Princess, while talking to you, will suddenly excuse herself, rise and throw her arms round the neck of her old *nourrice*, who walks about amongst the highest of the Court ladies. The accident of high birth demands specially cultured conversation, kindness, and fine manners towards persons of humbler birth, argues the Turkish woman, and the *snobbery* which is so frequent in our Western countries has never existed here.

But suddenly one becomes conscious of a certain movement amongst the ladies, who, in spite of the music of the Imperial orchestra playing in the garden of the palace, in spite of the Hasnadar's merry laugh and her encouraging request to be "patient," have been growing weary of waiting. The Sultan has arrived! He has taken a particularly long rest this day, changed the uniform in which he received the Ottoman officials for a simple morning coat, and is seated in an armchair in the big salon waiting the arrival of the ladies in the order which the Hasnadar should see fit to introduce them. A procession of four ladies at a time, headed by the Hasnadar, we enter the room where Mehmeth V. is seated. But it is a ceremony so intimate, so unlike the ceremony we had dimly seen a few hours before through the latticed windows, that I cannot bring myself to think this good-natured, unceremonious old gentleman is the Sultan of a great Empire.

To me, we had the appearance of four students going to an examination, and I felt this more when, after kneeling before the Caliph, as etiquette demands, and kissing his hand, we were requested to rise and be introduced. "Your Majesty, our Sultan, Commander of the Faithful," began the Hasnadar, with bent head, and leaning on her stick of office, "this is the daughter of—and the wife of—" Then the Sovereign Caliph congratulated her on being the daughter of—and the wife of—,said he was delighted to make her acquaintance, and passed on to the next lady, who was introduced in the same manner. When Fâtima's name was made known to his Majesty, he asked her to be seated, and, again kneeling before the Sultan, she gave him news of her father, and answered the many questions he asked.

This was the first time Fâtima had made the acquaintance of the Sultan. "He was delighted," he said with Eastern courtesy, and Fatima rose and asked permission to introduce me herself. I was not introduced as the daughter or wife of a well-known Pasha, but as Fâtima's "English sister," who had come to share her existence for a while, and who had now come with her to pay homage to the Sovereign of the country. Many questions the Sultan asked about me, about my country, and all the while he talked I was thinking of the poor captive, Prince Réchad, who for thirty-three years had been imprisoned within those walls, and who now was the Sultan seated before me. He was weary. Early rising, perhaps, suited him as little as it suited me. He frequently pulled himself up, forced his eyes open, said he was delighted to make our acquaintance. Then we rose, and the Hasnadar escorted us from the room, and on the same occasion four more Court ladies were led into the Imperial presence.

It is interesting naturally to meet the ruler of a country, of an empire of such tradition, of a land which will be for so many years to come the subject of the greatest interest, but the meeting of the present Sultan did not stir me as did the meeting of the ex-Sultan Abdul Hamid—Abdul Hamid, who pretended not to know one word of the French language, which he speaks fluently, who always played his part, and took particular care that part should be well played before foreigners. All the nicest-sounding words were chosen from the Turkish language to delight their ears. He humbly requested that the distinguished foreigner for a short while staying within the capital of his "dear" land would make known to him the manner in which the Government could be of service in helping the foreigner on his or her journey. His great, big, brown eagle eyes were wide awake, he *unpacked* the distinguished visitor, whilst the interpreter translated into the language he knows so well, and this hideous tyrant became a being of fascination. The present Sultan is a "fatalist." Could he be otherwise with such an agonizing past? He who was obedient to his brother is now obedient to the Constitution; perhaps for Turkey it is better he should be so.

* * * * *

We drove home in silence, Fâtima and I. She had explained so many things to me that day; now she was tired. A long, tiring, but interesting day it was. I was almost sorry it had to end. Miss Chocolate, in her gaudy attire, is sitting in front of us in the carriage, weeping at the honour conferred on her, for she, with all the other slaves, has kissed the ground on which the master's feet were resting. ... Cannon are firing to announce that the time for evening prayer has come; the fat, unexercised horses are ploughing their way up the hill; the shops, which at 4.30 are pulling down their shutters for the night as we drive by, have had a day of rest. ... What a wonderful change it is to be a Turkish woman for a while. ... Surely Fate was kind to me when she crossed my destiny with that of little Fâtima.

CLAUDE SCUDAMORE JARVIS
(1879–1953)

Son of an East London insurance clerk, C.S. Jarvis achieved success as a colonial administrator in Egypt despite not coming from the usual social background and being without a public school education. When 17 he joined the merchant navy as an apprentice, fought as a trooper in the South African War between 1899 and 1902, and in the Great War served in France, Egypt and Palestine reaching the rank of major. Having acquired a good knowledge of Arabic he joined the Egyptian frontiers administration in the Western Desert and was transferred to Sinai in 1922 where he was governor until his retirement in 1936. Thereafter he made a new career for himself writing, drawing upon the knowledge and experience he had acquired during his years among the Arabs in the Egyptian deserts. The Royal Central Asian Society awarded him its Lawrence Memorial Medal in 1938, but he was not a believer in the causes Lawrence espoused. He claimed to have had ample experience of the real Bedouin character and in his books gave many instances of their factiousness, laziness and lust for money.

From:

Three Deserts (1936)

A practical administrator who contributed to desert reclamation during his fourteen years in Sinai, Jarvis argues that the Bedouin were in part responsible for reducing scrub land to desert because they allowed their animals to destroy its trees and vegetation. He also contends that the wandering life is no longer sustainable in the modern world and blames the romantic ideas of the desert travellers for influencing colonial administrators in their misguided policy of protecting native customs and laws instead of assimilating the empire's 'dependent races' to European ways, as did the French and Italians.

Arab Days and Arab Ways

There is a saying in the Near East that those who work with the Arabs "either get to like them or get like them," and there is a considerable amount of truth in this. There are, however, exceptions to every rule, and, though I have administered Arabs for almost half a lifetime, I do not think that I come under either category. To become like an Arab one must, in the first place, rid oneself absolutely of the idea that time is of consequence, and adopt an entirely fatalistic attitude in every matter; and this I have never been able to do. I believe in a Deity, but I am not conceited enough to think that He takes any great personal interest in me or my work, nor that He is willing to alter the weather to suit my convenience—as far as weather goes it has always seemed to me to be designed specially to upset my arrangements and spoil my crops. The Arab, however, believes firmly that Allah arranges everything from the point of view of the race to which he belongs, and, although the weather is frequently most unpropitious, he would regard any complaint about it as a form of criticism, and any attempt to fight against existing conditions as amounting to blasphemy. This attitude may possibly be dictated by his religion, but it is probable that his natural sloth has a considerable amount to do with it, as it must be very comforting to the conscience to be able to attribute all one's failings to one's devotion to the Faith. My view is that Nature is a hard taskmaster and has no intention of making things easy for human beings, and any success one may achieve with crops or animals must be won by dint of hard work and by making provision against the worst happening.

The desert is, I admit, a fairly hopeless place for any man to cope with, but it can be improved by various methods, such as terracing wadis, running channels for rain-water into depressions, etc., and the proof of this exists in Central Sinai and Southern Palestine where all the wadis show signs of dams erected by the more virile race that occupied these areas prior to the Arab invasion. In Southern Trans-Jordan around the Petra country every mountain is terraced for vines and olives, and in those days it must have resembled Southern Italy or Sicily, but to-day not a tree exists, whilst along the whole of the Mariut coast are signs of the most intensive cultivation in Roman times, the greater part of which has been allowed to go back to waste land.

The Arab is sometimes called the Son of the Desert, but, as Palmer said, this is a misnomer as in most cases he is the Father of the Desert, having created it himself, and the arid waste in which he lives and on which practically nothing will grow is the direct result of his appalling indolence, combined with his simian trait of destroying everything he does not understand. A great part of the country in which, he now ekes out his haphazard existence was at one time fairly prosperous and productive and, by failing to repair damage done by wear and tear of weather and by wantonly wrecking conduits and cisterns he was too lazy to use, he has succeeded in creating a sun-scorched, treeless desert which will remain a wilderness so long as he encumbers the land.

In his campaign of destruction the Arab has been most loyally supported by his animals, the camel and the goat. There is an Arab proverb: "Tie up your camel and trust it to God," which means: "Hobble it and let it do its damnedest"; and this is a most iniquitous proceeding as the camel is an iconoclast and Philistine by nature and takes a positive delight in biting the heart out of a young tree, while the goat is even worse as it will eat down every living thing to the very roots. In the Old Testament the goat is frequently referred to as an evil beast—a leader in mighty wickedness—and it would seem that the inhabitants of the Near East in those days were fully alive to the harm that the goat can do and has done. There is definite proof that about a thousand years ago Sinai was reasonably wooded, with big tamarisk and thorny acacia trees, not to mention a variety of scrub bushes that grew to great size and covered a large area of ground. Both the tamarisk and acacia are disappearing rapidly, for the very simple reason that no young trees can possibly survive, as immediately they show above the surface of the soil they are bitten off by grazing goats, whilst existing trees are hacked to bits by Arabs who break off the branches to provide fodder for their animals. The Beduin thoroughly appreciates shade, and every jutting rock that provides cover from the sun is used as a camping-ground, but the sight of a tree appears to incense him and he is not happy until he has destroyed it utterly by snapping off its branches and burning its trunk through to the core.

In the vicinity of my garden in El Arish I have three acres of desert sand that has been enclosed for fourteen years and which, owing to the fact that it is protected from goats and camels, has become a dense mass of scrub bushes, some of them eight feet high with a diameter of twenty feet, whilst the soil between the growth is covered with a thick layer of rotten vegetation so that the sand is thoroughly stabilized and does not move in the strongest gales. This gives one an idea of what Sinai must have been before the Arab came to lay it waste with his grazing flocks, and there is no doubt whatsoever that the responsibility for the sand-dune area which has advanced over a mile on a 120-mile frontage during the time I have been in the Peninsula rests at the door of that accursed animal, the goat, ably assisted by his ruthless companion, the camel, and connived at by their feckless owner, the Beduin Arab.

Another failing of the Arab is his avarice, and his love of money is such that he loses all sense of proportion whenever currency is discussed, whilst if actual coins and notes are displayed before him he not only loses his sense of proportion but his self-control as well. As an instance of this, I may mention the case of a Government surveyor who, being detailed for map-making in Southern Sinai, was driven nearly frantic by the demands of the local Arabs, who were disagreeing among themselves during the whole period of his stay as to the number of camels he should take from each tribe. There used to be a system in Sinai by which travellers and surveying parties hired their camels and guides from the tribe occupying the area in which the party was operating, but owing to the manner in which it was abused by the Arabs and the annoyance caused to the hirers I had to discountenance the arrangement. In those days the system was still observed, and as the surveyor was going to work for the first month in the Mezeina tribe area, then two months in the Terrabin country, finishing up with a further month with the Mezeina, and as he did not wish to change camels twice, I arranged with the sheikhs that he should hire a Mezeina caravan and guides for the first two months irrespective of where he worked, and a Terrabin party for the second two months. This seemed a perfectly fair and suitable arrangement and would have worked admirably with any race other than the Beduin, but the uncontrolled avarice of these people upset everything and eventually I had to send a strong police patrol to maintain order, as the Mezeina, having supplied the caravan for the first two months—one of which had been spent in Terrabin country—flatly refused to allow the Terrabin to take over later, whilst the Terrabin themselves further increased the impasse by failing to send camels capable of carrying a load.

When it came to the question of payment there was an indescribable scene with yelling and gesticulating Arabs confusing the issue, so that in the end the frantic and bewildered surveyor paid nobody and instead lodged the full amount with the office at Tor and asked me to settle it. I happened to be at Tor a month later and took the matter up, and as the Arabs had broken their word, had let me down, and had nearly driven a hard-working official into a lunatic asylum, I was not in a particularly sweet frame of mind about the business. After five minutes listening to the yelling mob, I adjourned the case for six months and told them that they must settle it among themselves, coming up to El Arish—a distance of 200 miles—to receive payment when everybody concerned stated that he was satisfied.

After four months they arrived in El Arish, and I asked them if they had agreed among themselves. As they stated that they had, I went to my safe and tipped out of a bag a huge pile of notes and coins due to them—and that finished it. The sight of the money upset all their good resolutions and in a moment the room was a yelling, disputing mass. I shoved the money into the bag again, put it into the safe, and told them to go back to Tor and return in six months' time, and then if they were agreed I would pay out. So back along the weary 200 miles the whole party travelled, and six months later when they arrived to accept payment they were in a chastened frame of mind. Nevertheless, when the coins were tipped out on to the desk there was a tense movement in the crowd and mouths opened to protest; but the sheikhs managed to exercise a controlling influence, until the last coin had been paid out. The strain, however, was too much for them, and immediately the party got outside my office the brawl started again and most of them spent the night in prison as the result.

There is a widespread belief that the Arab is a naturally courtly and stately individual, combining a charm of manner with a dignified restrained bearing. To a certain extent I agree, for there is no gainsaying his courtesy and charm, but I am definitely at issue with those who emphasize his dignity and restraint. One reads even in books written by people who know the Arab—such as Lawrence's *Seven Pillars of Wisdom*—of the dignified and well-bred calm of Arab sheikhs that makes the more voluble Englishmen appear at a disadvantage. The truth is that the Arab has an assumed air of detachment and dignity when the matter at issue is of no importance to him whatsoever, but the most regal of them throw all restraint to the winds when a question arises that affects them either financially or personally. I have attended Arab meetings in the Western Desert of Egypt, Sinai, Trans-Jordan, and Palestine, and if I were asked I should say that the most marked feature of such assemblies has always been the unrestrained and undignified yelling and gesticulating of all the litigants, some of whom have worked themselves up to the verge of hysteria and epilepsy, and this being the case I cannot understand the grounds on which the supposition of restraint and dignity is based.

The Arab's love of litigation is extremely exasperating to anyone who realizes that time has a value, as the procedure of their desert law is deliberately framed to make a case last as long as possible, but if adopted in reasonable proportions it is a perfectly sound and suitable ordinance for a primitive nomad race dwelling in deserts where the maintenance of public security by ordinary methods is an impossibility.

The trouble is that some Administrators find Arab law an all-engrossing subject and are vastly intrigued by some of the queer customs that date back possibly to the days of Abraham. Many of these customs have been discarded by the Beduin themselves as unsuitable to present-day conditions, for, though the march of time has affected the Arab less than any race in the world, the advent of the motor-car and more rapid means of communication has had a civilizing, or, perhaps it would be more correct to say, restraining influence on them. However much one may be accused of iconoclasm and spoiling the natural charm of a nomad race, it is the duty of an administrating official to do what he can to improve the lot of the Arab and also to maintain public security. It is an impossible situation to have towns inhabited by townspeople, settled areas with irrigated lands, and a system of roads linking them up, whilst there is roaming in the vicinity a primitive race who still consider it their absolute birthright to raid and rob the settled cultivator who has worldly possessions. The Arab must either conform to present-day conditions or remove himself to Central Arabia where his lawless methods will not interfere with the well-being of others.

These young and enthusiastic Administrators do a considerable amount of harm in encouraging the Arab to revive many of his old-time customs that he has discarded of his own accord. The situation rather suggests a sympathetic grown-up walking into the nursery and evincing an interest in the toys of the children—the toy-cupboard is at once opened up and the floor littered with old forgotten friends. If the Arab finds an Englishman is enthusiastic about his laws, he will be only too delighted to revive all the barbaric customs of the past, such as trial by ordeal—the ordeal consisting of applying a red-hot spoon to the tongue—and the handing over of young girls as payment of fines. And the trouble will not end there, for the Arab will enter into the spirit of the thing thoroughly, reviving every age-old case in the history of the tribes, so that the official will find himself forced to spend his whole time listening to utterly fatuous lawsuits concerning insults offered half a century ago and disputes about completely useless tracts of land that have never borne a crop and never will. There is too much useful work waiting to be done in an Arab province for any man to waste his time by encouraging unnecessary Beduin litigation, and moreover he will find all the legal difficulties he wants without the slightest encouragement.

Those who have visited the French possessions in North Africa and the new Italian Colony in Libya cannot fail to be struck by the very vast difference in the colonizing methods employed by these two Powers as compared with our own. Both France and Italy apparently aim at the gradual but complete obliteration of the customs, laws, language, and even the religion of the people they administer, the substitution of their own standards and the ultimate creation of a race that will know French or Italian nationalism and no other. We, on the other hand, work in the opposite direction entirely. Our young Administrators are exhorted to teach our dependent races to develop along their own lines—native customs and laws are to be encouraged, and in some cases revived; the teaching of the English language, so far from being compulsory, is frequently considered a doubtful policy; whilst the religion is sacrosanct and no opportunity is to be lost in strengthening its hold.

In fact, the object aimed at appears to be to encourage a backward and uncivilized race to remain backward and uncivilized, except in so far as purely material matters are concerned, and to instil into them not a desire for British citizenship but a vague longing for nationalism and self-determination. The result is that we receive no credit whatsoever for our benign and easy rule; in some cases we merely arouse feelings of contempt for what is mistaken for weakness and fear, and so far from inspiring a native race with friendship we— in the light of recent events—appear to instil into them instead a desire for complete independence and the removal of British influence. I am not suggesting that we should imitate either Italian or French methods, and I do not want to see Senegalese *sous-officiers* spitting betel-nut juice through gold-set teeth on Claridge's carpets, but I should like to hear occasionally a coal-black sergeant slap his chest and say, "I am a British soldier and citizen," or a Cypriot just for once insist on his British nationality on some other occasion than his appearance in an Egyptian police-court on a contraband charge.

I have met so often Libyan Arab soldiers, Moroccans, and Algerians who have insisted with pride on their Italian or French citizenship, and, though we are credited with being the most successful colonizing nation in the world, we seem to have failed altogether to arrive at the state of affairs where our dependent races grasp the fact that they are active members of the Empire.

The idea at the back of the minds of our Administrators is that the unspoilt, uneducated native is so infinitely preferable and so much more useful in every way in his primitive state than the civilized product. There is no argument about this, and if one could keep the native indefinitely very much as one originally found him it would most certainly be better for him and everybody else, but the trouble is that in these days of quick transport, aeroplanes, and wireless sets, this is absolutely impossible—the wild races of Africa are as keen on education and what they think is advancement as everybody else. One must, therefore, accept the situation and endeavour to guide our subject races along paths that will lead them to be useful citizens of the Empire—and this, I think, in many cases is what we are failing to do.

THOMAS HODGKIN (1910–1982)

Born into a family of academics – his grandfather was Master of Balliol and his father Provost of Queen's College, Oxford – Thomas graduated from Balliol in 1932. Deciding against an academic career he applied for the colonial service but instead of Palestine, his preference, was offered a post in the Gold Coast. Later an esteemed historian of Africa, Hodgkin opted to travel to Palestine as an unpaid assistant on an archaeological project at Jericho. His period as an archaeology student between January 1932 and July 1933 was unsuccessful career-wise, but he used it to travel around Palestine and parts of Syria and Transjordan. In May 1934 he was back as a cadet in the Palestine civil service. Hodgkin's political views were formed out of the maelstrom of events in the 1930s. Siding with the Left and opposed to imperialism he soon found it unconscionable to be involved in the British suppression of the Palestinian Arab revolt, which began in 1936 and which he supported. He resigned leaving Palestine in the summer of 1936. Edited by his brother E.C. Hodgkin, *Letters from Palestine 1932–36* was published only in 1986. Unlike Duff Gordon's *Letters from Egypt* or Bell's *Persian Letters*, Hodgkin's letters were not intended for publication and so remain unpolished.

From:

Letters from Palestine 1932–36 **(1986)**

Rather like the young Disraeli's *Home Letters* (*Lothair* and *Tancred* were actually fresh in Thomas' mind when he wrote them) these letters display qualities of vivid immediacy and youthful effervescence. In addition, in spite of their author's youth, they are valuable for the picture they give of a hopelessly fractured society in process of passing out of the hands of its colonial master.

TO ECH　　　　　　　　　　　　　　　　　　　　TANTUR
17 MAY 1933

I have this interval between sleeping at a lecture and sleeping at a play. Père Barrois, the delightful Dominican who took us to the Jebel Druse, had been lecturing on the Jebel Druse: the mixture of slides, French and a wet steamy atmosphere kept me asleep throughout. From time to time a little black Jesuit beside me propped me up in my place and I saw half a slide—but always out of focus. This getting up at half-past five—though healthy—makes me very sleepy at almost any hour of the day. You will find me when we meet I'm afraid almost more slothful than when we parted.

In a few minutes I go on to sup on a simple Wiener Schnitzel with an intelligent but lonely friend from the Museum called Lambert, and then to see the Habima act a play called *Rahab*: rather my subject I feel, to see if I can pick any archaeological holes in the production. They are Bolshevik players I think, modelling themselves on the Russian Ballet—intense stylization. But I'll tell you about it afterwards. They've done *12th Night* which I wish I'd seen, partly just to know that it wasn't as good as us.

I must tell you of my Sunday's ride—a rather shameful thing. Really a judgement for riding on Sunday during Church time, which I'd forgotten when I ordered my horse that it would be. And had to slink past the English cathedral looking like a Jew who had kept a pious Sabbath yesterday, or a Moslem who'd kept a holy Friday the day before. I rode up through Hinnom (I think it's Hinnom, but any divinity note will tell you) up towards the Hebrew University, having promised to see a professor, don, there called Billig ('alles noch billiger'—do you remember, in Klagenfurt?) who has made up his mind from a chance enthusiastic remark that I am going to Persia, and loads me with German books about it which I am very grateful for but have no time to read.

I tethered my horse (a large well-built chestnut) to a post in a shed, carefully choosing for him a nice bit of shade, and went to find Billig. But as soon as my back was turned I heard a crash and saw that my horse had detached the bit from his mouth and was cantering away. I tried to go after him gently and entice him to come back to me, but when he wouldn't be enticed I ran. But of course he being a horse could run faster. When I was tired of running I luckily found a little Jew student bicycling quickly in a hurry to get to his lecture, and borrowed, or rather commandeered, his bicycle. What's the use of belonging to a ruling nation if you can't be a little high-handed in an emergency?

Meanwhile my horse had broken out of a canter into a gallop. A procession of mixed Jew students was parading, as they often do, in gay clothes, with over-healthy bare legs and arms—about 200 of them, rather truculent, some arm in arm, a great many playing mouth-organs, all marching jauntily down the road to Jerusalem. My horse careered through the middle of them (being an Arab it was obviously fiercely nationalist and anti-Jew) while I bicycled at a tremendous pace a couple of hundred yards behind shouting to the young women to get out of the way, and the young men to catch my horse—curse them all for cowards.

Then I, like Pharaoh but more successfully, tried to dash through the gap made in the children of Israel by my horse before it closed up again. I got through but my horse easily gained on me. So I saw a passing taxi, hailed it, and told it to drive like the devil—throwing my bicycle, that is to say the little Jew student's bicycle, to a little Arab boy to mind. We drove on after the horse, having lost sight of it through all this, asking each policeman which way it had gone, and cursing him for not stopping it. It was a bit foolish of them. Surely the first thing a policeman learns is how to stop a runaway horse.

Anyhow in the end we found it frothing and sweating caught by a bold young Arab townee outside Barclay's Bank. But even then I had to go back returning everyone their property and compensating most of them. I had to give 5 piastres (I felt it would let English horsemanship down if I gave less, and I had already let it down far enough) apiece to:

The man who caught the horse
The man who happened to have a bit of old rope about him and led it back to the stables where I was too ashamed to appear)
The boy who had looked after the bicycle
The boy who rode the bicycle back to the owner of the bicycle
The owner of the bicycle (hot cross and late poor fellow. He'd had the worst time. But, honour to Jewry, he was the only one of them who refused my five piastres).

TO DFH   c/o THE MOTHER SUPERIOR
6 JUNE 1933   TANTUR HOSPICE
                                BETHLEHEM

Today I have spent mostly in the shelter of a closed car, a luxus Chrysler, belonging to a Russian Jew with the typically Russian name of Joshua Gordon. Have I mentioned him already? Very fat and square, a huge bulgy face with small blue eyes shining like a pair of expressive sultanas in a rather nondescript helping of suet pudding. He is the showman and liaison officer with the Government of the Jewish Agency, so that one can feel that his motor car was ground off the faces of poor dispossessed Arabs.

He's a friend of Eastwood's; that was how I first got to know him—took us both the other day to look at Jewish life and culture in Tel-Aviv. It's all very efficient but gruesomely go-ahead—what I imagine England must have been like in the Lancashire parts in the last century, and America till quite lately. Rather like the five towns—everything bubbling over with expansion—great maps of Tel-Aviv showing in coloured inks how huge was the increase in the increase of population every year; ghoulish German architecture. Sprightly people, but all fearfully dignity of labour conscious. Of course it is very dignified—and these trodden people from the ghettos have a right to be proud, but it's rather nauseous in a way, this bristling prosperity—and absolutely unscrupulous. They even say that there are times in any nation's history when it must simply go straight forward and realize itself as a nation and let everything else—the rights of other races—go to the devil. All this civic pride is very healthy I'm sure. We had tea with the Mayor who gave me a signed picture of his bust, as ugly as sin, and the town-clerk, and the conversation was all the time of this sort:

Pause
ONE OF THEM: Yes—there is a greater average consumption of water per head per day than in any of the great capitals of Europe.
I: Really?
ANOTHER OF THEM: Yes, Sir. Let me tell you that every Tel-Aviv citizen consumes 500 pints of water a day. Berlin comes second with 400 pints. London, third with 250 pints. Paris, last with 40 pints.
ANOTHER OF THEM: When one of the children runs home dusty from school or from Kindergarten the first thing he does is to demand from his father or mother a thorough shower bath. 'Mother,' he says, 'I want a good wash all over.'—and so on.

But it grates on one when one belongs to a country becoming poorer, and it makes one feel thankful for poverty, and almost for dirt. One can understand how all this bumptious prosperity must grate on the Arabs who see it. For the ones who profit from the Jews being here (which Jews say everyone must do) are only the town ones, most of them Christians, who drive buses to Jaffa, that sort of thing. The labourers have their lands sold over their heads and become really unemployed, but so long as they have a patch of ground they're not registered. So Norman Bentwich in the *New Statesman* can still point proudly to figures. Yesterday (it's now Wednesday morning) this Joshua took me to Tel Mond—900 acres of oranges and a statue, of the late Lord Melchett, in the position of a policeman on point-duty, as Progress. The idea is that you begin working for the company with a back garden and your back garden increases and by degrees you become a private owner—hence no proletariat. That they seem sensibly to aim at everywhere, giving everyone an acre or two for their spare time so as to have a part in the land. To see them in the streets it is almost what one expects Moscow is like—all of them being so consciously not proletariat, swinging along with open shoulders, open necks and girls on their arms. But yesterday at Tel Mond they were discussing an eviction of a Bedu from ground he thought he had rights on—and probably had—and being told they had better keep Jews out of the way on eviction day. All this they excuse by saying that the less civilized must always give way to the more civilized. Probably true but wicked.

I'm sorry—but you don't often have politics. I expect I ought to mention these topics more often. But as you know they're not my strong point, though my increasing admiration for Gladstone makes me feel they ought to be. Anyhow I feel I can face the politically minded in England now without utter ignorance.

I've had a busy week and done too little ordinary work, alas. Friday and Saturday at Sebastiya, Samaria that is, Crowfoot delightful—friendly in a rather gnarled way—gave me very kindly almost a day of his time showing me buildings and explaining them, which is more than that old curmudgeon Garstang would have done for anyone short of a Duke. And the people seemed pleasant there, mostly young women. The daughter seemed a delightful and well-featured young woman. Mrs Crowfoot very ill-mannered and never passed the cake. Some sprightly little Jews like sparrows. Mr (? Dr) Lake with his trembling lower lip talking about the Shakespearian *variae lectiones* and thinking how lucky he was not to have got a fellowship at Oxford because it had left him so much more time for writing. Enormous Mrs Lake, the housekeeper, providing excellent food, so that one really looked forward to meals.

A fairly profitable expedition from the thesis point of view—and some jolly 12th-century Byzantine paintings of John the Baptist. It was there, you remember, that poor John the Baptist lost his head, and the fact has been commemorated with two tasteful shrines. I am becoming (like Teddy) excited by early Christian architecture and mean to read Stzrygowski—at present I have only got as far as reading about him. There are very good 5th and 6th-century churches near Aleppo which I mean to visit, either with Boase or alone—a glorious one for Saint Simon Stylites to judge from the pictures. I feel that he will be a good object for a pilgrimage.

I am thankful to hear that my devoted native servant, Isma'in the Turk, is willing to leave the Sultan's employment for mine for that month, which will be useful if we cross the frontier over into Turkey, though I'm certain that he'll be arrested there poor fellow:

This face of his I do remember well…
Here in the streets, desperate of shame and state
In private brabble did we apprehend him…

Notable pirate, thou salt-water thief,
What foolish boldness brought thee to their mercies
Whom thou in terms so bloody and so bold
Hast made thine enemies?

(I hope Isma'in won't get into any private brabble. I told you about him didn't
I—deserter from the Turkish army after the war—killed 70 Frenchmen with
a machine gun in the Druse revolt, when he was part of a small sniper force
and they were a battalion marching in column. A price on his head in both
countries. A charming absolutely faithful and lovable person in spite of this
bloodthirsty record.)

Other events have been a happy dinner and a miserable garden party at
Government House. I have enough snobbery to revel in going there. Beautiful
singing we went to afterwards, a Yemmanite (Jew from SW Arabia), a lovely
actress, a little like Ruth Draper but less varied, singing love songs like Theocritus
and battle songs and songs about flowers—beautiful sudden subtle changes of
mood and character. She sang with bare feet and a great shapeless dress high at
the neck so that only head and feet showed. We agreed that we'd never seen
anyone with a more beautiful inside to her mouth, like a Cathedral with nave and
choir—a dark choir and a brighter nave—she opened it wide as she sang. We sat
gloriously in the front row so could see into it well. We were almost clapped too
when we entered but just not. These Yemmanites were expelled from Spain in
the 15th century and one can see that part of their history from their singing, and
shawls that she danced with and things. Tonight to a Jewish satirical drama—
Gordon taking me again—he promises that it is like Aristophanes.

TO DFH   TANTUR
19 JUNE 1933

A fairly hot very windy dusty ill-tempered sort of day—the kind that makes
you unpleasant to servants, and, alas, in Palestine there are always plenty of
servants to be unpleasant to. It was on the whole a satisfactory visit [to Beirut].
Baldwin was a beautiful host—a lovely man, simple and most hospitable, if
anything too ready to love worms—the usual Junior Consular sort of worm.
He had one living with him with a small moustache, small stature and what
he believed was a dashing manner.

I hardly know how to travel or when or with whom. No I'm not really as
hopeless as I sound, but it is hard to combine places that I must see with any
particular route. At last though I have decided that I shall go from Hama to
Aleppo and leave Transjordan and SE Syria—they're both very ugly (or SE
Syria is, all volcanic rock). I've seen part of them (the Jebel Druse) already, and

finally I must be content to be an amateur in travelling. It's no good trying to travel to find out things that other people don't know. I must simply try to find out some of the things which they do. And I might as well look at the best, and they (as far as early Christian churches are concerned) are almost all in this district N of Hama. Neither journey would really help my thesis; so I might as well go for my own pleasure, through lovely country and buildings. It's perfectly safe. I asked a high French official at Beirut about that—a diplomat with a bent nose. He guaranteed me Hama to Aleppo, and he knows.

Another trouble is that I have half hired two faithful and devoted bearers—more than one I can't afford. Besides if there were two they would probably intrigue with one another and stop being faithful. And one is at Kerak—he's the one I like most but that's so hard to get at and the other is at Samaria and that's not much easier. God will send some beautiful and easy solution—or I shall find some bad one.

My present idea is to go to Jerash (good 2nd- and 3rd-century Roman town and nice churches) the day after tomorrow early (Saturday), return Sunday evening, set off with one of the Devoteds on Tuesday, have all my luggage sent on to Alexandretta, be met in N Syria about the 17th of July by Boase and Richmond after a month's dirty travelling, have a week's clean travelling with them, and then about the 25th set off for Europe.

Yesterday was a long exhausting bargaining irritable day here. I'm afraid I became rather the intolerable sort of Englishman who curses quite ineffective quiet people to prevent his being taken advantage of. Of course I always was taken advantage of.

Then I travelled the last part of the way with a fanatical Moslem from Hebron who had strong views about the immorality of the Jews. I think he was really shocked by them. He categorized me about who sent us food and money and who sent the birds food and the Jews punishment and I after a few hesitations realized that I was expected each time to answer 'Allah'. But I was scored off when he asked if Allah didn't see the differences between his life and a Jew's, and I answered 'Surely God will reward you for your holy life and will punish the wicked Jew', and he pounced on me at once and said, 'How do you know that? Only God knows who will be rewarded and who punished. Who are you to say that I shall be rewarded?' Which was very crushing. He also gave me a list of the Four Things which man would never know but God knew. They were:

(1) Whether you will get money tomorrow
(2) Whether you will die tomorrow
(3) Whether the child of a pregnant woman will be a boy or a girl
(4) Whether it will rain tomorrow.

The last seemed rather bathos. We discussed a little the immorality of Americans. I offered sententious remarks about riches not making you happy or good, which he thank Heavens approved of, but most of the time we discussed his own morality—very like a Cromwellian. I quoted some of the first verses of Saint John's Gospel (the only Arabic I know by heart) which seemed to bear on the subject, but he didn't seem much affected. Perhaps I pronounced them wrong.

ARABIA

Historical Background

Arabia entered the twentieth century still a relatively unknown, backward and inhospitable region. However the spread of the telegraph and railway enabled the Ottoman Empire to reassert its claim of sovereignty over parts of the peninsula. Construction of the Hijaz railway from Damascus to Medina (opened 1908) meant the Ottoman government was able to exercise 'more direct control' over the Sherif of Mecca and 'restore its direct presence in Yemen' (Hourani 1991: 280). In Central Arabia though, the pro-Ottoman Ibn Rashid were eclipsed by the rising Sultan Abdul Aziz ibn Saud, while British agreements entered into with rulers of the Gulf sheykhdoms at the end of the nineteenth century prevented Turkish expansion in that area.

Turkey's late decision to join the Axis powers on the eve of the First World War meant she would be fighting against her old ally Britain in the Middle East. Serious British reverses at Gallipoli and in Mesopotamia were offset by the Sherif of Mecca's decision to open up a front against Turkey in the Hijaz. The Arab Revolt (1916–1918) led eventually not only to the removal of the Turks from the Hijaz but also to the Arab tribes' conquest of Syria. However Arab nationalist aspirations were dashed when after the war, the Allies acted on the Sykes–Picot agreement and divided Greater Syria. French armies ejected Faysal's supporters from Damascus in 1920, while Faysal's father, the embittered King Husayn, who expecting to rule over a much larger swathe of Arab territory had declared himself 'King of the Arabs', was confined to the Hijaz. Forced to leave in 1925 by the victorious armies of Abdul Aziz ibn Saud, he spent his last years in Amman, capital of Transjordan, which the British had set up under his eldest son, Abdullah. The Saudi ruler, now protector of the twin holy cities, expanded his power into Asir, in the south-west, having already wrested Al-Hasa from Ottoman rule in the Great War. But although now the dominant power in the peninsula Saudi Arabia, as the country became officially known in 1932, was still very poor. Arabia had therefore entered a new era in which tenuous loyalty to the Muslim Ottoman Empire had been replaced by a now completely independent Yemen and the newly created nation state of Saudi Arabia. Along the Arabian Gulf a string of tiny sheykhdoms remained effectively British protectorates, as did the even smaller sultanates sustained by Britain in the Hadramaut which together with Aden detracted from Yemen's territorial integrity. The discovery of oil in Bahrain in early the 1930s presaged the vast transformation of the deeply conservative Arab societies of the peninsula, but only began to have a real impact in the 1950s.

Travellers and their Narratives

During World War One the circumstances surrounding the Arab Revolt and Britain's subsequent between-the-wars 'moment in the Middle East' produced a series of travel texts with a strong political colouring. This ranged from the ambiguously 'pro-Arab' orientations of T.E. Lawrence's *Seven Pillars of Wisdom* and Harry St. John Philby's *Heart of Arabia*, to the outright Pan-Arabism of the Lebanese-American Ameen Rihani's Arabian trilogy. Bertram Thomas's *Arabia Felix* is still overtly colonial. In *Arabia Phoenix*, an account of a diplomatic visit to Riyadh in 1935, Gerald De Gaury adverts to the now illustrious tradition of English travel in Central Arabia. He writes of the traveller's 'strange elation' and 'pride in his isolation...remember[ing] the nearest Europeans are some five hundred miles away...his only fear is that he will be forced to return to the crowded Western world' (De Gaury 1946: 75). Nevertheless, De Gaury's party moved not by camel but by car. The original mode of travel would be jealously appropriated by the last great British desert traveller, Wilfred Thesiger. His writings attest to the persistence of the traditional ways right to the end of the period, in the teeth of change being brought by the exploitation of oil.

PERCY ZACHARIAH COX (1864–1937)

Born into Essex landed gentry, Cox decided on military a career, graduating from Sandhurst in 1884. He joined the Cameronians (Scottish Rifles) and went to India where he quickly learned Hindustani before starting Arabic and Persian. Following a well-trodden path for imperial administrators he decided to become a 'politico', and was appointed temporary assistant political resident in British Somaliland Protectorate at Zeila. At this point in his life he was 'devoted to his studies of bird life, Somali clans and conchology' (Graves 1941: 33). In 1899 Curzon offered Cox the position of political agent and consul at Muscat. This was the making of him; he honed his diplomatic skills during a period of tension with the French in the Gulf and established an influence over the Sultan of Muscat that continued when in 1904 he was promoted to acting political resident in the Persian Gulf and consul-general for southern Persia. It was during this period that Cox, following on from earlier travellers in Oman, James Wellsted, Colonel S.B. Miles, and the Dutch missionary Samuel Zwemer, performed two journeys in the interior. On the first he started out from Abu Dhabi, reaching Muscat via the desert oasis of Buraimi and the desert side of the Jebel Akhdar. The second, from Ras al Khaimah to Buraimi, returning to Muscat by steam boat via Sohar, involved transporting a chronometer along the caravan route in order to set the latter's longitude and latitude. 'Part of his route, a matter of 400 miles, had not been traversed by any European' (Graves, 78). In spite of his later prominence as acting minister to Tehran (1918–20) and high commissioner of Iraq (1920–1923), a high point for Cox the traveller must have been after his retirement when he was elected to the presidency of the Royal Geographical Society in 1933. It was before this society in 1925 that he delivered his paper 'Some Excursions in Oman', and was complimented by no less an authority than St. John Philby for his achievement of fixing the geographical coordinates for Buraimi.

From:

'Some Excursions in Oman' (1925)

Cox's paper begins with a description of Muscat then narrates the two journeys mentioned above. The extract below comes from the first, from the portion Buraimi to Muscat via Ibri and Nizwa, stopping at the mountain village of Shuraija. His patrician manner rarely ruffled by the Arabs, Cox nearly pays a high price however for racing his camel against one of them. Besides reporting the warmth and inquisitiveness of the Omanis, he also notes how blood feuds and tribal antagonisms still made theirs an unsettled land. Also noticeable but usual for an RGS lecture are the corrections of previous travellers' mappings; as a former colonial official and diplomat though, Cox is low key about the worth of his own exploration.

Baraimi to Sharaija

We got away in due course on May 7, steering due east *via* Muthariz and the Shaikh of Abu Dhabi's new settlement at Jahali, and thence to the camp at the village of Ain (3½ miles), which lies at the north end of a spur of Jabal Hafit. Jahali had only been in existence for about six years; it possessed a nice new fort and a walled date and fruit orchard, at that time in its infancy, but very promising. It extends to the foothills of Jabal Hafit. Ain is also one of Shaikh Zaid's villages, and he keeps a Jemadar or caretaker there. Across the plain to the north are to be seen the Naim villages of Jimi, Qatara, Baraimi and Su'ara. On arrival at Ain I was as usual deposited in the guest tent, and found it extraordinarily hot. People crowded in till I felt almost suffocated. While we were sitting there, waiting for the inevitable coffee, one among some Awamir Badawi, who were sitting amongst the company talking to me or about me, pulled off his chefiyeh, or headcloth, and out of a loosely tied knot produced a live scorpion, which he and his companions proceeded to toss to one another and allowed to crawl about all over them. I thought it had probably had a piece of thread tied round the base of its sting, as I had often seen done in India, but they declared not, and certainly none was detectable. Then another Amiri, at the request of the audience, mumbled a long poem, the recital of which was said to prevent any harm ensuing front the sting of the scorpion! I was a good deal worried here by the behaviour of my followers. I had brought plenty of food of my own and had no intention of sponging on any one, and the hire I paid for the camels was specifically calculated and expected to include food for the camels and men, but these camel-men thrust themselves upon the hospitality of any habitations they passed, delaying the caravan to eat hot meals and expecting me to make the necessary return to the Shaikh. There was no end to it, but it seemed the only way to get along. Next day we got up at 6.30 a.m., and trekked for 2¾ hours, about 8 miles, in a direction parallel to Jabal Hafit, bivouacking among the tents of some of Naeim and Awamir Badawi. The former go to the gardens at Hafit during the date season, but live in tents during the rest of the year....

While here a messenger reached me from my *locum tenens* at Muscat, *viâ* Sohar, informing me that all was well, but announcing that H.M. first-class cruiser *Amphitrite* was expected (on her way out to China), and urging my early return to meet her. This was not very welcome news in the circumstances, nor did I see how I was going to get back in time without changing all my plans. However I replied that I would do my best, and having dismissed the messenger we started off again, making almost due south to Hafit village, which we reached after one hour's trot. We then struck across to the left through bush country to Qabil, where we spent the night, going on to Bizaili next morning. On the way we were fired on from a Badawi encampment, the occupants taking us for a raiding party, but no harm was done. The country we were now passing through reminded me greatly of the Haud of Somaliland, but without the charm of always being in sight of game, and it continued almost till we reached Dhank, three and a half hours' journey from Bizaili. At Dhank we camped outside the town in the open. The usual simoom blew all the afternoon, and the heat was excessive. About 4 o'clock, however, I went to the top of the hill behind the town and scanned the surrounding country towards Ibri and Jabal Hafit. The latter was just visible and nearer due north than I had expected. Dhank possesses some fine date gardens and a running stream. There is no proper bazaar, but as at Baraimi there is a public place where goods are put up for auction or exposed for sale. There was no apparent reason why we should not have camped in the date gardens, but I had the greatest difficulty all along in getting my companions to sleep in the vicinity of the towns; they always wanted to get away into the open, and I came to realise that they had reason on their side, bred of experience.

My next halt was Mazum, a small settlement of Baluchis allied and inter-married with the Bani Qitab. It consists of about three hundred houses. It was at this village that Miles experienced some incivility, but I had better luck. *En route* however I had a little misadventure. My pilot had previously been expressing his views as to the pace of our respective camels, and I had agreed that as soon as we came to a stretch of good going, I would match my mount against his. I may mention that I had a very fine and well-bred riding-camel lent me by the Shaikh of Abu Dhabi. The morning after leaving Dhank we came on a suitable bit of going, and accordingly we decided to have our match and started our camels off at full gallop. My camel was fresh, and in trying to pull her up the headstring came away in my hand, and she went away with me into the blue. Sitting as I was behind the hump, according to the approved method of riding in Oman, I could do nothing to stop her, and I was fully occupied in keeping my seat and holding on to my sketching case, compass, etc., and trying to ward off mimosa thorns. The direction she was taking was at right angles to our line of route, and if in my wild career I had happened upon a strange Badawi encampment it might have gone hard with me. I could only just reach the camel's cheek or neck with the end of my riding-cane, and the best I could do was to keep her more or less on a wide circular course by poking at her neck and endeavouring to guide her gradually back towards our starting-point. At last in the course of half an hour I had gradually got her head in the right direction, and my pilot Hamud and another were able to cut in in front of me and head her off. I was somewhat exhausted, my clothes torn, and face and hands badly scratched with thorns, but I was otherwise none the worse. I did not offer to race any more, however!

The method of riding in Oman on a mere skin on the lightest of trees behind the hump is quite different to our method in India, and elsewhere, and though certainly less hard on the camel, needs more efficiency in the rider, and you will realize my plight when the headstring came away.

Once again on the march to Ibri we were fired on from a distant encampment, and bullets whizzed across our bows, but I was now used to this little amenity, which appeared to be the ordinary practice of a Badawi community—based on the assumption that any strange mounted party seen approaching must be enemies on the raid. Apparently the etiquette is to stop and return the fire if you really are an enemy, otherwise ride on and take no notice.

As we neared the town, which had evidently received warning of our coming, a number of horsemen galloped out and gave us a demonstrative welcome, continuing to perform weird evolutions in front of us until we reached the broad shingly wadi just outside the town, where some two hundred men were drawn up in line and fired a sort of *feu de joie*—and not at all badly. We were then escorted into the town by a very friendly if very dirty crowd. The whole populace seemed to have turned out, and women and children lined the path. Burkas (yashmaks) were not much in evidence, and the ladies seemed comely as a whole, but the greasy dirtiness of their apparel was indescribable. Every one, man, woman and child, insisted on shaking hands, in spite of the heat, and would take no refusal.

As I proposed to remain here a day or two, I insisted on camping in a date garden instead of out in the open in the sun, as my companions would have preferred. In the course of time a suitable place was chosen. The inhabitants were very friendly and good tempered—in fact, too much so, for they crowded round my tent all day and allowed me no privacy whatever. Some of them never left me even for food or prayers, and when I suggested that their dinner would be getting cold, they received the hint with an amused smile, but pleaded to be allowed to remain as they had never seen anything like me before. (And the present generation probably had not.) Wherever I went I was accompanied by a small crowd. In the afternoon, when it got cool enough, I walked up to the top of the hill overlooking Ibri from the south-west and took a number of angles to various points. At the top of this hill one gets a good view over the plain embracing the villages of Ghabbi, Araqi, Bait al 'Ainain, Dariz, and the Jabal Misht and the Jabal al Kor, pronounced "Keör." At dusk the ladies of the place were again present in force, and sat round and watched me attentively while I had my dinner. As soon as I had finished the local Shaikh came in, accompanied by four or five other men who were to act as night guards on my camp. Before turning in we discussed Oman affairs and the general insecurity of life which prevailed. Here, in a large town like Ibri, the townspeople are fairly immune from the operation of blood feuds so long as they remain within the town, and they do not allow parties of outsiders to sleep inside the walls. They are afraid of visitors and visitors of them. In fact, in many places where tribal feuds exist men never sleep in their own houses, but always somewhere outside. The reason for this is that if a man is known to sleep at home his enemies know where to find him, and it is a common ruse for treacherous enemies to come to a house at night and call up the occupant, who jumps up without thinking, and the intruders are thus sure of their man. On the other hand, sleeping outside one man cannot be distinguished from another, and thus all are collectively safer.

Ibri is the most important settlement in the Dhahira district, and boasts a tremendous expanse of date groves, a good bazaar, and a fine mosque. It used to have the reputation in Miles' time of being a thieves' market, but seems to have since turned over a new leaf. I was told, however, that in spite of their time-honoured Wahabi associations a good deal of date wine was manufactured here at Ibri; while indigo is extensively grown for home use, half the community having their fingers and faces stained with it. As before explained, from here onwards I was to be the responsibility of the Sultan of Muscat, and it had been arranged that his representative, Shaikh Rashid Bin Uzaiz, should meet me at Ibri, while my camels for the onward journey were to be supplied by the Daru tribe from Tana'am. Shaikh Rashid joined me in due course, and as soon as we had secured our new camels, on May 15 I resumed my journey. Our first stage was Salaif, a picturesque village having a situation very much like that of Ibri, in a narrow gorge-like wadi with a tower perched above the village on a precipitous overhanging rock. As usual we slept outside away from the habitations, but next morning, the 16th, after taking early tea I had my paraphernalia shifted to a shady date grove, and then went up to the top of the hill with two local guides to take some bearings with my compass. On the crest of this hill there were the remains of some stone fortifications and embrasures, said to have been erected by the Wahabis when they were here early in the nineteenth century. They apparently captured Ibri, but were unable to reduce Salaif. My informants spoke of Al Mutairi as the Wahabi general, and declared that there were persons still alive who remembered the episode.

From Salaif we marched to Kubara, following the Wadi Salaif for 10 miles and then turning south. Kubara is under the lee of Jabal al Kor and about 10 miles distant from it. We found the inhabitants of this village in a very bad way owing to drought. They had had no rain for three years, and their water was failing and date trees not bearing fruit. Poor people! we found them very civil and friendly, and for the first time during our trip we were spontaneously offered chickens and eggs for sale. It was pitiful to see the effects of the last three years' widespread drought: Fuluj failing, date trees drooping, and much land gone out of cultivation. In the morning, while the tents were being struck, I beat a retreat to the nearest date garden for shade, and there I was soon surrounded by a party of housewives from the village. One middle-aged dame did most of the talking, and asked me many questions about my country and discussed the burning question of the drought. They were a very nice, polite lot, and for a wonder did not ask me for medicines or regale me with their ailments. After about half an hour's edifying conversation one of my men came to say that the caravan was ready, so with a "God speed you" from the ladies I went my way.

Both at Baraimi and onward through Dhahira I noticed that the natives, when addressing me or referring to me in conversation, either when not aware of my identity or not sufficiently sure of themselves to address me as "Consul" (or "Balyooz," which is the term used for Consul in Oman and the Gulf ports), always applied to me the word "Nasarani" = Christian: for instance, "Good morning, O Christian," or "Hie! Christian, there is no road that way!" The term did not appear to be said or meant disdainfully, as the speakers were quite friendly, and I took it to be merely a relic of Wahabi fanaticism which was of course predominant in this district in the last century.

From Ibri onwards, or rather from Dhank onwards, the route which I followed differed very little from that of Col. Miles, so I do not propose to deal with it in great detail. There are one or two points, however, wherein the field-book and compass sketch which I made of my route give the lie of certain features somewhat differently to that given by Col. Miles in the map accompanying his paper in the Society's *Journal* in August and October 1910...[*corrections of Miles' mapping*]

On this part of the march one of the escort riding in front did a smart bit of business: he dropped out of the line ahead of us, shot at and killed a hare with his rifle, retrieved it, and mounted again without losing more than a dozen places in the marching line.

The descent into the Jauf of Oman was down a torrent bed, and took us half an hour. On reaching the bottom the path turned right round to the left, that is, to the north-east, along the south side of Jabal al Kor. It was 8 o'clock before we got to Saifam, which lies in a wadi bed of the same name right under the peak at the highest point of Jabal al Kor and not far from the southern mouth of the Najd al Barak, or "Pass of the Lightning," which can be discerned if one moves a little out into the plain. This was the alternative route taken by Miles.

On our arrival at Saifam Shaikh Rashid learnt that the Shaikh Nasir bin Hamad, the 'Utubi Shaikh of Bahla, had come down to Jabrin to meet us, and was awaiting my arrival there, so Shaikh Rashid thought we ought to push on first thing in the morning. We accordingly started off at 6.30, and reached Jabrin, 7 ½ miles away, at 8 o'clock, the caravan coming in at leisure.

Jabrin is State property, and is now merely the summer quarters of Shaikh Nasir and a few other Bahia people. The fort looks imposing from the outside. On arrival we were met by a relative of the Shaikh and taken through the village to an open space outside under a fine acacia tree, where they had some camel and horse races for our edification. I noticed that the population here seemed to be mostly negroes. As I was only staying until the afternoon, it was not worth while pitching a camp, and they had a room carpeted in an outhouse in one of the date gardens for us to rest in. People dropped in and out all day. About 2 o'clock I started off with one of my escort and a petty Bani Riyam Shaikh from Tanuf to see Bahla. It was about a 4-mile ride, partly through a thickly wooded glen. It is a most imposing place with a very fine old castle, of which Miles gives a description and a photograph in his paper. I only rode through the town and went over the fort to enjoy the view from the top, and then returned to Jabrin to pick up my caravan. From Jabrin I marched to Nizwa, with a halt halfway at Radda. Radda and Farq to the north are both in the Wadi Nizwa, while facing southwards you are looking towards Manah and Adam, the former being visible in the distance. The whole plain in which Bahla, Jabrin, Kubara, and Nizwa lie is like a large crater studded with low volcanic hills, bounded on the north by the Jabal al Kor, on the east by the Jabal Akhdhar, and on the west to south by the Jabal Hamra, the habitat of the Daru tribe. This latter small range looks geologically of a completely different character to the surrounding systems, and appeared of a bright terra cotta colour.

At Nizwa we had the usual preliminary reception. The Wali was one of the Muscat Royal Family named Saiyid Saif bin Hamad. He it was who got the Nizwa back into the possession of the family by murdering Hilal bin Zahir (for whom see Col. Miles' paper). He received us at the fort gate, and after giving us coffee took me to a date garden where a comfortable shed had been prepared for me. The caravan came in in due course, and after the hard travelling of the last few days I was glad to get into comfortable quarters.

To-day I bade good-bye to some of the men who formed my escort from Ibri. During the journey I had talked a great deal with them of the nature of the Great Desert and the possibility of crossing it, and two of my companions, Shaikh Muhammad bin Mansur of the Al Wahibah and Mazar bin Naif of the Awamir, had repeatedly protested their readiness to take me across, declaring that in the winter we should have no difficulty with good camels and a good bundobust. They would propose to take 15 men, 5 Al Wahibah, 5 Awamir, and 5 Daru, and of course only picked Badawi camels able to go for many days without water. They declared that as far as getting me across was concerned they could guarantee success; all the misgiving they had was as regards our reception by the Badawi when we reached the other side: that, they said, must be my responsibility and would need careful previous arrangement in order to ensure friendly treatment. These conversations imbued me with serious thoughts of contriving an expedition to attempt the crossing from Adam or the furthest possible base on the desert fringe in that direction, but my transfer to Bushire soon afterwards, and the publication of an article by Mr. Bacon suggesting a crossing by balloon, turned my thoughts in other directions. Probably the riddle will be solved by air in the course of time, but it does not appear to be a practicable proposition for the existing aeroplane.

After a quiet night I went out early with the Akid or commander of the fort to look round Nizwa and take a few photos, including one of the old Persian Bazaar known as the "Suq el Faris." I also took a picture of a cultivator churning indigo vats in the date gardens, and a view of two of the main street and fort. I then entered the fort with the Wali and was shown all over it, taking a view from the top and a photo of one of the Hazrami garrison occupying his leisure, in these piping times of peace, at the loom, in one of the gun embrasures.

Wellsted has given a description of Nizwa fort. It is a very strong one and renowned in the annals of Oman. It contains a capacious water reservoir, but at present no battery to speak of; there is, however, an interesting old gun in the basement bearing the Portuguese arms, but with a Persian inscription round the touch-hole mentioning the name of Padshah Shah Abbas. The Wali says the gun is said to have been brought from the island of Hormuz, and that would seem probable.

While at Nizwa I received another letter from Muscat telling me that H.M.S. *Amphitrite* had not left England till May 6, so she could not reach Muscat for some days after the date first announced: this was a great relief to me. Shaikh Rashid also received a letter from the Sultan by the same messenger, in which H.H. gave him the news that 200 Omanis had been killed by the Portuguese in East Africa. On this occasion a fleet of Omanis dhows from Sur, while engaged in loading up a very large consignment of slaves, was cornered by a Portuguese man-of-war and all captured or killed and upwards of 700 slaves released. 150 of the Omanis who were captured were sent to the Portuguese penal settlement in Angola on a sentence of twenty-five years, and I imagine that those who survived are still there.

During the forenoon of this day, May 20, it clouded over and in the afternoon some nice rain fell. Every one was transported with delight at this welcome visitation, as there had been a long-continued drought. Birds and frogs held high revel, and it was the greatest pleasure to feel and smell the rain.

I noticed that the population in general were in a highly nervous state and easily alarmed. One only had to hear a rifle-shot or two and every one got the wind up. It was significant of the unsettled state of the country and unsatisfactory relations prevailing between one tribe and another. For example, while out for a walk on the outskirts of the town, I said I should like to go up to the top of a nice-looking tower about 500 yards off to get a view of the oasis, but my companion said it would not be safe to go as it was a Bani Riyam tower, and we should certainly be fired at—and this was within a stone's throw of his own house.

I was sorry to leave Nizwa where everybody had been very friendly and civil to us. Between Nizwa and Samad al Kindi, my next stop, only 2 miles away, is an unbroken stretch of date gardens. It was considered politically desirable that I should halt at Samad al Kindi for the following reasons: The Shaikh of the place, Hamdan bin Saif, who proved to be a fair aristocratic young man of about thirty, was at feud with his cousin at Tanuf. In the days when their grandfather Shaikh Sulaiman ruled both Tanuf and Samad al Kindi, his two sons, Saif and another, had a bitter quarrel. It developed into a resort to firearms, and in the fray Saif shot his brother and his brother's daughter and lost one or two of his own adherents. He thereupon fled to Samad al Kindi and remained there, while the dead brother's family stayed on at Tanuf. The feud of course smouldered on, and one day Himyar, son of the dead brother and brother of the dead girl, succeeded in shooting his uncle Saif dead while at prayers, and then returned to his stronghold at Tanuf. The result is that both families now go in fear of their lives, and venture out very little. It was feared that if I paid attention only to one branch the others might lay themselves out to defeat my plans in order to do a bad turn to their rival. I had to spend the night at Samad al Kiudi, and as the gardens were full of mosquitoes, Shaikh Rashid and I went and slept out in the open plain. In the morning I got off betimes and arrived at Tanuf, a distance of about 7 miles, in a couple of hours, our direction seeming to be due north the whole way. Tanuf is situated at the base of the mountains blocking and commanding the entrance to the ascent up the Wadi Tanuf to the plateau of the Jabal Akhdhar.

I found Shaikh Himyar a fair-complexioned young man of much the same age and type as his cousin in Samad al Kindi, but smaller in stature. He gave me a salute from his tower with an old cannon, and there were the usual evolutions outside the town, followed by a gathering in the guest house, a long building (50 feet by 15 feet), while coffee was being served. Small talk for public consumption on these occasions soon gets exhausted and the long waits are very boring. Arabs themselves do not seem to mind sitting speechless for an indefinite time, tapping the ground with their canes, but it is extremely boring for Europeans.

As soon as I could I adjourned to my own quarters. The Shaikh came in to see me after breakfast. I had difficulty in getting him down to anything definite as regards my journey, and we parted without having arrived at an understanding. I came to the conclusion that greed was at the bottom of his intractability, and that he was out for blackmail, and this was soon confirmed. On leaving me he went to my pilot, Shaikh Rashid, and said that the Sultan some time ago had promised him a Lee-Metford rifle but had never sent it, and he wanted to know why. Shaikh Rashid offered him his own, saying he knew nothing about the Sultan's promise, but in any case would send him a new one from himself and me when we got back to Muscat. The Shaikh did not come in to me again during the day, but was busy making every sort of ridiculous difficulty, including the old chestnut which I had so often heard, that as the result of Col. Miles' visit five and twenty years before, a blight had fallen on the fruit. Also that the people were alarmed by my camera and prismatic compass—all bunkum. Finally, he made specific pecuniary demands on this and that score, which amounted in all to 500 Maria Theresa dollars, about £50, to be paid in advance. I replied that I was the Sultan's friend, travelling for my own pleasure and enjoyment in H.M. country, accompanied by his most well-known and respected retainer, and bearing all necessary letters of introduction, and I absolutely refused to pay any blackmail, either 500 dollars or any sum at all. He must either let me through without any offensive conditions or I would go straight back to Muscat and lay the matter before the Sultan. I heard no more that night, and turned in somewhat worried but hoping for the best. In the morning with the dawn donkeys were produced and our frugal baggage loaded up, and about 6 a.m. in came the Shaikh in a most amiable mood, smiling as if there had never been any unpleasant question between us, and announced that he was going to accompany me himself. Accordingly, at 6.30 we started on our way, Shaikh Rashid, Shaikh Himyar, my servant, and I, all on foot, with four donkeys with our food and bedding following on behind. The ascent was very steep to begin with, and distressing for the first two hours owing to the heat and the sun blazing straight into our eyes. At 8.15 we had an easy while the Arabs had a cold breakfast of dates and dried shark flesh. They cut or hammered off great chunks of the shark meat, and after beating it into a fibrous state picked it to pieces and ate it. After about four hours' walking at 2½ miles an hour we came to a rain-water cistern in the rocks, formed by blocking up the side of a deep cranny in the nullah. Here under the shadow of an over-hanging rock we halted for the hot noon-day hours, and in the afternoon intended to do the second half of our journey to Saiq; but about 1 o'clock, just as I was ready to start, some villagers brought in a goat, and it appeared absolutely necessary to my party that the goat should be eaten immediately, so we were considerably delayed in getting off, and after walking for two and a half hours at about 3 miles an hour, we found it was too late for us to reach Saiq that night. (I may mention that my companions generally used the diminutive form of Suwaiq for this village.) Meanwhile we reached the Wadi Habib, which gives its name to a small village of about thirty houses of Bani Riyam. It was built up the side of a deep nullah and reminded me very much of a Kashmir village. As we descended the series of steps down the side of the nullah in single file, the villagers all passed up one by one, each clasping our hand in one or both of theirs and uttering their rustic greeting, "Marhaba-Bakum" ("welcome to you"). On getting down to the bottom of the nullah we were shown to an open carpeted platform (for the entertainment of guests) in the bed of the wadi, surrounded by a mass of pomegranate and walnut trees. One fine walnut tree formed a canopy to the guest house, as the acacia tree did at Jabrin. All this time it was thundering and lightning and the sky looked very threatening. Our hosts inquired if I would like to sleep out in the open or under the trees. I replied, as it looked like rain I would prefer being under the tree or even in the shelter of a house. They assured me it was not going to rain, but our donkeys had hardly arrived and shot my things down under the tree when it came on to rain in torrents, and our baggage got very wet before we could get it into shelter. The villagers were very kind and friendly, however, and helped us to carry our things into shelter and fetched water and wood for us, and with a change of clothes and a fire we were all soon comfortable and ready to turn in. I did not sleep very well, as I was tormented by some biting insect which attacked my hands and wrists; I could not hear any buzzing, so concluded that my visitors were those of the silent order.

In the morning I got my tea at daybreak, and then strolled out with my camera and gun and collected one or two birds while the donkeys were loading up.

Saiq proved to be only 4 miles distant, and I found it a disappointing place, like the ordinary Baltistan village: stone houses plastered with reddish earth and with flat mud roofs, and with a succession of orchards in front. There was a certain amount of wheat and barley cultivation in terraces, and a good show of mulberries, peaches, and apricots, but the main cultivation was in the form of a fine show of pomegranates. After halting for a short time to look round we continued our march to the village of Sharaija—so pronounced by the inhabitants.

Miles and Wellsted spell the name Shiraizi, connecting it with Shiraz. ... It is a larger and more picturesque village than Saiq, situated at the head of a fine canyon facing south-west and looking down towards Birkat al Moz. The sides of the wadi are very massive and steep, and it is altogether a grand bit of scenery.... My poor old pilot Shaikh Rashid was beginning to look very tired and sorry for himself; probably he had never had to walk so much before in his life. After partaking of the usual coffee we were conducted through the busy portion of the town to the so-called guest house, two compartments on the ground floor which had been used as stables being set apart for our use, one for our donkeys and the other for ourselves. The floor was covered with litter, which we proceeded to clear away as far as possible. I expect this is the place that Wellsted mentions, and in which he would not stay. The villagers told him this was where travellers were always accommodated. Since Miles' visit in 1885, only one European had visited Sharaija, one whom they called "Butros." They referred no doubt to the missionary Peter Zwemer, the brother of the Rev. Samuel Zwemer whom I mentioned at the beginning of this paper as having travelled from Abu Dhabi to Baraimi. Peter Zwemer died of fever in America very soon afterwards.

Just below the guest house was a fine circular reservoir, fed by a spring, in which at the time several lads were bathing. The season, it will be remembered, was the end of May and excessively hot in the sun. I sat and looked on longingly until our donkeys came, when I got out my bathing suit and had a dip, but the spring water was too ice-cold for me to stay in long. While sitting at the pool I talked to some villagers, and one of them of course repeated the old story about Col. Miles and the blighted fruit trees. I tried to demonstrate the foolishness of it, and went on to say that anyhow on this occasion please God my coming was propitious, for wherever I had stopped I had brought rain after prolonged drought, as for instance at Nizwa and at Wadi Habib last night. The words were hardly out of my mouth when a storm began to work up overhead, and before long we had heavy rain, and it continued all the afternoon; pleasant for them but not convenient for me, as it obscured the view and greatly hampered my photographic activities. My Tanuf friend Shaikh Himyar here took his leave, as he feared for his life if he went further afield then Sharaija, saying that if his hostile relations heard that he had got down to Muti they would be able to cut him off. He apologized humbly for his uncouth conduct at Tanuf, and pleaded that it was due to his ignorance of our usages! He certainly had been very helpful since we started, and his presence had ensured me a friendly reception on the Jabal, and so on Shaikh Rashid's advice, which I felt bound to follow, he was promised a Lee-Metford rifle and 100 dollars, to be handed over to his representative on our arrival at Samail. He sent a local Shaikh, Yunas by name, to represent him as far as Muti, which was the limit of the Bani Riyam.

T.E. LAWRENCE (1888–1935)

A controversial figure to this day, Lawrence was born in Caernarvonshire and moved to Oxford when he was eight. Educated at the City of Oxford High School and Jesus College, he graduated from Oxford with first class honours in 1910. During vacations in 1909 and 1910 he went to Syria and Palestine to research crusader castles for his Oxford thesis. Between 1911 and 1913 he worked with D.G. Hogarth on a British Museum archaeological dig at Carchemish. It has been suggested that these trips, apart from their archaeological significance, were part of intelligence work. With his knowledge of the Sinai Lawrence was an obvious candidate to join the Military Intelligence Department in Cairo shortly after outbreak of war in 1914. In 1916 he was involved in the Arab Revolt against the Turks, which formed the subject matter of *The Seven Pillars of Wisdom*, first published in a limited edition in 1922. An abridged version with the title *Revolt in the Desert* was a huge popular success in 1927, but Lawrence withdrew it before a second edition could be put out. The same year *Seven Pillars* first appeared, Lawrence joined the RAF under an assumed name, and a year later the army tank corps as 'Private Shaw'. He both enjoyed and affected to disdain the 'Lawrence myth' disseminated by the lectures of the American publicist Lowell Thomas. His last foreign posting was in India in 1927. Discharged from the RAF in 1935, he died in a motorcycle accident near his Dorset home.

From:

Revolt in the Desert (1927)

Taken from the more 'straight narrative' (Trevelyan 1986: 6) *Revolt in the Desert* (as compared with *Seven Pillars*), the chapter combines the detailed description of terrain and the atmospherics of the desert for which Lawrence is famed. The incident at the water well, especially the use of dialogue, recalls Doughty. (A strong advocate of Doughty – Lawrence wrote a preface to the 1922 reprinting of *Arabia Deserta*).

Riding up to Feisal

Next morning I left Jidda by ship for Rabegh, the headquarters of Sherif Ali, Abdulla's elder brother. When Ali received his father's 'order' to send me at once up to Feisal, he was staggered, but could not help himself. So he prepared for me his own splendid riding-camel, saddled with his own saddle, and hung with luxurious housings and cushions of Nejd leather-work pieced and inlaid in various colours, with plaited fringes and nets embroidered with metal tissues. As a trustworthy man he chose out Tafas, a Hawazim Harb tribesman, with his son, to guide me to Feisal's camp.

Ali would not let me start till after sunset, lest any of his followers see me leave the camp. He kept my journey a secret even from his slaves, and gave me an Arab cloak and headcloth to wrap round myself and my uniform, that I might present a proper silhouette in the dark upon my camel. I had no food with me; so he instructed Tafas to get something to eat at Bir el Sheikh, the first settlement, some sixty miles out, and charged him most stringently to keep me from questioning and curiosity on the way, and to avoid all camps and encounters.

We marched through the palm-groves which lay like a girdle about the scattered houses of Rabegh village, and then out under the stars along the Tehama, the sandy and featureless strip of desert bordering the western coast of Arabia between sea-beach and littoral hills, for hundreds of monotonous miles. In daytime this low plain was insufferably hot, and its waterless character made it a forbidding road; yet it was inevitable, since the more fruitful hills were too rugged to afford passage north and south for loaded animals.

The cool of the night was pleasant after the day of checks and discussions which had so dragged at Rabegh. Tafas led on without speaking, and the camels went silently over the soft flat sand. My thoughts as we went were how this was the Pilgrim Road, down which, for uncounted generations, the people of the north had come to visit the Holy City, bearing with them gifts of faith for the shrine; and it seemed that the Arab Revolt might be in a sense a return pilgrimage, to take back to the north, to Syria, an ideal for an ideal, a belief in liberty for their past belief in a revelation.

We endured for some hours, without variety except at times when the camels plunged and strained a little and the saddles creaked: indications that the soft plain had merged into beds of drift-sand, dotted with tiny scrub, and therefore uneven going, since the plants collected little mounds about their roots, and the eddies of the sea-winds scooped hollows in the intervening spaces. Camels appeared not sure-footed in the dark, and the starlit sand carried little shadow, so that hummocks and holes were difficult to see. Before midnight we halted, and I rolled myself tighter in my cloak, and chose a hollow of my own size and shape, and slept well in it till nearly dawn.

As soon as he felt the air growing chill with the coming change, Tafas got up, and two minutes later we were swinging forward again. An hour after and it grew bright, as we climbed a low neck of lava drowned nearly to the top with blown sand. This joined a small flow near the shore to the main Hejaz lava-field, whose western edge ran up upon our right hand, and caused the coast road to lie where it did. The neck was stony, but brief: on each side the blue lava humped itself into low shoulders, from which, so Tafas said, it was possible to see ships sailing on the sea. Pilgrims had built cairns here by the road. Sometimes they were individual piles, of just three stones set up one above the other: sometimes they were common heaps, to which any disposed passer-by might add his stone—not reasonably nor with known motive, but because others did, and perhaps they knew.

Beyond the ridge the path descended into a broad open place, the Masturah, or plain by which Wadi Fura flowed into the sea. Seaming its surface with innumerable interwoven channels of loose stone, a few inches deep, were the beds of the flood water, on those rare occasions when there was rain in the Tareif and the courses raged like rivers to the sea. The delta here was about six miles wide. Down some part of it water flowed for an hour or two, or even for a day or two, every so many years. Underground there was plenty of moisture, protected by the overlying sand from the sun-heat; and thorn trees and loose scrub profited by it and flourished. Some of the trunks were a foot through: their height might be twenty feet. The trees and bushes stood somewhat apart, in clusters, their lower branches cropped by the hungry camels. So they looked cared for, and had a premeditated air, which felt strange in the wilderness, more especially as the Tehama hitherto had been a sober bareness.

In the early sunlight we lifted our camels to a steady trot across the good going of these shingle-beds among the trees, making for Masturah well, the first stage out from Rabegh on the Pilgrim Road. There we would water and halt a little. My camel was a delight to me, for I had not been on such an animal before. There were no good camels in Egypt; and those of the Sinai Desert, while hardy and strong, were not taught to pace fair and softly and swiftly, like these rich mounts of the Arabian princes.

Yet her accomplishments were today largely wasted, since they were reserved for riders who had the knack and asked for them, and not for me, who expected to be carried, and had no sense of how to ride. It was easy to sit on a camel's back without falling off, but very difficult to understand and get the best out of her so as to do long journeys without fatiguing either rider or beast. Tafas gave me hints as we went: indeed, it was one of the few subjects on which he would speak. His orders to preserve me from contact with the world seemed to have closed even his mouth. A pity, for his dialect interested me.

Quite close to the north bank of the Masturah, we found the well. Beside it were some decayed stone walls which had been a hut, and opposite it some little shelters of branches and palm—leaves, under which a few Beduin were sitting. We did not greet them. Instead, Tafas turned across to the ruinous walls, and dismounted; and I sat in their shade while he and Abdulla watered the animals, and drew a drink for themselves and for me. The well was old, and broad, with good stone steyning, and a strong coping round the top. It was about twenty feet deep; and for the convenience of travellers without ropes, like ourselves, a square chimney had been contrived in the masonry, with foot and hand holds in the corners, so that a man might descend to the water, and fill his goatskin.

Idle hands had flung so many stones down the shaft, that half the bottom of the well was choked, and the water not abundant. Abdulla tied his flowing sleeves about his shoulders; tucked his gown under his cartridge belt; and clambered nimbly down and up, bringing each time four or five gallons which he poured for our camels into a stone trough beside the well. They drank about five gallons each, for they had been watered at Rabegh a day back. Then we let them moon about a little, while we sat in peace, breathing the light wind coming off the sea. Abdulla smoked a cigarette as reward for his exertions.

Some Harb came up, driving a large herd of brood camels, and began to water them, having sent one man down the well to fill their large leather bucket, which the others drew up hand over hand with a loud staccato chant.

As we watched them two riders, trotting light and fast on thoroughbred camels, drew towards us from the north. Both were young. One was dressed in rich Cashmere robes and heavy silk embroidered headcloth. The other was plainer, in white cotton, with a red cotton head-dress. They halted beside the well; and the more splendid one slipped gracefully to the ground without kneeling his camel, and threw his halter to his companion, saying, carelessly, 'Water them while I go over there and rest.' Then he strolled across and sat down under our wall, after glancing at us with affected unconcern. He offered a cigarette, just rolled and licked, saying, 'Your presence is from Syria?' I parried politely, suggesting that he was from Mecca, to which he likewise made no direct reply. We spoke a little of the war and of the leanness of the Harb she-camels.

Meanwhile the other rider stood by, vacantly holding the halters, waiting perhaps for the Harb to finish watering their herd before taking his turn. The young lord cried 'What is it, Mustafa? Water them at once.' The servant came up to say dismally, 'They will not let me.' 'God's mercy!' shouted his master furiously, as he scrambled to his feet and hit the unfortunate Mustafa three or four sharp blows about the head and shoulders with his riding-stick.

'Go and ask them.' Mustafa looked hurt, astonished, and angry as though he would hit back, but thought better of it, and ran to the well.

The Harb, shocked, in pity made a place for him, and let his two camels drink from their water-trough. They whispered, 'Who is he?' and Mustafa said, 'Our Lord's cousin from Mecca.' At once they ran and untied a bundle from one of their saddles, and spread from it before the two riding-camels fodder of the green leaves and buds of the thorn trees. They were used to gather this by striking the low bushes with a heavy staff, till the broken tips of the branches rained down on a cloth stretched over the ground beneath.

The young Sherif watched them contentedly. When his camel had fed, he climbed slowly and without apparent effort up its neck into the saddle, where he settled himself leisurely, and took an unctuous farewell of us, asking God to requite the Arabs bountifully. They wished him a good journey; and he started southward, while Abdulla brought our camels, and we went off northward. Ten minutes later I heard a chuckle from old Tafas, and saw wrinkles of delight between his grizzled beard and moustache.

'What is upon you, Tafas?' said I.

'My Lord, you saw those two riders at the well?'

'The Sherif and his servant?'

'Yes; but they were Sherif Ali ibn el Hussein of Modhig, and his cousin, Sherif Mohsin, lords of the Harith, who are blood enemies of the Masruh. They feared they would be delayed or driven off the water if the Arabs knew them. So they pretended to be master and servant from Mecca. Did you see how Mohsin raged when Ali beat him? Ali is a devil. While only eleven years old he escaped from his father's house to his uncle, a robber of pilgrims by trade; and with him he lived by his hands for many months, till his father caught him. He was with our lord Feisal from the first day's battle in Medina, and led the Ateiba in the plains round Aar and Bir Derwish. It was all camel-fighting; and Ali would have no man with him who could not do as he did, run beside his camel, and leap with one hand into the saddle, carrying his rifle. The children of Harith are children of battle.' For the first time the old man's mouth was full of words.

While he spoke we scoured along the dazzling plain, now nearly bare of trees, and turning slowly softer under foot. At first it had been grey shingle, packed like gravel. Then the sand increased and the stones grew rarer, till we could distinguish the colours of the separate flakes, porphyry, green schist, basalt. At last it was nearly pure white sand, under which lay a harder stratum. Such going was like a pile-carpet for our camels' running. The particles of sand were clean and polished, and caught the blaze of sun like little diamonds in a reflection so fierce, that after a while I could not endure it. I frowned hard, and pulled the headcloth forward in a peak over my eyes, and beneath them, too, like a beaver, trying to shut out the heat which rose in glassy waves off the ground, and beat up against my face. Eighty miles in front of us, the huge peak of Rudhwa behind Yenbo was looming and fading in the dazzle of vapour which hid its foot. Quite near in the plain little shapeless hills seemed to block the way. To our right the steep ridge of Beni Ayub, toothed and narrow like a saw-blade, fell away on the north into a blue series of smaller hills, soft in character, behind which lofty range after range in a jagged stairway, red now the sun grew low, climbed up to the towering central mass of Jebel Subh with its fantastic granite spires.

A little later we turned to the right, off the Pilgrim Road, and took a short cut across gradually rising ground of flat basalt ridges, buried in sand till only their topmost piles showed above the surface.

Along this we held our way till sunset, when we came into sight of the hamlet of Bir el Sheikh. In the first dark as the supper fires were lighted we rode down its wide open street and halted. Tafas went into one of the twenty miserable huts, and in a few whispered words and long silences bought flour, of which with water he kneaded a dough cake two inches thick and eight inches across. This he buried in the ashes of a brushwood fire, provided for him by a Subh woman whom he seemed to know. When the cake was warmed he drew it out of the fire, and clapped it to shake off the dust: then we shared it together, while Abdulla went away to buy himself tobacco.

They told me the place had two stone-lined wells at the bottom of the southward slope, but I felt disinclined to go and look at them, for the long ride that day had tired my unaccustomed muscles, and the heat of the plain had been painful. My skin was blistered by it, and my eyes ached with the glare of light striking up at a sharp angle from the silver sand, and from the shining pebbles. The last two years I had spent in Cairo, at a desk all day or thinking hard in a little overcrowded office full of distracting noises, with a hundred rushing things to say, but no bodily need except to come and go each day between office and hotel. In consequence the novelty of this change was severe, since time had not been given me gradually to accustom myself to the pestilent beating of the Arabian sun, and the long monotony of camel pacing. There was to be another stage tonight, and a long day tomorrow before Feisal's camp would be reached.

So I was grateful for the cooking and the marketing, which spent one hour, and for the second hour of rest after it which we took by common consent; and sorry when it ended, and we remounted, and rode in pitch darkness up valleys and down valleys, passing in and out of bands of air, which were hot in the confined hollows, but fresh and stirring in the open places. The ground under foot must have been sandy, because the silence of our passage hurt my straining ears, and smooth, for I was always falling asleep in the saddle, to wake a few seconds later suddenly and sickeningly, as I clutched by instinct at the saddle post to recover my balance which had been thrown out by the irregular stride of the animal. It was too dark, and the forms of the country were too neutral, to hold my heavy-lashed, peering eyes. At length we stopped for good, long after midnight; and I was rolled up in my cloak and asleep in a most comfortable little sand-grave before Tafas had done knee-haltering my camel.

Three hours later we were on the move again, helped now by the last shining of the moon. We marched down Wadi Mared, the night of it dead, hot, silent, and on each side sharp-pointed hills standing up black and white in the exhausted air. There were many trees. Dawn finally came to us as we passed out of the narrows into a broad place, over whose flat floor an uneasy wind span circles, capriciously, in the dust. The day strengthened always, and now showed Bir ibn Hassani just to our right. The trim settlement of absurd little houses, brown and white, holding together for security's sake, looked doll-like and more lonely than the desert, in the immense shadow of the dark precipice of Subh, behind. While we watched it, hoping to see life at its doors, the sun was rushing up, and the fretted cliffs, those thousands of feet above our heads, became outlined in hard refracted shafts of white light against a sky still sallow with the transient dawn.

We rode on across the great valley. A camel-rider, garrulous and old, came out from the houses and jogged over to join us. He named himself Khallaf, too friendly-like. His salutation came after a pause in a trite stream of chat; and when it was returned he tried to force us into conversation. However, Tafas grudged his company, and gave him short answers. Khallaf persisted, and finally, to improve his footing, bent down and burrowed in his saddle pouch till he found a small covered pot of enamelled iron, containing a liberal portion of the staple of travel in the Hejaz. This was the unleavened dough cake of yesterday, but crumbled between the fingers while still warm, and moistened with liquid butter till its particles would fall apart only reluctantly. It was then sweetened for eating with ground sugar, and scooped up like damp sawdust in pressed pellets with the fingers.

I ate a little, on this my first attempt, while Tafas and Abdulla played at it vigorously; so for his bounty Khallaf went half-hungry: deservedly, for it was thought effeminate by the Arabs to carry a provision of food for a little journey of one hundred miles. We were now fellows, and the chat began again while Khallaf told us about the last fighting, and a reverse Feisal had had the day before. It seemed he had been beaten out of the head of Wadi Safra, and was now at Hamra, only a little way in front of us; or at least Khallaf thought he was there: we might learn for sure in the next village on our road. The fighting had not been severe; but the few casualties were all among the tribesmen of Tafas and Khallaf and the names and hurts of each were told in order.

We rode seven miles, to a low watershed, crossed by a wall of granite slivers, now little more than a shapeless heap, but once no doubt a barrier. It ran from cliff to cliff, and even far up the hillsides, wherever the slopes were not too steep to climb. In the centre, where the road passed, had been two small enclosures like pounds. I asked Khallaf the purpose of the wall. He replied that he had been in Damascus and Constantinople and Cairo, and had many friends among the great men of Egypt. Did I know any of the English there? Khallaf seemed curious about my intentions and my history. He tried to trip me in Egyptian phrases. When I answered in the dialect of Aleppo he spoke of prominent Syrians of his acquaintance. I knew them, too; and he switched off into local politics, asking careful questions, delicately and indirectly, about the Sherif and his sons, and what I thought Feisal was going to do. I understood less of this than he, and parried inconsequentially. Tafas came to my rescue, and changed the subject. Afterwards we knew that Khallaf was in Turkish pay, and used to send frequent reports of what came past Bir ibn Hassani for the Arab forces.

We turned to the right, across another saddle, and then downhill for a few miles to a corner of tall cliffs. We rounded this and found ourselves suddenly in Wadi Safra, the valley of our seeking, and in the midst of Wasta, its largest village. Wasta seemed to be many nests of houses, clinging to the hillsides each side the torrent-bed on banks of alluvial soil, or standing on detritus islands between the various deep-swept channels whose sum made up the parent valley.

Riding between two or three of these built-up islands, we made for the dar bank of the valley. On our way was the main bed of the winter floods, a sweep of white shingles and boulders, quite flat. Down its middle, from palm grove on the one side to palm grove on the other, lay a reach of clear water, perhaps two hundred yards long and twelve feet wide, sand-bottomed, and bordered on each brink by a ten-foot lawn of thick grass and flowers. On it we halted a moment to let our camels put their heads down and drink their fill, and the relief of the grass to our eyes after the daylong hard glitter of the pebbles was so sudden that involuntarily I glanced up to see if a cloud had not covered the face of the sun.

We rode up the stream to the garden from which it ran sparkling in a stone-lined channel; and then we turned along the mud wall of the garden in the shadow of its palms, to another of the detached hamlets. Tafas led the way up its little street (the houses were so low that from our saddles we looked down upon their clay roofs), and near one of the larger houses stopped and beat upon the door of an uncovered court. A slave opened to us, and we dismounted in privacy. Tafas haltered the camels, loosed their girths, and strewed before them green fodder from a fragrant pile beside the gate. Then he led me into the guest room of the house, a dark clean little mud-brick place, roofed with half palm logs under hammered earth. We sat down on the palm-leaf mat which ran along the dais. The day in this stifling valley had grown very hot; and gradually we lay back side by side. Then the hum of the bees in the gardens without, and of the flies hovering over our veiled faces within, lulled us into sleep.

Before we awoke, a meal of bread and dates had been prepared for us by the people of the house. The dates were new, meltingly sweet and good, like none I had ever tasted. Afterwards we mounted again, and rode up the clear, slow rivulet till it was hidden within the palm gardens, behind their low boundary walls of sun-dried clay. In and out between the tree roots were dug little canals a foot or two deep, so contrived that the stream might be let into them from the stone channel, and each tree watered in its turn. The head of water was owned by the community, and shared out among the landowners for so many minutes or hours daily or weekly according to the traditional use. The water was a little brackish, as was needful for the best palms; but it was sweet enough in the wells of private water in the groves. These wells were very frequent, and found water three or four feet below the surface.

Our way took us through the central village and its market street. There was little in the shops; and all the place felt decayed. A generation ago Wasta was populous (they said of a thousand houses); but one day there rolled a huge wall of water down Wadi Safra, the embankments of many palm-gardens were breached, and the palm trees swept away. Some of the islands on which houses had stood for centuries were submerged, and the mud houses melted back again into mud, killing or drowning the unfortunate slaves within. The men could have been replaced, and the trees, had the soil remained; but the gardens had been built up of earth carefully won from the normal freshets by years of labour, and this wave of water—eight feet deep, running in a race for three days—reduced the plots in its track to their primordial banks of stones.

A little above Wasta the valley widened somewhat, to an average of perhaps four hundred yards, with a bed of fine shingle and sand, laid very smooth by the winter rains. The walls were of bare red and black rock, whose edges and ridges were sharp as knife blades, and reflected the sun like metal. They made the freshness of the trees and grass seem luxurious. We now saw parties of Feisal's soldiers, and grazing herds of their saddle camels. Before we reached Hamra every nook in the rocks or clump of trees was a bivouac. They cried cheery greetings to Tafas, who came to life again, waving back and calling to them, while he pressed on quickly to end his duty towards me.

Hamra opened on our left. It seemed a village of about one hundred houses, buried in gardens among mounds of earth some twenty feet in height. We forded a little stream, and went up a walled path between trees to the top of one of these mounds, where we made our camels kneel by the yard-gate of a long, low house.

Tafas said something to a slave who stood there with silver-hilted sword in hand. He led me to an inner court, on whose further side, framed between the uprights of a black doorway, stood a white figure waiting tensely for me. I felt at first glance that this was the man I had come to Arabia to seek—the leader who would bring the Arab Revolt to full glory. Feisal looked very tall and pillar-like, very slender, in his long white silk robes and his brown headcloth bound with a brilliant scarlet and gold cord. His eyelids were dropped; and his black beard and colourless face were like a mask against the strange, still watchfulness of his body. His hands were crossed in front of him on his dagger.

I greeted him. He made way for me into the room, and sat down on his carpet near the door. As my eyes grew accustomed to the shade, they saw that the little room held many silent figures, looking at me or at Feisal steadily. He remained staring down at his hands, which were twisting slowly about his dagger. At last he inquired softly how I had found the journey. I spoke of the heat, and he asked how long from Rabegh, commenting that I had ridden fast for the season.

'And do you like our place here in Wadi Safra?'

'Well; but it is far from Damascus.'

The word had fallen like a sword into their midst. There was a quiver. Then everybody present stiffened where he sat, and held his breath for a silent minute. Some, perhaps, were dreaming of far off success: others may have thought it a reflection on their late defeat. Feisal at length lifted his eyes, smiling at me, and said, 'Praise be to God, there are Turks nearer us than that.' We all smiled with him; and I rose and excused myself for the moment.

AMEEN RIHANI (1876–1940)

Although not as well-known a figure within English travel literature as he should be, to the researcher into Middle East societies of the inter-war years such as Bahrain, Saudi Arabia, or Yemen, the writings of Ameen Rihani constitute a valued and authoritative source. Born in Freike a small village in Lebanon in 1876, Rihani migrated to New York as a boy of 12. As a young man the United States gave him the freedom to develop himself as an individual, and as a person of Middle Eastern ethnicity to research into and choose his own identity. Moving beyond the narrow sectarian Maronite Lebanese background into which he had been born, Rihani found, as he later claimed, a larger Arab allegiance through reading the travel writing of Doughty and Burton in the New York public libraries. Returning to Syria in the first decade of the twentieth century, Rihani tapped into an emerging Arab nationalist discourse, while back in the United States he carved out a niche for himself as an exotic writer and reporter on Arabian culture. It was, however, when this novelty value wore off on the American public and he found it difficult to place his work that he decided to travel in Arabia. From late 1922 through 1923 he journeyed to the main cities and through the great deserts of the Arabian Peninsula, meeting rival Arab kings, emirs, sultans, and imams, and trying to enlist them in the cause of peace and Pan-Arabism. When he got back to America he wrote up these journeys in Arabic in *Muluk al-Arab* (Arab Kings), and in English in *Ibn Sa'oud of Arabia: His People and His Land*, *Around the Coasts of Arabia*, and *Arabian Peak and Desert: Travels in Al-Yaman*. Altogether these works provide a unique insight into the conservative Arabian societies on the verge of modernity, before the discovery of vast oil reserves (which Rihani helped conserve for Saudi Arabia) changed them forever. Knowing Arabic and Middle Eastern in appearance, Rihani was able to view the peninsula Arabs from the inside, while as a naturalised American citizen with a sympathetic eye he delineated their backwardness as well as the strides being made toward the modern world by his chief Arab hero, Abdul Aziz ibn Saud.

From:

Ibn Sa'oud of Arabia: His People and His Land (1928)

As a traveller on camel through the deserts of Central Arabia, Rihani performed journeys that compare with those of the Blunts, Doughty, and his contemporaries Bertram Thomas and Harry St. John Philby. He went to Riyadh the then capital of Nejd, where he spent a month as guest of Abdul Aziz ibn Saud, much of the time ill with malaria. There he gained an intimate view of the workings of what was soon to become the kingdom of Saudi Arabia. The visit confirmed him as an ally and interpreter of the most important Arab leader of his time.

In the Palace

I had, in fact, heard of the Georgian women in Ar-Riyadh, and when I went to visit the Sultan's father, the Imam Abd'ur-Rahman, who is about eighty and dyes his beard with *henna,* I was told that he had in his harim two Gurjiyahs (Georgian girls) and that one of them had recently given him a son. I do not know how many real Georgians, who are much prized in Najd for their alabaster beauty, were among the Armenian girls that were bought in Syria in the year of the red terror, when many thousands of that race were expelled from their homes by the Turks and driven east and south into the wilderness. The traders of Najd, who are always travelling between Al-Qasim and Damascus, bought seventy or eighty Armenian girls that year and sold them as slaves in Haiel, Buraidah and Ar-Riyadh. The Sultan purchased some of them, gave away a few to his relatives and friends, and had two with him in Al-Hasa when we were there. They have been made to embrace Al-Islam these girls, and were taught the Koran. The Chief Steward of the Sultanate of Najd, the Quartermaster-General and Finance Minister, Shalhoub, once told me a story which I would have deemed incredible had it been told by and about some one else. But the burly and ever busy Shalhoub, who would have one of his children, 'a boy of inflammable wit,' educated at the American University of Beirût, is a man of veracity and in spite of his position of modest demeanour. Nor does he indulge in ribaldry or brag. He had come to see me when I was sick, bringing with him a package of tea packed in India—'the best quality,' he said, 'in our stores.' Saiyed Hashem then came in, and as he was still looking for a wife he prodded the dear man with questions about women and slave-girls. Whereupon, to escape the prodding he told the following story.

Said Shalhoub: 'The Sultan Abd'ul-Aziz, Allah lengthen his days, once presented me a Gurjiyah. She was brought to him from Buraidah, and after he had 'entered upon her,'—one night only—he gave her to me, sent her to the house. And when I went to her room on the evening of that day I stood before the door with my heart in my hand (that is, trembling with fear); I entered, *bismillah*. But what I beheld—*wallah, billah!* every word I utter is truth—what I beheld tied my tongue, and I felt moreover as if I had received a blow on my head. I sat down and gazed upon her as upon an image.

'She held down her head after she had seen me. And I—never in my life have I seen or heard of such beauty, such august beauty. Her skin?—white as alabaster. Her hair?—like cataracts of melted gold. Her lips?—red as a pomegranate seed. Her forehead?— lofty and glowing like the dawn. And those honey-coloured eyes, so soft, so demure, so appealing to the honour of man. And I have nothing, O long-of-days, O *Ustaz*, but my honour that is of any worth. Yes, *billah*, I still have something more, which the years I thought had smuggled away from me. I sat before that image of beauty like a child—I tell you, like a child— and I felt the flame of shame upon me. I was ashamed to touch her, or to approach her, or even to speak to her. I got up and walked out of the room; and on the following day I sold her to a man from Kuwait for four hundred reals, aye, *wallah*, only four hundred.'

Saiyed Hashem looked at Shalhoub significantly, dubiously, and laughed. And Shalhoub, getting up to go: 'I swore by Allah, *ya Saiyed*. Are you a believer? Fear Allah then, and doubt not a believing brother.' A few days later the doubting Saiyed came to me and said: '*Wallah*, the story of Shalhoub is true.'

But the Sultan Abd'ul-Aziz is not always milk and honey to Shalhoub, nor does he always offer him odalisques of ineffable—untouchable—beauty. One day His Highness took me up to the roof of the Palace to show me the tower from which the great *atrik*—incandescent lamp—sends out at night penetrating white rays to the palm-groves encircling Ar-Riyadh;—a beacon to those who come from the desert or from the wadi. But Shalhoub is the keeper of the key to the tower, which was then closed. He was therefore called, and straightway he appeared. 'Where is the key?' the Sultan asked. The Quartermaster-General mumbled his reply. 'Get it,' His Highness darted out. 'In haste, Allah hasten thine end.' And Shalhoub running down the stairs tripped and fell on his hands: 'Allah has heard thee, O thou long-of-days,' The Sultan laughed.

He cherishes his Finance Minister and therefore likes to bully him. But it goes at times even beyond that. Once he committed a grave mistake, and the Sultan's ire was unleashed. He is terrible at such moments. His word, which is law, is likely to be anything save death. For this is in the hand of the Judge; and in his, too, when he sits in judgment. But he was very angry, in that instance, with his Chief Steward and Finance Minister Shalhoub; and after cursing him and his forefathers back and forth he exclaimed 'Go! Walk to Al-Hasa barefoot.' And poor Shalhoub, a man in the sixties, set out there and then, leaving his sandals at the door. He walked until he had reached the Dahna—two days—when a *najjab* with the Sultan's order overtook him there and brought him back. It was after that, me-thinks, that he presented him with the odalisque—the golden odalisque whom he did not deem himself worthy to touch.

Yet, he is a man of real worth, and to the Sultanate of Najd of great service. He has to feed from 200 to 300 guests a day; he has to provide 150 families, the Sa'ouds, the Rashids, and the fallen Eminences of Ar-Riyadh with provisions;—rice, butter, coffee, sugar, dates, flour, wood, charcoal, tea, and an extra allowance in money for meat;—he has to keep account of the *zeluls* and camels that come and go; to dole out also oats for the horses—more than fifty grooms gather at his door every day about sunset; and he has to pray five times a day and devote, Allah keep thee, an hour to his harim.

Of a certainty, Shalhoub is the busiest man in Ar-Riyadh, in all Najd, except of course the Sultan Abd'ul-Aziz; for he, in addition to his own work, has to supervise the work of Shalhoub. Everything, the smallest detail, goes through his hand. The Master of Ceremonies makes a list every day of the visitors who arrive—their names, tribes, towns, also the object of their visits, is set down— and presents it to the Sultan (the copy of one of the lists, which the Master of Ceremony gave me as a souvenir is of more than a hundred names). Now the Sultan goes over the list, marks near each name, what the man is to receive in clothes, in provision, and in money. He knows the place and rank of every one it seems, and his gifts are always appropriate. The list then goes to Shalhoub for execution—Shalhoub the Upright, Shalhoub the Virtuous.

I visited him one day in his office, that is in his stores, on the ground floor of the Palace. He sat on a rug crosslegged with bags of silver before him and two book-keepers to his right, while to his left were two clerks, one of whom had charge of the clothes, the other of the money. Shalhoub counted out the rupees or the Marie Theresa dollars to those who came with orders, and then handed to them the clothes. 'Write in the book,'—this to the book-keeper of the treasury, 'Ahmad ibn Jaber of Tharmadah, 250 rupees. And thou write,'—this to the book-keeper of the stores, 'A Persian *busht*, an Indian *zuboun*, two cotton *gutrahs.'* And so, throughout the day, saving the intervals of prayer.

He took me around, showing me the various Departments: provisions— flour and rice and dates; the saddlery—everything that is needed for the *zelul* and the pack-camel; the ammunition—rifles of every make, old and new, and hundreds of boxes of cartridges; the coffee, tea and sugar store; the tents; the rugs; the clothes—*gutrahs* and *zubouns* and *bushts*; and—another article which you do not find at Wanamaker or Selfridge—a store of large metal vats, five feet deep by two feet in diameter, all full of clarified butter.

This butter is one of the three articles of food, of which they consume immense quantities in Central Arabia the other two are rice and dates.

Shalhoub showed me three qualities of rice; and of the best, which is for the Sultan and all the Sa'ouds and the Rashids, he had a stock of over five hundred bags (200 lbs. each). The rice is cooked with the butter, steeped in it; and the Arabs are lavish, wasteful, in the use of both. They never serve rice in plates, but always, even to one guest, in large tray-like platters of metal or wood. Eat what you can, and give away what you can't.

But most amazing of all of Shalhoub's departments is the booty-room, where old pieces of brass-ware, odds and ends of rusty cannons and guns, bits of rugs, metal water-cans, army boots, belts, broken swords, and what not, are thrown pell-mell, heaped on top of each other. One large box was still unopened. 'What is in it, O Shalhoub,' I asked. '*Wallah*, I do not know. I have not yet had time to open it.' The confusion and disorder, however, are not the exclusive features of this great junk-shop only but everywhere in the other departments I found something akin to them, something that suggested the junk- shop—and much that was covered with dust. But Shalhoub's idea of the matter does not exactly correspond with ours. 'Everything is kept in order, and clean,' he said. Which reminded me of the beduin who came one day, when we were crossing the desert, to our leavings of rice; and after he had made away with what was left, he wiped his greasy hands with the edge of his long tapering sleeve, saying: 'The Bedu are clean—cleaner than the *hadhar* (town Arabs).' After all is said, however, it's a colossal job, that of Shalhoub; and his responsibilities are great. But here again his own idea of the matter does not exactly correspond with ours. 'I do most of the work,' he said, in a plain, matter-of-fact manner, 'A simple thing. A thousand comes in: we write it in the book. A thousand goes out: we write it in the book. And the result,' he stroked one palm against the other,— 'nothing.'

Besides the stores on the ground floor of the Palace are the refectories, and a waiting hail where the visitors are received before they are admitted to the *mqjlis* upstairs. The Palace itself was not built on a preconceived plan; but it grew in a free and spontaneous manner, which is often short-sighted and quite characteristic of the Arabs. It took me many days to find my bearings in it, so tortuous are its halls and corridors, and so ramified. There are at least ten big buildings connected together, not by subterranean passages, but by high walled bridges. The Sultan can thus make his daily tour without being seen or without going through the streets. There is a bridge from the Palace to the Grand Mosque; a bridge to the Harim; bridges between the houses of the several wives and concubines, etc. Some of the citizens of Ar-Riyadh also indulge in this caprice, or rather enjoy this convenience. One house is built, and as the family grows with the growth of the harim another house is necessary, which often has to be built across the street and connected by a bridge with the main establishment. Looking immediately around the Palace, from its tower, you get the impression that Ar-Riyadh is a city of bridges; and looking southward as far as the oasis of Al-'Ared reaches, about five miles, you behold in the haze the spectral form of the ancient town of Manfouhah.

After showing me the tower, the Sultan took me through another wing of the Palace to show me on the parapeted roof of an adjacent building the cannons and machine guns. These were about fifty in all, of English and German make, which he had won from the King of Al-Hijaz as well as from the Turks and Ibn 'ur-Rashid. They were all kept clean; and the men who were in charge realizing this looked very proud. But the Ikhwan, who have a deep contempt for cannons—they prefer cold steel—have no objection to them as booty. One of their favourite feats of heroism is to stride the gun while it is being fired and slay the gunner at his job. How else can they conquer the *mushrekin* and win *Al-Jannat?*

On our return from the artillery exhibition, the Sultan, wishing to show me that he also cared for books, ordered Shalhoub who accompanied us to open a certain room. But the Quartermaster-General opened the wrong room, and we were in the drug store instead of the Library. The stock-room rather, which was full of boxes from England—boxes full of medicines—opened, half-opened, broken, and all in a state of woeful neglect. 'These are the boxes of Dr. Mann,'[1] said His Highness with a tinge of disdain. No, they care not very much for medicine the Arabs of Najd. Besides, there was at that time but one man in Ar-Riyadh, Dr. Abdullah—and he was in Al-Hasa—who understood the use of these drugs. Waste, sheer waste. The books in the adjacent room reminded me of a corner in a second-hand book-shop, where the odds and ends, stray leaves and torn volumes are left pell-mell to the mercy of the moth and the dust.

His Highness would do better I thought if he showed me a corner of the harim quarters. He must have read my mind; for on the evening of that day, instead of calling on me as usual, he accorded me the privilege of sipping coffee with him in one of his very private apartments—after the odalisque from the north had vacated it. I do not think His Highness realized that he had been cruel. For although a Christian girl had embraced Al-Islam—but why dwell further on the subject? Sufficient for thy sins, the perfumes of the Gurjiyah and her diwan.

The apartment is on the floor below, and we had to go through a labyrinth to reach it. A lamp hung in the vestibule which led to a pleasant little room, furnished as usual with carpets, cushions, and *masnads*. It has no windows, not even apparently an aperture. But the Sultan, who does not disdain to show the hidden virtues of his living rooms, got up and pulled a cord which opened

---

[1] Dr. Mann was the representative of the Sultan of Najd in London; and he and Major Holmes came together to see the Sultan in Al-Hasa three months before I was there.

a square aperture in the wall near the ceiling. 'For the sun and air,' he said. He then pointed to a sword which was hanging on a peg. 'It is the most cherished of all my possessions.' He ordered a slave to bring it down. The hilt is of chased gold, the scabbard of silver; and since it is the sword of the Great Sa'oud it must be more than a hundred years old. The blade looks even older. The Sultan took it in his hand and told us how he killed with it one of his bitterest foes. It was a revenge—a lawful and honoured custom. 'I struck him first on the leg and disabled him; quickly after that I struck at the neck;—the head fell to one side—the blood spurted up like a fountain: the third blow at the heart:—I saw the heart, which was cut in two, palpitate like that.' He illustrated with a shiver of his hand. 'It was a joyous moment—I kissed the sword.'

He then brought out a leather case of perfumes, and insisted on perfuming me from the various bottles: one on my beard, another on my *gutrah*, a third on my breast—and they were all as heavy as undiluted ottar of roses. As for Saiyed Hashem, he helped himself to them all recklessly, without a thought to what was happening to his *rafiq*. The room itself reeked with the dazing essences; my head began to swim; I was ready to faint. The Sultan laughingly chided Saiyed Hashem—'a Saiyed never knows his limits,' he said,—and offered me a fan. He then ordered a glass of water for me. 'While Your Highness is giving orders,' I said, indulging the banter of the moment, please order Saiyed Hashem out.' I little thought that he would do so in earnest; and I felt a satisfaction, when the Saiyed was at the door, of being able and willing to intercede for him.

The laughter was refreshing, reviving; and I was able to ask the Sultan a few questions, and take notes as usual while he related of a certain battle in his career of conquest, the causes and results of which were not clear to me. He is an excellent *raconteur,* and I have no doubt that he tells all the truth—all the truth that an honest monarch can possibly tell, when he feels that he personally is not yet finished with history. More than once he looked at the clock; and as soon as it struck four (9 p.m.) he stopped. No one after this hour and no affairs of State can claim his attention or favour. During his evening visits to me he seemed to know instinctively when to get up; and invariably as I looked at my watch it was nine o'clock or five minutes before or after. This is the harim hour, and he must go to one of his wives. A word he often said, in connection with the one waiting for him and his evening visit to me, which cannot be rendered into English. The nicety of it is in the pun and the alliteration.

Before going out that evening he showed us through the Gurjiyah's apartment:—the bedroom with a bed and mosquito-netting, the dressing-room, the bath-room, and a private stairs leading to a reception chamber which gives on the roof. The full moon saw us salaam and separate, he going through the iron gate across the bridge and we going back to our quarters between high roof-walls, and walls even higher of envy and desire.

On the following day we got a better view of what was beyond the iron gate; for continuing our tour of the Palace, the Sultan still acting as guide, we crossed three roofs, two bridges, and several corridors to his own private apartment, from which we beheld a row of four or five massive buildings columned and crenelated. 'That is the harim,' said His Highness; 'each one has a house of her own.' In the vestibule—a sort of ante-chamber—where we had coffee are two doors, one leading to the private *masjid* where the Sultan prays—he goes to the Grand Mosque on Friday only—the other leading to the apartment which no woman ever enters. It is furnished like the other we have seen, except that it has also a fire-place and niches with doors decorated in red and yellow and blue. There is an adjoining room, which is used as a wardrobe—his robes were hanging on pegs—and a bath-room divided into two sections, one containing the samovar, the other a tub and metal-pans. The water is brought in skins, which is the custom, without exception in Ar-Riyadh. But in the Palace my attention was called to the cast-iron pipes which carry the waste water under ground outside the city.

The Sultan, I have said before, is a man of surprises. Out of his private apartment he led us across a roof and a bridge to a house, in the corridors of which as we entered there were some women. They scampered like sheep when they saw us. But one of them in a red robe and a black veil, which she pulled quickly over her face, found herself right in front of the Sultan, and did not know like a lost lamb which way to turn. His Highness waved his staff in the direction of one of the doors. 'Stupid slave-girls,' he said, 'who cannot see what is even before them.'

We were passing through the servants' quarter adjoining another private apartment. The Sultan preceded us into the vestibule, and hearing a noise within sent ahead of us one of the accompanying blacks. We followed half a minute later, and as usual we were greeted with the unctuousness of Oriental perfumes; and the usual furniture—carpets, cushions, and *masnads*. The apartment consists of the same number of rooms, whose windows are latticed, and the door of one of which was closed. For the lady had to hide till the stranger—an infidel, withal—had seen her living quarters,—had been, in fact, through her prison. The ceiling of these rooms, as well as the two grand reception halls, are covered with red or dotted cloth to match the covers of the cushions. There is also a punka in the living room, and an alcove in one of the adjoining rooms for the bedding. In very truth, I was in the apartment of one of the Sultan's legal wives, and the servants who scampered away from us as we came in attend exclusively upon her. I was told afterwards that she is the ex-wife of Sa'oud ibn 'ur-Rashid, the third from the last ruler of Haiel, and that the Sultan Abd'ul-Aziz married her and adopted her children as a political measure.

Before leaving us that day he showed me the place, a gallery of one of the quadrangles below, from which I might take a picture of the wedding feast. For there was a wedding in the Palace the day or the night before; but I had heard nothing of it or about it, since weddings like funerals in Ar-Riyadh now take place quietly without any singing, ululuing, or music. The groom is a young Sa'oud—a boy of thirteen, in fact;—'he wanted to get married,' said the Sultan nonchalantly, 'and we got him married,'—and his wife is his cousin a girl of twelve. The Sa'ouds rarely marry outside of their own house, except it be into the house of *the* Sheikh (*i.e.* the descendants of Ibn Abd'ul-Wahhab).

The marriage ceremony like everything else in Wahhabism is very simple. The parents of the bride and the bridegroom gather at the house of the former, where the formula is pronounced in their presence by a sheikh or a judge. A few days after the visitors and the invited guests come to the house of the bridegroom, where they are entertained with coffee, tea, and Turkish delights, and are perfumed and incensed. They then accompany him to the Mosque to pray and thence to the house of the bride's parents, where a similar reception is held. After which he is conducted into a private apartment, where for the first time he meets his bride, and where after the marriage is consummated he may live with her for two or three days, before he takes her to his own home.

The relatives of the married couple as well as their parents slay sheep and camels for those who may come besides the invited guests. Every one is welcome. And it was the Sultan, in this instance, who had to give the wedding feast. Over three thousand people gorged themselves at four or five sittings with rice and lamb. Shalhoub supplied the exact figures. 'Wallah!' he swore, 'they gave me but one day to prepare; and you saw the result. ... O yes; we have vessels that hold a whole camel—We slaughtered eighty sheep and thirty camels. And we emptied twenty bags of the best rice.'

Besides the refectories three open courts in the Palace were filled. People of all classes sat in rows opposite each other, and a sort of table-and-tray combined made of metal was placed over a round mat between each group of ten or fifteen. No sooner was this done than the lines formed into circles. The large trays of rice and lamb were then brought in, and every one tucked his sleeves and waited for the Sultan, who sat among one of the groups, to begin. He had to give a sign. He spoke. He uttered a prayer. And it was the shortest and the most effective prayer I have ever heard. 'Think of Allah,' said he in a loud voice, 'and Allah will think of you.' The hands of the guests were held still for a moment over the bounty of the day, and then they fell to, silently digging into the rice and tearing at the meat.

Saiyed Hashem and I were watching from the gallery above; and I tried, by setting the camera in one of the loopholes of the crenelated parapet, to take a picture. Light there was still; and also many watchful eyes among the Ikhwan, who resent being photographed. Hence, alternately through hesitation and haste the attempt failed. But the joy of the adventure was at the end of the feast, when the Sultan came up and surprised us on the stairs. He laughed like a schoolboy who had taken part in a successful conspiracy against the schoolmaster.

Later towards evening I met Shalhoub, the wise and virtuous and strenuous Shalhoub, and he spoke thus 'Thou hast seen with thy two eyes. Now write down in thy book, for what I tell thee is truth—write, Allah keep thee! Every king in the world is supported by his people; but the people of Najd are supported by their king.'

FREYA STARK (1893–1993)

With Lady Anne Blunt and Gertrude Bell, Freya Stark completes the triumvirate of renowned British women travellers to Arabia. Like Doughty, her motivation to travel may have been to escape an unhappy background as well as to find freedom in unfamiliar and exotic places. Brought up in Asolo in northern Italy – where she lived with her mother and sister – at the age of 12 Freya was injured in an accident in the basket factory her mother had set up for her Italian lover. Educated at Bedford College, London, she spent the early years of the Great War as a nurse, only starting to travel in the Middle East relatively late when in her early thirties, having studied briefly at the London School of Oriental Studies in 1927. She then lived for periods in Damascus and Baghdad, her first piece of writing, *Baghdad Sketches*, appearing in 1933 and *Letters from Syria* in 1942. Two books on her travels in southern Arabia are: *The Southern Gates of Arabia* and *Winter in Arabia* (1940). While frequently celebrated for her romantic view of Eastern lands and closeness to the peoples amongst whom she travelled, and for her spirit of independence that resulted in run-ins with British colonial officials ('she was denounced for having challenged authority and forsaken her European character' (En-Nehas, LTE: 1136)) it is sometimes overlooked that during her earlier Middle East travels, Stark was actually working for the British government.

From:

The Southern Gates of Arabia (1936)

Installed in Aden since the 1830s, Britain maintained its strategic interests in the Hadramaut by supporting a series of puppet sultans, such as the Sultan of Makalla, from whose small domain described below Stark began her journey.

Life in the City

> *"The merchants of Sheba and Raamah, they were thy merchants: they occupied in thy fair, with chief of all spices, and with all precious stones, and gold...."*
>
> (Ezekiel 27, V. 22.)

The Indian agent to whom I was recommended did not do very much on my behalf. I met him near his office by the custom house a day or two after my arrival, and he excused himself for not having called.

"A baby of mine died," said he.

I was sorry to hear this, but he brushed the subject aside with his silver-headed cane.

"It does not matter," he said. "It was a small one, and I have lots more. The women make a fuss about it."

Condolence seemed out of place. I left him and continued to explore the city with an Afghan chauffeur whom the Governor had kindly placed at my service together with his car. He used to drive slowly along the High Street, stopping to let me look into dark doors of shops, their wares exposed against the outer wall. There is not much to be bought in Makalla, and most of it is food of some sort set out in open baskets and made invisible by flies. There is no local manufacture except that of the curved daggers and of baskets large and vividly dyed. The drying of fish, of sea-slugs (*Holothuria edulis*) and of sharks' fins for China, the dyeing with indigo, and pressing of sesame oil, comprise the industry of the town: the Indian Ocean is a good highway, and most things come by sea; and the little business there is centres round the harbour, where dhows show their rigging and high sterns against the background of cliff, and black slaves with huge naked limbs lie asleep on the bales of the custom house, waiting for a load.

The whole town is one crowded street parallel with the sea: its western end is going to be a boulevard, but is still no more than an obstacle course of holes and blocks of stone along the sea front. The side streets climb at right angles to this main thoroughfare and end almost immediately against the cliff. The houses cling there one above the other, white and grey, with carved doors and windows, but often ruinous on a nearer view. Here are the oil presses, about twelve open sheds built for shade, where blindfolded camels—a little basket covering each eye—walk slowly in circles for ten hours every day and pull a pole weighted with boulders, by which the upper millstone grinds the seed. The seed is in a sort of funnel in the centre, which holds about 36 lb. and is filled five times a day. The camel carries on his dreary circular task with his usual slow and pompous step and head poised superciliously, as if it were a ritual affair above the comprehension of the vulgar; and no doubt he comforts himself for the dullness of life by a sense of virtue, like many other formalists beside him.

The Sultan's old palace is near the harbour, and is now a public building where the Governor holds his divan, the Qadhis give judgment, and the Treasury and such offices are lodged. The revenue comes from customs and land tax in the interior: Makalla itself has no taxable land. The law is the Muhammedan shari'a, and the Sultan is its ultimate appeal.

To the east, where the town opens out on a little headland beyond the cemetery, I visited the prison. It was an ordinary whitewashed house on the outside, with carved and sun-bleached door: a toothless old guard opened when my Afghan knocked, his thin face shaded by an immense green turban, and a key in his sash. He was pleased to show us his prison, though he could not remember how many prisoners there were: no one went among them, he told me. Their food was pushed through a hole under the door, and one might see them from the roof above. We climbed, and looked over a low parapet into a sort of pit, pillared and dark, where ten or twelve tribesmen and as many children squatted among heaps of refuse. They leaped up when they saw us outlined against their blue square of sky.

"Peace be upon you," we said.

They replied in chorus and, seeing the camera in my hand, began to argue blusteringly among themselves for and against a photograph. Their black figures scarce showed against the dusky background and the children danced about like imps of darkness crying: "Take, take a picture!" Some stretched out their arms and pretended to point rifles at us. "Now shoot," said they, and I took my picture without waiting further. All the children and most of the men were hostages, taken from tribes who misbehave; they are changed every month or two. Cases of illness (which one would imagine to be constant under the circumstances) are put in hospital, and once a week the whole establishment is led to bathe in the sea before it says its Friday prayer. Makalla is not one of the states that send delegates to International Prison Conferences: and perhaps it is as well, for I feel sure that these beduin prefer their unhygienic misery in common, to solitary comfort in a model cell.

As for the system of hostages, it is not easy to suggest an alternative in countries where the writ of government has to run over wildernesses. Forty years ago, when Hirsch travelled in the Hadhramaut, the beduin used to levy toll to the gate of Makalla itself and make about 550 dollars a year; the contrast of order and peaceful commerce now is very great. But I was haunted for the rest of the day by that vision of darkness and squalor and sent an offering to be distributed next morning—an effort greeted with approval by my friends in Makalla, who hold that the sufferings of the poor are part of the necessary furniture of the world, a sort of perpetual gymnasium where the rich can practise virtue when they feel so inclined.

By the end of my stay in the town, the mixed people of the High Street, Beduin, Arab and Negro, had begun to grow accustomed to the sight of me, but even then their excitement was great enough to gather a crowd whenever I left the defences of the car: they were friendly, but I am only five foot two, and a way had to be cleared whenever I wished to see anything beyond their hot tumultuous faces. Only once did I make for the town on foot and then gave it up as a bad job and turned to the cliff in search of solitude; about fifty children pursued, calling "Nasrani" in a monotonous but not insulting way, till the climb took their breath. The cliff was very steep; when we reached the ledge where the four forts are, the weaklings had dropped off, and those that remained had developed the friendliness of sharers in an exploit.

We came to one of the little forts, with a small and useless gun beside it. A carved door opened half-way up, and its pyramid sloping walls were finished off with a battlement flourish at each corner. These watch-towers are called Kuts. They are all aligned on a plateau ledge which must have been quite recently inhabited, as it still has plain traces of square fields, and the top of the hill above is covered with untidy graves, not very ancient. It took some tact and persuasion to make the Somali slave who was attending me reach this hill top, and of the eleven small boys who still clung to us not one had ever been so far before; and yet the whole ascent only took an hour and a half. The truth is that mountaineering is not looked upon as a treat along the coast of South Arabia,—there are too many empty hill tops all about.

From the top we had a fine but barren view over inland rust-coloured waves of landscape, to small villages north of us in palms, where Makalla goes for summer coolness, and to the valleys that lead by long ridges to Do'an. East of us was the mound-like hill of Shihr, and Wadis Buwash and Rukub between; west of us, Fuwa, where the R.A.F. have a landing-ground, and below us the sea, with porpoises playing in it. Our hill had a wide rounded top; the pinkish veined surface of its rock looked as if it had been smoothed with a giant plane, so sharp were the edges of its honeycombed cavities; I am no geologist, but I imagine that this peculiar surface is the work of strong sand-whirling winds that scoop and wear the rock like emery. It is at all events of a most unyielding hardness; my barefoot troop grew tired as we followed a naked little gulley down the northern slope, and came out on the inland road where two forts guard the approaches to the sea and look well in the wrinkled passage of the hills, their walls the same hill-colour.

Above them is the town's water supply and the Sultan's garden, a green enclosure with a raised tank in the middle of it and a dilapidated summer palace. I drove here on my first day in Makalla, and wandered under the trees among squares of vegetables—aubergines, ladies' fingers, peppers, bidan trees with big leaves and nut-like fruit of which they eat the red pulp, pomegranates, bananas, vines and other things unrecognized—but no mere flowers. Two small dark gardeners followed me about, like ghosts still plying their prehistoric craft, which the earliest dwellers in this land must have practised—probably in exactly the same way, making with bare feet the small ridges of earth that separate one water runnel from the next.

As we came away we picked up a lanky young sheikh out for a walk and glad of a lift: he had been praying for a car, he said.

"Allah must have sent us," I remarked.

He agreed dubiously, not very sure of an unbelieving woman as an instrument of Allah. But he relaxed gradually, and told me that he would like to travel, but was poor.

"That," said I, "is because you are learned. All the learned are poor. If they were not poor, they would stop being learned."

To this he also agreed, reluctantly and sadly. He was not cut out for books, and would have been much happier as a soldier. I mentioned that I had visited the al-Azhar university in Cairo and that the term of study there is thirteen years—to which he remarked very sensibly that this was too long.

"You have studied, and your life—where is it?" he asked.

We were distracted from this rather sad review of the student's lot by the sight of a fine bushy fox under a rock; he did not move, but waited, and watched us as we passed, ready to run, his body alert and intelligent—a lucky creature, not made to be religious against his will. The young sheikh drew his cotton shawl close round his shoulders in the slight chill of evening: he was anæmic and pale. He left me at the gate of the town, anxious not to compromise himself by such doubtful company: the little human flicker disappeared; his sheikly manner returned; and he strode away with a formal word and sudden mask-like face, a religious model in all but his walk, which was still that of a free and wild young animal under the clumsy gown.

One day my Afghan took me to Fuwa to see the R.A.F. landing-ground. It is one of many which we have dotted about the Arabian coasts, and it is in a wide open landscape leading to Wadis Khirbe and Hajar in the north. The cairns of loose stones that mark it are whitewashed to make them conspicuous in the general red and brown of the landscape, and by the natural development of history they will no doubt eventually become shrines to commemorate celestial visitations, long after the actual aeroplanes are forgotten. The place is thirteen miles from Makalla and the way lies partly by the water's edge on the sands and partly inland in stony valleys, naked and red, where fan-shaped samr trees grow in the flat places, grey as lichen or granite, and decorative in a barren way. Euphorbias, too, grow there, and dry and dusty statice, and straggling clumps of thorns, but nothing human except one little house and dying garden, and women who come out from Makalla—eight miles or so—to gather the thorns with naked thighs and kilted gowns, and eyes shining above a thick face cloth which veils them.

Between Makalla and Bir Au—a distance of some 70 miles—there is nothing but this and the village of Barum on the coast. It is a poor little place with no good houses, and a population disposed to kindness by the friendly influence of the R.A.F. They seemed much mixed with African, and gathered round us, and could not think of anything to show us in their small township except the school—a windowless earthen basement where twelve small boys sat in semi-darkness reading at random out of red Qurans. Some read, and some pretended to read, with a droning noise and swaying body: their negro teacher in the doorway aired his naked torso and short white beard, benevolent and pleased with the hum of learning. When I asked him which was his best pupil, he pointed at once to the ugliest of all.

As we drove back by the sea, along the strip of wet sand at the edge of the waves, gulls rose like a fluttering grey ribbon before us and sank again behind. They live here in countless numbers. They seem black and white as raindrops when they fly against the water. On the white sands they look like white pearls, and like grey pearls on the brown, and they swim strung out like pearls upon the waves. Now, as their barrage rose and fell, they made a canopy of shadow with their wings. They rose only just high enough to clear us, wheeling and almost touching; and one misjudged his distance and hit me and fell stunned in my lap. I picked him up, stiff with fear; only his eyes moved, surrounded by a delicate black beading like the glass of a miniature; his beak was red, its upper point curved over the lower; his feet were webbed and pale; and as I let his body slip away to freedom, the grey feathers felt cool and smooth as the sea they live on.

I visited three other schools in Makalla before I left. The new and handsome one, only five years old, is paid for by the Sultan and provides six years of education free to all who want it; but the teachers told me that they can very rarely persuade a boy's parents to leave him for more than four years, for there is no material advantage in education.

The teachers were young and eager, with that love of learning for its own sake of which the East is not yet ashamed. There were thirteen of them, to about 300 boys in six classes. The two smallest classes sat cross-legged on the floor; the older ones had benches, and all—from the tiniest—could produce a welcoming poem, uttered with appropriate gestures and more or less acute signs of misery, but with an obvious feeling for social obligations behind it. The children were ragged, and unintelligent to look at, as is the way of insanitary towns: and books, that come from Egypt, were few. The great treasure was a globe on a stand, kept in a bag for great occasions; two big maps, a few readers, and many Qurans provided the pasture; and five of the subjects taught were various aspects of the Quran: the rest were reading, grammar, dictation, composition, drawing, arithmetic, geometry, geography, history, and signalling with flags—the culminating point of education, and kept for the last and most advanced class as a climax to be looked forward to across the arid spaces of five preliminary years. Sayyid 'Omar, the assistant head, who took me round, was kind and gentle and fond of his children: he had the long face, little chin beard, almond-shaped eyes and large and well-cut mouth which is typical in Hadhramaut—an aristocratic type Van Dyck might have painted: and his enthusiasm and that of Shaikh 'Abdullah, who kept the school register, gave a pleasant feeling to the place in spite of the poverty of the scholars and the gigantic task undertaken with means so inadequately slender.

The old government school was on the same lines, but the third was a private venture conducted by an Indian Christian missionary, who had fifty-five pupils, much cleaner and better dressed than Sayyid 'Omar's flock, but all more or less fatally affected by that disease of smugness which oriental Christians often seem to take over inadvertently from the Pharisees. No one had wanted the Missionary in Makalla, which prides itself on admitting no Jews and hardly any Christians, and he had had to wait many months before being allowed to settle there at all; and now here he was with kind conscientious face and yellow teeth and spectacles, getting sixty rupees a month from the Sultan to run his school, provide his scholars with stationery and all they might require, and keep himself and his family alive. In his lodging upstairs he had two rows of books well thumbed to guide him on his way, a thin little wife who tried to make the best of things and not to regret Aden too deeply, and small girls whose mission lessons in embroidery were, said the wife, being all forgotten. I saw the embroidery, and did not think this an unmixed evil: some things are better forgotten. But I admired the heroism that fed the struggling spirit, wrestling alone to impart an unassimilated civilization in an unwilling land. The assembled classes sang me "God Save the King," in English and then in Arabic: I listened with some misgiving, wondering if this might not be misinterpreted as one of these subtle British arts of propaganda which we are always hearing about—but I afterwards learned that "God Save the King" is an accomplishment of which all Makalla is proud, and has no territorial implications.

The most amusing performance in the school was an English dialogue between two of the younger scholars, about a chair.

"I have bought a chair," said one.

"What is it like?" asked the other.

"It is made of wood," … etc. etc.

It sounds a peaceful and amicable conversation. But the two lads pitched into it as if it were a battle, at the top of their voices and with incredible fury, leaning towards each other as if the physical interposition of thirty odd fellow scholars alone kept them from each other's throats. It was only by listening carefully that I felt reassured as to its being merely the description of a chair.

I came away from these oases of western influence a little sadly, feeling as some indifferent lover may feel who sees the poverty of his own second-rate sentiments being taken for pure gold and can do nothing about it, and I was glad when my Afghan stopped outside a sort of marquee made of reed matting and asked if I would like to look at a wedding inside. He took me to the door and left me, and I slipped in through a fold and found myself in a chaos of women, packed in hot and dense twilight, and as far removed from anything to do with modern education as it is possible to be.

Slave women stood in an outer crowd, while the ladies in the centre squatted knee to knee on their heels and someone beat a drum. I was pushed into the middle, and a tumult arose: I found myself opposite an indignant lady with blue lips and a yellow veil who asked to right and left why the Nasrani was there. I spoke volubly and directly to her, with all the politeness in my vocabulary. Things hung in the balance for a few seconds; but the situation was more than she could deal with, for she was trying to talk politely *to* me and angrily *about* me, and she subsided suffocated: I squatted down: one or two, between curiosity and kindness, began to look more friendly; and I was able to examine the strangeness of the gathering.

It was a dense female parterre, glittering and gorgeous, ringed by a black slave crowd. The dresses were brocade or tinsel, stiff with embroidered silver breastplates and necklaces in rows; and heavy anklets, bracelets and girdles, and five or six ear-rings in each ear. The ladies came in with a yellow kerchief tied over their head, but this was soon taken off and then they showed the elaborate works of art—their face and hands and hair. They wore about a hundred tiny plaits tight to the head from a smooth straight parting painted orange with henna; on their forehead the hair was plastered to a point shining with grease; their chins were bright yellow; the palms of their hands reddish brown with heavily scented henna and oil and painted outside in a brown lacework pattern, like a mitten. Their eyebrows were painted brown and a curling brown pattern darted from each temple; a brown line ran down the forehead and chin. Some were very pretty, with pointed faces and long small chins; but they were inhuman, hieratic and sacrificial; not women, but a terrifying, uncompromising embodiment of Woman, primæval and unchanging. And more so when they stood up to dance, one or two at a time. They did not move their feet, but threw their heads and upper bodies stiffly about, and made patterns like wheels in the air with their pigtails. A clinging scent came from their bodies; the drums beat; the bracelets and girdles jingled; the heat was almost unbearable. When one arose, it was like a flower, some many-coloured tulip, opening as she slipped from her dark street wrapping and stood to let her finery be seen, nonchalant but not without an ear for the murmur of discriminating praise. The bride was, of course, invisible in an upper room. More guests kept on arriving: space was made for them, impossible as it seemed: the drum went on beating with its subtle excitement of monotony; more and more dancers stood up knee deep in the female sea: and I slipped out as quietly as I could, oppressed with a mystery so ancient and fundamental, so far more tenacious in its dim, universal, roots than the transitory efforts of that incurably educational creature, Man.

BERTRAM THOMAS (1892–1950)

Thomas emerged from humble origins to become in 1930 the first Westerner to cross the Empty Quarter in Arabia. He fought on the Western Front in 1914–15 and survived. Transferred to Mesopotamia in the last two years of the war he caught the eye of Arnold Talbot Wilson, then acting civil commissioner in the Persian Gulf. Wilson – to whom he dedicated *Arabia Felix* – was the inspiration behind his later travels in Arabia. As a traveller Thomas acted on his own initiative, dressed like the locals, and spoke the native tongue. Working in the sultanate of Oman he was able to make his extensive journeys into the interior of Oman 'that contributed substantially to the geographical and ethnological knowledge of the region' (DNB). Thomas sustained a successful career as a colonial officer: he was later a public relations officer in Bahrain, 1942–3, and Director of the Middle East Centre for Arabic Studies.

From:

Arabia Felix (1938)

The issue as to who was the 'real' Bedouin and what his racial characteristics were exercised a number of European travellers such as Burton. The ethnological 'research' of skull-measuring which Thomas details in the following extract from *Arabia Felix* unfortunately cannot be disconnected from the practice of the pseudo-science pursued in Nazi Germany at almost the same time. But the piece also highlights interesting cultural differences between the African slaves and their Omani masters.

Skull-Measuring and Devil Dancing

'From what Arabs are you?' Thus has the question been put to me in the desert, by natives conscious that I was of a race different from theirs, for the word Arab is used by them to denote 'people' rather than the particular race we mean.

But is it so certain that the Arabs are themselves racially one? Neither Glaser the scholar, nor Burton the traveller thought so. The former held the South Arabian to be Hamitic and not Semitic. The latter declared that he had found proof of three distinct races. Whatever the case, Burton's anticipation that 'physiological differences sufficient to warrant our questioning the common origin of the Arab family would be found' was a sound one. Such differences I discovered in abundance in this central region of South Arabia: not merely physiological, but cultural and linguistic differences that constitute collectively a serious challenge to the conception of a single racial entity for the entire peninsula.

I came indeed prepared with head callipers to make and record skull measurements, for such measurements are vital to anthropologists. Of importance too are visual observations of the foreigner domiciled for some years in Arabia, for his mind becomes unconsciously stamped with the physical characteristics of the natives, and is therefore acutely aware of aberrations from racial types when he meets them. Thus it was that after continuous residence in Arabia from 1915 onwards, serving in capacities that brought me into close touch with the Arabs of Mesopotamia, Transjordan and the Persian Gulf, I was impressed on meeting the natives of central South Arabia – the Dhufar 'bloc,' with a feeling of some fundamental difference. The Political Resident in Aden, Major-General Maitland, recorded a similar impression in the following terms:

'The people of Arabia belong to two distinct and apparently quite different races. The common idea of the Arab type…tall bearded men with clean-cut hawk-like face. The Arabs of South Arabia are smaller, darker, coarser featured and nearly beardless. All authorities agree that the southern Arabs are nearly related by origin to the Abyssinians. Yet strange to say it is the Egypto-African race who are the pure Arabs, while the stately Semite of the north is Musta'rab… Arab by adoption and residence rather than by descent.'

Arab scholars themselves have inherited a tradition that their race is derived from two stocks, Qahtan and Adnan, but tribes scattered over the peninsula to-day claiming descent from one or other of these ancestors are of indistinguishable racial types. On the other hand, differences noted by Burton and Maitland and Glaser, and in our own generation by Rathjens, are well marked, and the tribes thus differentiated do not coincide with the Qahtan-Adnan demarcation.

None of these Europeans, moreover, could have been familiar with the group of Dhufar tribes I encountered, which there is very strong anthropological and linguistic evidence for regarding as at most racially peculiar, at least racially different.

Inscriptions and ruined cities in South-west Arabia bear witness to ancient Minaean and Sabaean civilisations that decayed before the rise of Islam in the seventh century of our era. We know too of early Abyssinian and Roman invasions and of Greek and Aramaean settlements. Who are these South Arabians? If the answer to the problem rests with anthropologists, as it assuredly does, the collection of relevant data was of never-failing interest to me on my travels.

I had early entertained hopes of unearthing and sending home ancient skulls, but the dangers of offending religious susceptibilities in Arabia were great. To disturb a body that has been given Muslim burial is the worst desecration, and has been a fruitful source of trouble as when, for instance, in Mesopotamia during the war, someone unwittingly drove a car through a derelict Arab cemetery. Hence also the rock tombs faced with loose stones which I had come upon in the Wadi Dhikur in 1927–28 were forbidden ground. On my 1929–1930 journey I had met with better fortune, for at Hasik we passed a cave whose entrance had been forced by a wolf or other wild animal. It was daylight and the presence of my Arab companions imposed restraint, but I contrived to halt near by, and no one knew next morning that a skull found in the cave was in my bedding – though the jawbone was missing and the rest of the skeleton had wholly disappeared. I took it to Muscat and thence to the Royal College of Surgeons in London. But in my house at Muscat where I unpacked the treasure, my servant Mabruk, a manumitted slave, became aware of his master's queer hobby, and announced next day that he had brought a present for me and produced from a bundle a complete human skull. Another Arab servant emerged sniggering from behind the door to explain that Mabruk had been overnight to his father's burial-place, and was presenting me with a once vital part of his revered parent. That night Mabruk, unrewarded and rebuked, restored it to its resting-place. Whether Arab feelings would have been hurt on religious grounds in such a case, it is impossible to tell, certainly slaves do not pray in this part of Arabia, and may not normally be regarded as good Muslims.

To return to Dhufar and head-measuring, it was no easy task to find willing subjects. There is always in the minds of rude people the fear of magic or worse, while the religious among them hate to be pawed by infidel hands. In the desert I would not have dared risk putting callipers over the head of a Badu – an uncouth tribesman might have drawn his dagger, for at times Badawin have turned against me for bringing out a camera at the wrong moment – but here in Dhufar I felt I could safely work upon prisoners, warders and old friends behind closed doors, and with these and some enlightened foreign traders I was able during my stay to make forty-five head-measurements, covering a wide geographical range and to take a hundred 'type' portraits.

The work was enlivened by many amusing episodes, but was physically unpleasant, for the specimens were either Badawin with tousled hair full of sandy and other accumulations or sedentary townsmen whose locks were a mass of grease from applications of coco-nut oil. One morning my clients were to be Somalis, a breed which crosses the Red Sea to set up as petty merchants in the bazaar or as middlemen to contract frankincense orchards. Six of them arrived, and averred in answer to my questions that they were *somal khalis, i.e.* Somalis on both sides of the family – a necessary condition, for specimens of mixed parentage are useless anthropologically, but on a closer study their squat noses and receding head axes were so obviously negroid that I dismissed them as unsuitable. 'Are you quite sure you are pure-bred?' I asked a Somali member of the police who was next. 'I claim to be,' he replied, 'but God is the knower, and then my mother.'

The wit enjoyed his own lewd joke and disappeared laughing down the roof-steps, promising to appear on the morrow with a number of equally uncontaminated fellow-specimens.

Next came the government *askaris*. These mercenary tribesmen of Hadhramaut or of the Aden hinterland who take service with the Sultan of Muscat, like the Nejdis of old, are labelled as *Hadharim* by the local Omanis. There were forty on duty at Dhufar, so I had little difficulty in finding six of undiluted tribal stock. These – of the Ahl Yazid, Yahar, and Ahl Sa'ad sections of the Yafa' confederation, I measured and photographed, but I was soon to discover that they objected to the term *Hadharim* as applied to themselves. '*Hadharim* to us, Sahib, are low-caste inhabitants of Shahar and other non-tribesmen: the genuine tribesman will be content only to be regarded as belonging to one of two rival confederations, Yafa' and Hamdan – none other!' they said.

Next day I was measuring a member of another race type, one 'Ali al Dhab'an, a Badawi of the Mashai' that roam the desert on the north side of the Hadhramaut. 'Ali, a very fine shot as Arabs go, had accompanied me on my last year's expedition to Mugshin, and was now my daily companion, and a fount of desert erudition. He knew the southern borderlands well, had shed Rashidi blood and later taken a Rashidi girl to wife to avoid their vengeance. From me he wanted a parting present before going into the Qara Mountains to demand four head of sheep from Al Kathir as part payment of blood-money for his son accidentally killed by one of their number the year before.

What he wanted turned out to be a modest fifty rounds of ammunition – the Badu will unblushingly ask for the moon!

'No,' I said, remembering 'Ali's record and propensities. 'Certainly not!'
'Ali was reputed to have taken fifteen lives; the last murder, three years before,
immediately followed a visit to my camp at Auhi: he had then shot an 'Amari
he met in the wilderness because he coveted the wretch's camel. The camel
did not, alas, survive the journey to Dhufar, and 'Ali had nothing to show for
his blood-guiltiness, which he ascribed cheerfully to Allah, and himself felt not
at all, but he dare not meet a man of that tribe again. 'I will give you three
dollars, 'Ali,' I added, 'if you will come on a shooting expedition into the
mountains next week: but ammunition, no! You want it for some evil purpose.
I will be no party to violence.'

'Then tell me how a man shall live?'

'Till the ground or fish.'

He looked at me incredulously. 'That is not a man's work,' he said.

'Then what is a man's work?'

'The rifle and janbiya (dagger).'

'Nonsense,' I returned. 'Fighting is all very well when the time for it comes,
but how do you think we English became strong if it was not by work? How do
you think we get our ships and our rifles?'

'Money!' he said laconically, and I knew it would be idle to argue. A pause.

'O 'Ali! if every one lived by his rifle and *janbiya*, whence would we get food?
We owe what we eat to the cultivator and the fisherman.'

'But what *qubaili* (tribesman) would stoop so low? Fishing! it is impossible!
Tilling! Yes, I will ask Saiyid Taimur (the Sultan) to give me a plot of land. Then
I will get a slave to till it for me.'

'But why not till it yourself?'

'Ah! never fear, I'll pay the slave,' said 'Ali, missing the point, but adding
ingenuously, 'and I shall live on the produce of the garden.'

How 'Ali was to come by a slave I had every reason to shrink from imagining.
Even in Dhufar three hundred dollars would be a moderate price for a slave,
and had 'Ali anything like that sum, the desert would call him and he would
invest the money in a she-camel. But 'Ali's flight of fancy had carried him into
the clouds and he now returned to earth.

'Give me fifty rounds, Sahib!' and he slithered the ammunition belt round
his body for me to see that it was all but empty. I suppressed a smile at the
incongruity of his utter poverty with his opulent optimism.

'*W'allahi!* I would rather ammunition than a camel,' he said. 'The camel
dies on her master's hands, but with ammunition! I can repel my enemies
when they come after me, and kill an oryx when I am hungry.'

'No, 'Ali! Come to-morrow and you shall have three dollars, but mark you!
behave yourself in the mountains, or this is the end of our friendship.'

'Let Saiyid Taimur put me on his pay-roll,' said 'Ali as he went away – he was, maybe, envisaging three dollars a month – 'and I will be a brother to all men.'

It was the Acting-Governor's custom to call on me each morning at the fort. Sa'id bin Saif was yellow-faced, with a long scraggy goatee and a miserable physique even for late middle-age. His conversation centred round the poverty of the *Hukuma* (government), the insufficiency of his pay, and the demands of a large family: and in contrast the vast sums of money the English must have, as shown by official salaries. Sa'id lamented his own miserable portion and attributed both extremes to Allah. Work he regarded as undignified, fit for slaves; his hands were pale and delicate as a woman's and his legs never carried him faster than a slow, dignified walk, attended by a squad of soldiers before and behind him. What he did diligently, albeit with extreme deliberation, was to pray five times a day. For the rest, he sat about aimlessly, his sleepy silences broken only with pious ejaculations '*Al hamdu' l'illah! al hamdu' l'illah*' – a most depressing companion.

There were distant sounds of revelry. A soldier rushed to the roof and came back to report it was the slaves. Drums in growing volume confirmed their approach and we now all went to look down on an interesting spectacle.

The occasion of it was merely a slave's death, but when a negro here dies and is buried, instead of two Muslim angels to share his tomb, an evil spirit enters to molest his slumbers, and so the drums and the devil-dance are invoked to drive away the tormentor.

'God forgive them!' murmured the sanctimonious Omani at my side.

'Drums aren't acceptable to you?' I questioned.

'No, nor pipes; but these are slaves and know no better.'

'Yet the Muqabil tribe in Oman have pipes?' I said.

'Yes! but they are Sunnis. We are Ibadhis, and in Ibadhi Oman we forbid these instruments of the devil.'

Meanwhile the procession was making its brave way to pay me respects inspired by hope of reward – a basket of dates, perhaps, for death with them, as at an Irish wake, is an occasion for feasting. The banner-carrier and drummers moved slowly forward; the main body of negroes about them, with staves held aloft, were dancing and chanting, and a party of negresses came tripping along in rear. As the fort gates were approached some of the men rushed forward threateningly in a mock attempt at forcing the doorway that was already open.

Within the courtyard a halt was cried and the rhythm changed. With the drums and banners for a centre, the men circled round in single file, hopping now on this foot, now on that, and chanting some wild Swahili gibberish while their women moved circumspectly around the outer edge with curious measured step, their mantles lifted suggestively before them. Other negroes detached themselves for a mock fight, one man who presumably impersonated the evil spirit lying on the ground lashing wildly about him, while would-be vanquishers assailed him from all sides.

So many sightseers pressed into the outer gateway that they made the exit of the Omani at my side impossible, and he remained an involuntary spectator. He stood aghast at this exhibition of paganism, which he would have suppressed if he could, while I felt that I was the object of his inward censure for my levity in taking a cine-picture of the proceedings.

In the afternoon I was to witness more elaborate ritual outside in the gardens, for the Sultan had forbidden the rite within city precincts and thereby won the praises of all True Believers.

'Did not these processions on the '*Id* of *Nayruz* (New Year's Day) with loud gibes enter the harlot's house carrying a kitten — her implied offspring? But,' said my pious informant, 'the Sultan's action in suppressing this may have been precipitate for, alas, since then promiscuity has increased.'

The negro community is almost self-contained, and the biggest single element in the population of the Dhufar capital. Awwadh, a Court slave and most exalted above his fellows, was their *ab*, a magistrate to whom negro disputes were usually referred for settlement. Nor was he without an assistant glorying in the high-sounding name of *naqib*, but the rank and file of slaves are *aulad* and *banat*, *i.e.* 'boys' and 'girls,' euphemistic terms when they are applied to wrinkled negroes and aged negresses.

Slaves may have their taboos. One here, for instance, is that they may not touch dead animals other than those properly slaughtered for food. It is the master and not the slave who would remove a dead cat from the house, and where is the Court slave who would willingly consent to drag away the carcass of a horse? For such and other infringements of their code there is punishment (normally ostracism) by communal sentiment, the decision being cried round the town with a conch – the slaves' alarm: while the offender's readmission is celebrated by the slaughter of a sheep in the blood of which he dips his foot.

Negro slaves in my experience are of a contented mind. They have a cheerful demeanour often lacking in their masters, so that they sing and dance apparently unmindful of their political and social disabilities. It is difficult for a European who has not lived in Muslim countries to form any considered opinion regarding slavery in practice. The lot of the slave must necessarily be compared with that of the freeman in the same environment. Judged by this standard, the life of the slave is not wholly pitiable. The general standard of life is so low – just above the line of bare sufficiency – that the slave-owner, in his own interests, has to feed and clothe the slave nearly as well as himself.

The fundamental difference between them lies in work. In the land of sloth, it is the slave who does the manual labour. He has to produce enough to support both of them, and the freeman sees that he does so. But to suppose that a difference of rewards exists as sharply defined as in the Southern States of the U.S.A. or the West Indian Colonies before the abolition of slavery would be a false assumption No such difference exists.

Slaves actually enjoy certain fortuitous social advantages. The male, for instance, escapes the perils of the blood-feuds that haunt the 'free' tribesman, and when he is caught in a raid and Arab kills Arab, his life will be spared. It is true he will find himself taken captive and sold to a fresh master, but his lot need not therefore be worsened. As regards females, the slave girl enjoys a social liberty that is in gratifying contrast to the 'free' Arab woman. The latter is probably married at fifteen to a spouse chosen by her father, without being consulted or even seeing him. Thereafter she is destined to close confinement in her house for the rest of her life except for rare excursions out of doors, where she goes closely veiled. The rigidity of the convention increases as her position rises in the social scale, while any sexual lapse – this in contrast to her husband's admitted licence – she will pay for with her life.

The slave girl, on the other hand, is fancy free, and although her marriage will be likewise arranged by her master with an eye only to his own profit, she will walk abroad unveiled throughout her life, and flirt and fraternise where she will.

A group of desert Badawin were interested spectators of the devil-dancing in the afternoon, and though professing Muslims all, none seemed to have any misgivings of conscience about it, in refreshing contrast to the narrow spirit of the semi-sophisticated Omani official. If the pastoral races of the desert have placed their gods in the skies because they were habitually looking upwards for rain, the giver of life, why should not the agricultural races, with their eyes always on the soil, have their earth-spirits? But with such ideas neither party would have had any sympathy.

It was before Hafa village, picturesque in its setting of coco-nut palms, that the *zenug* rites were customarily performed three days after a death. The sound of well-played drums drew me to the throng. In the midst was a clearing spacious as a riding-school. At one end sat the drummers, a fire before them for the purpose of tuning their drums. Round about them danced the 'drum boys,' a dozen or so stalwart negroes of splendid muscular development. They were naked but for their loin-cloths; about their knees was a rattle of dried mangoes. This *khish khish* swished to the beating of the drums, as the dancers stamped and gyrated.

Across the circle opposite stood the *naqib*. His hands were to his lips as he chanted his incantations – 'Y'Allah ya malengi, y'Allah ya malengi' – while a chorus of a dozen companions, standing facing him in a row, took up the responses.

Around the inner edge of the circle Awwadh the *ab*, master of ceremonies, ran hither and thither, slashing with a whip in his hand before the naked feet of spectators, wherever they pressed too closely.

A dozen paces within the ring was the path of the main performers – a stream of young negroes and negresses, who came sweeping round and round the circle in grand parade – young slave girls, singly or in pairs, sturdy, black as ebony, and high of bosom, selected doubtless for their superior graces in the eyes of men. A black muslin veil shrouded each girl's head and drooped about the shoulders, of so flimsy a material that it did not conceal, but rather accentuated the effect of her flashing eyes, her thick scarlet-painted lips, her nose-ring, ear-rings and necklaces of gold. Her dress, new doubtless for the occasion, was a single mantle of starched indigo that glistened in the sun. One end of its long sweeping train she held up fastidiously between finger and thumb, the arm outstretched level with her shoulder, the other arm lay close to her side with the hand poised a span or so from the hip and palm turned back at almost right angles to the wrist. And thus she moves; her head motionless, her face turning neither to right nor left, her body moving by some subtle shuffle-step that has the sinuous slide of a skater. Before her leaps an eager youth, in his hand a drawn sword that quivers with a flick of the wrist; now on this side, now on that, now turning about to face her – spellbound he seems, like the moth to the candle. Other male slaves, threes and fours in line, rifles held above their heads, stalk round in the more deliberate measure of the horse-dance and looking straight to their front regardless of beauty.

The afternoon wears on. More and more candidates enter the drum-throbbing ring. The moment for the climax of the rite approaches. The spirit molesting the corpse must be drawn forth and take possession of a 'drum boy' chosen for his powers, who now draws apart from his companions. All eyes are turned upon him. The stamping grows wilder; the spirit-possessed puts forth all the frenzy of which his body is capable. His face is hideously contorted, his eyes wildly stare, he rolls himself on the ground and rubs his head in the dust, he slobbers with his lips as though in a fit. He is clearly overcome by exhaustion, and I, sickened by the sight of the orgy, depart as rifles are discharged into the air, to add to the general tumult.

The *mu'edhdhin's* 'Credo' would put an end to the ceremony if the spirit-possessed slave did not, before then, swoon, symbolizing the passing of the spirit that otherwise would have given the corpse no rest. But he has fallen and lies motionless; and now the *aulad* and *banat* gather up his limp body and bear it home, thence they joyfully disperse.

WILFRED THESIGER (1910–2003)

Described by Harry St. John Philby as 'probably the greatest of all explorers' Thesiger lived to see the traditional ways and the last unfilled spaces of the Middle East disappear. Born and until the age of eight brought up in Abyssinia where his father was consul-general and minister plenipotentiary, he imbibed from his earliest days the best traditions of the colonial service's dedication to service in foreign lands. After an undistinguished education at Eton and Oxford, he joined the Sudan political service in 1935. To his early exploration in Abyssinia was added several years trekking in the deserts of western Sudan and Libya. The Second World War campaign against the Italians brought him back to Abyssinia; he also saw service in Syria, North Africa and Palestine. But it was in the years immediately after the war that Thesiger embarked on his now celebrated journeys in Oman and the Empty Quarter. His first crossing took place in 1946–7, beginning and ending at Salalah on the coast of south-west Arabia. On this, the second crossing of 1947–8, as well as on further journeys in 1949 and 1950, Thesiger travelled with two Bedouin youths, Salim bin Kabina and Salim bin Ghabaisha. He wrote *Arabian Sands*, his narrative of these journeys a decade later. This and *The Marsh Arabs* (1964), the product of yearly visits to the marshes of southern Iraq until 1958, brought fame and acclamation.

From:

***Arabian Sands* (1959)**

Besides the spare descriptive style for which it is justly celebrated, Thesiger's narrative foregrounds the human qualities of fearlessness and comradeship that, in spite of the hint of deference in the incident of the rabbit's liver, transcend differences of tribe, race or nation.

The First Crossing of the Empty Quarter

The others were awake at the first light anxious to push on while it was still cold. The camels sniffed at the withered tribulus but were too thirsty to eat it.

In a few minutes we were ready. We plodded along in silence. My eyes watered with the cold; the jagged salt-crusts cut and stung my feet. The world was grey and dreary. Then gradually the peaks ahead of us stood out against a paling sky; almost imperceptibly they began to glow, borrowing the colours of the sunrise which touched their crests.

A high unbroken dune-chain stretched across our front. It was not of uniform height, but, like a mountain range, consisted of peaks and connecting passes. Several of the summits appeared to be seven hundred feet above the salt-flat on which we stood. The southern face confronting us was very steep, which meant that this was the lee side to the prevailing winds. I wished we had to climb it from the opposite direction, for it is easy to take a camel down these precipices of sand but always difficult to find a way up them.

Al Auf told us to wait while he went to reconnoitre. I watched him walking away across the glistening salt-flat, his rifle on his shoulder and his head thrown back as he scanned the slopes above. He looked superbly confident, but as I viewed this wall of sand I despaired that we would ever get the camels up it. Mabkhaut evidently thought the same, for he said to Musallim, 'We will have to find a way round. No camel will ever climb that.' Musallim answered, 'It is al Auf's doing. He brought us here. We should have gone much farther to the west, nearer to Dakaka.' He had caught a cold and was snuffling, and his rather high-pitched voice was hoarse and edged with grievance. I knew that he was jealous of al Auf and always ready to disparage him, so unwisely I gibed, 'We should have got a long way if you had been our guide!' He swung round and answered angrily, 'You don't like the Bait Kathir. I know that you only like the Rashid. I defied my tribe to bring you here and you never recognize what I have done for you.'

For the past few days he had taken every opportunity of reminding me that I could not have come on from Ramlat al Ghafa without him. It was done in the hope of currying favour and of increasing his reward, but it only irritated me. Now I was tempted to seek relief in angry words, to welcome the silly, bitter squabble which would result. I kept silent with an effort and moved apart on the excuse of taking a photograph. I knew how easily, under conditions such as these, I could take a violent dislike to one member of the party and use him as my private scapegoat. I thought, 'I must not let myself dislike him. After all, I do owe him a great deal; but I wish to God he would not go on reminding me of it.'

I went over to a bank and sat down to wait for al Auf's return. The ground was still cold, although the sun was now well up, throwing a hard, clear light on the barrier of sand ahead of us. It seemed fantastic that this great rampart which shut out half the sky could be made of wind-blown sand. Now I could see al Auf, about half a mile away, moving along the salt-flat at the bottom of the dune. While I watched him he started to climb a ridge, like a mountaineer struggling upward through soft snow towards a pass over a high mountain. I even saw the tracks which he left behind him. He was the only moving thing in all that empty, silent landscape.

What were we going to do if we could not get the camels over it? I knew that we could not go any farther to the east, for al Auf had told me that the quicksands of Umm al Samim were in that direction. To the west the easier sands of Dakaka, where Thomas had crossed, were more than two hundred miles away. We had no margin, and could not afford to lengthen our journey. Our water was already dangerously short, and even more urgent than our own needs were those of the camels, which would collapse unless they were watered soon. We *must* get them over this monstrous dune, if necessary by unloading them and carrying the loads to the top. But what was on the other side? How many more of these dunes were there ahead of us? If we turned back now we might reach Mughshin, but I know that once we crossed this dune the camels would be too tired and thirsty to get back even to Ghanim. Then I thought of Sultan and the others who had deserted us, and of their triumph if we gave up and returned defeated. Looking again at the dune ahead I noticed that al Auf was coming back. A shadow fell across the sand beside me. I glanced up and bin Kabina stood there. He smiled, said 'Salam Alaikum', and sat down. Urgently I turned to him and asked, 'Will we ever get the camels over that?' He pushed the hair back from his forehead, looked thoughtfully at the slopes above us, and answered, 'It is very steep but al Auf will find a way. He is a Rashid; he is not like these Bait Kathir.' Unconcernedly he then took the bolt out of his rifle and began to clean it with the hem of his shirt, while he asked me if all the English used the same kind of rifle.

When al Auf approached we went over to the others. Mabkhaut's camel had lain down; the rest of them stood where we had left them, which was a bad sign. Ordinarily they would have roamed off at once to look for food. Al Auf smiled at me as he came up but said nothing, and no one questioned him. Noticing that my camel's load was unbalanced he heaved up the saddle-bag from one side, and then picking up with his toes the camel-stick which he had dropped, he went over to his own camel, caught hold of its head-rope, said 'Come on', and led us forward.

It was now that he really showed his skill. He picked his way unerringly, choosing the inclines up which the camels could climb. Here on the lee side of this range a succession of great faces flowed down in unruffled sheets of sand, from the top to the very bottom of the dune. They were unscalable, for the sand was poised always on the verge of avalanching, but they were flanked by ridges where the sand was firmer and the inclines easier. It was possible to force a circuitous way up these slopes, but not all were practicable for camels, and from below it was difficult to judge their steepness. Very slowly, a foot at a time, we coaxed the unwilling beasts upward. Each time we stopped I looked up at the crests where the rising wind was blowing streamers of sand into the void, and wondered how we should ever reach the top. Suddenly we were there. Before slumping down on the sand I looked anxiously ahead of us. To my relief I saw that we were on the edge of rolling downs, where the going would be easy among shallow valleys and low, rounded hills. 'We have made it. We are on top of Uruq al Shaiba', I thought triumphantly. The fear of this great obstacle had lain like a shadow on my mind ever since al Auf had first warned me of it, the night we spoke together in the sands of Ghanim. Now the shadow had lifted and I was confident of success.

We rested for a while on the sand, not troubling to talk, until al Auf rose to his feet and said 'Come on'. Some small dunes built up by cross-winds ran in curves parallel with the main face across the back of these downs. Their steep faces were to the north and the camels slithered down them without difficulty. These downs were brick-red, splashed with deeper shades of colour; the underlying sand, exposed where it had been churned up by our feet, showing red of a paler shade. But the most curious feature was a number of deep craters resembling giant hoof-prints. These were unlike normal crescent-dunes, since they did not rise above their surroundings, but formed hollows in the floor of hard undulating sand. The salt-flats far below us looked very white.

We mounted our camels. My companions had muffled their faces in their head-cloths and rode in silence, swaying to the camels' stride. The shadows on the sand were very blue, of the same tone as the sky; two ravens flew northward, croaking as they passed. I struggled to keep awake. The only sound was made by the slap of the camels' feet, like wavelets lapping on a beach.

To rest the camels we stopped for four hours in the late afternoon on a long gentle slope which stretched down to another salt-flat. There was no vegetation on it and no saltbushes bordered the plain below us. Al Auf announced that we would go on again at sunset. While we were feeding I said to him cheerfully, 'Anyway, the worst should be over now that we are across the Uruq al Shaiba.' He looked at me for a moment and then answered, 'If we go well tonight we should reach them tomorrow.' I said, 'Reach what?' and he replied, 'The Uruq al Shaiba', adding, 'Did you think what we crossed today was the Uruq al Shaiba? That was only a dune. You will see them tomorrow.' For a moment, I thought he was joking, and then I realized that he was serious, that the worst of the journey which I had thought was behind us was still ahead.

It was midnight when at last al Auf said, 'Let's stop here. We will get some sleep and give the camels a rest. The Uruq al Shaiba are not far away now.' In my dreams that night they towered above us higher than the Himalayas.

Al Auf woke us again while it was still dark. As usual bin Kabina made coffee, and the sharp-tasting drops which he poured out stimulated but did not warm. The morning star had risen above the dunes. Formless things regained their shape in the first dim light of dawn. The grunting camels heaved themselves erect. We lingered for a moment more beside the fire; then al Auf said 'Come', and we moved forward. Beneath my feet the gritty sand was cold as frozen snow.

We were faced by a range as high as, perhaps even higher than, the range we had crossed the day before, but here the peaks were steeper and more pronounced, rising in many cases to great pinnacles, down which the flowing ridges swept like draperies. These sands, paler coloured than those we had crossed, were very soft, cascading round our feet as the camels struggled up the slopes. Remembering how little warning of imminent collapse the dying camels had given me twelve years before in the Danakil country, I wondered how much more these camels would stand, for they were trembling violently whenever they halted. When one refused to go on we heaved on her head-rope, pushed her from behind, and lifted the loads on either side as we manhandled the roaring animal upward. Sometimes one of them lay down and refused to rise, and then we had to unload her, and carry the water-skins and the saddlebags ourselves. Not that the loads were heavy. We had only a few gallons of water left and some handfuls of flour.

We led the trembling, hesitating animals upward along great sweeping ridges where the knife-edged crests crumbled beneath our feet. Although it was killing work, my companions were always gentle and infinitely patient. The sun was scorching hot and I felt empty, sick, and dizzy. As I struggled up the slope, knee-deep in shifting sand, my heart thumped wildly and my thirst grew worse. I found it difficult to swallow; even my ears felt blocked, and yet I knew that it would be many intolerable hours before I could drink. I would stop to rest, dropping down on the scorching sand, and immediately it seemed I would hear the others shouting, 'Umbarak, Umbarak'; their voices sounded strained and hoarse.

It took us three hours to cross this range.

On the summit were no gently undulating downs such as we had met the day before. Instead three smaller dune-chains rode upon its back, and beyond them the sand fell away to a salt-flat in another great empty trough between the mountains. The range on the far side seemed even higher than the one on which we stood, and behind it were others. I looked round, seeking instinctively for some escape. There was no limit to my vision. Somewhere in the ultimate distance the sands merged into the sky, but in that infinity of space I could see no living thing, not even a withered plant to give me hope. 'There is nowhere to go', I thought. 'We cannot go back and our camels will never get up another of these awful dunes. We really are finished.' The silence flowed over me, drowning the voices of my companions and the fidgeting of their camels.

We went down into the valley, and somehow – and I shall never know how the camels did it – we got up the other side. There, utterly exhausted, we collapsed. Al Auf gave us each a little water, enough to wet our mouths. He said, 'We need this if we are to go on.' The midday sun had drained the colour from the sands. Scattered banks of cumulus cloud threw shadows across the dunes and salt-flats, and added an illusion that we were high among Alpine peaks, with frozen lakes of blue and green in the valley, far below. Half asleep, I turned over, but the sand burnt through my shirt and woke me from my dreams.

Two hours later al Auf roused us. As he helped me load my camel, he said, 'Cheer up, Umbarak. This time we really are across the Uruq al Shaiba', and when I pointed to the ranges ahead of us, he answered, 'I can find a way through those; we need not cross them.' We went on till sunset, but we were going with the grain of the country, following the valleys and no longer trying to climb the dunes. We should not have been able to cross another. There was a little fresh *qassis* on the slope where we halted. I hoped that this lucky find would give us an excuse to stop here for the night, but, after we had fed, al Auf went to fetch the camels, saying, 'We must go on again while it is cool if we are ever to reach Dhafara.'

We stopped long after midnight and started again at dawn, still exhausted from the strain and long hours of yesterday, but al Auf encouraged us by saying that the worst was over. The dunes were certainly lower than they had been, more uniform in height and more rounded, with fewer peaks. Four hours after we had started we came to rolling uplands of gold and silver sand, but still there was nothing for the camels to eat.

A hare jumped out from under a bush, and al Auf knocked it over with his stick. The others shouted 'God has given us meat.' For days we had talked of food; every conversation seemed to lead back to it. Since we had left Ghanim I had been always conscious of the dull ache of hunger, yet in the evening my throat was dry even after my drink, so that I found it difficult to swallow the dry bread Musallim set before us. All day we thought and talked about that hare, and by three o'clock in the afternoon could no longer resist stopping to cook it. Mabkhaut suggested, 'Let's roast it in its skin in the embers of a fire. That will save our water – we haven't got much left.' Bin Kabina led the chorus of protest. 'No, by God! Don't even suggest such a thing'; and turning to me he said, 'We don't want Mabkhaut's charred meat. Soup. We want soup and extra bread. We will feed well today even if we go hungry and thirsty later. By God, I am hungry!' We agreed to make soup. We were across the Uruq al Shaiba and intended to celebrate our achievement with this gift from God. Unless our camels foundered we were safe; even if our water ran out we should live to reach a well.

Musallim made nearly double our usual quantity of bread while bin Kabina cooked the hare. He looked across at me and said, 'The smell of this meat makes me faint.' When it was ready he divided it into five portions. They were very small, for an Arabian hare is no larger than an English rabbit, and this one was not even fully grown. Al Auf named the lots and Mabkhaut drew them. Each of us took the small pile of meat which had fallen to him. Then bin Kabina said, 'God! I have forgotten to divide the liver', and the others said, 'Give it to Umbarak.' I protested, saying that they should divide it, but they swore by God that they would not eat it and that I was to have it. Eventually I took it, knowing that I ought not, but too greedy for this extra scrap of meat to care.

Our water was nearly finished and there was only enough flour for about another week. The starving camels were so thirsty that they had refused to eat some half-dried herbage which we had passed. We must water them in the next day or two or they would collapse. Al Auf said that it would take us three more days to reach Khaba well in Dhafara, but that there was a very brackish well not far away. He thought that the camels might drink its water.

That night after we had ridden for a little over an hour it grew suddenly dark. Thinking that a cloud must be covering the full moon, I looked over my shoulder and saw that there was an eclipse and that half the moon was already obscured. Bin Kabina noticed it at the same moment and broke into a chant which the others took up.

> God endures for ever.
> The life of man is short.
> The Pleiades are overhead.
> The moon's among the stars.

Otherwise they paid no attention to the eclipse (which was total), but looked around for a place to camp.

PERSIA/IRAN

Historical Background

The long reign of Nasir al-Din Shah ended with his assassination in 1896. His death at the hands of a disciple of the revolutionary agitator Jamal al-Din 'al-Afghani' reflected a deep popular discontent both with the monarch himself, the Qajar dynasty in general, and the overall stagnation of the country. Reform was urgently required, but the combination of arbitrary and despotic rule and Western penetration of the economy generated an unnatural opposition alliance of radicals and conservative *ulama*. This had manifested itself in 1891 in the popular protests against the Shah's selling of the tobacco monopoly to an Englishman and would emerge again when Muzzafar al-Din Shah was forced to grant a *majlis* (parliament) in December 1905. The so-called *mushrutih*, or Persian constitutional revolution, lasted until 1911 when Russian pressure effectively ended it. Although the British legation in Tehran had been generally sympathetic to the revolution, the British government signed a convention with Russia in 1907 partitioning the country. In allowing Russia a free hand in the north this effectively doomed Persia's experiment in modern government to failure. In the south, where Britain's influence invariably predominated, oil had been discovered and in 1901 a Briton, William Knox D'Arcy, had been granted the concession for exploration. In 1914 the British government acquired a majority of the shares in the company holding the concession.

Foreign intervention in Persia intensified during the Great War when, faced with attempted German penetration, Britain and Russia occupied the country. With Russia's withdrawal from the war on the outbreak of the Bolshevik Revolution, Britain became the dominant power. Now Foreign Secretary, Curzon endeavoured to force the weak politicians in Tehran into 'a treaty amounting to a British protectorate' (Keddie 1981: 81–2). But in 1921, commander of the Persian Cossack regiment Reza Khan came to power in a coup backed by the British who now saw that a protectorate was not viable. The new dictator managed to put down separatist movements and establish a strong central government. In 1925 the Qajar dynasty was ended and a new Pahlavi one declared by the former Cossack leader. Reza Shah ruled until 1941 when his pro-German tendencies led the British and Russians to invade the country once more and replace him by his son Muhammad Reza. Although he employed nationalist rhetoric Reza Shah 'did not end Iran's dependence on the West or undermine foreign interests in Iran' (Keddie 1981: 109). He pursued a policy of modernization from above modelled on Atatürk's reforms in Turkey, but never gained the admiration the latter won in Western circles. Although his policies favoured the landowning class and his bureaucratization programme helped create a new middle class, Reza Shah's outlawing of the veil and crude implementation of a measure that insisted all Iranian women wear Western-style dress went further than Atatürk and helped build up resentment later to resurface against his son.

Travellers and their Narratives

The two best-known travel books on Persia of the 1890s were written by young men who when it came to Britain's policy toward the country adopted polar positions. E. G. Browne, author of *A Year Amongst the Persians*, developed a strong antipathy toward the Qajars and during the Persian revolution actively propagandized on its behalf in Britain. Browne's love affair with Persia fully embraced its peoples while notably excluding its rulers, but it would not be too much of an exaggeration to say George Nathaniel Curzon went there to establish personal diplomatic relations with the Shah and his ministers much as he did with the Amir of Afghanistan. His encyclopaedic two-volume *Persia and the Persian Question* established an Eastern expertise that helped secure him the position of viceroy of India in 1899. Although Curzon perpetuated an Orientalist 'Hajji Baba' view of Persians, he joined the anti-imperialist Browne in opposing the Liberal government's appeasement policies towards Russia's intervention in the country after 1907. Other *fin-de-siècle* travellers were Captain Percy Sykes, author of the first history of Persia in English since John Malcolm's, and his sister Ella, who wrote *Through Persia on a Side-Saddle* (1898). Isabella Bird Bishop, who spent time as a missionary amongst the Armenians and was the first woman to address the Royal Geographic Society, published *Journeys in Kurdistan* in 1891.

At the beginning of the new century, the same strategic factors that had inflected Curzon's work, now amplified by the country's acceleration into chaos, exercised journalists Valentine Chirol in *The Middle East Question* (1903) and David Fraser in *Persia and Turkey in Revolt* (1910). Also inspired by Curzonian imperialist politics was Arnold Wilson whose *South West Persia: A Political Officer's Diary* (1941) revisits his experiences as a young army officer from 1907–14, a crucial point in the development of of oil exploration. 'The fantastic anachronisms and inconsistencies of a dying dynasty, the last remnants of medieval Persia'

(Arberry [1947] 2005: xx) having largely disappeared, between the wars Iran (as the country was now officially known) seemed to change its character as a destination for Western travellers. Vita Sackville-West in 1926 still found the dress of the Kurdish tribesmen she encountered near the border with Iraq 'medieval...they might have been stragglers from some routed army' (Sackville-West 2007, 68). But she came prepared to see the country with new eyes. Already an original exponent of Byzantine art, Robert Byron turned to the Islamic architecture of Persia and Afghanistan and during the high tide of European modernism, with a stylistic originality as striking as Kinglake's had once been, made this the subject of a modernist classic: *The Road to Oxiana*. However, enthusiastic for Islamic civilization, Byron displays contempt on aesthetic grounds for non-European countries like Iran making efforts to enter the twentieth century. In some ways this seems a modernist variant of the Victorian Orientalism of Curzon. Ella Maillart's *The Cruel Way* displays a comparable modernist consciousness to Byron's in paralleling the outward journey with the inner one, though hers was concerned less with aesthetic discovery, more with personal struggle, as represented in her companion's unsuccessful battle to escape drug addiction. But like Byron, Maillart also expresses European snobbishness towards Iran, categorizing it as one of 'the newly reformed countries' where 'it pays to pretend one is much impressed by its officials' (Maillart [1947] 1986: 29).

GEORGE NATHANIEL CURZON
(1859–1925)

On the whole an undistinguished family, the Curzons of Keddleston Hall, an imposing eighteenth-century mansion in Derbyshire, traced their aristocratic lineage back to the Norman Conquest. George Curzon was however considered exceptional by his prep school headmaster and he lived up to his early promise at Eton and Balliol (though unaccountably he left Oxford without a first class degree). Already tipped for high office he made the tour of Greece and the Holy Land in 1883, then four years later, between 1887 and 1894, started a series of journeys, one round the world, and all taking in the East. Curzon had been from his schooldays an ardent imperialist and these travels had a political purpose. In 1891 he was briefly under-secretary at the India Office in Salisbury's short-lived government. At the same period the aspiring politician was busy writing letters to the *Times* about Britain's foreign policy in the East. There followed three books each mixing travel narration with observations on the political and strategic issues raised by the different areas through which the author had travelled. Both *Russia in Central Asia* (1889) and *Persia and the Persian Question* (1892) focus on the 'Great Game', or Britain and Russia's clash of interests in the East with the defence of India the core concern. *Problems of the Far East* (1894) surveyed Britain's possessions in the Far East and the growing threat of Japan. At the same time, these works develop Curzon's personal aesthetic of travel, strongly connected with imperial satisfaction and an imaginative Orientalism that delighted in the exotic whilst at the same time emphasizing Oriental decay. Later in his career, especially as viceroy of India (1899–1905), and as British Foreign Secretary (1919–1924), Curzon appeared to apply this 'expertise' in Eastern matters. The great Calcutta Durbar of 1903, which he personally organized, perfectly demonstrated his political and aesthetic enjoyment of the East as imperial spectacle.

From:

Persia and the Persian Question (1892)

Curzon's introduction to *Persia and the Persian Question* is in many ways a classic statement of both Victorian imperialism and Orientalism. It intentionally sets out to epitomize the binaries of a powerful expansive Western civilization coming up against a static and decaying Orient. Travel is constructed as an act that produces aesthetic and political meanings, but is bounded by irrefutable facts, most notably the Great Game and the decline of the Islamic world, and the aesthetic attraction of the East is enhanced by its incorporation into the British Empire. Characteristically, Curzon commences with self-quotation – from his first letter written from Persia to the *Times* expatiating on Anglo-Persian relations and the visit of the Shah to Britain in 1889.

Introductory

In the above paragraphs is indicated with sufficient precision the political aspect of this work. I need not conceal the fact that it is in the elucidation of that aspect that personally I am most concerned and that I would sooner be the author of a political treatise that commended itself to the well-informed than of a book of travel that caught the ephemeral taste of the public. Nor do I make this admission merely because success if attained in the one department may have some permanence, while in the opposite case it can scarcely be other than fugitive, but because, in the contemplation of the kingdoms and principalities of Central Asia, no question, to my mind, is comparable in importance with the part which they are likely to play or are capable of playing in the future destinies of the East. Turkestan, Afghanistan, Transcaspia, Persia—to many these names breathe only a sense of utter remoteness or a memory of strange vicissitudes and of moribund romance. To me, I confess, they are the pieces on a chessboard upon which is being played out a game for the dominion of the world. The future of Great Britain, according to this view, will be decided, not in Europe, not even upon the seas and oceans which are swept by her flag, or in the Greater Britain that has been called into existence by her offspring, but in the continent whence our emigrant stock first came, and to which as conquerors their descendants have returned. Without India the British Empire could not exist. The possession of India is the inalienable badge of sovereignty in the eastern hemisphere. Since India was known its masters have been lords of half the world. The impulse that drew an Alexander, a Timur, and a Baber eastwards to the Indus was the same that in the sixteenth century gave the Portuguese that brief lease of sovereignty whose outworn shibboleths they have ever since continued to mumble; that early in the last century made a Shah of Persia for ten years the arbiter of the East; that all but gave to France the empire which stouter hearts and a more propitious star have conferred upon our own people; that to this clay stirs the ambition and quickens the pulses of the Colossus of the North. In the increasing importance with which domestic politics are invested in our own public life and in the prevailing tendency to turn westwards, and to seek both for the examples and the arena of statesmanship amid younger peoples and a white-skinned race, room may yet he found for one whose fancy is haunted by 'the ancient of days;' who reminds his countrymen that, while no longer the arbiters of the West, they remain the trustees for the East, and are the rulers of the second largest dark-skinned population in the world; and who argues that no safeguard should be omitted by which may be secured in perpetuity that which is the noblest achievement of the science of civil rule that mankind has yet bequeathed to man.

History and Geography

Whilst, however, the connection of Persia with the larger problems of Asiatic politics is the first object which I have had in view, a second, scarcely less important, has ever been before me, and has gradually swollen in scope and dimensions, until of itself I would fain believe that it might justify these volumes. This is a desire to depict Persia as she now is, apart from her foreign relations; to give a succinct account of her provinces and peoples, her institutions and features, her sights and cities, her palaces, temples, and ruins; to trace her entry, in the present century, and particularly during the last half-century (a period nearly coterminous with the reign of the present king), into the diplomatic comity of nations, and her efforts to accommodate herself to the ill-fitting clothes of a civilisation that sits but clumsily upon her: so that any man, anxious to ascertain in any respect what is the Persia of Nasr-ed-Din Shah, how to reach it, whither to go when he gets there, what to ask for and to see, what has been done or explored or said by others before him, what there remains for him to do, may discover that which he seeks in these pages, finding therein, not merely an account of the *status quo*—the fleeting record of a moment—but, pieced together, fragment by fragment, the processes and means by which that state has been produced, and by a knowledge of which alone will he be able either to comprehend the resultant issue or to frame a forecast as to the future. In a word, I shall endeavour to do here for Persia what far abler writers have done for most other countries of equal importance, but what for two hundred years no single English writer has essayed to do for Iran, viz. to present a full-length and life-size portrait of that kingdom.

Travel

Finally, I shall add whatever of variety or incident may be possible to a text that might otherwise prove somewhat solid of substance, by describing the wayfarer's life in the East and the ever-fresh, if seldom momentous, incidents of travel.

It ought not to be difficult to interest Englishmen in the Persian people.[1] They have the same lineage as ourselves. Three thousand years ago their forefathers left the uplands of that mysterious Aryan home from which our ancestral stock had already gone forth, and the locality of which is still a frequent, if also the most futile, battlefield of science.[2] They were the first of the Indo-European family to embrace a purely monotheistic faith. Amongst them appeared Zarathustra, or Zoroaster, the second in date of the great religious teachers of the East, if indeed, he ever appeared at all.[3] Thence sprang the ennobling creed of Ormuzd and Ahriman. Then the Avesta took shape, and there was kindled the fire that, all but extinguished on its parent altars, still lights a subdued but steadfast flame in the rich and comfortable exile of Bombay.

As we descend the stately flight of Persian history we encounter many a name familiar to us from childhood. Dismissing the legendary as appertaining to a **rama** region of myth more nebulous in the case of Iran than of almost any country, **f** we are confronted with the illustrious figures of Cyrus, Darius, and Xerxes, **ersian** whose handwriting still echoes their fame from the halls where they ruled and **iistory** feasted. A succession of meteoric phenomena, the wonder or the scourge of humanity, an Alexander, a Jenghiz Khan, a Timur, a Nadir Shah, pass, at

---

[1] In the minds of a great many English folk I fear that Persia awakens few other images than a recollection of the tales of Herodotus, the verses of Moore, and the diamonds of the Shah. On the whole, Herodotus more often wrote history than story; while the quality of the Shah's jewels is unimpeachable. But I regret to say that a heavy weight of responsibility lies at the door of Moore, whose descriptions of Persia are about as much like the original as the Alhambra of Leicester Square is like the exquisite palace of Boabdil. The roses of Bendemeer's stream are equally illusory with the nightingales; 'Kishma's amber vines' are in comical contrast with the treeless sterility of the real Kishm ; and when Luttrell wrote–

'I am told, dear Moore, your lays are sung
(Can it be true, you lucky man?)
By moonlight in the Persian tongue
Along the streets of Ispahan,'

he must have been confiding in the ignorance, as well as humouring the egoism of the poet.
[2] I am aware that it is now asserted that the Aryans never came from Asia at all. But, for the present, I hesitate to adopt either the Sarmatian theory (Dr. Schrader, *Prehistoric Antiquities of the Aryan Peoples*, translated by F. B. Jevons, 1890; and Canon I. Taylor, *Tue Origin of the Aryans*, 1890) or the Scandinavian theory (Herr Penka, *Die Herkunft der Arier*, 1886), for fear of being presently invited to surrender them for a third and, as yet, undiscovered alternative. In the meantime, therefore, I prefer the old Asian hypothesis, to which Professor J. Schmidt has gallantly rallied in an essay published in 1890 in the *Transactions of the Royal Academy of Berlin.*
[3] Again a necessary qualification, seeing that so learned an authority as Professor Darmesteter has found in the personality of Zoroaster nothing more substantial than 'a product of the ubiquitous storm-myth.'

different epochs, in a trail of fire and blood across the scene. The direst day of the later Roman Commonwealth was when the legions of Crassus were strewn on the plain of Carrhæ. Twice did a Roman Cæsar surrender to a Persian or semi-Persian conqueror; when the Emperor Valerian bowed his neck beneath the heel of Shapur I.; and when the Emperor Romanus Diogenes fell a prisoner to the Seljuk Alp Arslan, the Great Lion. The death in battle of a third, the renowned Julian, was a triumph more precious than a battlefield to the second Shapur. Twice also, in the days of the famous Chosroes, or Nushirwan, and again under his grandson, the second Chosroes or Parviz, the borders of Iran were extended to the Mediterranean, and the terror of her arms to the walls of Byzantium. Then fell the sword of Omar and the devouring flame of the Koran. In the ensuing ages great names—Avicenna (Abu-ibn-Sena), Firdusi, Omar-el-Khayam, Sadi, and Hafiz—adorned her literary annals, and have left her a legacy of imperishable renown. Finally a native dynasty and a naturalised religion appeared; and the name of Shah Abbas the Great is to this hour associated with anything that is durable or grandiose during the last three centuries of Persian history. A record of inferior names, of internecine conflict and international struggle, in the course of which Russia and England enter upon the scene, brings us down to the present time, when a dominion, greatly contracted, but withal much consolidated, acknowledges a Turkish dynasty, and parades before the world the now familiar figure of Nasr-ed-Din Shah. If Persia had no other claim to respect, at least a continuous national history for 2,500 years is a distinction which few countries can exhibit.

Anglo-Persian Connection

There is, further, in the special connection of Persia with this nation at different epochs, and more especially during the present century, a claim upon Englishmen's attention which no student of his country's history should be willing to ignore. As long ago as the reign of Edward I. an accredited plenipotentiary was deputed from Great Britain to the court of the Mongol sovereign Arghun, in whose dominions Persia was included. Nearly three centuries later an envoy bore letters from Queen Elizabeth to the second Sefavi monarch. An ambassador from Charles I. reached Persia only to die. In the sixteenth and again in the seventeenth centuries gallant attempts were made by British agents to establish a trade with Persia by the north of Europe and the Caspian. Between the two periods the growing maritime ascendency of Great Britain had opened to her first a share, and presently the control, of the commerce of the Persian Gulf. Finally, with the dawn of the present century, emerged a policy of close Anglo-Persian relationship, which, though twice suspended by diplomatic rupture, and once by war, has remained in existence ever since; which has given birth to a few deservedly great reputations; and which, though it has been signalised by many follies and by some shame, by spasms of prodigal concern succeeded by intervals of unreasoning apathy, has yet bound the two nations in a closer bond of political interest than unites this country with any other independent sovereignty in Asia.

The memorials of many of these ages, the handiwork of some of these men, will come under notice in the narrative to which I shall presently turn. My journey was divided into four portions, each of which will be found to possess a historical interest or a political importance, as well as physical idiosyncrasies, of its own. They will deal respectively with the north-east, the central, and the south-west provinces of Persia, and with the maritime highway on the south, the thread upon which will be strung whatever of information I have been able to collect, either with regard to the regions actually traversed or to those bordering thereupon, being supplied by the description of my own travels, which consisted of (1) a ride of 850 miles through the frontier province of Khorasan and thence to the capital, Teheran; (2) the more familiar journey of 800 miles, also on horseback, from Teheran to Bushire; (3) the ascent of the Shat-el-Arab and the Karun River; and (4) the navigation of the Persian Gulf.

In the first case I shall conduct my readers to the last remaining possession of the once mighty principality of Khorasan—a dominion that embraced Merv, extended to Khiva, included Herat and Kandahar, and was laved by the Oxus. Though shorn of its high estate, this province, fortified by savage mountains and inaccessible ravines, interspersed with plains that sustain the relics of famous capitals, and possessing one city at least of world-wide renown, will be found to present many problems of undiminished and imperial interest. For hundreds of years it has been the battle-ground of races and the prey of a rapine less merciful than sustained war. More persons have probably died a violent death in Khorasan than in any other territory of equal size in Asia. There, moreover, at this moment, on the north and east, the eagles are again gathered together, and in the barracks of Transcaspia and the council-tents of Turkestan is being debated the destiny of Meshed.

While treating of this portion of my journey it will be both natural and necessary to the scope of these volumes that I should give the latest information about the adjacent-provinces or districts; information the bulk of which was derived from inquiries made by myself while in the neighbourhood, and the whole of which has been supervised by the most competent authorities. This will apply to the Perso-Afghan border and Seistan question on the east, where a political crisis is always possible and sometimes acute, and where the Indian Frontier question emerges as a formidable factor in the situation; to the maritime provinces of Persia on the Caspian, where such an amazing difference of natural conditions exists that they might be mistaken for the antipodes, instead of a physical continuation, of Persian soil; and to the north-western and western provinces, containing great cities, an alien and divided population, and indestructible remains of antiquity. Similarly, when I come to the southern parts of the country, information will be forthcoming about those more distant and little known provinces in the south-east and south-west, which have held out the longest against the centralizing tendencies of the age, and which still, in some sort, exhibit an image of the nomad turbulence that was once a uniform characteristic of Iranian society.

Resuming my journey at Teheran the opportunity will await us of seeing something of a court whose splendour is said to have formerly rivalled that of **2. Central Provinces** the Great Mogul, of a Government which is still, with the exception of China, the most oriental in the East, and of a city which unites the unswerving characteristics of an Asiatic capital with the borrowed trappings of Europe. Thence the high road—only ninety miles of which is a road in any known sense of the word—will lead us across the successive partitions of the great plateau, possessing a mean elevation of 4,000 to 5,000 feet above the sea, that occupies the heart of Persia; and whose manifold mountain ridges intervene, like the teeth of a saw, between the northern and southern seas. In the plains of greater or less extent lying at their base we shall find, in the shape of large but ruined cities, the visible records of faded magnificence, of unabashed misrule, and of internal decay. Kum, from behind its curtain of fanaticism and mystery, will reveal the glitter of the golden domes that overhang the resting-place of saints and the sepulchre of kings. Isfahan, with its wreck of fallen palaces, its acres of wasted pleasaunce, its storeyed bridges that once rang beneath the tread of a population numbered at 650,000, will tell a tale of deeper pathos, although in its shrill and jostling marts we may still observe evidence of mercantile activity and a prospering international trade. Shiraz, which once re-echoed the blithe anacreontics of Hafiz, and the more demure philosophy of Sadi, preserves and cherishes the poets' graves; but its merry gardens, its dancing fountains, and its butterfly existence have gone the way of the singers who sang their praises, and are now only a shadow and a lament. In this neighbourhood, and in eloquent juxtaposition to these piles of modern ruin, occur at intervals the relics of a grander imagination and a more ancient past. Here on the plain still stands the white marble mausoleum that, in all probability, once held the gold coffin and the corpse of Cyrus. At no great distance the rifled sepulchre of Darius gapes from its chiselled hollow in the scarp of a vertical cliff. Opposite the princely platform of Persepolis lifts its dwindling columns, and amid piles of *débris* displays the sculptured handiwork that graced the palace of Xerxes and the halls of Artaxerxes.

I shall not be reproached if I linger awhile amid these renowned, and often commemorated, relics of the past. They show us that, just as mediæval Persia **monu-ments of antiquity** was far removed from modern Persia in its pageantry and wealth, so ancient Persia—the Persia of Herodotus and Xenophon—was immeasurably superior to mediæval Persia in its attributes, and is even now more respectable in its ruin. Though in dealing with these ancient and historic monuments I shall not recapitulate architectural or topographical details, which can be found better displayed in other and more technical works, I shall yet avail myself of the latest scientific knowledge and research, having no sympathy with those who rush through a country that has elicited the services of profound and famous writers, and who think the ignorant jottings of a tourist's note-book good enough to supersede the labours of a long line of scholars and men of science. A historian of travel who possesses any self-respect will thankfully profit by their researches, in the spirit of the seventeenth century editor of Tavernier, who wrote that 'he was sufficiently imbued in his intellectuals with all due knowledge of sciences, languages, and geography, and precedent travellers' maps and books, without all which common travellers cannot conceive so soon and so orderly, nor reap so much benefit for themselves or others.' At the same time he will endeavour, by the exercise of personal observation and of honest criticism, to give an independent account of what has passed before his own eyes.

In the extreme south-west I shall invite attention to a part of the country where nature has been lavish of gifts that man has alternately blessed and despised; where navigable rivers flow through plains once enriched with a superb vegetation, though now relapsed into stony wastes; and where great engineering works, enduring memorials of a hydraulic ingenuity, and a public-spirited zeal, to which later centuries afford no parallel, now raise their shattered piers amid a waste of untended waters and uncultivated lands. There great cities once adorned the river banks; great palaces reared their colonnades and halls upon the summit of elevated mounds; great kings, a Cyrus, a Darius, an Alexander, a Shapur, either swept past on the stormy tide of conquest, or paused to taste the splendid luxury of repose. Here I shall halt to notice the newly revived sparks of industry and trade, which the present generation should not pass without fanning into a livelier flame. This romantic region abuts upon one still more famous in the annals of the past. Its borders are washed by the broad estuary down which the Euphrates and Tigris roll their commingled waters to the Gulf. Here we are in a land of equal honour in sacred legend and profane history. We may sail past the traditional Garden of Eden to the mysterious site where, amid colossal mounds of pottery and brick, the alphabet of Nebuchadnezzar speaks loudly from the ruins of sculptured palaces, of terraced temples, and Babylonian towers, where Daniel prophesied, where Israel wept, where Alexander perished. We are on the river threshold of Busrah, the Balsorah of Sinbad the Sailor, that Arab Columbus of an earlier age. We may fringe the soaring arch of Ctesiphon and descry on the horizon the minarets and palm trees of Baghdad.

outh-
tern
vinces

Finally, skirting in a vessel the southern and maritime borders of Persia, I shall ask attention to a country and a sea little known at home, to warring **The** Arab tribes and piratical professions, to seaports, now dead and deserted, **Persian** whose fame once sounded through Europe; to waters that have been ploughed **Gulf** by the rival argosies of Portugal, Holland, and Great Britain. If I am there tempted to unravel some few of the threads that have been woven into a web of history, intensely personal to our own country and race, I shall also be able to show that Great Britain sustains, in a less acquisitive and martial age, the prestige which she gained at the dawn of her career of Asiatic conquest, and that the British name is still on these distant waters a synonym for order and freedom.

These will provide what I may call the pictorial aspects of my narrative; mingled with the normal and yet uncommon episodes of travel in the East, they may win a hearing even from the desultory reader. Nor shall I despair of **Change-** arousing his concern when I turn from a past, however eventful, to a present, **lessness** however degenerate and sad. A country that possesses no railways is *ipso facto* **of the** the possessor of a great charm. Here may still in many parts be found a **East** people retaining the indigenous customs and modes of Asiatic life, and as yet unawakened to the summons that is beating at their doors. Fifty years hence the outlying towns of Persia may have taken on some of the varnish of the capital, and have lost their peculiar individuality of combined dignity and decay. But for the present Persia is of the East, most Eastern; and though the Persian nobleman may ride in a Russian brougham, the Persian merchant carry a French watch, and the Persian peasant wear a Manchester blouse, yet the heart of the nation is unregenerate, and is fanatically (and not always unfortunately) attached to the ancient order of things. We may still re-echo the words of the philosophic Chardin:—

> That it is not in Asia as in our Europe, where there are frequent changes more or less in the forms of things, as the habits, buildings, gardenings and the like. In the East they are constant in all things. The habits are at this day in the same manner as in the precedent ages; so that one may reasonably believe that in that part of the world the exterior forms of things (as their manners and customs) are the same now as they were 2,000 years since, except in such changes as may have been introduced by religion, which are nevertheless very inconsiderable.

Its And here let me endeavour in some sort to explain to others what I am **abiding** sometimes conscious of having only imperfectly explained to myself, viz. the **charm** wonderful and incalculable fascination of the East. Mr. Stanley in one of his letters spoke of the mysterious Soudan fever which drew Gordon and many another brave spirit to perish in the dim recesses of Africa, and which will require how many more human hecatombs before its appetite be appeased? Just such another, though a less perilous contagion is that which tempts the traveller into Asia, makes him regardless of the petty restraints of distance and time, animated only by a burning desire to go on. Perhaps it is that in the wide landscape, in the plains stretching without break to mountains, and the mountains succeeded by plains, in the routes that are without roads, in the roads that are without banks or ditches, in the unhampered choice both of means of progression and of pace, there is a joyous revulsion from the sterile conventionality of life and locomotion at home. Something, too, must be set down to the gratified spirit of self-dependence, which legions of domestics have not availed to subdue, and to the love of adventure, which not even the nineteenth century can extinguish. Or is it that in the East, and amid scenes where life and its environment have not varied for thousands of years, where nomad Abrahams still wander with their flocks and herds, where Rebecca still dips her water skin at the well, where savage forays perpetuate the homeless miseries of Job, western man casts off the slough of an artificial civilisation, and feels that he is mixing again with his ancestral stock, and breathing the atmosphere that nurtured his kind?

ntrast
tween
e East
d West
Upon the vivid and never failing contrast between the picture and the furniture of existence in the East and West, as an element of attraction, it is needless to enlarge. The most casual visitor to the true East is no stranger to its strange intensity.

Countries which have no ports or quays, no railways or stations, no high-roads or streets (in our sense of the term), no inns or hotels, no bedsteads or tables or chairs, but where a traveller is sufficiently equipped so long as he is provided with a saddle and some soap, are severed by a sufficiently wide gap from our own to appeal to the most glutted thirst for novelty. Do we ever escape from the fascination of a turban, or the mystery of the shrouded apparitions that pass for women in the dusty alleys? How new to us is a landscape where there are no hedgerows or timber, no meadows or fields; where in the brilliant atmosphere minute objects can be distinguished for many miles,[4] where the cities are not swathed in smoke, and the level roofs are not broken by shafts or chimneys. How mute and overpowering the silence that prevails over the lone expanse, so different from the innumerable rural sounds that strike upon the ear at home. And how grateful a climate where fogs and vapours never strangle, but where the sun strikes with straight lance from the zenith.

---

[4] I have seen a small object, such as a single hut or building, for at least twenty miles before reaching it; and every traveller in Persia will confess to the frequent exasperation of hope thus baffled and delayed.

In no Oriental country that I have seen is the chasm of exterior divergence between Oriental and European scenery more abrupt than in Persia. It is difficult to bring home to English readers, whose ideas of nature are drawn exclusively from the West, the extremity of the contrast that meets the eye. Mountains in Europe are for the most part blue or purple in colour; in Persia they are flame-red, or umber, or funereal drab. Fields in Europe, when not decked with the green of grass or crops, are crimson with upturned mould. In Persia they are only distinguishable from the brown desert by the dry beds of the irrigation ditches. A typical English village consists of detached and often picturesque cottages, half hidden amid venerable trees. A typical Persian village is a cluster of filthy mud huts, whose outline is a crude combination of the perpendicular and the horizontal, huddled within the protection of a decayed mud wall. Outside the Caspian provinces and a few mountain valleys there is not a forest, and barely a wood in Persia that is worthy of the name. One may travel for clays without seeing a blade of grass. Rivers do not roll between trim banks, nor do brooks babble over stones. Either you are stopped by a foaming torrent, or you barely moisten your horse's fetlocks in fording a pitiful thread.

Extreme in Persia

For my own part—so normal and blunted after a while do these sensations become—I find a more abiding charm in the contrast existing, not between the lives of the East and West, but in the elements and conditions of Oriental life itself. It is a contrast equally visible in the inanimate and in the human world. Extensive plains are suddenly terminated, almost without slope or undulation, by gaunt and forbidding peaks. A drear and colourless desolation in winter is succeeded by riotous, though ephemeral, verdure and a thousand tints of flowers in the spring. Even in the green and cultivated spots, the moment we leave the charmed circle of water distribution the stark desert recommences, and the transition is as awful as from life to death. An entrancing warmth by day is expiated in the autumn and winter months by biting cold at night and in the hours immediately preceding sunrise. Nature seems to revel in striking the extreme chords upon her miraculous and inexhaustible gamut of sound.

Intrinsic contradiction

And how faithfully do the cities and people respond to the suggestion that is always eloquent around them. Majestic ruins that tell of a populous and mighty past rear their heads amid deserted wastes and vagabond tents. Tiny and ill-nurtured children grow up into robust men. Conversely, female beauty in early youth is followed by a premature decay and ugliness beyond words. Just as from a distance a town surrounded by its orchards looks a gem of beauty, but shrinks upon nearer approach into a collection of clay hovels; and just as in the exterior of these houses, consisting of blank and unsightly walls of mud, there is no hint of the flower-beds and tanks, of the taste and comeliness that sometimes prevail within, so does the human exterior tell a contradictory tale

The lies of life

of its inmate. *Splendide mendax* might be taken as the motto of Persian character. The finest domestic virtues co-exist with barbarity and supreme indifference to suffering. Elegance of deportment is compatible with a coarseness amounting to bestiality. The same individual is at different moments haughty and cringing. A creditable acquaintance with the standards of civilisation does not prevent gross fanaticism and superstition. Accomplished manners and a more than Parisian polish cover a truly superb faculty for lying and almost scientific imposture. The most scandalous corruption is combined with a scrupulous regard for specified precepts of the moral law. Religion is alternately stringent and lax, inspiring at one moment the bigot's rage, at the next the agnostic's indifference. Government is both patriarchal and Machiavellian—patriarchal in its simplicity of structure, Machiavellian in its finished ingenuity of wrong doing. Life is both magnificent and squalid; the people at once despicable and noble; the panorama at the same time an enchantment and a fraud.

EDWARD GRANVILLE BROWNE
(1862–1926)

Born in Gloucestershire into a family with strong engineering connections (his father was director of a shipbuilding firm in Newcastle-upon-Tyne), Browne attended Eton and graduated from Cambridge in the Natural Sciences in 1882, qualifying as a practitioner of medicine in 1887. In between, he travelled briefly to Istanbul (1883) and took the Indian languages tripos at Cambridge in 1884. His background of wealth and liberal orientations gave him scope to follow a career in Oriental Studies rather than medicine, and adopt radical postures on the East. Successively the Turks and then the Iranians became objects of his ardour, and he actively promoted their cultural and political causes. He developed a particular rapport with Iranians after his visit to Iran in 1887–8; though this would be his only visit it featured in one of the best travel works of the nineteenth century, *A Year Amongst the Persians*, which appeared in 1893. Browne was made Sir Thomas Adam's Professor of Arabic in 1902 and spent the rest of his life as a Cambridge don. However, his bitter criticism of the foreign policy of the Liberal Government, especially its position on the Iranian constitutional revolution between 1906 and 1911, harmed his reputation among the political establishment. Independent means and a remarkable grasp of Oriental languages made Browne a formidable adversary. A love for Persian language and culture strongly informs *A Year Amongst the Persians*, in spite of its being the work of a young man. It 'enabled him in large measure to surmount the handicaps of being a foreigner and an infidel, suspected inevitably by the Persians – of all nations, the most prone to conspiracy theories of history and politics – of being either a British spy or a treasure-hunter' (Bosworth 2001: 80*)*. The book presents topics and themes that would exercise Browne in later years. These include: his fascination with the extremities of Iranian religious ideas, his opposition to the ruling Qajar dynasty, and his belief in an imagined Persian spirit that incarnated itself from age to age in Iranian history, in essence the subject of his four volume *Literary History of Persia*.

From:

A Year Amongst the Persians **(1893)**

Towards the end of his stay in Persia Browne arrived in Kerman where he encountered 'the strangest and wildest of men whose endless talk on metaphysics and mysticism [he] brilliantly recorded' (Arberry 1960: 167).

Kirmán Society

> "*Har chand ki az rúyi karímán khajilím,*
> *Gham níst, ki parvardé-i-ín áb u gilím:*
> *Dar rúyi zamín níst chú Kírmán ja'í;*
> *Kírmán dil-i-'álam-ast, ú má ahl-i-dilím!*"

> "Although we stand abashed in the presence of the noble,
> It matters not, since we have drawn nourishment from this earth and water:
> On the face of the earth there is no place like Kirmán;
> Kirmán is the heart of the world, and we are men of heart."

In no town which I visited in Persia did I make so many friends and acquaintances of every grade of society, and every shade of piety and impiety, as at Kirmán. When I left I made a list of all the persons who had visited me, or whom I had visited, and found that the number of those whom I could remember fell but little short of a hundred. Amongst these almost every rank, from the Prince-Governor down to the mendicant dervish, was represented, as well as a respectable variety of creeds and nationalities—Belúchís, Hindoos, Zoroastrians, Shí'ites and Sunnís, Sheykhís, Ṣúfís, Bábís, both Behá'í and Ezelí, dervishes, and *kalandars* belonging to no order, fettered by no dogma, and trammelled by but few principles. Hitherto I had always been more or less dependent on the hospitality of friends, whose feelings I was obliged to consult in choosing my acquaintances; here in Kirmán the garden where I dwelt was open to all comers, and I was able without let or hindrance to pursue that object which, since my arrival in Persia, had been ever before me, namely, to familiarise myself with all, even the most eccentric and antinomian, developments of the protean Persian genius. I succeeded beyond my most sanguine expectations, and, as will presently be set forth, found myself ere long in a world whereof I had never dreamed, and wherein my spirit was subjected to such alternations of admiration, disgust, and wonder, as I had never before in my life experienced.

All this, however, did not come to me at once, and would not, perhaps, have come at all but for a fortunate misfortune which entirely altered all my plans, and prolonged the period of my stay at Kirmán from the fortnight or three weeks which I had originally intended to a couple of months. For just as I was about to depart thence (having, indeed, actually engaged a muleteer for the journey to Shíráz by way of Sírján, Khír, and Níríz), I fell a victim to a sharp attack of ophthalmia, which for some weeks compelled me to abandon all idea of resuming my travels. And this ophthalmia, from which I suffered no little pain, had another result tending to throw me more than would otherwise have been the case into the society of dervishes, dreamers, and mystics. Judge me not harshly, O thou who hast never known sickness—ay, and for a while partial blindness—in a strange land, if in my pain and my wakefulness I at length yielded to the voice of the tempter, and fled for refuge to that most potent, most sovereign, most seductive, and most enthralling of masters, opium. Unwisely I may have acted in this matter, though not, as I feel, altogether culpably; yet to this unwisdom I owe an experience which I would not willingly have forfeited, though I am thankful enough that the chain of my servitude was snapped ere the last flicker of resolution and strenuousness finally expired in the Nirvana of the opium-smoker. I often wonder if any of those who have returned to tell the tale in the outer world have wandered farther than myself into the flowery labyrinths of the poppy-land, for of him who enters its fairy realms too true, as a rule, is the Persian opium-smoker's epigram—

> "*Ḥaẓrat-i-afyún-i-má har maraẓí-rá rewást,*
> *Lík chú 'ádí shudí, khud maraẓ-i-bí-dewást.*"

> "Sir Opium of ours for every ill is a remedy swift and sure,
> But he, if you bear for a while his yoke, is an ill which knows no cure."

Although it was some while after my arrival in Kirmán that I became numbered amongst the intimates of the aforesaid Sir Opium, he lost no time in introducing himself to my notice in the person of one of his faithful votaries, Mírzá Ḥuseyn-Ḳulí of Bam (a pleasant, gentle, dreamy soul, of that type which most readily succumbs to the charm of the poppy), who came to visit me in Ná'ib Ḥasan's company on the very day of my entry into the garden. Soon after this, too, I came into daily relations with another bondsman of the all-potent drug, one 'Abdu'l Ḥuseyn, whom Ḥájí Ṣafar, in accordance with the agreement made between himself and myself at Yezd, had hired to look after my horse. He was far advanced on the downward path, and often, when sent to buy bread or other provisions in the shops hard by the city-gate, would he remain away for hours at a time, and return at last without having accomplished his commission, and unable to give any account of how the time had passed. This used to cause me some annoyance till such time as I too fell under the spell of the poppy-wizard, when I ceased to care any longer (because the opium-smoker cares not greatly for food or indeed for aught else in the material world save his elixir), nay, I even found a certain tranquil satisfaction in his vagaries. But I must leave for a while these delicious reminiscences and return to the comparatively uneventful fortnight with which my residence at Kirmán began. Of this I shall perhaps succeed in giving the truest picture by following in the main the daily entries which I made in my diary.

On the day of my instalment in the garden (*Wednesday, 5th June, 25th Ramazán*) I received several visitors besides the opium-smoker of Bam. Chief amongst these was a certain notable Sheykh of Ḥum, whose doubtful orthodoxy had made it expedient for him to leave the sacred precincts of his native town for happy, heedless Kirmán. Here he had succeeded in gaining the confidence and esteem of Prince Náṣiru'd-Dawla, the Governor, in whose society most of his time was passed, either in consultation on affairs of state, or in games of chance, for which he cared the less because he was almost invariably the loser. He was a burly, genial, kind-hearted gentleman, with but little of the odour of sanctity so much sought after in his native town, and a fund of wit and information. I afterwards saw much of him, and learned that he was an Ezelí Bábí, so far as he was anything at all (for by many he was accounted a free-thinker, "*lá-madhhab*"); but in this first interview he gave no further indication of his proclivities than to enquire whether I had not a copy of Mánakjí's *New History* of the Bábí Theophany. With him came two brothers, merchants of Yezd, whom I will call Áḳá Muhsin and Áḳá Muḥammad Ṣádiḳ. Of the former, who was an orthodox Shí'ite, I saw but little subsequently; but with the younger brother, a man of singular probity and most amiable disposition, I became rather intimate, and from him I met with a disinterested kindness which I shall not omit to record in its proper place. He too was a Bábí, but a follower of Behá, not of Ezel; as also was a third brother, who, being but a lad of fifteen or sixteen, was suddenly so overcome by a desire to behold the face of Behá that he ran away from Kirmán with only five *túmáns* in his pocket, with the set purpose of making his way to Acre, on the Syrian coast, in which project, thanks to the help of kindly Zoroastrians at Bandar-i-'Abbás, and the Bábís of Bombay and Beyrout, he was successful. I subsequently made the acquaintance of another lad whose imagination was so stirred by this exploit that he was determined to imitate it at the first opportunity, though whether or no his plan was realised I cannot say.

Thursday, 6th June, 26th Ramazán. – Soon after I was up I received a visit from Ná'ib Hasan (who, indeed, lost no time in establishing himself in the position of my guide, philosopher, and friend, and who seldom allowed a day to pass without giving me the pleasure of his society for a good many hours, including at least one meal). With him came Rustam, the young Zoroastrian of whom I have already spoken, who, on this occasion, outstayed the Ná'ib. This Rustam was a well-mannered and intelligent lad, whose only fault was an unduly deferential manner, which at times I found rather irksome. He asked me many questions about my country and about America ("*Yangi-dunyá*," "the New World"), in which, like several other Persians whom I met, he appeared to take an extraordinary interest; for what reason I know not, since he had not the excuse of supposing, like some Muḥammadans, that thence, by some underground channel, Antichrist (*Dajjál*) shall reach the well in Iṣfahán from which, at the end of time, he is to appear.

In the afternoon I went into the town, accompanied by Ḥájí Ṣafar and Mírzá Yúsuf, notwithstanding a message which I received from the Sárdar of Sístán informing me of his intention of paying me a visit. We passed the walls, not by the adjacent *Derwázé-i-Náṣiriyya*, but by another gate called *Derwázé-i-Masjid* ("the Mosque Gate"), lying more to the west, from which a busy thoroughfare (thronged, especially on "Friday eve," with hosts of beggars) leads directly to the bazaars, and paid a visit to my Zoroastrian friends in the caravansaray of Ganj 'Alí Khán (where, for the most part, their offices are situated) and to the post-office. In the bazaars I met a quaint-looking old Hindoo, who persisted in addressing me in his own uncouth Hindi, which he seemed to consider that I as an Englishman was bound to understand. We returned about sunset by the way we had come, and met crowds of people, who had been to pay their respects to a deceased saint interred in a mausoleum just outside the Mosque Gate, re-entering the city.

On reaching the garden I found another visitor awaiting me—an inquisitive, meddlesome, self-conceited scion of some once influential but now decayed family, who, in place of the abundant wealth which he had formerly possessed, subsisted on a pension of 150 *túmáns* allowed him by the Prince-Governor in consideration of his former greatness. For this person, whose name was Ḥájí Muḥammad Khán, I conceived a very particular aversion. He manifested a great curiosity as to my rank, my income, and the object of my journey, and presently assured me that he detected in me a remarkable likeness to the Prince of Wales, with whom, he declared, he had struck up an acquaintance one evening at the Crystal Palace. "Don't attempt to deceive me," he added, with many sly nods and winks: "I understand how one of noble birth may for a time be under a cloud, and may find it expedient to travel in disguise and to forgo that state and circumstance to which he is justly entitled. I am in somewhat the same position myself, but I am not going to continue thus for long. I have had a hint from the *Aminu's-Sulṭán*, and am wanted at Ṭeherán. There are those who would like to prevent my reaching the capital," he continued mysteriously, "but never fear, I will outwit them. When you leave Kirmán for Shíráz, I leave it in your company, and with me you shall visit Shahr-i-Bábak and many other interesting places on our way thither." Ná'ib Hasan fooled him to the top of his bent, unfolding vast and shadowy pictures of my power and affluence, and declaring that I had unlimited credit with the Zoroastrian merchants of Kirmán; which falsehoods Ḥájí Muḥammad Khán (whom copious libations of beer were rendering every moment more credulous and more mysterious) greedily imbibed. When he had gone I remonstrated vigorously with the Ná'ib for his mendacity. "I suppose it is no use for me to remind you that it is wicked to tell lies," I remarked, "but at least you must see how silly and how futile it is to make assertions whereof the falsity cannot remain hidden for more than a few days, and which are likely to land me in difficulties." But the Ná'ib only shook his head and laughed, as though to say that lying was in itself an artistic and pleasurable exercise of the imagination, in which, when there was no reason to the contrary, he might fairly allow himself to indulge. So, finding remonstrance vain, I presently retired to rest in some disgust.

Friday, 7th June, 27th Ramazán.—In the morning I was visited by an old Zoroastrian woman, who was anxious to learn whether I had heard in Teherán any talk of Aflátún ("Plato") having turned Musulmán. It took me some little while to discover that the said Aflátún was not the Greek philosopher but a young Zoroastrian in whom she was interested, though why a follower of "the good Mazdayasnian religion" should take to himself a name like this baffles my comprehension. In the afternoon I was invaded by visitors. First of all came a Belúch chief named Afẓal Khán, a picturesque old man with long black hair, a ragged moustache, very thin on the upper lip and very long at the ends, and a singularly gorgeous coat. He was accompanied by two lean and hungry-looking retainers, all skin and sword–blade; but though he talked much I had some difficulty in understanding him at times, since he spoke Persian after the corrupt and vicious fashion prevalent in India. He enquired much of England and the English, whom he evidently regarded with mingled respect and dislike. "Ḳal'at-i-Náṣirí is my city," he replied, in answer to a question which I put to him; "three months' journey from here, or two months if your horse be sound, swift, and strong. Khán Khudádád Khán is the Amír, if he be not dead, as I have heard men say lately." He further informed me that his language was not Belúchí but Bráhú'í, which is spoken in a great part of Belúchistán.

The next visitors to arrive were the postmaster, Áḳá Muḥammad Ṣádik? (the young Yezdí merchant of whom I have already spoken), and the eldest son of the Prince-Telegraphist. The last upbraided me for taking up my abode in the garden instead of in the new telegraph-office, which his father had placed at my disposal; but his recriminations were cut short by the arrival of a Tabrízí merchant, two Zoroastrians, an Ezelí Bábí (whom I will call Mullá Yúsuf, to distinguish him from my Tabrízí satellite Mírzá Yúsuf), who appeared on this occasion as a zealous Musulmán, and undertook to convince me on some future occasion of the superiority of Islam to Christianity; and a middle-aged man of very subdued demeanour (how deceptive may appearances be!), dressed in a long *jubbé*, fez, and small white turban, after the manner of Asiatic Turks, to whom, under the pseudonym of Sheykh Ibráhím of Sulṭán-ábád, I shall have frequent occasion to refer in this and the succeeding chapter. These, in turn, were followed by four more Zoroastrians, including Gushtásp, Ferídún, and Rustam, who outstayed the other visitors, and did not depart till they had pledged me in wine after the rite of the Magians, after which I had supper with Ná'ib Hasan, and sat talking with him till nearly midnight.

Saturday, 8th June, 28th Ramazán.—In the morning I visited one of the shawl-manufactories of Kirmán in company with Rustam, Ná'ib Hasan, and Mírzá Yúsuf of Tabríz. Our way lay through the street leading to the Mosque Gate, which, by reason of the Saturday market (*Bázár-i-Shanba*), was thronged with people. The shawl-manufactory consisted of one large vaulted room containing eleven looms, two or three of which were standing idle. At each loom sat three workers, one skilled workman in the middle, and on either side of him a *shágird* or apprentice, whom he was expected to instruct and supervise. There were in all twenty-five apprentices, ranging in years from children of six and seven to men of mature age. Their wages, as I learned, begin at ten *túmáns* (about £3) a year, and increase gradually to twenty-four or twenty-five *túmáns* (about £7 10s). In summer they work from sunrise to sunset, and in winter they continue their work by candle-light till three hours after sunset. They have a half-holiday on Friday (from mid-day onwards), thirteen days' holiday at the *Nawrúz*, and one or two days more on the great annual festivals, while for food they get nothing as a rule but dry bread. Poor little Kirmánís! They must toil thus, deprived of good air and sunlight, and debarred from the recreations and amusements which should brighten their childhood, that some grandee may bedeck himself with those sumptuous shawls, which, beautiful as they are, will evermore seem to me to be dyed with the blood of the innocents! The shawls manufactured are of very different qualities. The finest, of three or three and a half ells in length, require twelve or fifteen months for their completion, and are sold at forty or fifty *túmáns* apiece; others, destined for the Constantinople market, and of much coarser texture, can be finished in a month or six weeks, and are sold for ten or fifteen *kráns*. Of late, however, the shawl trade had been on the decline; and the proprietor of this establishment told me that he was thinking of closing his workshops for a year, and making a pilgrimage to Kerbelá, hoping, I suppose, to win by this act of piety the Divine favour, which he would have better merited by some attempt to ameliorate the condition of the poor little drudges who toiled at his looms.

I next visited the one fire-temple which suffices for the spiritual needs of the Kirmán Zoroastrians, and was there received by the courteous and intelligent old Dastúr and my friend Ferídún. I could not see the sacred fire, because the *múbad* whose business it was to tend it had locked it up and taken the key away with him. In general appearance this fire-temple resembled those which I had seen at Yezd. I enquired as to the manuscripts of the sacred books preserved in the temple, and was shown two: a copy of the Avesta of 210 leaves, transcribed in the year A.H. 1086 (A.D. 1675–6), and completed on "the day of Abán, in the month of Bahman, in the year 1044 of Yezdigird," by the hand of Dastúr Marzabán, the son of Dastúr Bahrám, the son of Marzabán, the son of Ferídún; and a copy of the Yashts, completed by the hand of Dastúr Isfandiyár, the son of Dastúr Núshírván, the son of Dastúr Isfandiyár, the son of Dastúr Ardashír, the son of Dastúr Ádhar of Sístán, on "the day of Bahman, in the month of Isfandarmad, in the year 1108 of Yezdigird," corresponding to A.H. 1226 (A.D. 1811). I found that the Dastúr was much interested in the occult science of geomancy (*'ilm-i-ramal*), which, he informed me, required the assiduous study of a lifetime ere one could hope to attain proficiency. He was also very full of a rare old book called the *Jámásp-náma*, of which he said only one copy, stolen by a Musulmán named Huseyn from the house of a Zoroastrian in Yezd, existed in Kirmán, though he had information of another copy in the library of the Mosque at Mashhad. This book he described as containing a continuous series of prophecies, amongst which was included the announcement of the return of Sháh Bahrám, the Zoroastrian Messiah, to re-establish "the Good Religion." This Sháh Bahrám... is believed to be a descendant of Hurmuz the son of Yezdigird (the last Sásánian king), who fled from before the Arab invaders, with Peshútan and other fire-priests, to China; whence he will return to Fars by way of India in the fullness of time. Amongst the signs heralding his coming will be a great famine, and the destruction of the city of Shushtar.

In the evening I went for a ride outside the city with Ferídún, Rustam, and the son of the postmaster. We first visited a neighbouring garden to see the working of one of the *dúlábs* generally employed in Kirmán for raising water to the surface. The *dúláb* consisted of two large wooden wheels, one set horizontally and the other vertically in the jaws of the well, cogged together. A blindfolded cow harnessed to a shaft inserted in the axle of the former communicated a rotatory motion to the latter, over which a belt of rope passed downwards into the well, to a depth of about five ells. To this rope earthenware pitchers were attached, and each pitcher as it came uppermost on the belt emptied its contents into a channel communicating with a small reservoir. The whole arrangement was primitive, picturesque, and inefficient.

From the *dúláb* we proceeded to the "old town" (*shahr-i-kadím*), situated on the craggy heights lying (if I remember rightly) to the west of the present city, and said to date from the time of Ardashír-i-Bábakán, the founder of the

Sásánian dynasty. There are a number of ruined buildings on these heights, including one known as the Ḳadam-gáh, where vows and offerings are made by the Kirmánís. From this place we proceeded to another valley, closed to the south by beetling cliffs studded with cavernous openings which are said to extend far into the rock. High up on the left of this valley is a little building known as Daryá-Ḳulí Beg, whither, leaving our horses below, we ascended, and there sat for a while drinking wine by the light of the setting sun. My companions informed me that formerly the mouth of the valley below had been closed by a *band* or dyke, and all the upper part of it converted into a gigantic lake whereon boat races, watched by the king and his court from the spot where we sat, took place on certain festal occasions.

As we rode homewards in the gathering twilight the postmaster's son craved a boon of me, which I think worth mentioning as illustrative of that strange yearning after martyrdom which is not uncommon amongst the Bábís. Bringing his horse alongside of mine at a moment when the two Zoroastrians were engaged in private conversation, he thus addressed me:—"Ṣáḥib, you intend, as you have told me, to visit Acre. If this great happiness be allotted to you, and if you look upon the Blessed Beauty (*Jemál-i-Mubárak, i.e.* Behá'u'lláh), do not forget me, nor the request which I now prefer. Say, if opportunity be granted you, 'There is such an one in Kirmán, so-and-so by name, whose chief desire is that his name may be mentioned once in the Holy Presence, that he may once (if it be not too much to ask) be honoured by an Epistle, and that he may then quaff the draught of martyrdom in the way of the Beloved.'"

Sunday, 9th June, 29th Ramaẓán.—To-day I received a demonstration in geomancy (*'ilm-i-ramal*) from a young Zoroastrian, Bahrám-i-Bihrúz, whom I met in Mullá Gushtásp's room in the caravansaray of Ganj–'Alí Khán. The information about myself with which his science supplied him was almost entirely incorrect, and was in substance as follows: —"A month ago you received bad news, and suffered much through some absent person…. Fifteen days ago some physical injury befell you…. By the next post you will receive good news…. In another month you will receive very good news…. You are at present in good health, but your caloric is in excess and the bilious humour predominates…. Your appetite is bad, and you should take some laxative medicine." This is a fair specimen of the kind of answer which he who consults the *rammál* (geomancer) is likely to get; but it is fair to say that Bahrám laid claim to no great proficiency in the science. However, he promised to introduce me to a Musulmán who was reputed an adept in the occult sciences, including the *taskhír-i-jinn*, or command of familiar spirits, and this promise, as will presently be set forth, he faithfully kept.

While Bahrám was busy with his geomancy, a dervish boy, who afterwards proved to be a Bábí, entered the room where we were sitting (for the dervish is free to enter any assembly and to go wherever it seemeth good to him), and presented me with a white flower. I gave him a *ḳrán*, whereupon, at the suggestion of one of those present, he sung a *ghazal*, or ode, in a very sweet voice, with a good deal of taste and feeling......

.....In the evening I received another visit from the garrulous Ḥájí Muḥammad Khán, who seemed to me rather less disagreeable than on the occasion of his first call. After his departure a temporary excitement was caused by the discovery of a theft which had been committed in the garden. A Shírází muleteer, who intended shortly to return home by way of Sírján and Níríz, had greatly importuned me to hire his mules for the journey and this I had very foolishly half consented to do. These mules were accordingly tied up in the garden near my horse, and it was their coverings which, as the muleteer excitedly informed us, had been removed by the thief. The curious thing was that my horse's coverings, which were of considerably more value, had not been touched, and I am inclined to believe that the muleteer himself was the thief. He caused me trouble enough afterwards; for when, owing to the ophthalmia with which I was attacked, I was obliged to rescind the bargain, he lodged a complaint against the poor gardener, whom he charged with the theft. A *farrásh* was sent by the *vazír* to arrest him; whereupon the said gardener and his wife, accompanied by the myrmidon of the law, came before me wringing their hands, uttering loud lamentations, and beseeching me to intercede in their favour. So, though my eyes ached most painfully, I was obliged to write a long letter to the *vazír* in Persian, declaring the gardener to be, to the best of my belief, an honest and worthy fellow, and requesting, as a personal favour, that he might be subjected to no further annoyance. I furthermore took the precaution of promising a present of money to the *farrásh* when he returned with the gardener, in case the latter had suffered no ill-treatment; and, thanks to these measures, I succeeded in delivering him from the trouble in which the malice of the muleteer threatened to involve him; but the effect of the exertion of my eyes in writing the letter was to cause a recrudescence of the inflammation, which had previously been on the decline. So the muleteer had his revenge, which, I suppose, was what he desired and intended......

.....*Tuesday, 11th June, 1st Shawwál.*—In the morning I had a visit from Rustam, the young Zoroastrian. He told me, amongst other things, of the persecutions to which his co-religionists were occasionally exposed. "Formerly," said he, "it would often happen that they carried off one of our boys or girls, and strove to compel them by threats and torments to become Musulmáns. Thus on one occasion they seized upon a Zoroastrian boy twelve years of age, carried him to the public bath, and forced him to utter the Muḥammadan profession of faith, and to submit to the operation of circumcision. On another occasion they abducted two Zoroastrian girls, aged fifteen and twenty respectively, and, by every means in their power, strove to compel them to embrace the religion of Islam. One of them held out against their importunities for a long while, until at last they turned her out almost naked into the snow, and she was ultimately compelled to submit."....

Wednesday, 12th June, 2nd Shawwál.—Towards evening I was visited by the Belúch chief, Afẓal Khán, and his son; Seyyid Ḥuseyn of Jandaḳ; the Sheykh of Ḳum, and his friend the young Bábí gunner; and Mullá Yúsuf the Ezelí. Between the last and Seyyid Ḥuseyn a violent dispute arose touching the merits and demerits of the first three caliphs (so called), 'Omar, Abú Bekr, and 'Othmán, whereby the other visitors were so wearied that they shortly departed, and finally the Seyyid was left in undisputed possession of the field, which he did not abandon till he had prayed the prayers of sundown (*maghrib*) and nightfall ('*ashâ*), and explained to me at length the significance of their various component parts, adding that if I would remain in Kirmán for one month he would put me in possession of all the essentials of Islam. Ná'ib Hasan and Ferídún had supper with me in the *chár-faṣl*, or summer-house, on the roof of which I sat late with the latter, and finally fell asleep, with the song of a nightingale, sweet-voiced as Isráfil, ringing in my ears.

GERTRUDE BELL (1868–1926)

Bell was the only daughter of a wealthy Durham industrialist upon whose death in 1904 she inherited a fortune. Encouraged by her family – both her father and stepmother (her mother had died when she was three) understood well her precocious talents – in 1888 she became the first woman to take a first in Modern History at Oxford. Family connections also opened doors in her ensuing career in the Middle East. After travelling in Persia she took up climbing in the Alps. More journeys followed: in the cause of archaeology she visited Asia Minor, while Syria provided her with opportunities to demonstrate her mastery of Arabic and to start accumulating knowledge of the different tribes and clans. From the travels emerged more writing – including *The Desert and the Sown* (1907), *The Thousand and One Churches* (1909), and *Amurath to Amaruth* (1911). Acutely aware of the hierarchies of the desert and enabled by the power brought by prodigious intellect, Bell revelled in the freedom from English social restraint such travel brought her. When the Great War began she enlisted in the Cairo Arab Bureau and took her place among the Arabic scholars working for British interests in the Middle East. After the war she became political advisor to Faysal in Iraq, and founder director of the National Museum in Baghdad. Unhappy in her personal life she died in Iraq in 1926 from an overdose.

From:

Persian Letters (1894)

Before establishing her reputation as an expert on the Arab tribes of the Fertile Crescent, Bell made a name for herself as a translator of the Persian poet Hafiz. In 1892, having already taken up the study of Farsi, she went to Persia where her uncle by marriage was ambassador. The letters she wrote home formed the basis of Bell's first travel piece, *Safar Nameh-Persian Letters*. This chapter raises the topic of Bell's attitude to women's issues, which should be viewed not only in her travel writing but through her later membership of the anti-women's suffrage league. The recurring use of the adjective "small" is an indicator of her patronizing view of the Persian Princess.

Three Noble Ladies

When the Shah takes a girl into his andarun it is said to be a matter of universal rejoicing among her family, not so much because of the honour he has done her, as because her relatives look to using her influence as a means of gaining for themselves many an envied favour. For aught I know to the contrary, the girl, too, may think herself a fortunate creature, and the important position of the one man she may possibly govern may console her for the monotony of her kingdom; but however delightful as a place of abode the royal andarun may be, in one respect it must fall short of the delights of the kingdom of heaven—there cannot fail to be endless talk of marrying and giving in marriage within its walls. The number of Shah's wives is great, and he is blessed with a proportionately large family; it must therefore be difficult to find a sufficiency of high-born suitors with whom to match his daughters. Moreover, there may be a trace of reluctance in the attitude of the suitors themselves, for the privilege of being the Shah's son-in-law is not without its disadvantages. If the nobleman selected happen to be wealthy, the Shah will make their close relationship an excuse for demanding from him large gifts; if at any subsequent period he should have a mind to take another wife, the etiquette of the Court will stand in his way; and still worse, if he be already married, he will find himself obliged to seek a divorce from his wife that he may obey the Shah's command. The negotiations preceding the match must be complicated in the extreme, and great must be the excitement in the andarun before they are concluded.

With one such household we were acquainted. The husband, whose title may be translated as the Assayer of Provinces, was a charming person, who had spent much of his youth (much also of his fortune) in Paris. He was a cultivated man and an enthusiast for sports; a lover of dogs, which for most Persians are unclean animals, and a devotee to the art of fishing. He had suffered not a little at the hands of his royal father-in-law, and had withdrawn in indignation from all public life, spending his days in hunting and shooting, in improving his breed of horses, and in looking after his estates. His residence abroad had made him more liberal-minded than most of his countrymen. He paid special attention to the education of his daughters, refused to allow them to be married before they had reached a reasonable age, and gave them such freedom as was consistent with their rank. They were two in number; we made their acquaintance, and that of the Princess their mother, one afternoon in Tehran.

Now, an afternoon call in Persia is not to be lightly regarded; it is a matter of much ceremony and it lasts two hours. When we arrived at the house where the three ladies lived, we were conducted through a couple of courts and a long passage, and shown into a room whose windows opened into a vine-wreathed veranda. There was nothing Oriental in its aspect: a modern French carpet, with a pattern of big red roses on a white ground, covered the floor; photographs and looking-glasses hung upon the walls; the mantelpiece was adorned with elaborate vases under glass shades, and on some brackets stood plaster casts of statues. We might have imagined ourselves in a French château, but for the appearance of the châtelaine.

The Princess was a woman of middle age, very fat and very dark; her black eyebrows met together across her forehead; on her lips there was more than the suspicion of a moustache; the lower part of her face was heavy, and its outline lost itself in her neck. The indoor costume of a Persian lady is not becoming. She wears very full skirts, reaching barely to the knee, and standing out round her like those of a ballet-dancer; her legs are clothed in white cotton stockings, and on her feet are satin slippers. These details are partly concealed by an outer robe, unfastened in front, which the wearer clutches awkwardly over her bulging skirts, and which opens as she walks, revealing a length of white cotton ankles. In the case of the Princess this garment was of pale blue brocade. She wore her hair loose, and a white muslin veil was bound low upon her forehead, falling down over the hair behind. She was too civilized a woman to have recourse to the cosmetics which are customary in the East; the orange-stain of henna was absent from her finger nails, and in the course of conversation she expressed much disapproval of the habit of painting the eyes, and great astonishment when we informed her that such barbarism was not unknown even in England.

It must not be imagined that the conversation was of an animated nature. In spite of all our efforts and of those of the French lady who acted as interpreter, it languished woefully from time to time. Our hostess could speak some French, but she was too shy to exhibit this accomplishment, and not all the persuasions of her companion could induce her to venture upon more than an occasional word. She received our remarks with a nervous giggle, turning aside her head and burying her face in her pocket-handkerchief, while the Frenchwoman replied for her, "Her Royal Highness thinks so and so." When the interview had lasted for about half an hour, cups of tea were brought in and set on a round table in the midst of us; shortly afterwards the two daughters entered, sweeping over the floor towards us in green and pink satin garments, and taking their places at the table. The younger girl was about sixteen, an attractive and demure little person, whose muslin veil encircled a very round and childish face; the other was two years older, dark, like her mother, though her complexion was of a more transparent olive, and in her curly hair there were lights which were almost brown. Her lips were, perhaps, a little too thick, though they were charmingly curved, and her eyes were big and brown and almond-shaped, with long lashes and a limpid,

pathetic expression as you see in the trustful eyes of a dog when he pushes his
nose into your hand in token of friendship. Nor did her confiding air belie
her: she took our hands in her little brown ones and told us shyly about her
studies, her Arabic, and her music, and the French newspapers over which she
puzzled her pretty head, speaking in a very low, sweet voice, casting down her
black eyelashes when we questioned her, and answering in her soft guttural
speech: "Baleh Khanum"—"Yes, madam," or with a little laugh and a slow,
surprised "Naghai-ai-r!" when she wished to negative some proposition which
was out of the range of her small experience.

During the course of the next hour we were regaled on lemon ices, and
after we had eaten them it was proposed that we should be taken into
the garden. So we wandered out hand-in-hand, stopping to speak to an
unfriendly monkey who was chained under the oleanders, and who turned a
deaf ear to all our blandishments. In the garden there was a large pond, on
the banks of which lay a canoe—an inconvenient vessel, one would imagine,
for ladies attired in stiff and voluminous petticoats! Tents were pitched on the
lawn, for our hostesses were on the eve of departure for their summer camp
in the mountains, and had been examining the condition of their future
lodgings. The garden, with its tents and its water, was like some fantastic opera
stage, and the women, in their strange bright garments, the masqueraders,
who would begin to dance a *pas de trois* before us as soon as the orchestra
should strike up. But the play was unaccountably delayed, and while we sat
under the trees servants appeared bringing coffee, a signal that the appointed
time of our visit had come to an end, and that we might be permitted to take
our leave. The girls accompanied us into the outer court, and watched us
through the half-open doors till we drove away, wishing, perhaps, that they
too might drive out into the world with such unfettered liberty, or perhaps
wondering at our unveiled shamelessness.

We went to see the three ladies again when we were in the mountains. Their
camp was pitched about a mile lower down the river than ours, on a grassy
plateau, from which they had a magnificent view down the long bare valley
and across mountains crowned by the white peak of Demavend. No sooner
had we forded the river in front of our tents than a storm of wind and rain
and hail broke upon us, but we continued dauntlessly on our way, for the day
of our visit had been fixed some time before, and it was almost pleasant after
the summer's drought to feel the rain beating on our faces. When we reached
the Persian camp we dismounted before a canvas wall which surrounded the
women's tents, a curtain was drawn aside for us by a negro slave, and we were
taken into a large tent, where the Princess was sitting on a rolled-up bed for
sofa. We greeted her with chattering teeth and sat down on some wooden
chairs round her, carrying on a laboured conversation in the French tongue,

while our wet clothes grew ever colder upon us. We remembered the steaming cups of tea of our former visit, and prayed that they might speedily make their appearance, but alas! on this occasion they were omitted, and lemon ices alone were offered to us. It is not to be denied that lemon ices have their merit on a hot summer afternoon, but the Persian's one idea of hospitality is to give you lemon ices—lemon ices in hail-storms, lemon ices when you are drenched with rain, lemon ices when a biting wind is blowing through the tent door—it was more than the best regulated constitution could stand. We politely refused them.

An important event had taken place in the household during the last two months: a marriage had been arranged between the eldest daughter and a young Persian nobleman, whose wealth and influence matched themselves satisfactorily with her rank. He, too, was spending the summer in the mountains; his camp lay a little beyond ours, and we were therefore able to observe the daily visits which took place between him and his future father-in-law, when they rode, attended by troops of mounted servants, backwards and forwards along the stony bridle-path on the opposite bank. Doubtless great discussions of the approaching marriage and of the art of fly-fishing took place in those August days. We stood in the centre of this Oriental romance, and felt as though we were lending a friendly hand to the negotiations. Certainly if good wishes could help them, we did much for the young couple.

The Assayer of Provinces spent most of his time trout-fishing. He used to make us presents of gaudy flies manufactured by his negro slave (himself a most successful fisherman), and we found that these attracted the trout of the Lar considerably more than our March browns and palmers. The eldest daughter shared her father's taste. When she and her sister joined us in her mother's tent that thundery afternoon, we fell into a lively discussion of the joys and the disappointments of the sport, comparing the number of fish we had killed and the size of our largest victims. The Persian girls had never gone far afield—they contented themselves with the pools and streams near their tents—but that they should fish at all spoke volumes for their energy. To throw a well-considered fly is a difficult art at best, but to throw it when you are enveloped from head to foot in sweeping robes must be well-nigh impossible.

This second visit passed more cheerfully than the first. The fresh mountain wind had blown away the mists of ceremony, there was no interpreter between us, and we had a common interest on which to exchange our opinions. That is the secret of agreeable conversation. It is not originality which charms; even wit ceases in the end to provoke a smile. The true pleasure is to recount your own doings to your fellow-man, and if by a lucky chance you find that he has been doing precisely the same thing, and is therefore able to listen and reply with understanding, no further bond is needed for perfect friendship.

Unfortunately, this tie was lacking between us and the monkey, who was also in villeggiatura by the banks of the Lar, and in consequence we got no further forward with him than before. Our presence seemed, indeed, to exasperate him more than ever. He spent the time of our visit making spiteful dashes at us, in the vain hope that the gods might in the end reward his perseverance and lengthen his chain sufficiently to allow him to bite us but once before we left.

But the gods have eternity in their hand, and we must hasten, for our time is short; long ere the monkey's prayer was answered we had risen and taken leave of the three ladies. We left them gazing after us from behind their canvas walls. Their prisoned existence seemed to us a poor mockery of life as we cantered homewards up the damp valley, the mountain air sending a cheerful warmth through our veins. The thunderstorm was past, the sun dropped in clear splendour behind the mountains, leaving a red glory to linger on the slopes of Demavend, and bearing the fullness of his light to the Western world—to our own world.

VALENTINE CHIROL (1852–1929)

The DNB tells us that although he was of French Huguenot descent 'and brought up in France and Germany, Chirol was a staunch English patriot, proud of his Anglo-Saxon Ashburnham [his mother's family] blood.' It was not until the Franco-Prussian War broke out that he and his mother resettled in England. Though trained as a barrister the young Chirol spent four years in the Foreign Office before turning to travel: he visited Egypt, Syria, Lebanon, and in 1880 Istanbul where he took up journalism. In 1882 he reported Wolseley's campaign against Urabi in Egypt for the London *Standard*, went to India and Persia (1884), and reported the events of 1885 in Sudan. Through his good connections he joined the newly opened *Times* foreign news department in 1891. After a spell as Berlin correspondent during which he became disillusioned with German politics, he returned to his desk at the *Times* where he was appointed foreign editor in 1899. It was while in this highly influential post that Chirol wrote *The Middle East Question*. Together with David Fraser, another journalist who worked under him at the *Times*, he helped promote what would now be considered a 'realist' line in which Britain's foreign policy interests were held to override the aspirations of Eastern nationalisms such as those of Persia and Turkey (Nash 2005: Ch 4). Although Chirol retired in 1912 he was 'useful to the Foreign Office during the war' (DNB) and published two volumes of memoirs before his death in 1929.

From:

The Middle East Question (1903)

After the two opening paragraphs lay before the reader the economic and strategic facts about the new, Russian-constructed Resht-Tehran road, the third turns to description of Shah Muzzafar al-Din Qajar's return from Europe, characterized by the author as an 'illustration of Persian mediævalism'. The rest is Orientalism in the Morier/Curzon register, summed up by the borrowed phrase from Kinglake – 'the havoc of the East – more especially the havoc'.

The 'Russian' Road to Tehran

The outlay has been enormous, for, in spite of the undeniable difficulties of construction—the road rises to an altitude of over 7,000 feet in crossing the mountain range—the cost, which is estimated at £300,000, must be pronounced excessive. It is, as I have said, about 220 miles long, and of these 220 miles some 90 miles on the level plain between Kazvin and Teheran had already been made, at least in a rudimentary fashion, by a Persian company, which was bought up by the Russians. The cost of improving that section of the road must have been relatively trifling, and the bulk of the total outlay must therefore be assigned to the section between Resht and Kazvin, which does not exceed 130 miles in length. This represents an average of over £2,000 a mile, and, though the road is fairly well built and the engineering difficulties encountered in climbing the steep slopes—at first so beautifully wooded and then so barren and precipitous—to the north of the range, and in threading a way through the gaunt and narrow gorges of sun-scorched rock which lead down on to the great plateau of Northern Persia, must have been very considerable, so heavy an expenditure can be accounted for only by the lavish extravagance and absence of all financial control which generally characterise Russian undertakings of this nature. This, however, is an aspect of the question upon which it would be ungrateful to dwell, and, for my part, I was much more disposed to regret that the Russians had not undertaken the exploitation as well as the construction of the road, instead of sub-letting the former to Persian contractors, who ran antediluvian carriages with wretchedly overworked and under-fed horses. The contractors, it is true, complained that, in spite of the heavy rates they charged, they are running the road at a loss, and I was assured that the Russians intended before long to relieve them of their contract and work the road themselves with an exclusively Russian staff.

Whether the result of the undertaking be financially successful or the reverse, we may be sure that the Russians have not been throwing their money away. What their objects are is sufficiently obvious. There is no reason to suppose that they have ever contemplated using this road for strategic purposes. The difficulties of approach from the sea are sufficient to dispose of any such idea. Moreover, as I shall show later on, from the strategic point of view, the north of Persia lies absolutely open to Russia in so many other directions that she might well have left the Resht road to take care of itself. Even without the road from Erivan to Tabriz, in North-Western Persia, for which the Russians have obtained a concession, they can at any moment pour their troops as easily from Transcaucasia into Azerbaijan as they can along the coast of the Caspian from Baku and Lenkoran into the province of Gilan. A few years ago, when there were troubles at Astrabad, to the south-east of the Caspian, the Russians gave

Persia a foretaste of what they could do in Mazenderan by despatching a few hundred men from Chikishliar, who remained for some months in occupation of the provincial capital. Further east, again, the Trans-Caspian or Central Asian Railway runs for some hundreds of miles close along the northern frontier of Persia, and dominates the whole of Khorasan, in the absence of any Persian force which can be dignified with the name of an army. It is therefore quite unnecessary to suggest strategic reasons for the construction of the Resht road to Teheran. But Russia, none the less, gets value for her money. Not only does the road serve the ends of Russian commercial policy, which is almost openly directed to the acquisition of an absolute monopoly in the trade of Northern Persia, but it is in itself a splendid and perfectly legitimate advertisement of Russian influence. Russian occupies the place of honour in every document drawn up in connection with transportation on the road. The names of all the stations figure conspicuously in Russian characters. The barriers at which the Russian company levies its tolls are in the hands of Russian officials. The Russians have the maintenance of the road, and all the gangs employed on repairs are under the orders of Russian overseers. Not only, therefore, is every Persian travelling along the main road from the north to the capital made to feel that the Russians hold the right of access to it, but the inhabitants of all the adjoining districts, who provide the requisite labour, are taught to look up to the Russians as their employers and their masters. But though the advantages which Russia thus reaps from this undertaking deserve to be noted, it would be unfair as well as futile to cavil at them. The whole position which Russia has acquired in the north of Persia deserves, I think, to be studied in a spirit, not of idle recrimination, but of dispassionate, and even friendly, consideration.

Whilst the road from Resht to Teheran affords a perfect illustration of Russian activity, it happened to afford, whilst I was passing over it, an accidental, but equally striking, illustration of Persian mediævalism. The Shah was on his way back from Europe, and in accordance with immemorial custom, the whole of his Court, numbering thousands of retainers, was hurrying down to welcome him at the frontier. It was the strangest and most picturesque spectacle which the eye of an artist enamoured of quaint contrasts, or of a student in search of a typical presentment of the unchanging East, could hope to light upon. For hours at a time there streamed past us a ceaseless procession of camels, mules, horses, carts and litters, laden with the *personnel* and the paraphernalia of an Eastern Court, which, though it has to some slight extent adopted a travesty of European fashions, and has lost from other causes much of its ancient splendour, is still in most respects as barbaric as when Tavernier's travels excited the wonder of the French people, accustomed to the magnificence of the *Roi Soleil*. An advanced guard of Persian Cossacks—a squadron of the brigade of Persian "Cossack" cavalry which, drilled and officered by Russians, alone stands for efficiency in the

Persian Army—opened the march with some show of ordered pomp. At some distance behind them came a regiment of Persian infantry, slouching along the road in every variety of patched or tattered uniform—once upon a time sky blue—some with two shoes of different patterns, many with only one, and most of them with none, the majority old men or mere boys, with a sprinkling of every other age, from extreme youth to extreme senility. Their rifles, marked by the same variety of pattern and condition, came afterwards, stuck promiscuously on to the pack of any unobjecting mule. Those who had fallen out hopelessly on the way, or had a few coppers to spare—or were they, perhaps, the officers?—we met later on, reclining in picturesque confusion on the top of cumbrous baggage carts. A military band was conveyed in an even more original fashion, each of the larger instruments—big drums, trombones, horns, etc.—crowning in solitary grandeur the load of a pack camel. What the endless strings of beasts of burden carried in the huge wooden chests and packages of every shape and size under which they slithered down the steep mountain slopes, one could only guess at when some mishap necessitated the repacking of a load in the middle of the road. Then one might get a glimpse of costly carpets and tent walls of many colours, of robes of honour and silken embroideries, of quilted bedding and cushions of soft texture. Here and there a silver ewer, or a piece of gaudy French furniture, which had been overlooked until the last moment, or had proved recalcitrant to Persian packing, was tied on loosely with a bit of string, and kept clanking on the side of the load as the unconscious mule disported himself along the road.

On brightly caparisoned horses officers of the household, with their silver staves of office stuck jauntily under the thigh, and a leather peak adjusted to their black lambswool cap at the proper angle to shield their eyes from the sun—a very practical adjustment, which, however, imparts to the wearer a curiously rakish air—Court attendants of various ranks—many of them, no doubt, generals of the first or second class, a rank which is liberally conferred in Persia for services entirely unconnected with the art of war—flunkeys in scarlet coats, with faded bravery of gold and silver lace, high officials of State in full-waisted black broadcloth coats of semi-European design, *mullahs* in green or white turbans, of different degrees of sanctity and learning, notabilities of the countryside from far and near, and hundreds of menials and camp followers of every description, real "beggars on horseback," jostled each other in bewildering confusion along the road, or sat in groups at the wayside resthouses, discussing the latest gossip over their waterpipes and tea. In hooded Russian carts drawn by four horses abreast, or in wooden panniers slung on either side of a camel, Persian ladies of high and low degree—their faces and their figures alike shrouded beyond any recognition in the ample black domino and thick white linen veil which all invariably wear out of doors—were following in the wake of their lords and masters. Further on, close to Teheran, we came across two huge camps in which the Shah's harem or *anderoon*, to use the Persian equivalent, which had been suddenly commanded by telegraph from Europe to wait upon his Majesty at the frontier, were resting after a night's march, during the heat of the day, in charge of Court officials and black eunuchs. At intervals the road was cleared for the passage of some Prince of the Blood or great officer of State, travelling down in an ancient brougham or *calèche*, with four or six horses *à la Daumont* and seedy postillions, followed by an uncouth retinue of pipe-bearers and *ferrashes* on horseback.

It was a wonderful succession of *tableaux vivants*, embodying the whole story of what "Eothen" terms the glory and the havoc of the East—more especially the havoc. If only one could have recorded the scene on a cinematograph for production at the Hippodrome, where the Shah had himself been seen but a few weeks before surrounded by the well-ordered pomp of the West, it would have helped not only the British public, but even responsible statesmen at home, to form some conception of men and things as they really are in Persia. Just imagine what a reckless waste of time and money this motley pilgrimage means! For a month at least the whole business of the State, such as it is, is at a standstill. The Shah was, of course, stated to have given emphatic orders, immediately upon his accession, that the Court was not to prey upon the country through which it moved, and that everything was to be paid for at full value. But how is the Shah to know whether his orders are carried out? Of-course they are not carried out, and no swarm of locusts lays a countryside more bare than this ceremonial army on the march. As for the drain on the Shah's exchequer, it is impossible to form any trustworthy estimate, but I was assured that the mere cost of moving the royal *anderoon* from Teheran to Resht amounted to 30,000 tomans, or about £6,000. The total expenditure probably did not fall far short of £40,000 or £50,000, and this in a country reduced to the utmost financial straits, of which the total public revenue for all purposes is not believed to exceed one and a half million sterling per annum. But it is an ancient custom, and, if it is a plague to the people of the country and a heavy drain upon the exchequer, it is a source of splendid profit to many powerful individuals, whose vested interests even the Shah must think twice before he touches. The East cannot, and should not, be judged by the standards of the West. But in this procession of a moribund past, with its strange mixture of magnificence and squalor, passing unconcernedly down the "Russian" road to the Persian capital, the most casual of Western observers could hardly fail to find a vivid reminder of the fateful writing on the wall, translated on this occasion into Russian characters.

ROBERT BYRON (1905–1941)

With Harold Acton, Byron was a key figure in the 1920s Oxford milieu described by Evelyn Waugh in *Brideshead Revisited* (DNB). He began establishing a reputation as a traveller and writer on Art with *Europe in the Looking-Glass* (1926), a youthful record of a journey made with two Oxford friends to Germany and Italy. He found himself honoured in Greece owing to his name (he *was* distantly connected to the poet). To understand Greece better he went to Mt. Athos where he believed the Byzantine spirit still lived on. *The Station* (1928) and *The Byzantine Achievement* (1929, repr. 1937) were statements of his belief that, in the words of his friend Christopher Sykes, 'the Byzantine Empire was the high noon of Hellenic greatness' (Sykes 1946: 103). According to Sykes, Byron was a 'fighter' who could however carry his opinions to extremes, as he did in his condemnation of Roman Catholicism. Byron's travels to the East began with a stint in India in 1929 as a correspondent for the *Daily Express*. *An Essay on India*, which appeared in 1931, laid out his ambivalence toward empire and modernity. He criticized the British Raj for its assumption of racial superiority and bitterly attacked Churchill for his opposition to India achieving dominion status, but he also reproved Indians, while acting under an unavoidable sense of inferiority, for attempting to be modern. Byron preferred non-Europeans not to copy Western material success. Sykes saw an unfortunate stylistic trait in his friend's writing where 'notes of facetiousness strike discords in serious exposition of a profoundly serious theme' (120). This occurs in *The Road to Oxiana* where Byron demonstrates ironic condescension towards Iran's ruler Reza Shah and his drive to acquire the apparel of modernity. Alongside a stylistic brilliance in re-opening the architectural jewels of classic Muslim civilization Byron can also write: 'His majesty's new railway, his impartial and open justice, his passion for lounge suits, offer hope to a distracted world. In fact, Shah Riza Pahlevi has left Firdaussi standing.' This mockery extends to Byron's public schoolboy dubbing of Reza Shah 'Marjoribanks'. It is difficult to see what alternative he envisaged for the East. Published in 1937, *The Road to Oxiana* has since become a monument to a precocious writer who in 1941 became a tragic victim of the Second World War.

From:

The Road to Oxiana (1937)

'This at last is that other Persia which so many travellers fell in love with'. Few have conjured the country's mystique as successfully as Robert Byron, writing here of Firuzabad in the far south, where the writ of Reza Shah does not seem to extend, where robbers find sanctuary, very few Pahlevi hats are worn, and the face of the governor's son displays 'the ideal beauty of the Persian miniaturist'. Note how the author's warmth and respect for the locals approaches his enthusiasm for Persian gardens and ancient, pre-Islamic ruins.

Firuzabad

Block-houses and motor-track ended at Kavar, a village belonging to Haji Abdul Karim Shirazi, who has just built himself a new house. This makes me unusually comfortable, though the mud on the walls is still wet. The pool in the courtyard is kept clear by a stream, which spurts from a stone gargoyle.

Outside the village, he has an old garden of about twelve acres. The gardener let me in by a wicket in a thatched wall, and I spent the afternoon wandering about the straight grass paths that divide Persian gardens into squares and oblongs. Each path is an avenue of poplars or planes, and is accompanied by irrigation runnels; inside these, each square contains fruit trees or bare plough. Squares sound formal; but really, plantation or wilderness is the proper word to describe a Persian garden. Winter and spring had met on this afternoon. A strong warm wind carried a sound of chopping with it and a rustle of dead plane-leaves; through those leaves, perked the green crooks of young ferns. Here and there the rose-leaves had budded too early, and were blackened with frost. The bare apple branches bore tangles of dead mistletoe; another such tangle in the fork of a massive chestnut some hundreds of years old, was the nest of a *palamdar* – according to the gardener; did he mean magpie or squirrel? its dome was of one or the other. The first butterflies were out: a dusty white, of a kind I did not know, newly hatched and flying in a puzzled sort of way as if the world was still too brown for it; and a painted lady, newly awakened, and surveying the garden it knew in September with familiar swoops from point to point. There were some flowers for them. A peach (or plum) was in blossom, and I caught my breath at the dazzle of its red buds, white transparent petals and black stalks defined by the shimmering blue sky. From over the wall peered the endless mountains, mauve and lion-coloured, deathly barren. The bleating of lambs and kids drew me to the gate again. A little girl was guarding them beside the village graveyard, where stood three giant weeping conifers of the cypress family. 'Those are called *Karj*,' said the Sultan, 'but why say they are big?

You have not seen the ones at Burujird in Luristan.' A grey owl flew out of the first, from a hole it was inspecting. On a marshy pond dotted with the yellow bullet-heads of water lilies, the moorhens were already nesting.

*

I am lying in bed over a bottle of vin rosé. Ali Asgar, who was cook to a British regiment in the War, is 'baking' a partridge in a pot. The cavalry have collected and horses been paraded. They say it is a two days' ride to Firuzabad, but I hope to do it in one.

Firuzabad (4400 ft), 22 February I did, with an effort; though it was hard on the rest of the party. Opinion at Kavar gave the distance as nine farsakhs, thirty-six miles. I rode eleven hours, excluding one stop for lunch, and as the good going and the bad were about equal, I can hardly have averaged less than four miles an hour. It must have been more than forty miles.

After the usual mishaps, a broken girth, luggage thrown to the ground by a bucking horse, we left at seven. A sounder of pig crossed the path, running in file according to size. The ground was too stony for us to head them off, though one of the escort tried; but a gallop along the path brought us level with them, and the man shouted, 'Do you want one?' The fact that I didn't, combined with some dim inhibition implanted by the English game-laws, made me hesitate. They veered away, and I lost my chance of seeing a Persian shoot from the saddle at full gallop.

The mountainside was covered with bushes and wild fruit trees in pink blossom. Beneath one lay a dead wolf. After a hard climb, ending in a glissade of shale which was difficult for the horses, we reached the top of the Muk Pass; thence we followed a stream whose banks were dotted with deep blue grape-hyacinths. This brought us to the Zanjiran gorge, a narrow gate between two overhanging cliffs and a famous place for robbers. The path disappeared. There was only room for the stream, which was blocked to an unusual depth by a confusion of crags, tree-trunks, and brambles, so that the horses could hardly force a passage. Directly the water escaped from the gorge, it was collected into irrigation channels branching this way and that at different levels.

A hot scrubby plain intervened, separated from another like it by a step of 100 feet, from whose brink we saw villages in the distance. A black cleft in the opposite mountains was our object: the Tang-Ab or Water Pass. At Ismailabad I sat under a tree on a patch of emerald grass strewn with ox bones, and ate a bowl of curds.

It was a tumbledown place, and the headman was frightened out of his wits; for the police are seldom seen in these parts. 'You should have gone to Ibrahimabad over there,' he said apologetically. When I asked him to fetch my horse, he misunderstood and thought I wanted a new one, which he produced.

This was too great a convenience to forgo. I gave him five crowns, which he was loath to accept, till I employed the unfailing formula: 'For your children.'

The cliffs of the Water Pass are stratified diagonally, as though the mountain had been cloven by an axe and would fit together again if pushed; I have seen nothing like it, or the gorge that followed, since those of Aghia Rumeli on the south coast of Crete. As we approached it, a river, which had come along the base of the hills from the east, suddenly turned at right angles into the gate, and seemed to be flowing rapidly uphill, an illusion which persisted during the whole four miles of the gorge. This extraordinary formation varies in width from half a mile to 100 yards; its cliffs are from 500 to 800 feet high. The path crosses and recrosses the river in its serpentine course. About the middle, I saw the first signs of antiquity: a Sasanian castle perched on a salient of the east cliff, and connected by a long wall with a lesser stronghold. These two buildings are known as the Kala-i-Dukhtar and Kala-i-Pisa. *Kala* means castle, and *Dukhtar* maiden, being the same as our word daughter. But I had forgotten this for the moment, and when I asked Ali Asgar what it was, he suddenly answered in English: 'Dukhtar, Sahib? Dukhtar – baby missis.'

Fantastic strata led up this eastern cliff, composed of huge rectangular blocks thirty feet long and twenty broad; I thought at first they were artificial roads, such as the Incas built to Cuzco. By now the light was going. Ali Asgar and the luggage were miles behind. He had three of the escort with him, but the two with me grew more and more worried.

'What is the matter?' I asked.

'Robbers.'

'But the great Riza Shah-in-Shah has destroyed all the robbers in Persia.'

'Oh, has he? Last month they shot four horses under me, and wounded me in the head. They would murder Your Excellency for a crown.'

We emerged at last by the south gate on the east bank of the river. There was just light enough to distinguish, half a mile away on the other, the vaulted phantom of Ardeshir's great palace, which my men called the Artish-Khana or House of Fire. And later, among the open fields, there was starlight enough to silhouette a minaret of enormous thickness. The men had no idea where the town was, but a village, where they wanted to stop, directed them in order to get rid of us. In half an hour we found ourselves among silent streets and moonwashed walls. A passing wraith showed us to the Governor's house.

I walked upstairs.

There was no furniture in the room. In the middle of the floor stood a tall brass lamp, casting a cold white blaze over the red carpets and bare white walls. It stood between two pewter bowls, one filled with branches of pink fruit blossom, the other with a posy of big yellow jonquils wrapped round a bunch of violets. By the jonquils sat the Governor, with his legs crossed and his hands folded in his sleeves; by the blossom his young son, whose oval face, black eyes and curving lashes were the ideal beauty of the Persian miniaturist. They had nothing to occupy them, neither book nor pen nor food nor drink. Father and son were lost in the sight and the smell of spring.

The irruption of the barbarian, dusty, unshaved, and lurching tired, was a trial of manners to which they rose, not without astonishment, but with a bustle and goodwill that must have hurt their mood of poetic contemplation. While I lowered myself to the floor, creaking and sprawling like a dog in a doll's-house, and feasted my nose in the jonquils, fire was kindled, the samovar relit, and thick red wine poured out; with his own hands the Governor chopped and skewered the meat to make me a kabob, and roasted it over the charcoal embers; then he was dismembering tangerines and sugaring them, for my pudding. In the end he went so far as to offer me his own bed. I explained that mine was coming, and begged the room below to put it in.

There are no police in this small tribal market town, neither Amniya nor Nasmiya; the Governor's safety depends on a few soldiers. People dress as they will, the men wearing striped gowns, loose cummerbunds stuck with weapons, and black bun-shaped hats without brims. The Pahlevi hat is a rare exception. This at last is that other Persia which so many travellers fell in love with, and having found it I would willingly stay here a week if I could. But if Christopher and I are to reach Afghanistan in time to forestall that much prophesied 'trouble in the spring', we ought to leave Teheran by 15 April, and I can't dawdle. Not that there is really much likelihood of trouble. But the mere rumour of it would be enough to close the country to foreigners for a month or two.

It was thus with an energy quite opposed to my inclinations that I set out to see the ruins this morning. The Governor offered me a horse, knowing mine must be tired. I thanked him, explaining that the mere mention of a saddle made me groan, and began to walk. Firuzabad is actually further south than Bushire. It was very hot. From outside the town I saw palms waving over the flat roofs. I had covered the two and a half miles to Gur, the city that Ardeshir founded about AD 220, and was regretting my refusal of a mount, when the clatter of horses in pursuit made me turn. First rode the Governor on a rearing brown stallion, followed by his son on a bucking grey; next the mayor and some other gentlemen; then a posse of armed soldiers, one mounted on a strawberry roan. In the middle of the cavalcade pranced a huge white ass, carrying a mountain of carpets but no rider. 'This,' said the Governor, 'is for you. Our guests do not walk.'

The 'minaret' of the night before proved to be a solid square shaft eighty to a hundred feet high, and twenty broad, built of coarse Sasanian masonry and having no entrance or trace of one. The sides gave evidence of an ascending ramp, which must have engaged the shaft in a four-sided spiral. I remember now that Herzfeld in his *Reisebericht* suggests that the ramp was enclosed in its turn, the whole thus forming a tower with an interior ascent of which only the core remains. Dieulafoy, more picturesque, believes the column served as a fire-altar and pictures the priests filing up its ramp in full view of the populace below, as though it were an Aztec teocalli. But neither theory explains what purpose, other than megalomania, can have prompted the erection of 40,000 cubic feet of solid stone in this form. Even the pyramids were slightly hollow.

The tower has no name, but is said to mark the site of a stone fallen from heaven. All round it, within a radius of half a mile, the ground shows the contours of Ardeshir's capital. Many of the foundations, or of the walls that fell on them, seem to be only a foot or two below the earth, and there is one platform still above it. This is built of rectangular blocks, neatly cut and fitted in the Achemenian way, and very different from the higgledy-piggledy masonry of the tower, where stones of any shape are embedded in a sea of mortar. I should like to dig here; it must be the richest site in Persia still untouched. Sasanian fragments are seldom beautiful. But they document an obscure passage of history at the junction of the ancient and modern worlds.

The others mounted their horses and I the ass, which beat the Governor's stallion by a nose at every corner, flapping its ears and hopping its ditches as if it could outpace any horse living. We stopped at a garden on the way back, to recline beneath a grove of old orange trees, and drink curds with nutmeg. Outside the town, three ragged children salaamed the Governor from the back of a camel. Reining back the stallion on his hindlegs, as though the scene were another Field of the Cloth of Gold, he gave them in return the polite formulas: 'Peace to you. Your Excellencies' health is good by the grace of God?' It was a great joke, we all laughed, and so did the children. But it was also a true benevolence, that warmed my heart towards Haji Seyid Mansur Abtahi Shirazi, the Governor of Firuzabad.

ELLA MAILLART (1903–1997)

Traveller, journalist and sportswoman, Maillart travelled extensively in Europe and Russia in the early 1930s. In 1932 she stayed six months in Russian Turkestan living amongst Kirghiz and Kazakh tribesman who she wrote about in *Turkestan Solo* (1938). In 1934 she went to Manchuria as correspondent of the magazine, *Petit Parisien*, for which she continued to write during her travels in Iran and Afghanistan in 1937. *Forbidden Journey*, the account of her travels in the Gobi desert and return journey via the Hindu Kush accompanied by Peter Fleming, was published in 1937. In the early months of 1939, Maillart and her travelling companion Christina traversed Turkey, Iran and Afghanistan, as the latter 'fought a hopeless battle against her addiction to drugs' (Russell 1986: xiii). Maillart's narrative of the journey, *The Cruel Way*, was published after the Second World War. She wrote both in French and English and also represented her native Switzerland at single-handed sailing in the 1924 Paris Olympics and later at ladies hockey and skiing.

From:

The Cruel Way (1947)

According to Mary Morris and Larry O'Connor, Maillart was 'one of the first writers to consider the inner journey'; her distinctiveness as a travel writer lay in her interweaving of 'political and historical details with the personal and the everyday' (Morris 1996: 243).

Meshed

We were walking towards the shrine, our cameras hidden under our arms for we had no permit to take photographs in Persia: the authorities in Teheran must have been too overworked to deal with us in spite of our reiterated calls. If I were caught I thought of trying to prevent confiscation by displaying a document two years out of date.

The broad avenues reminded me of Tashkent. Tired women, hatless and in drab overcoats, went to market with a basket over their arm. Droshkies gave a Russian touch to the scene; the white manes of their paired horses were tinged with flame-colour like the beards of old men—a sure sign that they had been bound with henna. At the cinemas, films were advertised in Russian and Persian and in shops every third man understood Russian. The new anti-religious propaganda also contributed to an otherwise superficial resemblance: like Kiev or Bokhara, Meshed had built its modern hospital with money levied from religious foundations.

Officially the shrine was open to non-Muslims but in practice there was much reluctance to enforce a rule that hurt the feelings of the majority. We didn't feel inclined to stroll through the great buildings: passed within the iron gates we felt nervous and self-conscious. We crossed the first court unobtrusively and went quickly towards the offices.

The main court, more than four hundred feet square, was enclosed all round by double rows of arcades. This courtyard was built at the beginning of the seventeenth century by Shah Abbas: coming from Isfahan on foot as a pilgrim, that cunning Shah had decided to advertise a shrine on Persian soil: it was unnecessary that a continual flow of pilgrims should enrich only the sacred places of Arabia and Irak.

In the middle of each side was a splendid *ivan*—the arched portico typical of Persian mosques. Every inch of the walls was shining with enamelled tiles. But the main feature of the courtyard was the gold that covered the tall minarets, lined the arched hollow of the *ivans* and shone with opulent brightness on the bomb-like dome above the sacred tomb. The joins of the square plates of gilded copper were clearly apparent: slightly convex, they reminded me of a sumptuously quilted upholstery. On the golden cupola, naked pink copper showed in a large band bearing historical inscriptions. How unearthly such gorgeousness must seem to the peasant who knows nothing but the sun-baked clay of his village hovels, nothing but the sun-scorched gravel of the desert!

The entrance to the actual tomb, a gold-vaulted recess in a great portal, was like the dark mouth of an ogival cave: it led to the heart of the golden summit.

We asked one of the officials to take us to the tomb-chamber; dallying, he first showed us the treasures of the library. Among the eighteen thousand books were some five thousand Qurans, many of them famous masterpieces. Every page of each of them displayed original designs and colourings, the margins filled with enough gold and azure arabesques, green and ruby floral *entrelacs* to inspire a cohort of modern artists in search of new patterns. Bound in snake's skin, Ali's Quran showed great Kufic writing. Walking along the shelves, I was astonished to see such books as Thiers' *Révolution Française* and even Dumas' *Les Trois Mousquetaires*.

In a big room hung with a portrait of Ali, we were shown rare carpets, among them "The Four Seasons" made in Kerman in 1650; it was full of lovely changing sheens as the attendant directed different parts of it towards the windows. The shrine, indeed, must contain many treasures: pilgrims have brought their offerings to the saint for ten centuries.

Ali ibn Musa ur Reza was born in 770. He became the head of the house of Ali, and thus Imam of the Shias, in 800, when Harun al Rashid was Caliph in Baghdad. The Caliph died of illness on his way to Samarkand to put down a rebellion. Trying to unite Shias and Sunnis, Mamun, the son of Harun, nominated Imam Reza heir to the Caliphate and married him to his daughter. Shias rejoiced. But the Sunnis of Baghdad revolted against so bold an innovation. Mamun was in a difficult position. But luckily for him Imam Reza died in 819 of a surfeit of grapes. Shias maintain that the fruit was poisoned, and when they visit the holy shrine they curse Harun and Mamun whose tombs are in a nearby cell.

Our chief wish was to enter the tomb-chamber on the ground floor, but our guide was deliberately slowing his conducted tour. From the choked uproar that reached us we knew that the number of pilgrims was great; but as I once more moved towards the narrow staircase, the attendant said it was now too late to go down and dangerous to mix with so many people.

We had been warned beforehand about the elusive ways of the shrine officials, but we did not know how to counter them. Through a bull's eye, Christina took a plunging view at a dark hall that seemed full of pilgrims. And I told her what I had seen there two years ago:

Four warders having taken me in tow, I was asked to imitate their gestures. We then entered the humming crowd of pilgrims, the huge crowd that moved like a stream, the crowd that wailed, chanted and prayed all at the same time. The noise grew into a loud clamour as we entered a resonant hall whose walls sparkled with innumerable mirror-facets. I progressed, squeezed within an avid multitude, a seething mass of hallucinated eyes. We reached the tomb-chamber.

Like my neighbours I had kissed a great silver door splendidly worked in repoussé, then a dark door of carved wood; like them I pressed my forehead against a wall of pink marble. Beyond that I could no longer imitate them. They were in a trance: they looked but seemed to see nothing. I, I was still able to observe details. The tomb, under a canopy in one corner of the room, was surrounded by a silver railing and covered with a pall of blue satin. In that confined space the uproar swelled, thundered and bounded back like the mighty sea in a cave. The silver bars were caressed, kissed and clasped in an outburst of adoration that devoured the whole being of the pilgrims: they were partaking of the holiness of the saint.

They mumbled, yelled and cried without knowing it. They shuffled along, rubbing their bundles along the sacred walls. Between a turned-up collar and a battered felt hat pulled down as much as possible, a woman's eye burned with fever. Turbaned men evoked wild, starving animals. They were not looking at this world: carried away by passion they had approached and touched something greater than themselves.

I had no place there. To observe them as I did in a relatively cold way was indiscreet, sacrilegious even. This must have been the greatest moment in their lives, a moment during which, wondrously, they went beyond themselves. Who was I to scrutinise them as I did?

Instead of looking through me as most of the pilgrims did, two bearded veterans watched me, saw me for what I was: they were so hurt, their faces expressed a pain so acute that I felt sorry. Had they lynched me I think I could perhaps have agreed with them. . . . I slipped out with undignified haste. I had seldom been so moved. I wondered if any of the great pilgrimages in Europe were causing such religious fervour.

In spite of my excitement—and this shows how detachedly one's mind works—I had been continually aware that, impassive, ugly and Japanese, a wall-clock had trivially ticked away second after second.

Leaving that confused roar behind us, Christina and I followed a narrow passage that took us to the peace of Gauhar Shad, the delightfully simple courtyard of that perfect mosque. Among the mass of shapeless clay houses of the great town, Gohar Shad was an unexpected pool of blue light: we basked in it, felt refreshed by it as by a dip in the clean high seas when the water is of a dense navy-blue with a white plume rising joyfully here and there.

Double tiers of arcades formed the sides of the court, each side enriched by the portal of an *ivan*, every surface covered with deeply coloured faience mosaics.

The main *ivan* was flanked by two minarets decorated with a network of dark lozenges; above the shaded entrance of the greatest portal, the spandrels were filled with a mass of light enamelled flowers. "From her private property and for the benefit of her future state, Gohar Shad built this great mosque" was the inscription inlaid into the façade. "Baisungur, son of Shah Rukh, son of Timur Gurkhan, wrote this with hope in Allah, dated 1418." (Gurkhan—universal Khan—is the supreme Turko-Mongol title that had been used by the Kerait, the Kara Khitai, etc.) Behind the main *ivan* rose the ellipse of an exquisite turquoise dome with sinuous white arabesques. A foam-white calligraphic frieze ran around and bound together these glazed walls of splendid hues. A tank for ritual ablution mirrored the radiant vision—happy proportions, good colours and lasting harmony.

Timur died in 1405 and the same year his daughter-in-law Gohar Shad started the building of this mosque. At Herat we were to see the tomb of that remarkable woman.

These mosaics were nearly as good as the much-ruined panels of the Blue Mosque at Tabriz. They were much more attractive than the tiled ensemble built by Shah Abbas for the great court of the shrine. The process adopted by Shah Abbas is called *haft-renghi:* it means that as many as seven colours may if necessary be applied side by side on a tile before it goes to the kiln. The result is that each coloured detail not being sharply separated from the next as it is when incrustation-mosaic is used, the general impression is more diluted, weaker. In the seven-colour process it is impossible to obtain a gamut of the densest tones since each colour has a different maximum firing-point.

I sat by the edge of the square pool.

That morning we had visited a carpet workshop. And now I felt that a richly coloured prayer-rug is a version in wool of the mosaic façade of an arched portal; and that in its turn is intimately related with the gorgeousness of Quranic illuminations. These three summits of Persian art can perhaps be traced to the bright flower-beds of Persian gardens—compact geometrical fields of multicoloured flowers that frame every moment of life in this sun-scorched land.

I felt I could grow fond of the place. And that raised a problem that interested me. So far I had always fallen in love with robust three-dimensional art—the Tower of Kabus, the charioteer of Delphi, China's Great Wall, the purity of Vezelay, the solidity of the Parthenon, the deep-rooted joy of Romanesque Tournus, the Trimurti of the Elephanta cave. What had I to do, then, with an Asian mosque, a lidless box whose inner surfaces alone are seen, shining with paint and lacquer?

I knew that Gohar Shad was "good" and it was casting a spell on me. Nevertheless, I still preferred the turquoise and ultra-marine glazes I had seen in Samarkand: Probably because it was there that I had first seen the rich glow that emanates from these two enamels when they are used side by side. There, near the Reghistan square, I watched the dying sun from the roof of the Tilla Kari medresseh where "Sovtourist" had allotted me a cell. An intimacy had grown between myself and the stubborn dome above its high drum girthed with huge Kufic characters. My Tilla Kari seemed to be a weak imitation but I was within a stone's throw of the perfect Ulugh Beg College named after the astronomer, son of Gohar Shad.

The old monuments of Samarkand have pathos, most of them being in ruins—the audacious cupola of Bibi-Khanum still challenging the bluish-green of a sunset sky, the vestigia of a beautiful arcade before Timur's mausoleum, the lane of tombs at Shah Zinda, palaces and hunting-boxes in the country crumbling into dust. Do we cherish better what is on the eve of vanishing? Would the Parthenon affect us equally were its paint and gilt still shining? Time, wars and earthquakes have badly mauled the Herat monuments, but the little that remains—a tomb with minarets in a wheat-field—touches me like the last smile of a friend.

In its good state of preservation, the mosque of Gohar Shad has none of these appealing qualities. I had to read Pope's *Introduction to Persian Art* to understand what was moving me. And I clearly see how knowledge "does both train and supple men the eye":

"Though it concerned itself with an art of design, the Persian æsthetic genius cannot therefore be relegated to a secondary rank. For in the same sense both music and architecture are arts of design, proof enough that design of a supreme quality attains a high seriousness and deep meaning that make it one of man's greatest achievements. The arts of design have no immediate appeal to sentiment and make no direct reference to nature; but their very abstractness, their detachment from a specific ideational content or emotional entanglement is a source of tranquil power. Nor are they merely a series of enticing forms. Like great music, they may characterise and reveal ultimate values and give expression to the basal and universal forms of the mind itself. Great design has the authority of logic. Design bears, indeed, the same relation to beauty that logic does to science and philosophy. It is the proper introduction to art, its indispensable framework, and perhaps also its finest achievement."

BIBLIOGRAPHY

Travel and Biographical Reference Works

DLB *Dictionary of Literary Biography* vol. 166: *British Travel Writers 1810–1875*; vol. 174: *British Travel Writers 1876–1909*. Edited by Barbara Brothers and Julia M. Gergits. Detroit: Gale. 1996–7.

DNB *Dictionary of National Biography*. Edited by Colin Matthew, Brian Harrison and Lawrence Goldman. Oxford: Oxford University Press. 2004. (Older editions are indicated by year of entry).

LTE *Literature of Travel and Exploration: An Encyclopaedia*. 3 vols. Edited by Jennifer Speake. New York: Fitzroy Dearborn. 2003.

Travel Writing – texts cited

Bell, Gertrude [1894] (1928) *Persian Pictures*. E.Benn.

———— (1907) *The Desert and the Sown*. London: William Heinemann.

Blunt, Lady Anne (1881) *A Pilgrimage to Nejd: The Cradle of the Arab Race, A Visit to the Court of the Arab Emir*...2 vols. London: John Murray.

Browne, Edward Granville [1893] (1950) *A Year Amongst the Persians: Impressions as to the Life, Character & Thought of the People of Persia*. A. & C. Black.

Burckhardt, John Lewis (1829) *Travels in Arabia: Comprehending an Account of Those territories in Hedjaz which the Muhammadans regard as Sacred*. London: Henry Colburn.

Burton, Richard [1855] (1893) *Narrative of a Pilgrimage to El-Medinah and Meccah*. 2 vols. (Memorial Edition) New York: Tylston and Edwards.

Buxton, Charles Roden (1909) *Turkey in Revolution*. London: T.F. Unwin.

Byron, Robert [1937] (1981) *The Road to Oxiana*. London: Pan Books.

Chirol, Valentine (1903) *The Middle East Question or Some Political Problems of Indian Defence*. London: Dutton.

Cox, Percy 'Some Excursions in Oman'. *Geographical Journal*, LXVI, 3, Sept. 1925: 193–2.

Curzon, George N. (1892) *Persia and the Persian Question*. 2 vols. Longmans Green.

Curzon, Robert [1849] (1897) *Visits to Monasteries of the Levant*. London: G. Newnes.

De Gaury, Gerald (1946) *Arabia Phoenix: An Account of a visit to Ibn Saud Chieftan of the Austere Wahhabis and Powerful Arabian King*. London: George D Harrap.

Doughty, Charles [1888] (1926) *Travels in Arabia Deserta*. London: Jonathan Cape.

Ellison, Grace (1915) *An Englishwoman in a Turkish Harem*. London: Methuen.

Fraser, James Baillie (1826) *Travels and Adventures in the Persian Provinces on the Southern Banks of the Caspian Sea*. London Longman, Hurst, Rees, Orme and Brown.

Gordon, Lucie Duff [1865] (1902) *Letters from Egypt*. London: Brimley Johnson.

Hodgkin, Thomas (1986) *Letters from Palestine 1932–36*, ed. E.C. Hodgkin. London: Quartet.

Hogarth, David George (1896) *A Wandering Scholar in the Levant*. London: John Murray.

Jarvis, C.S. (1936) *Three Deserts*. London: John Murray.

Kinglake, Alexander (1844) *Eothen, or Traces of Travel Brought Home from the East*. London: J. Ollivier.

Layard, Austen Henry (1887) *Early Adventures in Persia, Susiana and Babylonia*. 2 vols. London: John Murray.

Lawrence, T.E. (1927) *Revolt in the Desert*. London: Jonathan Cape.

Maillart, Ella (1947) *The Cruel Way*. London: William Heinemann.

Malcolm, John (1828) *Sketches of Persia*. 2 vols. London: John Murray.

Martineau, Harriet (1848) *Eastern Life, Present and Past*. 3 vols. London: Edward Moxon.

Morier, James (1812) *A Journey Through Persia, Armenia and Asia Minor to Constantinople, in the Years 1808 and 1809*. London: Longman, Hurst, Rees, Orme and Brown.

Palgrave, William Gifford (1863) *Narrative of a Year's Journey Through Central and Eastern Arabia (1862–63)*. 2 vols. London: Macmillan.

Rihani, Ameen (1928) *Ibn Sa'oud: His People and His Land*. London: Constable.

Sackville-West, Vita [1926] (2007) *Passenger to Teheran*. London: Tauris Parke.

Sheil, Lady (1856) *Glimpses of Life and Manners in Persia*. London: John Murray.

Stark, Freya (1936) *The Southern Gates of Arabia: A Journey in the Hadramaut*. London: John Murray.

Sykes, Mark (1904) *Dar-ul-Islam: A Record of a Journey Through Ten Provinces of Asiatic Turkey*. London: Bickers.

Thomas, Bertram (1938) *Arabia Felix: Across the Empty Quarter of Arabia*. London: Jonathan Cape.

Urquhart, David (1838) *Spirit of the East: A Journey of Travels through Roumelia*. 2 vols. London: Henry Colburn.

Vambery, Arminius (1864) *Travels in Central Asia. Being the Account of a Journey from Teheran Across the Turkoman Desert on the Eastern Shore of the Caspian to Khiva, Bokhara and Samarcand, Performed in the Year 1863*. London: John Murray.

———— [1914] (1973) *Arminius Vambery: His Life and Adventures*. New York: Arno Press.

Warburton, Eliot (1845) *The Crescent and The Cross*. London: Henry Colburn.

Wellsted, J. R. (1838) *Travels in Arabia*. 2 vols. London: John Murray.

Wilson, Arnold. (1941) *South West Persia: A Political Officer's Diary*. London: Oxford University Press.

Biographical, Historical and Critical Writing Works cited

Adelson, Roger (1975) *Mark Sykes: Portrait of an Amateur*. London: Jonathan Cape.

Amanat, Abbas. *Pivot of the Universe: Nasir al-Din Shah Qajar and the Iranian Monarchy, 1851–1896*. London: I.B. Tauris.

Arberry, A. J. (1960) *Oriental Essays: Portraits of Seven Scholars*. London: Allen & Unwin.

———— [1947] (2005) Preface to Gertrude Bell, *Persian Pictures*. London: Anthem.

Assad, Thomas (1964) *Three Victorian Travellers, Burton, Blunt, Doughty*. London: Routledge and Kegan Paul.

Ballantyne, Tom (2002) *Orientalism and Race: Aryanism in the British Empire*. London: Macmillan.

Behdad, Ali (1994) *Belated Travelers: Orientalism in the Age of Colonial Dissolution*. Durham, N.C.: Duke University Press.

Bidwell, Robin (1976) *Travellers in Arabia*. London: Hamlyn.

Birkett, Dea (2004a) *Off the Beaten Track: Three Centuries of Women Travellers*. London: National Portrait Gallery.

_____ (2004b) *Spinsters Abroad: Victorian Lady Explorers*. Phoenix Mill Thrupp, Gloucestershire: Sutton Publishing.

Bosworth C. Edmond (2001) *A Century of British Orientalists 1902–2001*. Oxford: British Academy and Oxford University Press.

Cleveland, William L. (2000) *A History of the Modern Middle East*, 2nd ed. Boulder, Colorado: Westview.

Curzon, George N. (1895) Introduction to James Morier, *The Adventures of Hajji Baba of Ispahan*. London: Macmillan.

Driver, Felix (2001) *Geography Militant: Cultures of Exploration and Empire*. London: Blackwell.

Duncan, James and Gregory, Derek, eds. (1999) *Writes of Passage: Reading Travel Writing*. London: Routledge.

Finch, Edith (1938) *Wilfrid Scawen Blunt: 1840–1922*. London: Jonathan Cape.

Foster, Shirley and Mills, Sara, eds. (2002) *An Anthology of Women's Travel Writing*. Manchester: Manchester University Press.

Frank, Katherine (1994) *Lucy Duff Gordon: A Passage to Egypt*. London: Hamish Hamilton.

Fraser, Ian H.C. (1986) *The Heir of Parham: Robert Curzon 14th Baron Zouche*. Alburgh, Harleston, Norfolk: Paradigm Press.

Gail, Marzieh (1951) *Persia and the Victorians*. London: George Allen & Unwin.

Gobineau, Comte Arthur de (1983) *Œuvres*, vol. 2. ed. Jean Gaulmier and Vincent Monteil. Paris: Gallimard.

Graham-Brown, Sarah (1985) Introduction to Gertrude Bell, *The Desert and The Sown*. London: Virago.

Graves, Phillip (1941) *The Life of Sir Percy Cox*. London: Hutchinson.

Gregory, Derek (1999) 'Scripting Egypt: Orientalism and the cultures of travel', in James Duncan and Derek Gregory, eds. *Writes of Passage: Reading Travel Writing*. London: Routledge: 114–150.

Hogarth, David George (1983) Introduction to Robert Curzon, *Visits to Monasteries of the Levant*. London: Century.

Hourani, Albert (1991) *A History of the Arab Peoples*. London: Faber.

Hulme, Peter and Tim Youngs, eds. (2002) *The Cambridge Companion to Travel Writing*. Cambridge: Cambridge University Press.

Javardi, Hasan (2005) *Persian Literary influence on English Literature*. Costa Mesa, CA: Mazda.

Kark, Ruth (2001) 'From Pilgrimage to Budding Tourism: The Role of Thomas Cook in the Rediscovery of the Holy land in the Nineteenth Century' in Sarah Searight and Malcolm Wagstaff, eds. *Travellers to the Near East*. Durham: Astene Publications: 155–74.

Keddie, Nikki R. (1980) *Iran: Religion, Politics and Society*. London: Frank Cass.

_____ (1981) *Roots of Revolution: An Interpretive History of Modern Iran*. New Haven: Yale University Press.

Kedourie, Elie (1956) *England and the Middle East*. London: Bowes.

Kramer, Martin, ed. (1999) *The Jewish Discovery of Islam: Studies in Honor of Bernhard Lewis*. Tel Aviv: Moshe Dayan Center for Middle Eastern and African Studies.

Leask, Nigel (2002) *Curiosity and the Aesthetics of Travel Writing 1770–1840*. Oxford: Oxford University Press.

Lewis, Reina (2004) *Rethinking Orientalism: Women, Travel and the Oriental Harem*. London: I.B.Tauris.

Longford, Elizabeth (1980) *A Pilgrimage of Passion: The Life of Wilfrid Scawen Blunt*. New York: Alfred A. Knopf.

Lowe, Lisa (1991) *Critical Terrains: French and British Orientalisms*. Ithaca: Cornell University Press.

Macfie, A.L., ed. (2000) *Orientalism: A Reader*. Edinburgh: Edinburgh University Press.

———— (2007) 'Representations of Lawrence of Arabia from Said's *Orientalism* (1978) to David Lean's Film'. *Journal of Postcolonial Writing*, 43, 1: 77–87.

Maehl, William H. Jr. (1981) 'David Urquhart', in *Biographical Dictionary of Modern Radicals* eds. Joseph Baylen and Norbert J. Grossman. Vol. 2. 1830–1870. Hassocks: Harvester: 506–12.

Mansfield, Peter (1971) *The British in Egypt*. New York: Holt, Reinhart and Winston.

———— (1992) *The Arabs*. 3rd edn. Harmondsworth: Penguin.

Mazzeo, Tijar J., ed. (2001) *Travels, Explorations and Empires: Writings from the Era of Imperial Expansion 1770–1835*, vol. 4, *Middle East*. London: Pickering & Chatto.

McLynn, Frank (1990) *Burton: Snow Upon the Desert*. London: John Murray.

Melman, Billie (1992) *Women's Orients: English Women and the Middle East, 1718–1918: Sexuality, Religion and Work*. London: Macmillan.

———— (2002) 'The Middle East/Arabia – the "cradle of Islam"', in Peter Hulme and Tim Youngs, eds. (2002) *The Cambridge Companion to Travel Writing*. Cambridge: Cambridge University Press: 105–121.

Mercer, Wendy (1999) 'Gender and Genre in Nineteenth-century Travel Writing: Leonie d'Aunet and Xavier Marmier', in Steve Clark, ed. *Travel Writing and Empire: Postcolonial Theory in Transit*. London: Zed: 147–163.

Momen, Moojan (1981) *The Babi and Baha'i Religions, 1844–1944: Some Contemporary Western Accounts*. Oxford: George Ronald.

Morris, Mary, ed. (1996) *The Virago Book of Women Travellers*. London: Virago.

Nash, Geoffrey (2005) *From Empire to Orient: Travellers to the Middle East, 1800–1926*. London: I.B. Tauris.

———— (2006) 'Politics, Aesthetics and Quest in British Travel Writing on the Middle East', in Tim Youngs, ed. *Travel Writing in the Nineteenth Century: Filling the Blank Spaces*. London: Anthem: 55–70.

———— (2007) 'Friends Across the Water: British Orientalists and Middle East Nationalisms', in Graham Macphee and Prem Poddar, eds. *Empire and After: Englishness in Postcolonial Perspective*. New York: Berghahn: 87–100.

———— ed. (2009) *Gobineau and Orientalism: Selected Eastern Writings*. Translated by Daniel O'Donoghue. London: Routledge.

———— (2010) 'Renan, Anti-Semitism, and Islam', in Francis O'Gorman, ed. *Victorian Literature and the Near East*. Aldershot: Ashgate.

Poliakov, Léon (1974) *The Aryan Myth: A History of Racist and Nationalist Ideas in Europe*. London: Chatto and Windus.

Renan, Ernest (1947–1961) 'L'Islamisme et la science', *Œuvres Completes*, vol. 1, ed. Henriette Psichari. Paris: Calmann-Levy: 945–952.

Robinson, Jane (1990) *Wayward Women: A Guide to Women Travellers*. Oxford: Oxford University Press.

Ronaldshay, The Earl of (1928) *The Life of Lord Curzon*. 3 vols. London: Ernest Benn.

Russell, Mary (1986) Introduction to Ella Maillart, *The CruelWay*. London: Virago Said,
    Edward (1978) *Orientalism: Western Conceptions of the Orient*. London: Routledge and
    Kegan Paul.
Searight, Sara (1979) *The British in the Middle East*. London: East-West Publications.
——— (1983) Introduction to Lucie Duff Gordon, *Letters from Egypt*. London: Virago.
Schiffer, Reinhold (1999) *Oriental Panorama: British Travellers in 19th Century Turkey*.
    Amsterdam: Rodopi.
Scholz, Fred (1978) Introduction to James Wellsted, *Travels in Arabia*. Graz: Akademische
    Druck- u.Verlagsanstalt.
Sykes, Christopher (1986) *For Studies in Loyalty*. London: Century Hutchinson.
Tidrick, Kathryn (1989) *Heart-Beguiling Araby: The English Romance with Arabia*. London:
    I.B. Tauris.
Trench, Richard (1986) *Arabian Travellers: The European Discovery of Arabia*. London:
    Macmillan.
Trevelyan, Raleigh (1986) Introduction to T.E. Lawrence, *Revolt in the Desert*. London
    Century.
Wilbur, Donald N. (1963) *Iran Past and Present*. Princeton, NJ: Princeton University Press.
Wright, Denis (1977) *The English Amongst the Persians*. London: I.B. Heinemann.
Yapp, M.E. (1987) *The Making of the Modern Near East 1792–1923*. London: Longman.
Youngs, Tim ed. (2006) *Travel Writing in the Nineteenth Century: Filling the Blank Spaces*. London:
    Anthem.

Printed in the United States
151363LV00006B/5/P